Twentieth-Century Short Story Explication New Series

Volume III 1993–1994

With Checklists of Books and Journals Used

Wendell M. Aycock
Professor of English
Texas Tech University

The Shoe String Press, 1997

First published by The Shoe String Press, Inc.,
North Haven, Connecticut 06473.

Library of Congress Cataloging-in-Publication Data

Walker, Warren S.
Twentieth-century short story explication : new series;
with checklists of books and journals used/
Warren S. Walker.
p. cm.
Includes bibliographical references and index.
Summary: Contains nearly 6000 entries that provide
a bibliography of interpretations for short stories
published between 1989 and 1990.
1. Short stories—Indexes. [1. Short stories—Indexes.]
I. Title
Z5917.S5W35 1993 [PN3373] 92-22790
016.8093′1—dc20 ISBN 0-208-02340-2 (v. 1)

Twentieth-Century Short Story Explication, with Checklists of Books and Journals Used	Coverage	Published	ISBN
Edited by Warren S. Walker			
Third Edition	1961–1975	1977	0-208-01570-1
Supplement I	1976–1978	1980	0-208-01813-1
Supplement II	1979–1981	1984	0-208-02005-5
Supplement III	1982–1984	1987	0-208-02122-1
Supplement IV	1985–1986	1989	0-208-02188-4
Supplement V	1987–1988	1991	0-208-02299-6
Index	1961–1991	1992	0-208-02320-8

Twentieth-Century Short Story Explication, New Series, with Checklists of Books and Journals Used			
Edited by Warren S. Walker			
Vol. 1	1989–1990	1993	0-208-02340-2
Edited by Wendell M. Aycock			
Vol. 2	1991–1992	1995	0-208-02370-4
Vol. 3	1993–1994	1997	0-208-02419-0

The paper in this publication meets the minimum
requirements of American National Standard for
Information Science—Permanence of Paper for
Printed Library Materials, ANSI Z39.48-1984 ♾

Printed in the United States of America

For
Diane, Daniel, and Andrew

Contents

Preface

This third volume of the New Series carries the coverage of *Twentieth-Century Short Story Explication* forward through December 31, 1994. It includes more than 5,100 entries. Of the 726 authors cited, 229 appear here for the first time, bringing to 3,051 the total number of authors represented in both the original and New Series of *Twentieth-Century Short Story Explication*. Recent interest in multiculturalism may partially account for the increasing numbers of explications of writers from Latin America and Asia. A quick glance at the entries will reveal that Jorge Luis Borges garnered the most explications in this volume, although scholars still manifest interest in writers such as Hawthorne, Melville, and Kipling.

No matter what language the short stories were originally composed in, the explications within are limited to those published in the major languages of Western Europe. Although certainly some explications are excluded by these parameters, the vast majority of the studies are written in these languages.

As in the past, this volume of *Twentieth-Century Short Story Explication* is a bibliography of interpretations that have appeared since 1900 of short stories published since 1800. The term *short story* here has the same meaning it carries in the Wilson Company's *Short Story Index*: "A brief narrative of not more than 150 average-sized pages." *Explication* is meant to suggest simply interpretation or explanation of the meaning of the story, including observations on theme, symbol, and sometimes structure. This definition excludes from the bibliography what are essentially studies of source, biographical data, and background materials. Occasionally there are explicatory passages cited in works otherwise devoted to these external considerations. All pages refer strictly to interpretative passages, not to the longer works in which they occur.

Over the years, Professor Warren Walker, who originated this bibliography, developed a very convenient, useful system for handling great numbers of explications. We continue to follow his system in this volume. Each book is cited by author or editor and a short title; the full title and publication data are provided in "A Checklist of Books Cited"—and 450 were used in the compilation of this volume. For an article in a journal or an essay in a critical collection, the full publication information is provided in the text the first time the study is cited. In subsequent entries, only the critic's or scholar's name and a short title are used as long as these entries appear under the name of the same short story author. If an article or essay explicates stories of two or more authors, a complete initial entry is made for each author. As in previous volumes, we have included a "Checklist of Journals Used"—and this time 358 were used. This information should be especially helpful to students who may not be familiar with titles of professional journals, much less the abbreviations for such titles.

Although most of the entries in Volume III were published during 1993 and 1994, there are some entries with earlier dates. A few of these are earlier interpretations that were either unavailable or overlooked previously. A few are reprintings of earlier studies and these are preceded by a plus sign (+). Any such entry can be located in the original series by consulting the *Index to the Third Edition and Its Five Supplements, 1961–1991*.

In preparing this book, I have been indebted to a number of people. Warren Walker has been a constant source of information, help, and encouragement. In addition, I must acknowledge the contributions from such journals as *PMLA*, *Studies in Short Fiction*, and *Journal of Modern Literature*. I depend constantly upon the considerable support and help from the Texas Tech University Library and the Interlibrary Loan Department of the Texas Tech University Library, especially from Carol Roberts, Delia Arteaga, and Dale Poulter. I also extend my appreciation for the considerable help of some very capable graduate students: Tag-Jung Kim, Chandrashekhar Veera, Elizabeth Martin SoRelle, and Kristian Rickard. I also wish to thank Joseph Unger for his valuable help with computer-related matters. Finally, for her patience, assistance, and encouragement, I thank my wife, Diane.

WENDELL AYCOCK
TEXAS TECH UNIVERSITY

MERCEDES ABAD

"Crucifixión de circulo"
Mandrell, James. "Mercedes Abad and La Sonrisa Vertical: Erotica and Pornography in Post-Franco Spain," *Letras Peninsulares*, 6, ii–iii (1993–1994), 288–289.

"Ese autismo tuyo tan peligroso"
Mandrell, James. "Mercedes Abad . . . ," 291.

"Juegos de niños"
Mandrell, James. "Mercedes Abad . . . ," 290–291, 292.

"Malos tiempos para el absurdo o las delicias de Onán"
Mandrell, James. "Mercedes Abad . . . ," 283–285, 290.

"Una mujer sorprendente: relato gastronómico"
Mandrell, James. "Mercedes Abad . . . ," 285–286.

"Pascualino y los globos"
Mandrell, James. "Mercedes Abad . . . ," 286–287.

ALICE ADAMS

"Roses, Rhododendron"
+Bohner, Charles H. *Instructor's Manual* . . . , 3rd ed., 1–2.

OPAL PALMER ADISA

"Bake-Face"
Flockemann, Miki. "Language and Self in Opal Palmer Adisa's 'Bake-Face and Other Guava Stories,' " *Ariel*, 24, i (1993), 60, 61, 63–72.

"Duppy Get Her"
Flockemann, Miki. "Language . . . ," 62–63.

JAMES AGEE

"Death in the Desert"
Lowe, James. *The Creative Process* . . . , 31–44.

"A Mother's Tale"
Lowe, James. *The Creative Process* . . . , 131–132, 133, 141–143, 145–146, 154–155.

"They That Sow in Sorrow Shall Reap"
Lowe, James. *The Creative Process* . . . , 31–44.

JONIS AGEE

"Side Road"
Gidmark, Jill B. "A Cutting Art: Sharpness of Image in the Fiction

of Jonis Agee," in Noe, Marcia, Ed. *Exploring the Midwestern* . . . , 131–132.

"Stiller's Pond"
Gidmark, Jill B. "A Cutting Art . . . ," 130–131.

SHMUEL [SHAY] YOSEF AGNON [SHMUEL YOSEF CZACZKES]

"Ad henna"
Ben-Dov, Nitza. "S. J. Agnon and the Art of Sublimation," in Patterson, David, and Glenda Abramson, Eds. *Tradition and Trauma* . . . , 92–105.

"And the Crooked Shall Become Straight"
Ben-Dov, Nitza. "S. J. Agnon and the Art . . . ," 40–43.

"Betrothed"
Aberbach, David. "Homosexual Fantasies in Mendele and Agnon," in Patterson, David, and Glenda Abramson, Eds. *Tradition and Trauma* . . . , 183–184.

"The Doctor and His Divorcée" [same as "The Doctor's Divorce"]
Aberbach, David. "Homosexual . . . ," 178–179.
Kubovy, Miri. "The Doctor's Dilemma: The Nature of Jealousy in Agnon's 'The Doctor and His Divorcée,' " *Hebrew Stud*, 30 (1989), 41–47.
———. "Sleeping Princes, Beggars of Love," in Patterson, David, and Glenda Abramson, Eds. *Tradition and Trauma* . . . , 188–190.

"Forevermore"
Sokoloff, Naomi. "Passion Spins the Plot: Agnon's 'Forevermore,' " in Patterson, David, and Glenda Abramson, Eds. *Tradition and Trauma* . . . , 9–26.

"Friendship"
Coffin, Edna A. "The Anatomy of 'Friendship': From Logical Constructs to Psychological Realities," in Patterson, David, and Glenda Abramson, Eds. *Tradition and Trauma* . . . , 143–168.

"The Garment"
Abramson, Glenda. "The Garment and the Loaf: Tales of the Unfinished Task," in Patterson, David, and Glenda Abramson, Eds. *Tradition and Trauma* . . . , 66–67, 71–79, 82–87.

"Giv'at ha-hol"
Kubovy, Miri. "Sleeping Princes . . . ," 190–191, 193–206.

"In the Prime of Her Life" [same as "In the Noontime of Her Days"]
Sokoloff, Naomi B. "Narrative Ventriloquism and Muted Feminine Voice: Agnon's 'In the Prime of Her Life,' " *Prooftexts*, 9, ii (1989), 115–137.

"A Whole Loaf"
Abramson, Glenda. "The Garment . . . ," 66–71, 76–78, 83–87.

MARJORIE AGOSÍN

"Church Candles"
Glickman, Nora. "Jewish Women Writers in Latin America," in Baskin, Judith R., Ed. *Women of the Word* . . . , 311.

"Plains"
Glickman, Nora. "Jewish Women Writers . . . ," 311–312.

"The Seamstress of St. Petersburg"
Glickman, Nora. "Jewish Women Writers . . . ," 310–311.

ROBERT AICKMAN

"Ravissante"
Andriano, Joseph. *Our Ladies* . . . , 139–142.

AMA ATA AIDOO

"Everything Counts"
Ogede, Ode. "The Defense of Culture in Ama Ata Aidoo's *No Sweetness Here*: The Use of Orality as a Textual Strategy," *Int'l Fiction R*, 21 (1994), 78–79.

"In the Cutting of a Drink"
Ogede, Ode. "The Defense . . . ," 79–80.

"The Message"
Ogede, Ode. "The Defense . . . ," 80–81.

"No Sweetness Here"
Ogede, Ode. "The Defense . . . ," 81–82.

"Two Sisters"
Ogede, Ode. "The Defense . . . ," 83–84.

CÉSAR AIRA

"El vestido rosa"
Mathieu, Corina S. " 'El vestido rosa' de César Aira: ¿Puro cuento o novela?" *Romance Lang Annual*, 5 (1993), 469–471.

CHINGIZ AITMATOV

"A Spotted Dog, Running by the Seashore"
Brown, Deming. *The Last Years* . . . , 54.

LOUISA MAY ALCOTT

"Behind a Mask, or a Woman's Power"
Elliott, Mary. "Outperforming Femininity: Public Conduct and

Private Enterprise in Louisa May Alcott's 'Behind a Mask,' " *ATQ*, 8, N.S. (1994), 299–310.

"Cupid and Chow-Chow"

Estes, Angela M., and Kathleen M. Lant. " 'We Don't Mind the Bumps': Reforming the Child's Body in Louisa May Alcott's 'Cupid and Chow-Chow,' " *Children's Lit*, 22 (1994), 27–42.

"Enigmas"

Kyler, Carolyn. "Alcott's 'Enigmas': Impersonation and Interpretation," *ATQ*, 7, N.S. (1993), 229–245.

"Fancy Friend"

Estes, Angela M., and Kathleen M. Lant. " 'Unlovely, Unreal Creatures': Resistance and Relationship in Louisa May Alcott's 'Fancy Friend,' " *Lion & Unicorn*, 18, ii (1994), 154–170.

RICHARD ALDINGTON

"Nobody's Baby: A Mystery Story"

Gates, Norman T. "The Stereotype as Satire in the Fiction of Richard Aldington," in Morris, John, Ed. *Exploring Stereotyped* . . . , 88–89, 90.

"Now Lies She There: An Elegy"

Gates, Norman T. "The Stereotype . . . ," 87–88, 90.

"Stepping Heavenward"

Gates, Norman T. "The Stereotype . . . ," 90–94.

CLARIBEL ALEGRÍA

"The Blue Theatre"

Molinaro, Nina L. "The Language of Bodily Pain and the Fiction of Claribel Alegría," in Boschetto-Sandoval, Sandra M., and Marcia P. McGowan, Eds. *Claribel Alegría* . . . , 180–181.

"Family Album"

Crosby, Margaret B. "The Internal Revolution: Struggling with and against the Self in 'Family Album,' " in Boschetto-Sandoval, Sandra M., and Marcia P. McGowan, Eds. *Claribel Alegría* . . . , 144–156.

March, Kathleen N. "The Real and the Fantastic in the Political Discourse of 'Family Album,' " in Boschetto-Sandoval, Sandra M., and Marcia P. McGowan, Eds. *Claribel Alegría* . . . , 159–173.

Molinaro, Nina L. "The Language of Bodily . . . ," 177–178.

"Village of God and the Devil"

Ruffinelli, Jorge. "Public and Private in Claribel Alegría's Narrative," in Boschetto-Sandoval, Sandra M., and Marcia P. McGowan, Eds. *Claribel Alegría* . . . , 15–19.

SHOLOM ALEICHEM [SHOLOM RABINOWITZ]

"A Yom Kippur Scandal"
Howe, Irving. . . . *A Critic's Notebook*, 23–24,

WOODY ALLEN

"The Kugelmass Episode"
Champion, Laurie. "Allen's 'The Kugelmass Episode,' " *Explicator*, 51 (1992), 61–63.
Davis, Robert M. "A Stand-Up Guy Sits Down: Woody Allen's Prose," *Short Story*, 2, ii, N.S. (1994), 64–66.

ISABEL ALLENDE

"The Gold of Thomas Vargas"
Hart, Patricia. "Magic Feminism in Isabel Allende's *The Stories of Eva Luna*," in Waxman, Barbara F., Ed. *Multicultural Literatures* . . . , 116–117.
"If You Touched My Heart"
Hart, Patricia. "Magic Feminism . . . ," 131–132.
"The Judge's Wife"
Hart, Patricia. "Magic Feminism . . . ," 120–127.
"The Proper Respect"
Hart, Patricia. "Magic Feminism . . . ," 110–111.
"Revenge"
Hart, Patricia. "Magic Feminism . . . ," 127–130.
"Toad's Mouth"
Hart, Patricia. "Magic Feminism . . . ," 107–110.
"Walimai"
Hart, Patricia. "Magic Feminism . . . ," 115–116.

JÚLIA LOPES DE ALMEIDA

"Did You Notice?"
Sadlier, Darlene J. "Modernity and Femininity in *He and She* by Júlia Lopes de Almeida," *Stud Short Fiction*, 30 (1993), 576–579.
"I Can't Have a Single Private Thought . . ."
Sadlier, Darlene J. "Modernity . . . ," 579–581.

HANAN AL-SHAYKH

"A Girl Called Apple"
Cooke, Miriam. "Apple, Nabila, and Ramza: Arab Women's

Narratives of Resistance,'' in Ross, Lena B., Ed. *To Speak or be Silent* . . . , 86–88, 95.

RAFAEL ALTAMIRA Y CREVEA

''En la sierra''
Ayala, María de los Ángeles. ''*Cuentos de mi tierra*, de Rafael Altamira,'' in Dendle, Brian, and José Belmonte Serrano, Eds. *Literatura de Levante*, 25.
''La fiesta del agua''
Ayala, María de los Ángeles. ''*Cuentos* . . . ,'' 23–24.
''Marina''
Ayala, María de los Ángeles. ''*Cuentos* . . . ,'' 22–23.
''El terruño''
Ayala, María de los Ángeles. ''*Cuentos* . . . ,'' 24.

IGNACIO MANUEL ALTAMIRANO

''Atenea''
Vargas, Margarita. ''Romanticism,'' in Foster, David W., Ed. *Mexican Literature* . . . , 94–95.

KINGSLEY AMIS

''Dear Illusion''
Fussell, Paul. *The Anti-Egotist* . . . , 17, 106, 159–160.
''I Spy Strangers''
Bergonzi, Bernard. *Wartime* . . . , 24–27.

ALFRED ANDERSCH

''Der Vater eines Mörders''
Baumgärtner, Alfred C. ''Alfred Andersch: Der Vater eines Mörders,'' in Kaiser, Herbert, and Gerhard Köpf, Eds. *Erzählen, Erinnern* . . . , 211–221.

HANS CHRISTIAN ANDERSEN

''The Red Shoes''
Wilson, Sharon R. *Margaret Atwood's* . . . , 123–127.
''The Shadow''
White, Duffield. ''Shvarts's *The Shadow*: The Andersen Story and the Russian Subtexts,'' *Slavic and East European J*, 38 (1994), 637–639.

"The Snow Queen"
Wilson, Sharon R. *Margaret Atwood's . . .*, 302–303.

SHERWOOD ANDERSON

"The Book of the Grotesque"
Fludernik, Monika. "*Winesburg, Ohio*: The Apprenticeship of George Willard," *Amerikastudien*, 32, iv (1987), 437–438.

"Death in the Woods"
Miller, William V. "Texts, Subtexts, and More Texts: Reconstructing the Narrator's Role in Sherwood Anderson's 'Death in the Woods,' " in Noe, Marcia, Ed. *Exploring the Midwestern . . .*, 86–98.

"Drink"
Fludernik, Monika. "*Winesburg, Ohio . . .*," 446–447.

"The Egg"
Charters, Ann. *Resources . . .*, 1.
Lubbers, Klaus. "Sherwood Anderson: 'The Egg,' " in Lubbers, Klaus, Ed. *Die Englische . . .*, 209–221.

"Godliness"
Fludernik, Monika. "*Winesburg, Ohio . . .*," 436–437, 448.
Weinstein, Arnold. *Nobody's Home . . .*, 94, 102.

"Hands"
Charters, Ann. *Resources . . .*, 2.
Getz, John. "Mary Wilkins Freeman and Sherwood Anderson: Confluence or Influence," *Midamerica*, 19 (1992), 79–83.

"I Want to Know Why"
+Bohner, Charles H. *Instructor's Manual . . .*, 3rd ed., 3–4.
Ellis, James. "Sherwood Anderson's Fear of Sexuality: Horses, Men, and Homosexuality," *Stud Short Fiction*, 30 (1993), 599–601.

"Loneliness"
Fludernik, Monika. "*Winesburg, Ohio . . .*," 445.

"A Man of Ideas"
Fludernik, Monika. "*Winesburg, Ohio . . .*," 442–443.
Weinstein, Arnold. *Nobody's Home . . .*, 103–105, 106.

"The Man Who Became a Woman"
Benfey, Christopher. "The Woman in the Mirror: Randall Jarrell and John Berryman," in Morgan, Thaïs E., Ed. *Men Writing . . .*, 123–124.
Ellis, James. "Sherwood Anderson's Fear . . .," 597–599.
MacGowan, Christopher. "The Heritage of the Fathers in Sherwood Anderson's 'The Man Who Became a Woman,' " *Cahiers de la Nouvelle*, 21 (1993), 29–36.

"Mother"
Fludernik, Monika. "*Winesburg, Ohio . . .*," 441–442.

"Paper Pills"
Getz, John. "Mary Wilkins Freeman . . . ," 84–85.
Weinstein, Arnold. *Nobody's Home* . . . , 97–99, 106.

"The Philosopher"
Fludernik, Monika. "*Winesburg, Ohio* . . . ," 443–444.
Weinstein, Arnold. *Nobody's Home* . . . , 99–102, 106.

"Queer"
Fludernik, Monika. "*Winesburg, Ohio* . . . ," 447.

"The Thinker"
Fludernik, Monika. "*Winesburg, Ohio* . . . ," 446.

ENRIQUE ANDERSON IMBERT

"Espiral"
Planells, Antonio. "Anderson Imbert y la grandeza de lo diminuto," *Revista Interamericana*, 43 (1993), 431–437.

IURII ANDRUKHOVYCH

"Rekreatsiia"
Shkandrij, Myroslav. "Polarities in Contemporary Ukrainian Literature," *Dalhousie R*, 72 (1992), 246.

ALBALUCÍA ANGEL

"Capax en Salamina"
Galván, Delia V. "Género literario / Género femenino: Cuentos en *¡Oh gloria inmarcesible!* de Albalucía Angel," in Arancibia, Juana Alcira, Ed. *Literatura del Mundo Hispánico* . . . , 167.

"Colombina, la golosina de verdad"
Galván, Delia V. "Género literario . . . ," 166–167.

"La crucifixión de Jairo Orlando García"
Galván, Delia V. "Género literario . . . ," 167–168.

"¡Oh gloria inmarcesible!"
Galván, Delia V. "Género literario . . . ," 166.

REINALDO ARENAS

"Arturo, la estrella más brillante"
Soto, Francisco. "La transfiguración del poder en 'La vieja Rosa' y 'Arturo, la estrella más brillante,' " *Confluencia*, 8, i (1992), 73–76.

"Mona"
Soto, Francisco. "Arenas, Reinaldo (Cuba; 1943–1990)," in Foster, David W., Ed. *Latin American Writers* . . . , 31.

———. " 'Mona' de *Viaje a La Habana*: hacia una lectura fantástica," in Sánchez, Reinaldo, Ed. *Reinaldo Arenas* . . . , 169–182.

"La puesta del sol"
Ocasio, Rafael, and Fiona Doloughan. "Literary Offspring: The Figure of the Child in Marcel Proust and Reinaldo Arenas," *Romance Q*, 41 (1994), 115.

"La punta del arco iris"
Ocasio, Rafael, and Fiona Doloughan. "Literary . . . ," 113–114.

"Que trine Eva"
Soto, Francisco. "Arenas, Reinaldo . . . ," 30–31.

"Viaje a La Habana"
Soto, Francisco. "Arenas, Reinaldo . . . ," 31–32.

"La vieja Rosa"
Soto, Francisco. "La transfiguración . . . ," 72–73, 75–76.

JOSÉ MARÍA ARGUEDAS

"La agonía de Rasu-Ñiti"
Usandizaga, Helena. "Las figuras especiales en un relato de J. M. Arguedas: Arquetipos de la verticalidad y dualismo andino," in Romera Castillo, José, Ed, *Actas del IV* . . . , 837–843.

MARCEL ARLAND

"Chez la veuve"
Chaoui, Mokhtar. "La Pensée incestueuse chez Marcel Arland," *Roman 20–50*, 18 (1994), 102.

"Le Lavoir"
Chaoui, Mokhtar. "La Pensée incestueuse . . . ," 101–102.

"Monsieur Léonard"
Chaoui, Mokhtar. "La Pensée incestueuse . . . ," 102–104.

"La Part Dieu"
Chaoui, Mokhtar. "La Pensée incestueuse . . . ," 104–105.

"La Veuve"
Chaoui, Mokhtar. "La Pensée incestueuse . . . ," 105–107.

[LUDWIG] ACHIM VON ARNIM

"Die Majoratsherren"
Riedl, Peter P. "Die Zeichen der Krise: Erbe und Eigentum in Achim von Arnims 'Die Majoratsherren' und E. T. A. Hoffmanns 'Das Majorat,' " *Aurora*, 52 (1992), 23–38.

"Der Tolle Invalide auf dem Fort Ratonneau"
Dickson, Sheila. "Preconceived and Fixed Ideas: Self-Fulfilling

Prophecies in 'Der Tolle Invalide auf dem Fort Ratonneau,' " *Neophilologus*, 44, i (1994), 109–118.

MIKHAIL ARTSYBASHEV

"The Crime of Doctor Lur'e"
Luker, Nicholas. " 'Wild Justice': Mikhail Artsybashev's *Mstitel'* Collection (1913)," *New Zealand Slavonic J* [n.v.] (1993), 74–77.

"Little Otto"
Luker, Nicholas. " 'Wild Justice . . . ," 67–69.

"Mstitel"
Luker, Nicholas. " 'Wild Justice . . . ," 64–67.

"On Jealousy"
Luker, Nicholas. " 'Wild Justice . . . ," 69–71.

"The Tale of a Certain Slap in the Face"
Luker, Nicholas. " 'Wild Justice . . . ," 71–74.

"The Wooden Idol"
Luker, Nicholas. " 'Wild Justice . . . ," 77–80.

IHSAN ASSAL

"House of Obedience"
Cooke, Miriam. "Apple, Nabila, and Ramza: Arab Women's Narratives of Resistance," in Ross, Lena B., Ed. *To Speak or be Silent* . . . , 86, 89–94, 95.

VIKTOR ASTAF'EV

"To Live One's Life"
Brown, Deming. *The Last Years* . . . , 87.

THEA ASTLEY

"Seeing Mrs. Landers"
+Bohner, Charles H. *Instructor's Manual* . . . , 3rd ed., 7–8.

GERTRUDE ATHERTON

"The Foghorn"
Pennell, Melissa M. "Through the Golden Gate: Madness and the Persephone Myth in Gertrude Atherton's 'The Foghorn,' " in Hayes, Elizabeth T., Ed. *Images of Persephone* . . . , 84–97.

MARGARET ATWOOD

"Betty"
Carrera Suarez, Isabel. " 'Yet I Speak, Yet I Exist': Affirmation of the Subject in Atwood's Short Stories," in Nicholson, Colin, Ed. *Margaret Atwood . . .* , 232.

"Bluebeard"
Wilson, Sharon R. *Margaret Atwood's . . .* , 266–270.

"Bluebeard's Egg"
Keith, W. J. "Interpreting and Misinterpreting 'Bluebeard's Egg': A Cautionary Tale," in Nicholson, Colin, Ed. *Margaret Atwood . . .* , 248–257.

"Death by Landscape"
Charters, Ann. *Resources . . .* , 4–5.

"Giving Birth"
Cosslett, Tess. *Women Writing Childbirth . . .* , 29–31, 36–38, 55–56, 75, 88–89, 129, 139–140, 150–151.
Carrera Suarez, Isabel. " 'Yet I Speak . . . ,' " 234–235.

"Hack Wednesday"
Hengen, Shannon. *Margaret Atwood's . . .* , 115–116.

"Hairball"
Hengen, Shannon. *Margaret Atwood's . . .* , 111.

"Loulou; or, The Domestic Life of the Language"
Carrera Suarez, Isabel. " 'Yet I Speak . . . ,' " 238–239.
Meindl, Dieter. "Gender and Narrative Perspective in Margaret Atwood's Stories," in Nicholson, Colin, Ed. *Margaret Atwood . . .* , 227.

"Polarities"
Bennett, Bruce. "Short Fiction and the Canon: Australia and Canada," *Antipodes*, 7, ii (1993), 111.
Carrera Suarez, Isabel. "'Yet I Speak . . . ,'" 232–233.
Nischik, Reingard. "Speech Act Theory, Speech Acts, and the Analysis of Fiction," *Mod Lang R*, 88 (1993), 298–306.

"Rape Fantasies"
+Bohner, Charles H. *Instructor's Manual . . .* , 3rd ed., 8–9.

"Scarlet Ibis"
Lutwack, Leonard. *Birds in Literature*, 235–236.

"Significant Moments in the Life of My Mother"
Carrera Suarez, Isabel. " 'Yet I Speak . . . ,' " 236.
Charters, Ann. *Resources . . .* , 5–7.

"Uglypuss"
Nischik, Reingard. "Speech Act . . . ," 297.

"The War in the Bathroom"
Meindl, Dieter. "Gender . . . ," 226–227.

"Weight"
Hengen, Shannon. *Margaret Atwood's . . .* , 112–113.

"Wilderness Tips"
Hengen, Shannon. *Margaret Atwood's . . .*, 113–115.

FRANCISCO AYALA

"El hechizado"
Sánchez Trigueros, Antonio. "El comentario textual como procedimiento narrativo: El narrador-crítico de 'El hechizado,' " in Sánchez Trigueros, Antonio, and Antonio Chicharro Chamorro, Eds. *Francisco Ayala . . .*, 279–283.

"Los usurpadores"
Richmond, Carolyn. "La autocrítica del crítico Ayala en el prólogo a 'Los usurpadores,' " in Sánchez Trigueros, Antonio, and Antonio Chicharro Chamorro, Eds. *Francisco Ayala . . .*, 125–131.

VELMIRO AYALA GAUNA

"La mariposa"
Foster, David W. "Prolegomenon to an Investigation of Regionalism in Argentine Literature," *Hispanic J*, 14, ii (1993), 15–17.

AZORÍN [JOSÉ MARTÍNEZ RUIZ]

"La estrella de Belén"
Martínez del Portal, María. "Lo inacabado en los desenlaces de la cuentística de José Martínez Ruiz," *Insula*, 48, 556 (April, 1993), 18–19.

"Fabia Linde"
Martínez del Portal, María. "Lo inacabado . . .," 18.

"La mano en la mano"
Martínez del Portal, María. "Lo inacabado . . .," 18.

"El viejo inquisidor"
Martínez del Portal, María. "Lo inacabado . . .," 18.

DODICI AZPADU

"Saturday Night in the Prime of Life"
Quinn, Roseanne L. "*Sorelle delle ombre*: Confronting Racism and Homophobia in Literature by Contemporary Italian-American Women," in Krase, Jerome, and Judith N. DeSena, Eds. *Italian Americans . . .*, 241–245.

MARIANO AZUELA

"Andrés Pérez, maderista"
Gyurko, Lanin A. "Twentieth-Century Fiction," in Foster, David W., Ed. *Mexican Literature . . .*, 249–250.

"The Underdogs"
Biermann, Karlheinrich. "Mariano Azuela: 'Los de abajo,' " in Roloff, Volker, and Harald Wentzlaff-Eggebert, Eds. *Der Hispanoamerikanische* . . . , 105–117.
Gyurko, Lanin A. "Twentieth-Century . . . ," 246–249.
Lindstrom, Naomi. *Twentieth-Century* . . . , 44–45.
Sklodowska, Elzbieta. " '¿A que no me lo cree?': coerciones discursivas en 'Los de abajo' de Mariano Azuela," *Hispamérica*, 23, lxix (1994), 23–36.

ISAAC [EMMANUILOVICH] BABEL

"Berestechko"
Eng, Jan van der. "*Red Calvary*: A Novel of Stories," *Russian, Croatian*, 33 (1993), 257–258.

"The Cemetery at Kozin"
Baak, Joost van. "Isaak Babel's 'The Cemetery at Kozin,' " *Canadian Slavonic Papers*, 36 (1994), 69–87.

"Di Grasso"
Erlich, Victor. "Art and Reality: A Note on Isaak Babel's Metaliterary Narratives," *Canadian Slavonic Papers*, 36 (1994), 110–111.

"Froim Grach"
Briker, Boris. "The Underworld of Benia Krik and I. Babel's *Odessa Stories*," *Canadian Slavonic Papers*, 36 (1994), 131–134.

"Guy de Maupassant"
Erlich, Victor. "Art and Reality . . . ," 109–110.

"In the Basement"
Erlich, Victor. "Art and Reality . . . ," 107–109.

"Konkin's Prisoner"
Eng, Jan van der. "*Red Calvary* . . . ," 259–260.

"A Letter"
Eng, Jan van der. "*Red Calvary* . . . ," 258–259.

"Line and Color"
Erlich, Victor. "Art and Reality . . . ," 111–113.

"My First Goose"
Shcheglov, Yuri K. "Some Themes and Archetypes in Babel's *Red Cavalry*," *Slavic R*, 53 (1994), 653–670.

"The Rebbe's Son"
Avins, Carol J. "Kinship and Concealment in *Red Cavalry* and Babel's 1920 Diary," *Slavic R*, 53 (1994), 705–707.
Hetenyi, Zsuza. "The Visible Idea: Babel's Modelling Imagery," *Canadian Slavonic Papers*, 36 (1994), 56–57.

"The Road to Brody"
Eng, Jan van der. "*Red Calvary* . . . ," 252.

"The Story of My Dovecote"
+Bohner, Charles H. *Instructor's Manual* . . . , 3rd ed., 10–11.

"The Widow"
Hetenyi, Zsuza. "The Visible Idea . . . ," 60, 64.

"Zamoste"
Avins, Carol J. "Kinship and . . . ," 704–705.
Eng, Jan van der. "*Red Calvary* . . . ," 258.
Hetenyi, Zsuza. "The Visible Idea . . . ," 65–66.

INGEBORG BACHMANN

"The Barking"
Achberger, Karen R. *Understanding Ingeborg Bachmann*, 154–156.

"Eyes to Wonder"
Achberger, Karen R. *Understanding Ingeborg Bachmann*, 153–154.

"Problems, Problems"
Achberger, Karen R. *Understanding Ingeborg Bachmann*, 150–153.

"A Step Towards Gomorrah"
Achberger, Karen R. *Understanding Ingeborg Bachmann*, 78–85.

"Three Paths to the Lake"
Achberger, Karen R. *Understanding Ingeborg Bachmann*, 156–162.

"Undine Goes"
Achberger, Karen R. *Understanding Ingeborg Bachmann*, 85–90.
Behre, Maria. "Ingeborg Bachmanns 'Undine geht' als Sprache einer besonderen Wahrnehmung," in Göttsche, Dirk, and Hubert Ohl, Eds. *Ingeborg Bachmann* . . . , 63–79.
Hempen, Daniela. "Das Bild der Wasserfrau bei Meyerhof, Bachmann und Röhner," *Seminar*, 30 (1994), 386–388.
Scrol, Veronica P. "Return to 'O': A Lacanian Reading of Ingeborg Bachmann's 'Undine Goes,' " *Stud Twentieth-Century Lit*, 18 (1994), 239–246.

"Word for Word"
Achberger, Karen R. *Understanding Ingeborg Bachmann*, 147–150.

DMITRII BAKIN

"Land of Origin"
Brown, Deming. *The Last Years* . . . , 178.

JACQUELINE BALCELLS

"La pasa encantada"
Agosin, Marjorie. " 'La pasa encantada' o las iras de la maternidad: Un cuento de Jacqueline Balcells," *Alba de América*, 6 (1988), 157–160.

JAMES BALDWIN

"Going to Meet the Man"
Leeming, David. *James Baldwin: A Biography*, 248–249.

"Previous Condition"
Charters, Ann. *Resources* . . . , 8.
Leeming, David. *James Baldwin: A Biography*, 53–54.

"Sonny's Blues"
+Bohner, Charles H. *Instructor's Manual* . . . , 3rd ed., 11–12.
Charters, Ann. *Resources* . . . , 9.
Joyce, Joyce A. *Warriors, Conjurers* . . . , 283–284.
Leeming, David. *James Baldwin: A Biography*, 135–136.
Pickering, James H., and Jeffrey D. Hoeper. *Instructor's Manual* . . . , 88–90.
Scruggs, Charles. *Sweet Home* . . . , 146–147.
Werner, Craig H. *Playing the Changes* . . . , 219–221.

"This Morning, This Evening, So Soon"
Leeming, David. *James Baldwin: A Biography*, 169–171.

JAMES GRAHAM BALLARD

"News From the Sun"
Brigg, Peter. "J. G. Ballard: Time Out of Mind," *Extrapolation*, 35 (1994), 55–59.

"The Voices of Time"
Brigg, Peter. "J. G. Ballard . . . ," 44–48, 55.

HONORÉ DE BALZAC

"Gambara"
Bell, David F. *Circumstances* . . . , 142–152.

"The Girl With the Golden Eyes"
Messol-Bedoin, Chantal. "La Charade et la chimère: Du récit énigmatique dans 'La Fille aux yeux d'or,' " *Poétique*, 23 (1992), 31–45.
Perry, Catherine. " 'La Fille aux yeux d'or' et la quête paradoxale de l'infini," *L'Année Balzacienne*, 14 (1993), 261–284.

"La Grande Bretèche"
Lukacher, Maryline. *Maternal Fictions* . . . , 4–7.

"La Maison du chat-qui-pelote"
Amar, Muriel. "Autour de 'La Maison du chat-qui-pelote,' " *L'Anné Balzacienne*, 14 (1993), 141–155.

"The Red Inn"
Sterne, Richard C. *Dark Mirror* . . . , 57–58, 60, 70–71.

TONI CADE BAMBARA

"A Girl's Story"
Wear, Delese, and Lois L. Nixon. *Literary Anatomies* . . . , 52–55.

"The Lesson"
+Bohner, Charles H. *Instructor's Manual* . . . , 3rd ed., 12–13.

"Witchbird"
Aiken, Susan H. "Telling the Other('s) Story, or, the Blues in Two Languages," in Aiken, Susan H., Adele M. Barker, Maya Koreneva, and Ekaterina Stetsenko, Eds. *Dialogues/Dialogi* . . . , 207–215.
Koreneva, Maya. "Children of the Sixties," in Aiken, Susan H., Adele M. Barker, Maya Koreneva, and Ekaterina Stetsenko, Eds. *Dialogues/Dialogi* . . . , 199–205.

RUSSELL BANKS

"Black Man and White Woman in Dark Green Rowboat"
Leckie, Ross. "Plot-Resistant Narrative and Russell Banks's 'Black Man and White Woman in Dark Green Rowboat,' " *Stud Short Fiction*, 31 (1994), 407–413.

"My Mother's Memoirs, My Father's Lie, and Other True Stories"
+Bohner, Charles H. *Instructor's Manual* . . . , 3rd ed., 13–14.

NATALYA BARANSKAYA

"Borya's Bicycle"
Kelly, Catriona. *A History of Russian* . . . , 402.

"By the Nikitsky Gates and on the Plyushchikha"
Kelly, Catriona. *A History of Russian* . . . , 406–407.

"Lyubochka"
Kelly, Catriona. *A History of Russian* . . . , 402.

"A Negative Giselle"
Kelly, Catriona. *A History of Russian* . . . , 402.
Žekulin, Nicholas G. "Changing Perspectives: The Prose of Natal'ia Baranskaia," *Canadian Slavonic Papers*, 35 (1993), 239.

"Partners"
Žekulin, Nicholas G. "Changing Perspectives . . . ," 238.

"A Quiet Night in Roosna"
Žekulin, Nicholas G. "Changing Perspectives . . . ," 237.

"The Sinner and the Righteous Woman"
Žekulin, Nicholas G. "Changing Perspectives . . . ," 240–241.

"A Week Like Any Other"
Kelly, Catriona. *A History of Russian* . . . , 362–364, 399, 403.
Žekulin, Nicholas G. "Changing Perspectives . . . ," 241–243.

"The Woman with an Umbrella"
Žekulin, Nicholas G. "Changing Perspectives . . . ," 235–236.

JULES-AMÉDÉE BARBEY D'AUREVILLY

"La Vengeance d'une femme"
Shryock, Richard. *Tales of Storytelling* . . . , 30–32, 50, 55–56, 58.
Toumayan, Alain. "Barbey d'Aurevilly, Balzac, and 'La Vengeance d'une femme,' " *French Forum*, 19 (1994), 35–43.

CLIVE BARKER

"The Age of Desire"
Hoppenstand, Gary. *Clive Barker's* . . . , 120–126.

"Babel's Children"
Hoppenstand, Gary. *Clive Barker's* . . . , 144–149.

"The Body Politic"
Hoppenstand, Gary. *Clive Barker's* . . . , 106–111.

"The Book of Blood"
Hoppenstand, Gary. *Clive Barker's* . . . , 45–47, 203–204.

"The Book of Blood (A Postscript): On Jerusalem Street"
Hoppenstand, Gary. *Clive Barker's* . . . , 168–170.

"Coming to Grief"
Hoppenstand, Gary. *Clive Barker's* . . . , 177–182.

"Confessions of a (Pornographer's) Shroud"
Hoppenstand, Gary. *Clive Barker's* . . . , 91–93.

"Down, Satan!"
Hoppenstand, Gary. *Clive Barker's* . . . , 116–120.

"Dread"
Hoppenstand, Gary. *Clive Barker's* . . . , 65–68, 203–204.

"The Forbidden"
Hoppenstand, Gary. *Clive Barker's* . . . , 134–140.

"Hell's Event"
Hoppenstand, Gary. *Clive Barker's* . . . , 68–71.

"How Spoilers Bleed"
Hoppenstand, Gary. *Clive Barker's* . . . , 155–160.

"Human Remains"
Hoppenstand, Gary. *Clive Barker's* . . . , 97–100.
Smith, Andrew. "Worlds that Creep upon You: Postmodern Illusions in the Work of Clive Barker," in Bloom, Clive, Ed. *Creepers* . . . , 184–185.

"In the Flesh"
Hoppenstand, Gary. *Clive Barker's* . . . , 127–134.

"The Inhuman Condition"
Hoppenstand, Gary. *Clive Barker's* . . . , 101–106.

"Jacqueline Ess: Her Will and Testament"
Hoppenstand, Gary. *Clive Barker's* . . . , 71–74.

"The Last Illusion"
Hoppenstand, Gary. *Clive Barker's* . . . , 164–168.

"The Life of Death"
Hoppenstand, Gary. *Clive Barker's* . . . , 151–155.

"Lost Souls"
Hoppenstand, Gary. *Clive Barker's* . . . , 171–176.

"The Madonna"
Hoppenstand, Gary. *Clive Barker's* . . . , 140–144.

"The Midnight Meat Train"
Hoppenstand, Gary. *Clive Barker's* . . . , 47–49.

"New Murders in the Rue Morgue"
Hoppenstand, Gary. *Clive Barker's* . . . , 78–81.

"Pig Blood Blues"
Hoppenstand, Gary. *Clive Barker's* . . . , 53–59.

"Rawhead Rex"
Hoppenstand, Gary. *Clive Barker's* . . . , 86–91.

"Revelations"
Hoppenstand, Gary. *Clive Barker's* . . . , 111–116, 183–184.

"Scape-Goats"
Hoppenstand, Gary. *Clive Barker's* . . . , 93–97.

"Sex, Death and Starshine"
Hoppenstand, Gary. *Clive Barker's* . . . , 59–61.

"The Skins of the Fathers"
Hoppenstand, Gary. *Clive Barker's* . . . , 75–78.

"Son of Celluloid"
Hoppenstand, Gary. *Clive Barker's* . . . , 83–86.
Smith, Andrew. "Worlds that Creep . . . ," 176–77, 180.

"Twilight at the Towers"
Hoppenstand, Gary. *Clive Barker's* . . . , 160–164.

"The Yattering and Jack"
Hoppenstand, Gary. *Clive Barker's* . . . , 49–53.

DJUNA BARNES

"Spillway" [Originally "Beyond the End"]
Gerstenberger, Donna. "Modern (Post) Modern: Djuna Barnes Among the Others," *R Contemp Fiction*, 13, iii (1993), 37–38.

"The Terrorists"
Schneider, Lissa. " 'This mysterious and migratory jewelry': Satire and the Feminine in Djuna Barnes's 'The Terrorists,' " *R Contemp Fiction*, 13, iii (1993), 62–69.

PÍO BAROJA Y NESSI

"La dama de Urtubi"
Dean-Thacker, Verónica P. "Witchcraft and the Supernatural in Six Stories by Pío Baroja," in Martín, Gregorio C., Ed. *Selected Proceedings* . . . , 115–117.

"El estanque verde"
Dean-Thacker, Verónica P. "Witchcraft . . . ," 117–118.

"Medium"
Dean-Thacker, Verónica P. "Witchcraft . . . ," 113–114.

"La sima"
Dean-Thacker, Verónica P. "Witchcraft . . . ," 114–115.

"La sombra"
Dean-Thacker, Verónica P. "Witchcraft . . . ," 113.

"El trasgo"
Dean-Thacker, Verónica P. "Witchcraft . . . ," 114.

DVORA BARON

"A Couple Quarrels"
Adler, Ruth. "Dvora Baron: Daughter of the Shtetl," in Baskin, Judith R., Ed. *Women of the Word* . . . , 102–103.

"Deception"
Adler, Ruth. "Dvora Baron . . . ," 100–101.

"Gilgulim"
Adler, Ruth. "Dvora Baron . . . ," 107–108.

JOHN BARTH

"Anonymiad"
Bowen, Zack. *A Reader's Guide* . . . , 63–64.
Slethaug, Gordon E. *The Play of the Double* . . . , 139–140.

"Bellerophoniad"
Bowen, Zack. *A Reader's Guide* . . . , 72–74, 76.

"Dunyazadiad"
Bowen, Zack. *A Reader's Guide* . . . , 68, 71–72.
Slethaug, Gordon E. *The Play* . . . , 131–132.

"Echo"
Bowen, Zack. *A Reader's Guide* . . . , 57–58.
Slethaug, Gordon E. *The Play* . . . , 141–142, 146–148.

"Life-Story"
Bowen, Zack. *A Reader's Guide* . . . , 60.

"Lost in the Funhouse"
+Bohner, Charles H. *Instructor's Manual* . . . , 3rd ed., 14–16.
Bowen, Zack. *A Reader's Guide* . . . , 55–57.

Carey, Michael. "Barth's 'Lost in the Funhouse,' " *Explicator*, 52 (1994), 119–122.
Coulthard, A. R. "Barth's 'Lost in the Funhouse,' " *Explicator*, 52 (1994), 180.
Slethaug, Gordon E. *The Play* . . . , 143–145.

"Menelaiad"
Bowen, Zack. *A Reader's Guide* . . . , 60–63.
Slethaug, Gordon E. *The Play* . . . , 145.

"Night-Sea Journey"
Slethaug, Gordon E. *The Play* . . . , 140–141, 142.

"Perseid"
Bowen, Zack. *A Reader's Guide* . . . , 74–75.

"Petition"
Bowen, Zack. *A Reader's Guide* . . . , 54–55.
Slethaug, Gordon E. *The Play* . . . , 142–143, 148.

DONALD BARTHELME

"Basil from Her Garden"
Charters, Ann. *Resources* . . . , 11–12.
Pickering, James H., and Jeffrey D. Hoeper. *Instructor's Manual* . . . , 122–123.

"Brain Damage"
Robertson, Mary. "Postmodern Realism: Discourse as Antihero in Donald Barthelme's 'Brain Damage,' " in Patterson, Richard F., Ed. *Critical Essays* . . . , 124–139.

"The Leap"
Charters, Ann. *Resources* . . . , 14.

"The Mothball Fleet"
Trussler, Michael. "Metamorphosis and Possession: An Investigation into the Interchapters of *Overnight to Many Distant Cities*," in Patterson, Richard F., Ed. *Critical Essays* . . . , 202–203.

"The New Member"
Stengel, Wayne B. "Irony and the Totalitarian Consciousness in Donald Barthelme's *Amateurs*," in Patterson, Richard F., Ed. *Critical Essays* . . . , 149–150.

"Report"
Harper, Phillip B. *Framing the Margins* . . . , 151–152.

"Robert Kennedy Saved from Drowning"
Zeitlin, Michael. "Father-Murder and Father-Rescue: The Post-Freudian Allegories of Donald Barthelme," *Contemporary Lit*, 34 (1993), 197–198.

"The School"
Stengel, Wayne B. "Irony . . . ," 146–148.

"A Shower of Gold"
Davis, Robert M. "A Stand-Up Guy Sits Down: Woody Allen's Prose," *Short Story*, 2, ii, N.S. (1994), 64.

"Some of Us Have Been Threatening Our Friend Colby"
Stengel, Wayne B. "Irony . . . ," 148–149.

"This Newspaper Here"
Harper, Phillip B. *Framing* . . . , 150–151.

"Views of My Father Weeping"
Zeitlin, Michael. "Father Murder . . . ," 186–197.

"Visitors"
Trussler, Michael. "Metamorphosis . . . ," 203.

GEORGES BATAILLE

"La Mort"
Versteeg, Jan. " 'La Mort' en peine," in Hillenaar, Henk, and Jan Versteeg, Eds. *George Bataille* . . . , 79–87.

BARBARA BAYNTON

"The Chosen Vessel"
+Bohner, Charles H. *Instructor's Manual* . . . , 3rd ed., 16–18.

ANN BEATTIE

"The Burning House"
Mangum, Bryant. "The World as Burning House: Ann Beattie and the Buddha," *Notes Contemp Lit*, 20 (March, 1990), 9–11; rpt. Montresor, Jaye B. *The Critical Response* . . . , 94–96.
Sprows, Sandra. "Frames, Images, and the Abyss: Psychasthenic Negotiation in Ann Beattie," in Montresor, Jaye B. *The Critical Response* . . . , 143–147.

"A Clever-Kid Story"
Gelfant, Blanche H. "Ann Beattie's Magic Slate or The End of the Sixties," *New England R*, 1 (1979), 379–380; rpt. Montresor, Jaye B. *The Critical Response* . . . , 25–26.
Ryan, Maureen. "The Other Side of Grief: American Women Writers and the Vietnam War," *Critique*, 36 (1994), 45–46.

"Dwarf House"
Gelfant, Blanche H. "Ann Beattie's . . . ," 377; rpt. Montresor, Jaye B. *The Critical Response* . . . , 23–24.

"Friends"
Olster, Stacey. "Photographs and Fantasies in the Stories of Ann Beattie," in Logsdon, Loren, and Charles W. Mayer, Eds. *Since Flannery O'Connor* . . . , 121–122; rpt. Montresor, Jaye B. *The Critical Response* . . . , 126.

"Gravity"
+McKinstry, Susan J. "The Speaking Silence of Ann Beattie's Voice," in Montresor, Jaye B. *The Critical Response . . .*, 135.

"Honey"
Hugus, Kathleen J. "The Slice of Life: Paring It Thin in *What Was Mine*," in Montresor, Jaye B. *The Critical Response . . .*, 215–217.

"Imagine a Day at the End of Your Life"
Hugus, Kathleen J. "The Slice of Life . . . ," 211–212.

"In the White Night"
+McKinstry, Susan J. "The Speaking . . . , " 137–139.

"It's Just Another Day in Big Bear City, California"
+Porter, Carolyn. "Ann Beattie: The Art of Missing," in Montresor, Jaye B. *The Critical Response . . .*, 81–82.

"Jacklighting"
Story, Kenneth E. "Throwing a Spotlight on the Past: Narrative Method in Ann Beattie's 'Jacklighting,' " *Stud Short Fiction*, 27 (1990), 106–109; rpt. Montresor, Jaye B. *The Critical Response . . .*, 90–93.

"Janus"
Pickering, James H., and Jeffrey D. Hoeper. *Instructor's Manual . . .*, 124–125.

"Learning to Fall"
+Porter, Carolyn. "Ann Beattie: The Art . . . ," 83–85.
Sprows, Sandra. "Frames, Images . . . ," 147–148.

"Marshall's Dog"
+Porter, Carolyn. "Ann Beattie: The Art . . . ," 80–81.

"The Octascope"
+Gerlach, John. "Through 'The Octascope': A View of Ann Beattie," in Montresor, Jaye B. *The Critical Response . . .*, 36–41.

"Running Dreams"
+Porter, Carolyn. "Ann Beattie: The Art . . . ," 85–86.

"Shifting"
DeZure, Deborah. "Images of Void in Beattie's 'Shifting,' " *Stud Short Fiction*, 26 (1989), 11–15; rpt. Montresor, Jaye B. *The Critical Response . . .*, 30–35.

"Sunshine and Shadow"
Olster, Stacey. "Photographs and Fantasies in the Stories of Ann Beattie," in Logsdon, Loren, and Charles W. Mayer, Eds. *Since Flannery O'Connor . . .*, 117–118; rpt. Montresor, Jaye B. *The Critical Response . . .*, 121–122.

"Tuesday Night"
Gelfant, Blanche H. "Ann Beattie's . . . ," 378; rpt. Montresor, Jaye B. *The Critical Response . . .*, 24–25.

"You Know What"
Hugus, Kathleen J. "The Slice of Life . . . ," 213–214.

"What Was Mine"
+Bohner, Charles H. *Instructor's Manual* . . . , 3rd ed., 18–19.
Hugus, Kathleen J. "The Slice of Life . . . ," 212–213.

"Where You'll Find Me"
Sprows, Sandra. "Frames, Images . . . ," 148–151.

"Winter: 1978"
+Porter, Carolyn. "Ann Beattie: The Art . . . ," 86–88.

"Wolf Dreams"
+Porter, Carolyn. "Ann Beattie: The Art . . . ," 79.

SIMONE DE BEAUVOIR

"Malentendu à Moscou"
Keefe, Terry. "'Malentendu à Moscou,' " *Simone de Beauvoir Stud*, 11 (1994), 30–41.

SAMUEL BECKETT

"Company"
Bersani, Leo, and Ulysse Dutoit. "Beckett's Sociability," *Raritan*, 12, i (1992), 10–19.

"Dante and the Lobster"
Pilling, John. "Beckett's English Fiction," in Pilling, John, Ed. *The Cambridge Companion* . . . , 22–23.
Ricks, Christopher. *Beckett's Dying Words* . . . , 29–32.
Vandervlist, Harry. "Nothing Doing: The Repudiation of Action in Beckett's *More Pricks Than Kicks*," in Fischlin, Daniel, Ed. *Negation, Critical Theory* . . . , 147–150.

"Ding-Dong"
Vandervlist, Harry. "Nothing Doing . . . ," 150–151.

"The End"
Ricks, Christopher. *Beckett's Dying Words* . . . , 66–69.

"Fingal"
Pilling, John. "Beckett's English . . . ," 23–25.

"How it is (Comment c'est)"
Abbott, H. Porter. "Beginning Again: the Post-Narrative Art of 'Texts for Nothing' and 'How it is,' " in Pilling, John, Ed. *The Cambridge Companion* . . . , 110–120.
Bersani, Leo, and Ulysse Dutoit. "Beckett's . . . ," 1–10.

"The Lost Ones"
Renton, Andrew. "Disabled Figures: From the *Residua* to *Stirrings Still*," in Pilling, John, Ed. *The Cambridge Companion* . . . , 170–171.

"Texts for Nothing"
Abbott, H. Porter. "Beginning Again . . . ," 106–110.

"Yellow"
Kiely, Robert. *Reverse Tradition . . .* , 46–47.

GUSTAVO ADOLFO BÉCQUER

"El rayo de luna"
Dowling, Lee H. "Lecturas y lectores: Una leyenda de Bécquer," *Foro Lit*, 8, xiii (1985), 33–38.

MAX BEERBOHM

"The Happy Hypocrite: A Fairy Tale for Tired Men"
Lane, Christopher. "Framing Fears, Reading Designs: The Homosexual Art of Painting in James, Wilde, and Beerbohm," *ELH*, 61 (1994), 943–949.

LEO BELLINGHAM

"In for the Kill"
Harvey, Stephanie. "Doris Lessing's 'One Off the Short List' and Leo Bellingham's 'In for the Kill,' " *Critical S*, 5, i (1993), 67–69, 71–75.

SAUL BELLOW

"Cousins"
Friedrich, Marianne. " 'Cousins': The Problem of Narrative Representation," *Saul Bellow J*, 11–12 (1993–1994), 80–107.
Halio, Jay L. "Saul Bellow's Fiction of Contemplation and 'What Kind of Day Did You Have?' " *Saul Bellow J*, 11–12 (1993–1994), 126–127.

"Him with His Foot in His Mouth"
Chavkin, Allan and Nancy F. "Shawmut's Hostile Joking and Stereotyping in 'Him with His Foot in His Mouth,' " *Saul Bellow J*, 11–12 (1993–1994), 22–29.

"Leaving the Yellow House"
Austin, Mike. "Saul Bellow and the Absent Woman Syndrome: Traces of India in 'Leaving the Yellow House,' " *Saul Bellow J*, 11–12 (1993–1994), 146–155.

"The Old System"
Berger, Alan. "The Logic of the Heart: Biblical Identity and American Culture in Saul Bellow's 'The Old System,' " *Saul Bellow J*, 11–12 (1993–1994), 133–145.
Pinsker, Sanford. "A New Look at 'The Old System,' " *Saul Bellow J*, 11–12 (1993–1994), 54–65.

"Seize the Day"
Simmons, Gaye M. "Atonement in Bellow's 'Seize the Day,' " *Saul Bellow J*, 11–12 (1993–1994), 30–53.

"What Kind of Day Did You Have?"
Halio, Jay L. "Saul Bellow's Fiction . . . ," 127–132.

"Zetland: By a Character Witness"
Snyder, Phillip A. "Artist-By-Artist (De)construction: Mediated Testimony in Bellow's 'Zetland: By a Character Witness,' " *Saul Bellow J*, 11–12 (1993–1994), 66–79.

MARIO BENEDETTI

"El césped"
Cunha-Giabbai, Gloria da. "*Despistes y franquezas*: Otro Benedetti, ¿o es el mismo?" *Anthropos*, 132 (1992), 73.

"Fidelidades"
Kason, Nancy M. "*Despistes y franquezas*: Hacia una nueva poética cultural," *Alba de América*, 12 (1994), 310–311.

"El hombre que aprendió a ladrar"
Kason, Nancy M. "*Despistes* . . . ," 313.

"Idilio"
Kason, Nancy M. "*Despistes* . . . ," 314.

"Lázaro"
Kason, Nancy M. "*Despistes* . . . ," 311.

"Memoria electrónica"
Kason, Nancy M. "*Despistes* . . . ," 313–314.

"Recuerdos olvidados"
Cunha-Giabbai, Gloria da. "*Despistes* . . . ," 72–73.
Kason, Nancy M. "*Despistes* . . . ," 311–312.

"Rutinas"
Kason, Nancy M. "*Despistes* . . . ," 314.

"Traducciones"
Kason, Nancy M. "*Despistes* . . . ," 313.

"Triángulo isósceles"
Kason, Nancy M. "*Despistes* . . . ," 310.

PAZ MARQUEZ BENITEZ

"Dead Stars"
Grow, L. M. "The Art of Paz Marquez Benitez," *Philippine Q*, 19 (1991), 3–10.

LERONE BENNETT

"The Convert"
Hurd, Myles R. "Hands and Fingers: Revisioning Booker T.

Washington in Lerone Bennett's 'The Convert,' " *Xavier R*, 13, ii (1993), 29–37.

NINA BERBEROVA

"The Accompanist"
Kelly, Catriona. *A History of Russian* . . . , 269.

"Roccanvale"
Kelly, Catriona. *A History of Russian* . . . , 269–270.

MICHA JOSEF BERDICHEWSKY [BIN GORION]

"The Two Camps"
Steinhardt, Deborah. "Figures of Thought: Psycho-Narration in the Fiction of Berdichewsky, Bershadsky, and Feierberg," *Prooftexts*, 8, ii (1988), 203–208.

JOHN BERRYMAN

"The Imaginary Jew"
Smith, Ernest J. "John Berryman's Short Fiction: Elegy and Enlightenment," *Stud Short Fiction*, 30 (1993), 311–313.

"The Lovers"
Smith, Ernest J. "John Berryman's . . . ," 310–311.

"Wash Far Away"
Smith, Ernest J. "John Berryman's . . . ," 313–315.

JOAQUÍN BESTARD VÁZQUEZ

"Atrapar la sombra de una garza"
Daniel, Lee A. "Introducción," in *Cuentos* . . . [by Joaquín Bestard Vázquez], 14–16.

"El candor del cielo"
Daniel, Lee A. "Introducción," 17.

"Las cenizas de don Chebo"
Daniel, Lee A. "Introducción," 11–12.

"Chich"
Daniel, Lee A. "Introducción," 13–14.

"A distancia de una señal"
Daniel, Lee A. "Introducción," 18.

"Los fantasmas de Simona"
Daniel, Lee A. "Introducción," 13–14.

"¡Fuego!"
Daniel, Lee A. "Introducción," 16–17.

"Las garras de tío Ix"
Daniel, Lee A. "Introducción," 12–13.

"La hora de Álvaro Poot Kan"
Daniel, Lee A. "Introducción," 14.

"Legado de dragón"
Daniel, Lee A. "Introducción," 16.

"El manatí"
Daniel, Lee A. "Introducción," 17–18.

"El viejo rodar de los gitanos"
Daniel, Lee A. "Introducción," 12.

ALEXANDER BESTUZHEV-MARLINSKY

"The Frigate *Hope*"
Leighton, Lauren G. *The Esoteric Tradition* . . . , 93–110, 120–121, 149–152.

DORIS BETTS

"Still Life With Fruit"
Cosslett, Tess. *Women Writing Childbirth* . . . , 28, 78, 127–128, 137.

AMBROSE BIERCE

"The Damned Thing"
Burleson, Donald R. "Bierce's 'The Damned Thing': A Nietzschean Allegory," *Stud Weird Fiction*, 13 (1993), 8–10.

"An Occurrence at Owl Creek Bridge"
+Bohner, Charles H. *Instructor's Manual* . . . , 3rd ed., 19–21.
Fusco, Richard. *Maupassant* . . . , 112–115.
Owens, David M. "Bierce and Biography: The Location of Owl Creek Bridge," *Am Lit Realism*, 26, iii (1994), 82–89.
Stoicheff, Peter. " 'Something Uncanny': The Dream Structure in Ambrose Bierce's 'An Occurrence at Owl Creek Bridge,' " *Stud Short Fiction*, 30 (1993), 349–357.

"Hades in Trouble"
Berkove, Lawrence I. " 'Hades in Trouble': A Rediscovered Story by Ambrose Bierce," *Am Lit Realism*, 25, ii (1993), 67–71.

"Moxon's Master"
Haynes, Roslynn D. *From Faust* . . . , 146–147.

"Parker Adderson, Philosopher"
Heller, Arno. "Ambrose Bierce: 'Parker Adderson, Philosopher'—Eine Erzählung vom falschen und richtigen Sterben," in Lubbers, Klaus, Ed. *Die Englische* . . . , 89–99.

"A Watcher by the Dead"
Fusco, Richard. *Maupassant* . . . , 116–117.

BING XIN

"Chaoren"

Larson, Wendy. "Female Subjectivity and Gender Relations: The Early Stories of Lu Yin and Bing Xin," in Liu Kang and Xiaobing Tang, Eds. *Politics, Ideology* . . . , 129–130.

"Posthumous Letters"

Larson, Wendy. "Female Subjectivity . . . ," 132–133.

HEINRICH BÖLL

"Like a Bad Dream"

+Bohner, Charles H. *Instructor's Manual* . . . , 3rd ed., 21.

MARÍA LUISA BOMBAL

"Braids"

Díaz, Gwendolyn. "Desire and Discourse in María Luisa Bombal's *New Islands*," *Hispano*, 112 (1994), 58–59.

"New Islands"

Díaz, Gwendolyn. "Desire . . . ," 59–61.

"That Tree"

Boyle, Catherine. "The Fragile Perfection of the Shrouded Rebellion (Re-reading Passivity in María Luisa Bombal)," in Davies, Catherine, Ed. *Women Writers* . . . , 27–28.

Díaz, Gwendolyn. "Desire . . . ," 57–58.

Parra, Teresita J. "Feminist Ideas in the Works of Clorenda Matto de Turner, Teresa de la Parra, and María Luisa Bombal," in Waxman, Barbara F., Ed. *Multicultural Literatures* . . . , 167–169.

"La última niebla"

Díaz, Gwendolyn. "Desire . . . ," 52–56.

González, Inés. "María Luisa Bombal: 'La última niebla,' " in Roloff, Volker, and Harald Wentzlaff-Eggebert, Eds. *Der Hispanoamerikanische* . . . , 191–201.

Méndez Rodenas, Adriana. "El lenguaje de los sueños en 'La última niebla': la metáfora del Eros," *Revista Iberoamericana*, 60 (1994), 935–943.

"The Unknown"

Díaz, Gwendolyn. "Desire . . . ," 59.

ARNA WENDELL BONTEMPS

"Boy Blue"

Jones, Kirkland C. "Bontemps and the Old South," *African Am R*, 27 (1993), 184.

"The Cure"

Jones, Kirkland C. "Bontemps . . . ," 183.

"A Summer's Tragedy"
Gaudet, Marcia. "Images of Old Age in Three Louisiana Short Stories," *Louisiana Engl J*, 1, i (1993), 62–64.

JORGE LUIS BORGES

"The Aleph"
Brodzki, Bella. "Borges and the Idea of Woman," *Discurso*, 10, ii (1993), 38–40.
Calinescu, Matei. *Rereading*, 3–16.
Irwin, John T. *The Mystery to a Solution . . .* , 15–17.
Kiely, Robert. *Reverse Tradition . . .* , 95–96, 97–98.
Lindstrom, Naomi. . . . *A Study of the Short Fiction*, 54–57.
Rojas, Santiago. "El desdoblamiento creador-personaje en Borges: Usos y logros de creación," *Discurso*, 10, ii (1993), 146–147.
Sarlo, Beatriz. *Jorge Luis Borges . . .* , 56–57.

"The Anthropologist"
Lindstrom, Naomi. . . . *A Study of the Short Fiction*, 94.

"The Approach to al-Mu'tasim"
Alazraki, Jaime. "El componente sufí de 'El acercamiento a Almotasim,' " *Crítica Hispánica*, 15, ii (1993), 21–27.
Lindstrom, Naomi. . . . *A Study of the Short Fiction*, 18–20.
———. *Twentieth-Century . . .* , 92–93.
Pérez, Alberto Julián. "Génesis y desarrollo de los procedimientos narrativos en la obra literaria de Jorge Luis Borges," in Blüher, Karl A., and Alfonso de Toro, Eds. *Jorge Luis Borges . . .* , 18–19.
Winchell, James. "The Oldest Trick in the Book: Borges and the 'Rhetoric of Immediacy,' " *Stud Twentieth-Century Lit*, 17 (1993), 197–221.

"Averroes' Search"
Irwin, John T. *The Mystery . . .* , 91–93.
Lindstrom, Naomi. . . . *A Study of the Short Fiction*, 77–78.
Molloy, Sylvia. *Signs of Borges*, 55.

"Biography of Tadeo Isidoro Cruz"
Sorzana de Toribio, Nelida Ana. "El polémico criollismo de la época borgiana, estudio intertextual en la 'Biografía de Isidoro Tadeo Cruz,' " in Arancibia, Juana Alcira, Ed. *Literatura como . . .* , 236–244.

"The Book of Sand"
Brant, Herbert J. "Dreams and Death: Borges' 'El libro de arena,' " *Hispano*, 107 (1993), 71–86.
Lindstrom, Naomi. . . . *A Study of the Short Fiction*, 100–101.

"Borges y yo"
Rojas, Santiago. "El desdoblamiento . . . ," 148–149.

"The Circular Ruins"
Caro Valverde, María Teresa. "El otro en el texto: La escena de 'Las ruinas circulares,' " in *Actas del IV . . .* , 327–335.

Irwin, John T. *The Mystery* . . . , 257–258.
Lindstrom, Naomi. . . . *A Study of the Short Fiction*, 42–44.
Roloff, Volker. "Aspectos estético-receptivos en el discurso onírico de los cuentos de Jorge Luis Borges," in Blüher, Karl A., and Alfonso de Toro, Eds. *Jorge Luis Borges* . . . , 80–81.

"The Congress"
Brodzki, Bella. "Borges . . . ," 46–48.
Lindstrom, Naomi. . . . *A Study of the Short Fiction*, 99.

"The Cult of the Phoenix"
Lindstrom, Naomi. . . . *A Study of the Short Fiction*, 38–39.

"The Dead Man"
Kiely, Robert. *Reverse Tradition* . . . , 91–95.
Lindstrom, Naomi. . . . *A Study of the Short Fiction*, 76–77.
Molloy, Sylvia. *Signs of Borges*, 49–53.

"Death and the Compass"
Bloom, Harold. *The Western Canon* . . . , 464, 465–466.
Hewitt, Julia C. "El círculo del cuadrado en el cuadrado del círculo: 'La muerte y la brújula' de Borges," *Crítica Hispánica*, 15, ii (1993), 69–83.
Irwin, John T. *The Mystery* . . . , 30, 35–36, 49, 51–53, 55–57, 59–63, 68–70, 150, 152, 158–160, 162–163, 176–177, 226, 376–377, 380, 388–389, 390, 421–423, 427–428, 436–437, 439–440, 445–449.
Kiely, Robert. *Reverse Tradition* . . . , 98–99.
Lindstrom, Naomi. . . . *A Study of the Short Fiction*, 27–29.
Molloy, Sylvia. *Signs of Borges*, 48–49.
Sarabia, Rosa. " 'La muerte y la brújula' y la parodia borgeana del género policial," *J Hispanic Philol*, 17 (1992), 7–17.

"Deutsches Requiem"
Irwin, John T. *The Mystery* . . . , 63–64, 93.
Kiely, Robert. *Reverse Tradition* . . . , 101.
Lindstrom, Naomi. . . . *A Study of the Short Fiction*, 63–66.
Sarlo, Beatriz. *Jorge Luis Borges* . . . , 85–87.

"The Disk"
Lindstrom, Naomi. . . . *A Study of the Short Fiction*, 104.

"Doctor Brodie's Report"
Lindstrom, Naomi. . . . *A Study of the Short Fiction*, 96–97.

"The Draped Mirrors"
Gonzalez, José E. "Borges's 'The Draped Mirrors,' " *Explicator*, 52 (1994), 175.

"The Dread Redeemer Lazarus Morell"
Lindstrom, Naomi. . . . *A Study of the Short Fiction*, 14.

"The Duel"
Brodzki, Bella. "Borges . . . ," 44–45.
Lindstrom, Naomi. . . . *A Study of the Short Fiction*, 92–93.

"Emma Zunz"
Aizenberg, Edna. "Feminism and Kabbalism: Borges's 'Emma Zunz,' " *Crítica Hispánica*, 15, ii (1993), 11–19.

Charters, Ann. *Resources . . .*, 16.
Irwin, John T. *The Mystery . . .*, 289–290.
Kiely, Robert. *Reverse Tradition . . .*, 102–103.
Lindstrom, Naomi. . . . *A Study of the Short Fiction*, 67–68.
Rojo, Grinor. "Sobre 'Emma Zunz,' " *Revista Chilena*, 45 (1994), 87–106.
+Wheelock, Carter. "Borges and the 'Death' of the Text," in Lindstrom, Naomi. . . . *A Study of the Short Fiction*, 139.

"The End"
Lindstrom, Naomi. . . . *A Study of the Short Fiction*, 51–52.
Sarlo, Beatriz. *Jorge Luis Borges . . .*, 39–42.
Stephens, Cynthia. "Allusion in the Work of Jorge Luis Borges," *Hispano*, 111 (1994), 53–55.

"The End of the Duel"
+Bohner, Charles H. *Instructor's Manual . . .*, 3rd ed., 22.

"An Examination of the Work of Herbert Quain"
Irwin, John T. *The Mystery . . .*, 78–80.
Lindstrom, Naomi. . . . *A Study of the Short Fiction*, 31–32.
Pérez, Alberto Julián. "Génesis . . . ," 19–20.

"Funes the Memorious"
Lindstrom, Naomi. . . . *A Study of the Short Fiction*, 39–42.
———. *Twentieth-Century . . .*, 93–94.
Molloy, Sylvia. *Signs of Borges*, 74–76, 115–118.
Sarlo, Beatriz. *Jorge Luis Borges . . .*, 30–31.

"The Garden of the Forking Paths"
Balderston, Daniel. . . . *Reality in Borges*, 39–55.
Charters, Ann. *Resources . . .*, 17–18.
Cooksey, Thomas L. "The Labyrinth in the Monad: Possible Worlds in Borges and Leibniz," *Comparatist*, 17 (1993), 55–57.
Hardy, Sarah. "A Poetics of Immediacy: Oral Narrative and the Short Story," *Style*, 27 (1993), 365–366.
Irwin, John T. *The Mystery . . .*, 58, 64–65, 75–78, 80, 85–91, 158, 269, 307.
Lindstrom, Naomi. . . . *A Study of the Short Fiction*, 29–31.

"God's Script" [same as "The Writing of the Gods"]
Balderston, Daniel. . . . *Reality in Borges*, 69–80.
Lindstrom, Naomi. . . . *A Study of the Short Fiction*, 74–75.

"The Gospel According to Mark"
Sarlo, Beatriz. *Jorge Luis Borges . . .*, 29–30.
+Wheelock, Carter. "Borges and the 'Death' of the Text," in Lindstrom, Naomi. . . . *A Study of the Short Fiction*, 134–136.

"Guayaquil"
Balderston, Daniel. . . . *Reality in Borges*, 115–131.
Lindstrom, Naomi. . . . *A Study of the Short Fiction*, 94–95.

"The House of Asterion"
Irwin, John T. *The Mystery . . .*, 158, 253–254.

Larrea, María I. "Borges y el palimpsesto: 'La casa de Asterión,' " *Estudios Filológicos*, 29, i (1994), 101–111.
Lindstrom, Naomi. . . . *A Study of the Short Fiction*, 61–63.
Planells, Antonio. "El centro de los laberintos de Borges," *Revista Interamericana*, 42, i (1992), 109–112.

"Ibn-Hakkan al-Bokhari, Dead in His Labyrinth"
Irwin, John T. *The Mystery* . . . , 37–38, 39–41, 40–42, 55–57, 64–65, 73–74, 119, 160, 183–184, 227–228, 280, 424–426, 431–433.
Lindstrom, Naomi. . . . *A Study of the Short Fiction*, 59–61.
Planells, Antonio. "El centro . . . ," 112.

"The Immortal"
Bloom, Harold. *The Western Canon* . . . , 472–475.
Lindstrom, Naomi. . . . *A Study of the Short Fiction*, 69–71.
Planells, Antonio. "El centro . . . ," 108–109.
Stephens, Cynthia. "Allusion . . . ," 48–51.
Stewart, Jon. "Borges on Immortality," *Philosophy & Lit*, 17 (1993), 95–301.

"Insulting Master of Etiquette Kotsuké no Suké"
Lindstrom, Naomi. . . . *A Study of the Short Fiction*, 15–16.

"The Intruder"
Altamiranda, Daniel. "Borges, Jorge Luis (Argentina; 1899–1986)," in Foster, David W., Ed. *Latin American Writers* . . . , 79–80.
Brodzki, Bella. "Borges . . . ," 41–44.
Lindstrom, Naomi. . . . *A Study of the Short Fiction*, 95–96.
+Wheelock, Carter. "Borges and the 'Death' of the Text," in Lindstrom, Naomi. . . . *A Study of the Short Fiction*, 137.

"Juan Muraña"
Lindstrom, Naomi. . . . *A Study of the Short Fiction*, 90–91.
+Wheelock, Carter. "Borges and the 'Death' of the Text," in Lindstrom, Naomi. . . . *A Study of the Short Fiction*, 140.

"The Library of Babel"
Ammon, Theodore G. "A Note on a Note in 'The Library of Babel,' " *Romance Notes*, 33 (1993), 265–269.
Irwin, John T. *The Mystery* . . . , 153–154.
Lindstrom, Naomi. . . . *A Study of the Short Fiction*, 32–35.
Sarlo, Beatriz. *Jorge Luis Borges* . . . , 70–73.
Schmitz-Emans, Monika. "Lesen und Schreiben nach Babel: Über das Modell de labyrinthischen Bibliothek bei Jorges Luis Borges und Umberto Eco," *Arcadia*, 27, i–ii (1992), 108–112.
Urraca, Beatriz. "Wor(l)ds Through the Looking-Glass: Borges's Mirrors and Contemporary Theory," *Revista Canadiense*, 17 (1992), 153–176.
Walther, Lutz. "Babel, Burton, Borges: Zur Melancholie in Jorge Luis Borges's 'La Biblioteca de Babel,' " *Germanisch-Romanische Monatsschrift*, 43, iv (1993), 456–460.

"Life of Isidoro Tadeo Cruz, 1829–1874"
Lindstrom, Naomi. . . . *A Study of the Short Fiction*, 66.

"The Lottery in Babylon"
Gurewitch, Morton. *The Ironic Temper . . .*, 45–47.
Kiely, Robert. *Reverse Tradition . . .*, 86.
Lindstrom, Naomi. . . . *A Study of the Short Fiction*, 35–36.
Sarlo, Beatriz. *Jorge Luis Borges . . .*, 74–78.

"The Man at the Pink Corner"
Rey, Elisa. "Barroco y Teatralidad en el Primer Borges," in Martínez Cuitiño, Luis, and Élida Lois, Eds. *Actas del III Congreso . . .*, 859–868.
Silvestri, Laura. "Borges y la pragmática de lo fantástico," in Blüher, Karl A., and Alfonso de Toro, Eds. *Jorge Luis Borges . . .*, 59–60.

"The Man on the Threshold"
Balderston, Daniel. . . . *Reality in Borges*, 98–114.
Lindstrom, Naomi. . . . *A Study of the Short Fiction*, 75–76.

"The Masked Dyer, Kakkim of Merv"
Lindstrom, Naomi. . . . *A Study of the Short Fiction*, 13.

"The Meeting"
+Wheelock, Carter. "Borges and the 'Death' of the Text," in Lindstrom, Naomi. . . . *A Study of the Short Fiction*, 140.

"The Mirror and the Mask"
Lindstrom, Naomi. . . . *A Study of the Short Fiction*, 101–102.
Sánchez, Hernán. "Lectura de 'El espejo y la máscara' desde la poésia de Borges," *La torre*, 7 (1993), 213–231.

"The Night of Gifts"
Lindstrom, Naomi. . . . *A Study of the Short Fiction*, 103–104.

"The Other"
Brant, Herbert J. "Dreams and Death: Borges's *El libro de arena*," *Hispano*, 107 (1993), 77–79.
Irwin, John T. *The Mystery . . .*, 290–291, 298–299.
Jaime-Ramírez, Helios. "La estructura de lo fantástico en *El libro de arena* de Jorge Luis Borges," in *Coloquio Internacional . . .*, I, 130–134.
Latella, Graciela. "El discurso borgesiano: enunciación y figuratividad en 'El Otro' y 'Veinticinco agosto, 1983,' " in Blüher, Karl A., and Alfonso de Toro, Eds. *Jorge Luis Borges . . .*, 92–93, 94–100.
Lindstrom, Naomi. . . . *A Study of the Short Fiction*, 105–106.
Silvestri, Laura. "Borges y la pragmática . . . ," 49–58.

"The Other Death"
Lindstrom, Naomi. . . . *A Study of the Short Fiction*, 72–73.

"Pedro Salvadores"
Lindstrom, Naomi. . . . *A Study of the Short Fiction*, 93–94.

"Pierre Menard, Author of *Don Quijote*"
Balderston, Daniel. . . . *Reality in Borges*, 18–38.
Dapía, Silvia G. " 'Pierre Menard: Autor del Quijote,' " *Romance Lang Annual*, 5 (1993), 376–380.
Irwin, John T. *The Mystery . . .*, 168–169, 303–305, 430–431.

Janaway, Christopher. "Borges and Dante: A Reply to Michael Wreen," *British J Aesthetics*, 32, i (1992), 72–76.
Lindstrom, Naomi. . . . *A Study of the Short Fiction*, 46–50.
Molloy, Sylvia. *Signs of Borges*, 27–32.
Pérez, Alberto Julián. "Génesis . . . ," 19.
Rabell, Carmen R. "Cervantes y Borges: Relaciones intertextuales en 'Pierre Menard, autor del *Quixote*,' " *Revista Chilena*, 42 (1993), 203–207.
Rincón, Carlos. "The Peripheral Center of Postmodernism: On Borges, García Márquez, and Alterity," *Boundary 2*, 20, iii (1993), 163–168.
Sarlo, Beatriz. *Jorge Luis Borges* . . . , 31–33.
Silvestri, Laura. "Borges y la pragmática . . . ," 60–61.
Woscoboinik, Julio "La búsqueda de la fantasía inconsciente en la obra literaria de Jorge Luis Borges," in Paolini, Gilbert, Ed. *La Chispa* . . . , 276.
Wreen, Michael. "Once Is Not Enough?" *British J Aesthetics*, 30, ii (1990), 149–158.

"The Secret Miracle"
Balderston, Daniel. . . . *Reality in Borges*, 56–68.
Lindstrom, Naomi. . . . *A Study of the Short Fiction*, 44–46.
Molloy, Sylvia. *Signs of Borges*, 36–37.

"The Sect of the Thirty"
Lindstrom, Naomi. . . . *A Study of the Short Fiction*, 104–105.

"The Shape of the Sword"
Lindstrom, Naomi. . . . *A Study of the Short Fiction*, 50–51.

"The South"
Charters, Ann. *Resources* . . . , 18–19.
Irwin, John T. *The Mystery* . . . , 171–175, 176.
Lindstrom, Naomi. . . . *A Study of the Short Fiction*, 52–53.
Sarlo, Beatriz. *Jorge Luis Borges* . . . , 44–48.

"Story of the Warrior and the Captive"
Balderston, Daniel. . . . *Reality in Borges*, 81–97.
Lindstrom, Naomi. . . . *A Study of the Short Fiction*, 68–69.
Malpezzi, Julia, and Iris R. Segovia. "Borges y la intertextualidad de la historia: Nosotros en los otros," in Arancibia, Juana Alcira, Ed. *Literatura como* . . . , 246–254.
Sarlo, Beatriz. *Jorge Luis Borges* . . . , 42–44.

"Streetcorner Man"
Lindstrom, Naomi. . . . *A Study of the Short Fiction*, 11.

"Tai An's Long Search" [in collaboration with Bioy-Casares]
Irwin, John T. *The Mystery* . . . , 427–428.

"The Theme of the Traitor and the Hero"
Acosta, Marta. "Borges and Bertolucci: Two Conceptions of the Traitor and the Hero," *Lucero*, 4 (1993), 65–69.
Lindstrom, Naomi. . . . *A Study of the Short Fiction*, 36–37.
Nélida de Juano, María. "Semiótica del discurso referido en 'El tema

del traidor y del héroe' de Jorge Luis Borges,'' in Balat, Michel, and Janice Deledalle-Rhodes, Eds. *Signs of Humanity . . .*, 711–716.

''There Are More Things''
Brant, Herbert J. ''Dreams and Death . . . ,'' 79–80.
Irwin, John T. *The Mystery . . .*, 293–296.
Lindstrom, Naomi. . . . *A Study of the Short Fiction*, 101–102.

''The Theologians''
Lindstrom, Naomi. . . . *A Study of the Short Fiction*, 71–72.

''Three Versions of Judas''
Lindstrom, Naomi. . . . *A Study of the Short Fiction*, 37–38.

''Tlön, Uqbar, Orbis Tertius''
Bedoya Montoya, Luis I. '' 'Tlön, Uqbar, Orbis Tertius' de Jorge Luis Borges: Diseminación infinita de topografía y tropografía,'' *Lingüística y Lit*, 12, xix–xx (1991), 99–108.
Duncan, Cynthia K. ''Hacia una interpretación de lo fantástico en el contexto de la literatura hispanoamericana,'' *Texto Crítico*, 16 (1990), 57–58.
Irwin, John T. *The Mystery . . .*, 130, 132, 134–135, 136–137, 274–275, 285–286, 287–288, 297–298.
Lindstrom, Naomi. . . . *A Study of the Short Fiction*, 25–27.
Molloy, Sylvia. *Signs of Borges*, 85–86, 87–88, 98–99.
Pérez, Alberto Julián. ''Génesis . . . ,'' 21.
Sarlo, Beatriz. *Jorge Luis Borges . . .*, 62–70.
Urraca, Beatriz. ''Wor(l)ds Through . . . ,'' 153–176.

''Tom Castro, the Implausible Imposter''
Lindstrom, Naomi. . . . *A Study of the Short Fiction*, 13–14.

''The Twelve Figures of the Word''
Irwin, John T. *The Mystery . . .*, 437–441.

''The Two Kings and Their Two Labyrinths''
Lindstrom, Naomi. . . . *A Study of the Short Fiction*, 61.
Lombardini, Hugo E. ''El nivel de la historia en un relato de J. L. Borges: Un análisis narratológico,'' *Letras*, 27–28 (January–December, 1993), 39–65.
Planells, Antonio. ''El centro . . . ,'' 112.

''Ulrike''
Brant, Herbert J. ''Dreams and Death . . . ,'' 76–77.
Brodzki, Bella. ''Borges . . . ,'' 45–46.
Jaime-Ramírez, Helios. ''La estructura . . . ,'' 134–138.
Lindstrom, Naomi. . . . *A Study of the Short Fiction*, 107.

''Undr''
Jaime-Ramírez, Helios. ''La estructura . . . ,'' 138–141.
Lindstrom, Naomi. . . . *A Study of the Short Fiction*, 102.

''The Unworthy Friend''
Lindstrom, Naomi. . . . *A Study of the Short Fiction*, 91–92.

''Utopia of a Tired Man''
Brant, Herbert J. ''Dreams and Death . . . ,'' 81–82.
Lindstrom, Naomi. . . . *A Study of the Short Fiction*, 106.

"Veinticinco agosto, 1983"
Latella, Graciela. "El discurso . . . ," 93.

"La visèra fatal"
Irwin, John T. *The Mystery* . . . , 300–301, 302.

"The Waiting"
Lindstrom, Naomi. . . . *A Study of the Short Fiction*, 73–74.

"The Widow Ching, Lady Pirate"
Lindstrom, Naomi. . . . *A Study of the Short Fiction*, 15.

"The Zahir"
Brodzki, Bella. "Borges . . . ," 37, 40.
Kiely, Robert. *Reverse Tradition* . . . , 95, 96–97, 99.
Lindstrom, Naomi. . . . *A Study of the Short Fiction*, 57–58.

HERMAN CHARLES BOSMAN

"Drieka and the Moon"
Medalie, David. "The Mocking Fugitive: Humour as Anarchy in the Short Stories of Herman Charles Bosman," *New Contrast*, 22, iii (1994), 83–84.

"Graven Image"
Medalie, David. "The Mocking . . . ," 87–88.

"The Home-Coming"
Medalie, David. "The Mocking . . . ," 88–89.

"The Missionary"
Medalie, David. "The Mocking . . . ," 87–88.

"Old Transvaal Story"
Medalie, David. "The Mocking . . . ," 90.

"The Picture of Gysbert Jonker"
Medalie, David. "The Mocking . . . ," 85–86.

"Veld Maiden"
Medalie, David. "The Mocking . . . ," 81–82.

JUVENAL BOTTO

"Un cuerpo desaparece"
Zlotchew, Clark M. "Las esperas y la autoridad en la cuentística de Juvenal Botto," *Alba de América*, 6 (1988), 142.

"El documento"
Zlotchew, Clark M. "Las esperas . . . ," 139–141.

"El expediente"
Zlotchew, Clark M. "Las esperas . . . ," 141–142.

"Fiesta patria"
Zlotchew, Clark M. "Las esperas . . . ," 143.

"El muro (los abismos)"
Zlotchew, Clark M. "Las esperas . . . ," 145.

"Precisión"
Zlotchew, Clark M. "Las esperas . . . ," 145–146.

"La vaca"
Zlotchew, Clark M. "Las esperas . . . ," 144.

"El viaje de Isabel"
Zlotchew, Clark M. "Las esperas . . . ," 143–144.

ELIZABETH BOWEN

"Ann Lee's"
Lassner, Phyllis. *Elizabeth Bowen* . . . , 20–21.

"The Apple Tree"
Lassner, Phyllis. *Elizabeth Bowen* . . . , 50–52.

"Attractive Modern Homes"
Lassner, Phyllis. *Elizabeth Bowen* . . . , 80–82.

"Aunt Tatty"
Lassner, Phyllis. *Elizabeth Bowen* . . . , 33.

"The Back Drawing-Room"
Lassner, Phyllis. *Elizabeth Bowen* . . . , 5, 11–12.

"Breakfast"
Lassner, Phyllis. *Elizabeth Bowen* . . . , 27–28.

"The Cassowary"
Lassner, Phyllis. *Elizabeth Bowen* . . . , 33–35.

"The Cat Jumps"
Lassner, Phyllis. *Elizabeth Bowen* . . . , 60–63.
Morris, J. A. "Elizabeth Bowen's Stories of Suspense," in Bloom, Clive, Ed. *Twentieth-Century* . . . , 122–124.

"Charity"
Lassner, Phyllis. *Elizabeth Bowen* . . . , 47–48.

"The Cheery Soul"
Lassner, Phyllis. *Elizabeth Bowen* . . . , 67–68.

"The Claimant"
Lassner, Phyllis. *Elizabeth Bowen* . . . , 67.

"Coming Home"
Lassner, Phyllis. *Elizabeth Bowen* . . . , 41, 42–43.

"The Confidante"
Lassner, Phyllis. *Elizabeth Bowen* . . . , 25–27, 29.

"The Contessina"
Lassner, Phyllis. *Elizabeth Bowen* . . . , 35–36.

"The Dancing Mistress"
Lassner, Phyllis. *Elizabeth Bowen* . . . , 36–39.

"A Day in the Dark"
Lassner, Phyllis. *Elizabeth Bowen* . . . , 79.

"Dead Mabelle"
Lassner, Phyllis. *Elizabeth Bowen . . .*, 59–60.

"The Demon Lover"
Calder, Robert L. " 'A More Sinister Troth': Elizabeth Bowen's 'The Demon Lover' as Allegory," *Stud Short Fiction*, 31 (1994), 91–97.
Lassner, Phyllis. *Elizabeth Bowen . . .*, 64–67.
Morris, J. A. "Elizabeth Bowen's . . .," 117–119.

"The Disinherited"
Lassner, Phyllis. *Elizabeth Bowen . . .*, 97–101.
McCormack, W. J. *Dissolute Characters . . .*, 242–244.

"The Dolt's Tale"
Lassner, Phyllis. *Elizabeth Bowen . . .*, 40.

"The Evil that Men Do—,"
Lassner, Phyllis. *Elizabeth Bowen . . .*, 87–88.

"Firelight in the Flat"
Lassner, Phyllis. *Elizabeth Bowen . . .*, 89.

"Flavia"
Lassner, Phyllis. *Elizabeth Bowen . . .*, 28–29.

"Foothold"
Lassner, Phyllis. *Elizabeth Bowen . . .*, 12–14.

"Gone Away"
Lassner, Phyllis. *Elizabeth Bowen . . .*, 95–96.

"The Good Earl"
Lassner, Phyllis. *Elizabeth Bowen . . .*, 16.

"Green Holly"
Barreca, Regina. *Untamed and Unabashed . . .*, 116–117.
Lassner, Phyllis. *Elizabeth Bowen . . .*, 55–57.

"Hand in Glove"
Lassner, Phyllis. *Elizabeth Bowen . . .*, 69–70.

"The Happy Autumn Fields"
Lassner, Phyllis. *Elizabeth Bowen . . .*, 105–110.

"Her Table Spread"
Gonzalez, Alexander G. "Elizabeth Bowen's 'Her Table Spread': A Joycean Irish Story," *Stud Short Fiction*, 30 (1993), 343–348.
Lassner, Phyllis. *Elizabeth Bowen . . .*, 15–16.

"Human Habitation"
Lassner, Phyllis. *Elizabeth Bowen . . .*, 16–18.

"I Hear You Say So"
Lassner, Phyllis. *Elizabeth Bowen . . .*, 95–96.

"The Inherited Clock"
Lassner, Phyllis. *Elizabeth Bowen . . .*, 23–24.

"In the Square"
Lassner, Phyllis. *Elizabeth Bowen . . .*, 5, 79–81.

"Ivy Grips the Steps"
Lassner, Phyllis. *Elizabeth Bowen* . . . , 91–92.
Morris, J. A. "Elizabeth Bowen's . . . ," 126–127.

"Joining Charles"
Lassner, Phyllis. *Elizabeth Bowen* . . . , 84–85.

"The Jungle"
Lassner, Phyllis. *Elizabeth Bowen* . . . , 47–48.

"Just Imagine"
Lassner, Phyllis. *Elizabeth Bowen* . . . , 55.

"The Last Night in the Old Home"
Lassner, Phyllis. *Elizabeth Bowen* . . . , 76–77.

"The Little Girl's Room"
Lassner, Phyllis. *Elizabeth Bowen* . . . , 49–50.

"Look at All Those Roses"
Lassner, Phyllis. *Elizabeth Bowen* . . . , 72–73.
Morris, J. A. "Elizabeth Bowen's . . . ," 119–121.

"Love"
Lassner, Phyllis. *Elizabeth Bowen* . . . , 70–72.

"A Love Story: 1939"
Lassner, Phyllis. *Elizabeth Bowen* . . . , 85–86.

"The Lover"
Lassner, Phyllis. *Elizabeth Bowen* . . . , 30–31.

"Lunch"
Lassner, Phyllis. *Elizabeth Bowen* . . . , 39.

"Making Arrangements"
Lassner, Phyllis. *Elizabeth Bowen* . . . , 57–59.

"The Man of the Family"
Lassner, Phyllis. *Elizabeth Bowen* . . . , 32–33.

"Maria"
Lassner, Phyllis. *Elizabeth Bowen* . . . , 50.

"Mrs. Moysey"
Lassner, Phyllis. *Elizabeth Bowen* . . . , 73–74.

"Mysterious Kôr"
Bergonzi, Bernard. *Wartime* . . . , 44–45.
Lassner, Phyllis. *Elizabeth Bowen* . . . , 93–95.
Morris, J. A. "Elizabeth Bowen's . . . ," 124–125.

"The Needlecase"
Lassner, Phyllis. *Elizabeth Bowen* . . . , 89–91.

"The New House"
Lassner, Phyllis. *Elizabeth Bowen* . . . , 30–31.

"No. 16"
Lassner, Phyllis. *Elizabeth Bowen* . . . , 87–88.

"Oh, Madam"
Lassner, Phyllis. *Elizabeth Bowen* . . . , 39–40.

"The Parrot"
Lassner, Phyllis. *Elizabeth Bowen* . . . , 33.

"Pink Biscuit"
Lassner, Phyllis. *Elizabeth Bowen* . . . , 48–49.

"A Queer Heart"
Lassner, Phyllis. *Elizabeth Bowen* . . . , 22–23.

"Recent Photograph"
Lassner, Phyllis. *Elizabeth Bowen* . . . , 21–22.

"Reduced"
Lassner, Phyllis. *Elizabeth Bowen* . . . , 68–69.

"Requiscat"
Lassner, Phyllis. *Elizabeth Bowen* . . . , 82–83.

"The Return"
Lassner, Phyllis. *Elizabeth Bowen* . . . , 47.

"The Secession"
Lassner, Phyllis. *Elizabeth Bowen* . . . , 19–20.

"The Shadowy Third"
Lassner, Phyllis. *Elizabeth Bowen* . . . , 14–15.

"Songs My Father Sang Me"
Lassner, Phyllis. *Elizabeth Bowen* . . . , 88–89.

"The Storm"
Lassner, Phyllis. *Elizabeth Bowen* . . . , 83–84.

"Summer Night"
Lassner, Phyllis. *Elizabeth Bowen* . . . , 101–105.
McCormack, W. J. *Dissolute Characters* . . . , 233–235.

"Sunday Afternoon"
Lassner, Phyllis. *Elizabeth Bowen* . . . , 75–76, 77–78.

"Tears, Idle Tears"
Lassner, Phyllis. *Elizabeth Bowen* . . . , 41–42, 45–46.

"Telling"
Lassner, Phyllis. *Elizabeth Bowen* . . . , 63–64.

"The Tommy Crans"
Lassner, Phyllis. *Elizabeth Bowen* . . . , 77–78.

"The Visitor"
Lassner, Phyllis. *Elizabeth Bowen* . . . , 45.

"The Working Party"
Lassner, Phyllis. *Elizabeth Bowen* . . . , 18–19.

JANE BOWLES

"Camp Cataract"
Gentile, Kathy J. " The Dreaded Voyage Into the World': Jane Bowles and Her Serious Ladies," *Stud Am Fiction*, 22 (1994), 50–52.

PAUL BOWLES

"Afternoon With Antaeus"
Hibbard, Allen. *Paul Bowles* . . . , 96–97.

"Allal"
Hibbard, Allen. *Paul Bowles* . . . , 94–96.

"At Paso Rojo"
Hibbard, Allen. *Paul Bowles* . . . , 20–22.

"At the Krungthep Plaza"
Hibbard, Allen. *Paul Bowles* . . . , 115–116.

"By the Water"
Hibbard, Allen. *Paul Bowles* . . . , 10–12.

"Call at Corazón"
Hibbard, Allen. *Paul Bowles* . . . , 27–29.

"The Delicate Prey"
Hibbard, Allen. *Paul Bowles* . . . , 12–15.

"Dinner at Sir Nigel's"
Hibbard, Allen. *Paul Bowles* . . . , 122.

"A Distant Episode"
Hibbard, Allen. *Paul Bowles* . . . , 16–18.

"Doña Faustina"
Hibbard, Allen. *Paul Bowles* . . . , 70–72.

"The Echo"
Hibbard, Allen. *Paul Bowles* . . . , 29–32.

"The Eye"
Hibbard, Allen. *Paul Bowles* . . . , 105–106.

"A Friend of the World"
Hibbard, Allen. *Paul Bowles* . . . , 48–50.

"The Frozen Fields"
Hibbard, Allen. *Paul Bowles* . . . , 76–84.

"The Garden"
Hibbard, Allen. *Paul Bowles* . . . , 69–70.

"He of the Assembly"
Hibbard, Allen. *Paul Bowles* . . . , 50–52.

"Here to Learn"
Hibbard, Allen. *Paul Bowles* . . . , 110–114.

"How Many Midnights"
Hibbard, Allen. *Paul Bowles* . . . , 37–39.

"Hugh Harper"
Hibbard, Allen. *Paul Bowles* . . . , 121–122.

"The Hyena"
Hibbard, Allen. *Paul Bowles* . . . , 67–69.

"If I Should Open My Mouth"
Hibbard, Allen. *Paul Bowles* . . . , 84–86.

"In Absentia"
Hibbard, Allen. *Paul Bowles . . .*, 128–130.

"In the Red Room"
Hibbard, Allen. *Paul Bowles . . .*, 116–118.

"Istikhara, Anaya, Medagan, and the Medaganat"
Hibbard, Allen. *Paul Bowles . . .*, 99.

"Julian Vreden"
Hibbard, Allen. *Paul Bowles . . .*, 120–121.

"Kitty"
Hibbard, Allen. *Paul Bowles . . .*, 114–115.

"Madame and Ahmed"
Hibbard, Allen. *Paul Bowles . . .*, 104.

"Massachusetts 1932"
Hibbard, Allen. *Paul Bowles . . .*, 125–126.

"Mejdoub"
Hibbard, Allen. *Paul Bowles . . .*, 97–98.

"New York 1965"
Hibbard, Allen. *Paul Bowles . . .*, 124–125.

"Pages from Cold Point"
Hibbard, Allen. *Paul Bowles . . .*, 32–36.

"Pastor Dowe at Tacaté"
Hibbard, Allen. *Paul Bowles . . .*, 24–25.

"Reminders of Bouselham"
Hibbard, Allen. *Paul Bowles . . .*, 91–94.

"Rumor and a Ladder"
Hibbard, Allen. *Paul Bowles . . .*, 106–107.

"The Scorpion"
Hibbard, Allen. *Paul Bowles . . .*, 8–10.

"Señor Ong and Señor Ha"
Hibbard, Allen. *Paul Bowles . . .*, 25–27.

"Sylvie Ann, the Boogie Man"
Hibbard, Allen. *Paul Bowles . . .*, 86–87.

"Tangier 1975"
Hibbard, Allen. *Paul Bowles . . .*, 122–124.

"Tapiama"
Hibbard, Allen. *Paul Bowles . . .*, 72–75.

"Tea on the Mountain"
Hibbard, Allen. *Paul Bowles . . .*, 5–8.

"The Time of Friendship"
Hibbard, Allen. *Paul Bowles . . .*, 53–62.

"Under the Sky"
Hibbard, Allen. *Paul Bowles . . .*, 22–24.

"Unwelcome Words"
Hibbard, Allen. *Paul Bowles . . .*, 126–128.

"The Water of Izli"
Hibbard, Allen. *Paul Bowles . . .*, 98.

"You Are Not I"
Hibbard, Allen. *Paul Bowles . . .*, 39–41.

"You Have Left Your Lotus Pods on the Bus"
Hibbard, Allen. *Paul Bowles . . .*, 90–91.

KAYE BOYLE

"The Astronomer's Wife"
Pickering, James H., and Jeffrey D. Hoeper. *Instructor's Manual . . .*, 69–70.

T. CORAGHESSAN BOYLE

"Greasy Lake"
Walker, Michael. "Boyle's 'Greasy Lake' and the Moral Failure of Postmodernism," *Stud Short Fiction*, 31 (1994), 247–255.

DIONNE BRAND

"I used to like the Dallas Cowboys"
Hunter, Lynette. "After Modernism: Alternative Voices in the Writings of Dionne Brand, Claire Harris, and Marlene Philip," *Univ Toronto Q*, 62 (1992–1993), 272–273.
Raiskin, Judith. "7 Days/6 Nights at 'Plantation Estates': A Critique of Cultural Colonialism by Caribbean Writers," in Rudin, Ernest, and Gert Buelens, Eds. *Deferring a Dream . . .*, 95–97.

MAX BRAND [FREDERICK SCHILLER FAUST]

"Internes Can't Take Money"
Bloodworth, William. "Introduction," *The Collected Stories . . .* [by Max Brand], xvii–xviii.

BETH BRANT

"The Long Story"
Gould, Janice. "Disobedience (in Language) in Texts by Lesbian Native Americans," *Ariel*, 25, i (1994), 36–37.

KAMAU BRATHWAITE

"4th Traveller"
Rohlehr, Gordon. "Dream Journeys," *World Lit Today*, 68 (1994), 768–770.

"Salvages"
James, Cynthia. "The Unknown Text," *World Lit Today*, 68 (1994), 759–760.
Rohlehr, Gordon. "Dream . . . ," 770–772.

VOLKER BRAUN

"Unvollendete Geschichte"
Reucher, Theo. "Volker Braun, 'Unvollendete Geschichte' " in Kaiser, Herbert, and Gerhard Köpf, Eds. *Erzählen, Erinnern . . .*, 149–171.

BERTOLT BRECHT AND KARIN MICHAËLIS

"Streitigkeiten"
Eddy, Beverley D. "Bertolt Brecht's and Karin Michaëlis's 'Streitigkeiten': Reflections on Old Age and Literature," *Germ R*, 69 (1994), 2–6.

CLEMENS BRENTANO

"Die Schachtel mit der Friedenspuppe"
Brantner, Christina. "Zur Problematik des Vaterländischen Freiheitsgedankens in Brentanos 'Die Schachtel mit der Friedenspuppe,' " *Germ Life & Letters*, 46 (1993), 13–21.
"The Supernumerary Wehmüllers and Hungarian National Visages"
Browning, Robert M. "Clemens Brentano's 'Die mehreren Wehmüller': Some Thoughts on Leading Motifs," *Carleton Germ Papers*, 22 (1994), 39–45.

VALERIJ BRJUSOV

"Mramornaja golovka' "
Hutchings, Stephen C. "The Phantoms of Narrative: Time, Passion and the Fantastic in Brjusov's Short Stories," *Russian, Croatian*, 35 (1994), 101–103.
"Poslednie stranicy iz dnevnika ženščiny' "
Hutchings, Stephen C. "The Phantoms . . . ," 97–99
"Poslednie mučeniki"
Hutchings, Stephen C. "The Phantoms . . . ," 109–110.
"Rhea Silvia"
Hutchings, Stephen C. "The Phantoms . . . ," 106–108.
"Sestry"
Hutchings, Stephen C. "The Phantoms . . . ," 94–95.
"V zerkale"
Hutchings, Stephen C. "The Phantoms . . . ," 95–96.

"Za sebja ili za druguju"
Hutchings, Stephen C. "The Phantoms . . . ," 99–101.

"Zaščita"
Hutchings, Stephen C. "The Phantoms . . . ," 103–105.

"Zemlja"
Hutchings, Stephen C. "The Phantoms . . . ," 109–110.

HAROLD BRODKEY

"Piping Down the Valleys Wild"
Bidney, Martin. "A Song of Innocence and of Experience: Rewriting Blake in Brodkey's 'Piping Down the Valleys Wild,' " *Stud Short Fiction*, 31 (1994), 237–245.

"The State of Grace"
Bidney, Martin. "An Unreliable Modern 'Mariner': Rewriting Coleridge in Harold Brodkey's 'The State of Grace,' " *Stud Short Fiction*, 31 (1994), 47–55.

FREDRIC BROWN

"And the Gods Laughed"
Seabrook, Jack. *Martians and Misplaced* . . . , 147–148.

"The Angelic Angelworm"
Seabrook, Jack. *Martians and Misplaced* . . . , 152–153, 154–155.

"Arena"
Seabrook, Jack. *Martians and Misplaced* . . . , 149–150.

"Blood of the Dragon"
Seabrook, Jack. *Martians and Misplaced* . . . , 25.

"Come and Go Mad"
Seabrook, Jack. *Martians and Misplaced* . . . , 164–165.

"Cry Silence"
Seabrook, Jack. *Martians and Misplaced* . . . , 95–96.

"Death in the Dark"
Seabrook, Jack. *Martians and Misplaced* . . . , 31.

"Death Is a Noise"
Seabrook, Jack. *Martians and Misplaced* . . . , 34–35.

"Death Is a White Rabbit"
Seabrook, Jack. *Martians and Misplaced* . . . , 151.

"Don't Look Behind You"
Seabrook, Jack. *Martians and Misplaced* . . . , 90–91.

"Each Night He Died"
Seabrook, Jack. *Martians and Misplaced* . . . , 97–98.

"The Four Blind Men"
Seabrook, Jack. *Martians and Misplaced* . . . , 93.

"The Freak Show Murders"
Seabrook, Jack. *Martians and Misplaced* . . . , 36–37.

"The Ghost of Riley"
Seabrook, Jack. *Martians and Misplaced* . . . , 37–38.

"The Hat Trick"
Seabrook, Jack. *Martians and Misplaced* . . . , 146, 154, 155.

"Homicide Sanitarium"
Seabrook, Jack. *Martians and Misplaced* . . . , 29–30.

"I'll Cut Your Throat Again, Kathleen"
Seabrook, Jack. *Martians and Misplaced* . . . , 92–93.

"Knock"
Seabrook, Jack. *Martians and Misplaced* . . . , 159–160.

"Last Curtain"
Seabrook, Jack. *Martians and Misplaced* . . . , 97.

"The Laughing Butcher"
Seabrook, Jack. *Martians and Misplaced* . . . , 93–95.

"Letter to a Phoenix"
Seabrook, Jack. *Martians and Misplaced* . . . , 166.

"Life and Fire"
Seabrook, Jack. *Martians and Misplaced* . . . , 28–29.

"Little Apple Hard to Peel"
Seabrook, Jack. *Martians and Misplaced* . . . , 31.

"Little Boy Lost"
Seabrook, Jack. *Martians and Misplaced* . . . , 30.

"A Little White Lye"
Seabrook, Jack. *Martians and Misplaced* . . . , 32.

"Miss Darkness"
Seabrook, Jack. *Martians and Misplaced* . . . , 91–92.

"The Moon for a Nickel"
Seabrook, Jack. *Martians and Misplaced* . . . , 23–24, 27.

"Murder Set to Music"
Seabrook, Jack. *Martians and Misplaced* . . . , 102.

"Murder While You Wait"
Seabrook, Jack. *Martians and Misplaced* . . . , 38.

"The New One"
Seabrook, Jack. *Martians and Misplaced* . . . , 157–158.

"The Nose of Don Aristide"
Seabrook, Jack. *Martians and Misplaced* . . . , 99.

"Nothing Sirius"
Seabrook, Jack. *Martians and Misplaced* . . . , 148.

"Not Yet the End"
Seabrook, Jack. *Martians and Misplaced* . . . , 145–146.

"The Numberless Shadows"
Seabrook, Jack. *Martians and Misplaced* . . . , 156–157.

"Pi in the Sky"
Seabrook, Jack. *Martians and Misplaced . . .*, 151–152.

"Placet Is a Crazy Place"
Seabrook, Jack. *Martians and Misplaced . . .*, 148–149.

"Premiere of Murder"
Seabrook, Jack. *Martians and Misplaced . . .*, 101–102.

"Puppet Show"
Seabrook, Jack. *Martians and Misplaced . . .*, 168.

"Red Is the Hue of Hell"
Seabrook, Jack. *Martians and Misplaced . . .*, 157–158.

"Rustle of Wings"
Seabrook, Jack. *Martians and Misplaced . . .*, 165–166.

"Something Green"
Seabrook, Jack. *Martians and Misplaced . . .*, 165.

"The Song of the Dead"
Seabrook, Jack. *Martians and Misplaced . . .*, 87–89.

"The Star Mouse"
Seabrook, Jack. *Martians and Misplaced . . .*, 147, 154.

"Tale of the Flesh Monger"
Seabrook, Jack. *Martians and Misplaced . . .*, 168–169.

"Teacup Trouble"
Seabrook, Jack. *Martians and Misplaced . . .*, 26, 39.

"This Way Out"
Seabrook, Jack. *Martians and Misplaced . . .*, 96–97.

"Town Wanted"
Seabrook, Jack. *Martians and Misplaced . . .*, 26, 39.

"Trouble Comes Double"
Seabrook, Jack. *Martians and Misplaced . . .*, 30.

"A Voice Behind Him"
Seabrook, Jack. *Martians and Misplaced . . .*, 89–90.

"The Waveries"
Seabrook, Jack. *Martians and Misplaced . . .*, 146–147, 150, 155.

"The Weapon"
Seabrook, Jack. *Martians and Misplaced . . .*, 237–238.

"Witness in the Dark"
Seabrook, Jack. *Martians and Misplaced . . .*, 99–100.

"A Word From Our Sponsor"
Seabrook, Jack. *Martians and Misplaced . . .*, 165.

CHRISTINE BRÜCKNER

"Bist du nun glücklich, toter Agamemnon?"
Komar, Kathleen L. "Klytemnestra in Germany: Revisions of Female

Archetype by Christa Reinig and Christine Brückner,'' *Germ R*, 69 (1994), 22–23.

GAËTAN BRULOTTE

''Les Messagers de l'ascenseur''
Morin, Lise. ''Quelques rouages de la machine fantastique dans 'Les Messagers de l'ascenseur,' '' *Voix et Images*, 19, i (1993), 132–150.

''Le Réve de tomates''
Fink, Béatrice. ''Pommes d'amour: L'Ecriture tomatique de Gaëtan Brulotte,'' *French R*, 67 (1994), 966–973.

CHARLES BUKOWSKI

''A Couple of Winos''
Harrison, Russell. *Against the American* . . . , 256–258.

''The Death of the Father II''
Harrison, Russell. *Against the American* . . . , 265–268.

''Decline and Fall''
Harrison, Russell. *Against the American* . . . , 259–263.

''Have You Read Pirandello?''
Harrison, Russell. *Against the American* . . . , 254–255.

''Head Job''
Harrison, Russell. *Against the American* . . . , 258–259.

''The Life of a Bum''
Harrison, Russell. *Against the American* . . . , 269–279.

''Some Hangover''
Harrison, Russell. *Against the American* . . . , 264–265.

CARLOS BULOSAN

''Be American''
Wong, Sau-ling C. *Reading Asian American Literature* . . . , 130–133.

DONALD R. BURLESON

''Ziggles''
Deleault, Arthur R. ''Perceptions: Campbell/Burleson,'' *Stud Weird Fiction*, 15 (1994), 18–19.

OCTAVIA E. BUTLER

''Bloodchild''
Helford, Elyce R. '' 'Would you really rather die than bear my

young?': The Construction of Gender, Race, and Species in Octavia E. Butler's 'Bloodchild,' " *African Am R*, 28 (1994), 259–271.

DINO BUZZATI

"Appointment with Einstein"
Haynes, Roslynn D. *From Faust* . . . , 282–283.

"Le notti difficili"
Capano, Daniel H. "Buzzati, dos en uno," *Letras*, 25–26 (1991–1992), 51–56.

GEORGE WASHINGTON CABLE

"Belles Demoiselles Plantation"
King, Kimball. "George W. Cable: 'Belles Demoiselles Plantation,' " in Lubbers, Klaus, Ed. *Die Englische* . . . , 79–88.

"Tite Poulette"
Bryan, Violet H. *The Myth of New Orleans* . . . , 15–17.

LYDIA CABRERA

"Historia verdadera de un viejo pordiosero que decía llamarse Mampurias"
Inclán, Josefina. "Una polifacética y transformista historica de Lydia Cabrera," *Círculo*, 22 (1993), 38–44.

GUILLERMO CABRERA INFANTE

"Josefina, atiende a los señores"
Peavler, Terry J. "Matters of Ethical Inference: Cabrera Infante's 'Josefina,' " *Siglo*, 11, i–ii (1993), 203–208.

ABRAHAM CAHAN

"The Imported Bridegroom"
Harris, Susan K. "Problems of Representation in Turn-of-the-Century Immigrant Fiction," in Quirk, Tom, and Gary Scharnhorst, Eds. *American Realism* . . . , 127–128, 137–139.

ERSKINE CALDWELL

"Crownfire"
Klevar, Harvey L. *Erskine Caldwell* . . . , 37–38.

"A Swell-Looking Girl"
Klevar, Harvey L. *Erskine Caldwell* . . . , 87–88.

HORTENSE CALISHER

"The Coreopsis Kid"
Snodgrass, Kathleen. *The Fiction of* . . . , 23–24.

"The Gulf Between"
Snodgrass, Kathleen. *The Fiction of* . . . , 26–27.

"The Middle Drawer"
Snodgrass, Kathleen. *The Fiction of* . . . , 33–35.

"Old Stock"
Snodgrass, Kathleen. *The Fiction of* . . . , 27–29.

"The Pool of Narcissus"
Snodgrass, Kathleen. *The Fiction of* . . . , 24–25.

"The Rabbi's Daughter"
Snodgrass, Kathleen. *The Fiction of* . . . , 29–31.

"The Watchers"
Snodgrass, Kathleen. *The Fiction of* . . . , 25–26.

ITALO CALVINO

"The Adventure of a Soldier"
Gabriele, Tommasina. *Italo Calvino* . . . , 94, 95–98.
Weiss, Beno. *Understanding Italo Calvino*, 155–156.

"All at One Point"
Easterbrook, Neil. " 'The reasons why living was beautiful': Delirium, Loss, and Fantasy in Italo Calvino's *Cosmicomics* and *t zero*," *Conference Coll Teachers Engl Stud*, 58 (1993), 32.
Weiss, Beno. *Understanding Italo Calvino*, 101.

"The Argentine Ant"
Weiss, Beno. *Understanding Italo Calvino*, 68–72.

"Avventura di un automobilista"
Gabriele, Tommasina. *Italo Calvino* . . . , 77–78.

"Avventura di una bagnante"
Gabriele, Tommasina. *Italo Calvino* . . . , 98–102.

"Avventura di un impiegato"
Gabriele, Tommasina. *Italo Calvino* . . . , 103–106.

"Avventura di una moglie"
Gabriele, Tommasina. *Italo Calvino* . . . , 102–103.

"Avventura di un poeta"
Gabriele, Tommasina. *Italo Calvino* . . . , 112–118.

"Avventura di due sposi"
Gabriele, Tommasina. *Italo Calvino* . . . , 109, 110–111.

"Avventura di un viaggiatore"
Gabriele, Tommasina. *Italo Calvino . . .*, 107–109.

"The Baron in the Trees"
Weiss, Beno. *Understanding Italo Calvino*, 47–56.

"The Cloven Viscount"
Weiss, Beno. *Understanding Italo Calvino*, 40–46.

"The Count of Montecristo"
Weiss, Beno. *Understanding Italo Calvino*, 121–125.

"The Crow Comes Last"
Weiss, Beno. *Understanding Italo Calvino*, 22–25.

"Death"
Weiss, Beno. *Understanding Italo Calvino*, 117–119.

"The Dinosaurs"
Weiss, Beno. *Understanding Italo Calvino*, 103–105.

"The Distance of the Moon"
Easterbrook, Neil. " 'The reasons . . .,' " 31–32.
Weiss, Beno. *Understanding Italo Calvino*, 97–99.

"The Enchanted Garden"
Weiss, Beno. *Understanding Italo Calvino*, 21.

"La finta nonna"
Hanne, Michael. "Peasant Storytelling Meets Literary Theory: The Case of 'La finta nonna,' " *Italianist*, 12 (1992), 46–54.

"The Form of Space"
Weiss, Beno. *Understanding Italo Calvino*, 101–102.

"From Opaqueness"
Weiss, Beno. *Understanding Italo Calvino*, 200–201.

"The Identity of Blood Ties"
Weiss, Beno. *Understanding Italo Calvino*, 21–22.

"A King Listens"
Weiss, Beno. *Understanding Italo Calvino*, 194–197.

"The Memory of the World"
Weiss, Beno. *Understanding Italo Calvino*, 126–128.

"Mitosis"
Weiss, Beno. *Understanding Italo Calvino*, 115–116.

"Mushrooms in the City"
Weiss, Beno. *Understanding Italo Calvino*, 32.

"The Name, The Nose"
Weiss, Beno. *Understanding Italo Calvino*, 189–191.

"The Nonexistent Knight"
Weiss, Beno. *Understanding Italo Calvino*, 56–64.

"One of the Three Is Still Alive"
Weiss, Beno. *Understanding Italo Calvino*, 22.

"Priscilla"
Gabriele, Tommasina. *Italo Calvino . . .*, 66–87.

"Remembering a Battle"
Weiss, Beno. *Understanding Italo Calvino*, 199.

"Santa's Children"
Weiss, Beno. *Understanding Italo Calvino*, 34–36.

"A Sign in Space"
Weiss, Beno. *Understanding Italo Calvino*, 99–100.

"Smog"
Weiss, Beno. *Understanding Italo Calvino*, 75–79.

"The Soft Moon"
Weiss, Beno. *Understanding Italo Calvino*, 112–114.

"The Spiral"
Easterbrook, Neil. " 'The reasons . . . ,' " 28, 30–31.
Gabriele, Tommasina. *Italo Calvino* . . . , 66–69, 72–74, 78.
Weiss, Beno. *Understanding Italo Calvino*, 105–107.

"t zero"
Weiss, Beno. *Understanding Italo Calvino*, 119–120.

"Under the Jaguar Sun"
Gabriele, Tommasina. *Italo Calvino* . . . , 130–148.
Weiss, Beno. *Understanding Italo Calvino*, 191–194.

"The Watcher"
Weiss, Beno. *Understanding Italo Calvino*, 79–86.

RAMSEY CAMPBELL

"The Little Voice"
Deleault, Arthur R. "Perceptions: Campbell/Burleson," *Stud Weird Fiction*, 15 (1994), 18–19.

ALBERT CAMUS

"La Femme adultère"
McGregor, Rob R. "Camus's 'La Femme adultère': A Metaphor of the Fall from the Absurd," *French R*, 67 (1994), 478–485.

"The Guest"
Dine, Philip. *Images of the Algerian War* . . . , 89–106.
Griem, Eberhard. "Albert Camus's 'The Guest': A New Look at the Prisoner," *Stud Short Fiction*, 30 (1993), 95–98.
Hurley, D. F. "Looking for the Arab: Reading the Readings of Camus's 'The Guest,' " *Stud Short Fiction*, 30 (1993), 79–93.

"The Renegade"
Barny, Roger. "Une lecture descriptive du 'Renégat,' " in Bourquin, Jacques, and Daniel Jacobi, Eds. *Mélanges* . . . , 141–156.
Fayad, Mona. "The Problem of the Subject in Africanist Discourse: Conrad's 'Heart of Darkness' and Camus' 'The Renegade,' " *Comp Lit Stud*, 27 (1990), 298–305, 307–312.

McGregor, Rob R. "Camus's 'Le Renégat': An Allegory of the Existentialist Pilgrimage," *French R*, 66 (1993), 742–751.

"The Stranger"

Brock, Robert R. "Meursault the Straw Man," *Stud Novel*, 25 (1993), 92–100.

Chaitin, Gilbert D. "The Birth of the Subject in Camus's 'L'Étranger,' " *Romanic R*, 84 (1993), 163–180.

Grégoire, Vincent. "Pour une explication du passage sur l'amabilité des Arabes en prison dans 'L'Étranger,' " *Romance Notes*, 34 (1994), 223–231.

Hunwick, Andrew. "Albert Camus, Meursault, et le lecteur 'dupé,' " *R Lettres Modernes*, 1123–1132 (1993), 153–179.

Kristeva, Julia. *Strangers to Ourselves*, 24–29.

Lapaire, Pierre J. "Un Style polarisé: éléments de la binarité stylistique chez Camus," *French R*, 66 (1993), 611–613.

Silhol, Robert. "'L'Étranger' et le désir de l'Autre," in Hillenaar, Henk, and Walter Schönau, Eds. *Fathers and Mothers . . .*, 201–209.

Sterne, Richard C. *Dark Mirror . . .*, 191–204.

ALEJO CARPENTIER

"El camino de Santiago"

García Yero, Olga. "*Guerra del tiempo* de Alejo Carpentier: Realidad y devenir," *Universidad*, 241 (1991), 111–118.

"Semejante a la noche"

García Yero, Olga. "*Guerra . . .*," 120–123.

Muñoz, Willy O. "Literatura e historia en 'Semejante a la noche' de Alejo Carpentier," *Siglo*, 11, i–ii (1993), 181–192.

———. "El viaje de las ideologías en 'Semejante a la noche' de Alejo Carpentier," in Kenwood, Alun, Ed. *Traveller's Tales . . .*, 91–97.

"Viaje a la semilla"

García Yero, Olga. "*Guerra . . .*," 118–120.

LEONORA CARRINGTON

"La Dama ovale"

Domenella, Ana Rosa. "Leonora Carrington, Escritora surrealista," *Alba de América*, 11 (1993), 293–298.

"La debutante"

Domenella, Ana Rosa. "Leonora Carrington . . .," 298–300.

ANGELA CARTER

"Black Venus"

Siegel, Carol. *Male Masochism . . .*, 29.

"The Bloody Chamber"
Kaiser, Mary. "Fairy Tale as Sexual Allegory: Intertextuality in Angela Carter's *The Bloody Chamber*," *R Contemp Fiction*, 14, iii (1994), 31–33.
Sheets, Robin A. "Pornography, Fairy Tales, and Feminism: Angela Carter's 'The Bloody Chamber,' " *J History Sexuality*, 1, iv (1991), 642–657.
Wisker, Gina. "At Home All was Blood and Feathers: The Werewolf in the Kitchen—Angela Carter and Horror," in Bloom, Clive, Ed. *Creepers* . . . , 169–170.

"The Cabinet of Edgar Allan Poe"
Charters, Ann. *Resources* . . . , 20–21.

"The Erl-King"
Linkin, Harriet K. "Isn't It Romantic?: Angela Carter's Bloody Revision of the Romantic Aesthetic in 'The Erl-King,' " *Contemp Lit*, 35 (1994), 305–323.

"The Fall River Axe Murders"
Charters, Ann. *Resources* . . . , 22–23.
Ducornet, Rikki. "A Scatological and Cannibal Clock: Angela Carter's 'The Fall River Axe Murders,' " *R Contemp Fiction*, 14, iii (1994), 37–39.

"Flesh and the Mirror"
Russo, Mary. *The Female Grotesque* . . . , 162–164.

"Love"
Smith, Patricia J. "All You Need Is *Love*: Angela Carter's Novel of Sixties Sex and Sensibility," *R Contemp Fiction*, 14, iii (1994), 24–29.

"The Loves of the Lady Purple"
Wisker, Gina. "At Home . . . ," 163–165.

"The Snow Child"
Kaiser, Mary. "Fairy Tale . . . ," 33–35.

ADA JACK CARVER

"The Old One"
Gaudet, Marcia. "Images of Old Age in Three Louisiana Short Stories," *Louisiana Engl J*, 1, i (1993), 63–64.

RAYMOND CARVER

"After the Denim"
Plath, James. " 'After the Denim' and 'After the Storm': Raymond Carver Comes to Terms with the Hemingway Influence," *Hemingway R*, 13, ii (1994), 43–49.

"The Bath"
Powell, Jon. "The Stories of Raymond Carver: The Menace of Perpetual Uncertainty," *Stud Short Fiction*, 31 (1994), 650–652.

"Blackbird Pie"
Matsuoka, Naomi. "Murakami Haruki and Raymond Carver: The American Scene," *Comp Lit Stud*, 30 (1993), 426–433, 436.
Powell, Jon. "The Stories . . . ," 654–656.
Trussler, Michael. " 'Famous Times': Historicity in the Short Fiction of Richard Ford and Raymond Carver," *Wascana R*, 28, ii (1994), 41–50.

"The Bridle"
Gentry, Marshall B. "Women's Voices in Stories by Raymond Carver," *CEA Critic*, 56, i (1993), 88–89.
Scofield, Martin. "Negative Pastoral: The Art of Raymond Carver's Stories," *Cambridge Q*, 23 (1994), 251–252.

"Cathedral"
+Bohner, Charles H. *Instructor's Manual* . . . , 3rd ed., 23.
Bullock, Chris J. "From Castle to Cathedral: The Architecture of Masculinity in Raymond Carver's 'Cathedral,' " *J Men's Stud*, 2 (1994), 343–351.
Charters, Ann. *Resources* . . . , 25–26.
Nesset, Kirk. "Insularity and Self-Enlargement in Raymond Carver's *Cathedral*," *Essays Lit*, 21 (1994), 124–127.
Pickering, James H., and Jeffrey D. Hoeper. *Instructor's Manual* . . . , 112–114.

"Chef's House"
Gentry, Marshall B. "Women's Voices . . . ," 90.

"Errand"
May, Charles E. "Reality in the Modern Short Story," *Style*, 27 (1993), 377–378.

"Fat"
Berland, Lauren. "America, 'Fat,' the Fetus," *Boundary 2*, 21, iii (1994), 157–165.
Gentry, Marshall B. "Women's Voices . . . ," 89.
Scobie, Brian. "Carver Country," in Massa, Ann, and Alistair Stead, Eds. *Forked Tongues* . . . , 280–283.

"How About This?"
Scofield, Martin. "Negative Pastoral . . . ," 258–260.

"I Could See the Smallest Things"
Gentry, Marshall B. "Women's Voices . . . ," 90.

"The Idea"
Gentry, Marshall B. "Women's Voices . . . ," 90.

"Intimacy"
Gentry, Marshall B. "Women's Voices . . . ," 93.

"Nobody Said Anything"
Scofield, Martin. "Negative Pastoral . . . ," 256–258.

"Popular Mechanics"
Powell, Jon. "The Stories . . . ," 650.

"Preservation"
Gentry, Marshall B. "Women's Voices . . . ," 92.

"A Small, Good Thing"
Gentry, Marshall B. "Women's Voices . . . ," 92–93.
Nesset, Kirk. "Insularity and Self . . . ," 121–124.
Powell, Jon. "The Stories . . . ," 650–654.

"So Much Water So Close to Home"
Gentry, Marshall B. "Women's Voices . . . ," 90–92.
Scofield, Martin. "Negative Pastoral . . . ," 246–247.

"Tell the Women We're Going"
Scobie, Brian. "Carver . . . ," 277–279.

"The Third Thing That Killed My Father Off"
Scofield, Martin. "Negative Pastoral . . . ," 255–256.

"The Train"
Charters, Ann. *Resources* . . . , 27–28.

"What's in Alaska?"
Scofield, Martin. "Negative Pastoral . . . ," 248–250.

"Where I'm Calling From"
Nesset, Kirk. "Insularity and Self . . . ," 117–121.

"Will You Please Be Quiet, Please?"
Powell, Jon. "The Stories . . . ," 648–650.

"Why Don't You Dance?"
May, Charles E. "Reality . . . ," 377.
Scobie, Brian. "Carver . . . ," 274, 280–281, 283–284.
Trussler, Michael. "The Narrowed Voice: Minimalism and Raymond Carver," *Stud Short Fiction*, 31 (1994), 29–34.

"Why, Honey?"
Gentry, Marshall B. "Women's Voices . . . ," 89.

ROSARIO CASTELLANOS

"Lección de cocina"
Hart, Stephen M. *White Ink* . . . , 45–53.

ROBERTO CASTILLO

"Anita la cazadora de insectos"
Salinas Paguada, Manuel. "El cuento hondureño contemporáneo," in Róman-Lagunas, Jorge, Ed. *La literatura centroamericana* . . . , 97.

JOSÉ LUIS CASTILLO-PUCHE

"Una mosca en Manhattan"
Belmonte Serrano, José. "Aproximación a la narrativa breve de J. L.

Castillo-Puche: Los cuentos,'' in Dendle, Brian J., and José Belmonte Serrano, Eds. *Literatura de Levante*, 36–37.

''Parábola del buen rey y la ciudad ingrata''
Belmonte Serrano, José. ''Aproximación . . . ,'' 35–36.

WILLA CATHER

''Behind the Singer Tower''
Kaye, Frances W. *Isolation and Masquerade* . . . , 36–37.

''The Bohemian Girl''
Stead, Alistair. ''Pastoral Sexuality in British and American Fiction,'' in Massa, Ann, and Alistair Stead, Eds. *Forked Tongues* . . . , 304.

''The Joy of Nelly Deane''
Kaye, Frances W. *Isolation and Masquerade* . . . , 38–41.

''The Marriage of Phaedra''
Lee, Hermione. ''Cather's Bridge: Anglo-American Crossings in Willa Cather,'' in Massa, Ann, and Alistair Stead, Eds. *Forked Tongues* . . . , 46–47.
Zitter, Emmy S. ''The Unfinished Picture: Willa Cather's 'The Marriage of Phaedra,' '' *Stud Short Fiction*, 30 (1993), 153–160.

''The Old Beauty''
Lee, Hermione. ''Cather's Bridge . . . ,'' 51–54.

''Old Mrs. Harris''
Kaye, Frances W. *Isolation and Masquerade* . . . , 9–15, 18–24.

''On the Divide''
Kaye, Frances W. *Isolation and Masquerade* . . . , 59–60.

''On the Gull's Road''
Kaye, Frances W. *Isolation and Masquerade* . . . , 42–47.

''Paul's Case''
+Bohner, Charles H. *Instructor's Manual* . . . , 3rd ed., 24–25.
Charters, Ann. *Resources* . . . , 29–30.
Love, Glen A. ''Willa Cather: 'Paul's Case,' '' in Lubbers, Klaus, Ed. *Die Englische* . . . , 134–140.

''The Sculptor's Funeral''
Charters, Ann. *Resources* . . . , 31–32.

''Tommy the Unsentimental''
Kaye, Frances W. *Isolation and Masquerade* . . . , 32–36.

''A Wagner Matinée''
Feldman, Jessica R. *Gender on the Divide* . . . , 146–151.

ADELBERT VON CHAMISSO

''Peter Schlemihl Wundersame Geschichte''
Pille, René-Marc. '' 'Peter Schlemihl' récit initiatique? Essai de

lecture anthropologique," *Cahiers d'Etudes Germ*, 21 (1991), 85–97.

Wambach, Annemarie. " 'Fortunati Wünschhütlein und Glückssäckel' in neuem Gewand: Adelbert von Chamissos 'Peter Schlemihl,' " *Germ Q*, 67 (1994), 173–182.

FRANÇOIS-RENÉ DE CHATEAUBRIAND

"Atala"

Hamilton, James E. "The Hero's Journey to Niagara in Chateaubriand and Heredia, French and Cuban Exiles," *Romance Q*, 41 (1994), 71–73.

Irlam, Shaun. "Gerrymandered Geographies: Exoticism in Thomson and Chateaubriand," *Mod Lang Notes*, 108 (1993), 900–906.

O'Neil, Mary A. "Chateaubriand's 'Atala': A Study of the French Revolution," *Nineteenth-Century French Stud*, 22 (1993), 1–14.

Wang, Ben. "Inscribed Wilderness in Chateaubriand's 'Atala,' " *Romance Notes*, 33 (1993), 279–287.

Wasserman, Renata R. M. *Exotic Nations* . . . , 121–153.

"René"

Waller, Margaret. *The Male Malady* . . . , 29–56.

JOHN CHEEVER

"The Country Husband"

Dessner, Lawrence J. "Gender and Structure in John Cheever's 'The Country Husband,' " *Stud Short Fiction*, 31 (1994), 57–68.

"The Enormous Radio"

+Bohner, Charles H. *Instructor's Manual* . . . , 3rd ed., 25–26.

Charters, Ann. *Resources* . . . , 33–34.

"The Five-Forty-Eight"

Charters, Ann. *Resources* . . . , 34–35.

"The Fourth Alarm"

Ward, David S. "King Lear and Human Dignity in John Cheever's 'The Fourth Alarm,' " *Short Story*, 1, ii, N.S. (1993), 64–67.

"O Youth and Beauty!"

Pickering, James H., and Jeffrey D. Hoeper. *Instructor's Manual* . . . , 84–85.

"Oh What a Paradise It Seems"

Rooke, Constance. " 'Oh What a Paradise It Seems': John Cheever's Swan Song," in Wyatt-Brown, Anne M., and Janice Rossen, Eds. *Aging and Gender* . . . , 204–225.

"The Swimmer"

Kozikowski, Stanley J. "Damned in a Fair Life: Cheever's 'The Swimmer,' " *Stud Short Fiction*, 30 (1993), 367–375.

Kruse, Horst. "John Cheever: 'The Swimmer,' " in Lubbers, Klaus, Ed. *Die Englische* . . . , 334–348.

ANTON CHEKHOV

"About Love"
Isenberg, Charles. *Telling Silence* . . . , 129–135.

"Agafya"
Johnson, Ronald L. *Anton Chekhov* . . . , 32–33.

"All Friends Together" [same as "A Visit to Friends"]
Johnson, Ronald L. *Anton Chekhov* . . . , 84–85.

"An Anonymous Story"
Johnson, Ronald L. *Anton Chekhov* . . . , 58–59.

"Anyuta"
Johnson, Ronald L. *Anton Chekhov* . . . , 36–37.

"Ariadne"
Johnson, Ronald L. *Anton Chekhov* . . . , 79–81.

"Art"
Johnson, Ronald L. *Anton Chekhov* . . . , 44–45.

"The Artist's Story"
Johnson, Ronald L. *Anton Chekhov* . . . , 81–83.

"At Sea—A Sailor's Tale"
Finke, Michael C. " 'At Sea': A Psychoanalytic Approach to Chekhov's First Signed Work," in Jackson, Robert L., Ed. *Reading Chekhov's Text*, 49–60.
Johnson, Ronald L. *Anton Chekhov* . . . , 5–6.

"An Awkward Business" [same as "A Trivial Matter"; "An Unpleasant Business"; "An Unpleasantness"]
Johnson, Ronald L. *Anton Chekhov* . . . , 70–71.

"Baby"
Popkin, Cathy. "Paying the Price: The Rhetoric of Reckoning in Čechov's 'Peasant Women,' " *Russian, Croatian*, 35 (1994), 203–222.

"Because of Little Apples"
Johnson, Ronald L. *Anton Chekhov* . . . , 3–4.

"The Bishop"
Johnson, Ronald L. *Anton Chekhov* . . . , 102–103.
Nilsson, Nils A. " 'The Bishop': Its Theme," in Jackson, Robert L., Ed. *Reading Chekhov's Text*, 85–95.

"The Black Monk"
Debreczeny, Paul. " 'The Black Monk': Chekhov's Version of Symbolism," in Jackson, Robert L., Ed. *Reading Chekhov's Text*, 179–188.
Johnson, Ronald L. *Anton Chekhov* . . . , 72–74.

"The Butterfly" [same as "The Grasshopper": "La Cigale"]
Johnson, Ronald L. *Anton Chekhov* . . . , 56–57.

"A Case History"
Johnson, Ronald L. *Anton Chekhov* . . . , 95–96.

"The Chemist's Wife"
Johnson, Ronald L. *Anton Chekhov* . . . , 27.

"The Chorus Girl"
Johnson, Ronald L. *Anton Chekhov* . . . , 27–28.

"Concerning Love" [same as "About Love"]
Johnson, Ronald L. *Anton Chekhov* . . . , 83.

"The Darling" [same as "Angel"]
+Bohner, Charles H. *Instructor's Manual* . . . , 3rd ed., 26–27.
Evdokimova, Svetlana. " 'The Darling': Femininity Scorned and Desired," in Jackson, Robert L., Ed. *Reading Chekhov's Text*, 189–197.
Johnson, Ronald L. *Anton Chekhov* . . . , 78–79.
Pickering, James H., and Jeffrey D. Hoeper. *Instructor's Manual* . . . , 41.

"The Death of a Civil Servant"
Johnson, Ronald L. *Anton Chekhov* . . . , 7–8.

"The Dependents"
Johnson, Ronald L. *Anton Chekhov* . . . , 40–41.

"Dr. Startsev"
Johnson, Ronald L. *Anton Chekhov* . . . , 85.

"Dreams"
Johnson, Ronald L. *Anton Chekhov* . . . , 35–36.

"A Dreary Story—From an Old Man's Memoirs"
Johnson, Ronald L. *Anton Chekhov* . . . , 53–54.

"Drunk"
Johnson, Ronald L. *Anton Chekhov* . . . , 24.

"The Duel"
Axelrod, Willa C. "The Biblical and Theological Context of Moral Reform in 'The Duel,' " *Russian, Croatian*, 35 (1994), 129–152.
Durkin, Andrew R. "Allusion and Dialogue in 'The Duel,' " in Jackson, Robert L., Ed. *Reading Chekhov's Text*, 169–178.
Johnson, Ronald L. *Anton Chekhov* . . . , 54–56.

"Easter Eve"
Axelrod, Willa C. "Passage from Great Saturday to Easter Day in 'Holy Night,' " in Jackson, Robert L., Ed. *Reading Chekhov's Text*, 96–102.
Johnson, Ronald L. *Anton Chekhov* . . . , 42–43.
+May, Charles E. "Chekhov and the Modern Short Story," in May, Charles E., Ed. *The New Short Story* . . . , 209–210.
Pervukhina, Natalia. "Chekhov's 'Easter Night' and the Ornate Style," *Canadian Slavonic Papers*, 35 (1993), 29–44.

"An Encounter" [same as "The Meeting"]
Johnson, Ronald L. *Anton Chekhov* . . . , 34.

"The Enemies"
Jackson, Robert L. "'The Enemies': A Story at War with Itself?" in Jackson, Robert L., Ed. *Reading Chekhov's Text*, 63–73.

"Excellent People"
Johnson, Ronald L. *Anton Chekhov* . . . , 23.

"Fat and Thin"
Reid, Robert. "Checkov's 'Tolstyj i tonkij,': The Disclosure of Hierarchy," *Russian, Croation*, 36 (1994), 391–402.

"Gooseberries"
+Bohner, Charles H. *Instructor's Manual* . . . , 3rd ed., 28–29.
Charters, Ann. *Resources* . . . , 36–37.
Isenberg, Charles. *Telling Silence* . . . , 125–129.
Johnson, Ronald L. *Anton Chekhov* . . . , 90–91.

"The Grasshopper"
Pahomov, George. "Čexov's 'The Grasshopper': A Secular Saint's Life," *Slavic & East European J*, 37 (1993), 33–45.

"Gusev"
Johnson, Ronald L. *Anton Chekhov* . . . , 67–68.

"Happiness"
Johnson, Ronald L. *Anton Chekhov* . . . , 34–35.

"A Hard Case" [same as "The Man in a Case"; "The Man in a Shell"]
Johnson, Ronald L. *Anton Chekhov* . . . , 88–89.

"He Understood"
Johnson, Ronald L. *Anton Chekhov* . . . , 11–12.

"Home" [same as "At Home"; 1887]
Golstein, Vladimir. " 'Doma': At Home and Not at Home," in Jackson, Robert L., Ed. *Reading Chekhov's Text*, 74–81.
Johnson, Ronald L. *Anton Chekhov* . . . , 21–22.

"Home" [1897]
Johnson, Ronald L. *Anton Chekhov* . . . , 86–87.

"The House with the Mansard"
Debreczeny, Paul. "Chekhov's Use of Impressionism in 'The House with the Mansard,' " in Anderson, Roger, and Paul Debreczeny, Eds. *Russian* . . . , 101–104, 108–121.

"The Huntsman" [same as "The Game-keeper"]
Johnson, Ronald L. *Anton Chekhov* . . . , 31–32.

"In Exile"
Jackson, Robert L. "Dantesque and Dostoevskian Motifs in Čechov's 'In Exile,' " *Russian, Croatian*, 35 (1994), 181–193.
Johnson, Ronald L. *Anton Chekhov* . . . , 63–64.
Peace, Richard. " 'In Exile' and Russian Fatalism," in Jackson, Robert L., Ed. *Reading Chekhov's Text*, 137–144.

"In the Cart"
Howe, Irving. . . . *A Critic's Notebook*, 131–137.
Johnson, Ronald L. *Anton Chekhov* . . . , 87–88.

"In the Hollow" [same as "In the Ravine"]
Johnson, Ronald L. *Anton Chekhov* . . . , 98–100.

"Ionych"
Mihailovic, Alexandar. "Eschatology and Entombment in 'Ionych,' " in Jackson, Robert L., Ed. *Reading Chekhov's Text*, 103–114.

"The Kiss"
Johnson, Ronald L. *Anton Chekhov* . . . , 26–27.

"The Lady of the Manor"
Johnson, Ronald L. *Anton Chekhov* . . . , 10–11.

"A Lady with a Dog" [same as "The Lady with the Pet Dog"]
+Bohner, Charles H. *Instructor's Manual* . . . , 3rd ed., 29–30.
Charters, Ann. *Resources* . . . , 38.
Johnson, Ronald L. *Anton Chekhov* . . . , 76–78.
Stanion, Charles. "Oafish Behavior in 'The Lady with the Pet Dog,' " *Stud Short Fiction*, 30 (1993), 402–403.

"The Letter"
Johnson, Ronald L. *Anton Chekhov* . . . , 43–44.

"Lights"
Johnson, Ronald L. *Anton Chekhov* . . . , 51–52.

"A Living Chattel" [same as "Living Goods"; "Living Merchandise"; "Wife for Sale"]
Johnson, Ronald L. *Anton Chekhov* . . . , 9–10.

"Man in a Case"
Isenberg, Charles. *Telling Silence* . . . , 118–119, 120–125.

"Mire"
Johnson, Ronald L. *Anton Chekhov* . . . , 29–30.

"Misery" [same as "Grief"; "Heartache"; "The Lament"]
Johnson, Ronald L. *Anton Chekhov* . . . , 36.

"A Misfortune"
Evdokimova, Svetlana. "The Curse of Rhetoric and the Delusions of Sincerity: Čechov's Story 'Misfortune,' " *Russian, Croatian*, 35 (1994), 153–169.
Johnson, Ronald L. *Anton Chekhov* . . . , 28–29.

"Murder"
Johnson, Ronald L. *Anton Chekhov* . . . , 100–101.

"My Life—A Provincial's Story"
Johnson, Ronald L. *Anton Chekhov* . . . , 91–94.

"My Wife"
Johnson, Ronald L. *Anton Chekhov* . . . , 56.

"Neighbors"
Johnson, Ronald L. *Anton Chekhov* . . . , 57–58.

"Nerves"
Johnson, Ronald L. *Anton Chekhov* . . . , 19.

"A Nervous Breakdown"
Johnson, Ronald L. *Anton Chekhov* . . . , 71–72.

"The New Villa"
Johnson, Ronald L. *Anton Chekhov* . . . , 96–97.

"A Nightmare"
Johnson, Ronald L. *Anton Chekhov* . . . , 41–42.

"Not Wanted"
Johnson, Ronald L. *Anton Chekhov* . . . , 21.

"On the Night of Christmas Eve"
Shrayer, Maxim D. "Conflation of Christmas and Paschal Motifs in Čechov's 'Roždestvenskuju noč,' " *Russian, Croatian*, 35 (1994), 243–259.

"On Official Business" [same as "On Official Duty"]
Johnson, Ronald L. *Anton Chekhov* . . . , 94–95.

"On the Road"
Johnson, Ronald L. *Anton Chekhov* . . . , 47–48.

"The Order of St. Anne"
Johnson, Ronald L. *Anton Chekhov* . . . , 81.

"Oysters"
Johnson, Ronald L. *Anton Chekhov* . . . , 14–15.

"The Party" [same as "The Birthday Party"]
Johnson, Ronald L. *Anton Chekhov* . . . , 52–53.

"Peasant Women" [same as "Peasant Wives"]
Johnson, Ronald L. *Anton Chekhov* . . . , 74–75.

"Peasants"
Johnson, Ronald L. *Anton Chekhov* . . . , 97–98.

"The Pipe" [same as "The Reed"; "The Shepherd's Pipe"]
Johnson, Ronald L. *Anton Chekhov* . . . , 41.

"The Privy Councillor"
Johnson, Ronald L. *Anton Chekhov* . . . , 18–19.

"The Requiem"
Johnson, Ronald L. *Anton Chekhov* . . . , 43.

"Rothschild's Fiddle"
Johnson, Ronald L. *Anton Chekhov* . . . , 66–67.

"The Russian Master"
Johnson, Ronald L. *Anton Chekhov* . . . , 61–62.

"A Slander"
Johnson, Ronald L. *Anton Chekhov* . . . , 4–5.

"Sleepy"
Johnson, Ronald L. *Anton Chekhov* . . . , 38.

"Sorrow"
Johnson, Ronald L. *Anton Chekhov* . . . , 40.

"The Steppe"
Björklund, Martina. *Narrative Strategies* . . . , 10–19, 48–321.
Johnson, Ronald L. *Anton Chekhov* . . . , 50–51.
Mihaychuk, George. "The Thread of Consciousness in Čexov's

'Step': The Relevance of Discourse Features," *Slavic & East European J*, 38 (1994), 574–590.

"The Student"
Charters, Ann. *Resources* . . . , 39–40.
Jackson, Robert L. "Chekhov's 'The Student,' " in Jackson, Robert L., Ed. *Reading Chekhov's Text*, 127–133.
Johnson, Ronald L. *Anton Chekhov* . . . , 68–69.
+May, Charles E. "Chekhov . . . ," 209–211.

"A Tale"
Turner, C. J. G. "Chekhov's Story without a Title: Chronotope and Genre," *Canadian Slavonic Papers*, 35 (1993), 329–334.

"The Teacher of Literature"
Sherbinin, Julie W. de. "Life Beyond Text: The Nature of Illusion in 'The Teacher of Literature,' " in Jackson, Robert L., Ed. *Reading Chekhov's Text*, 115–126.

"Thieves" [same as "The Horse Stealers"]
Johnson, Ronald L. *Anton Chekhov* . . . , 74.

"Three Years"
Johnson, Ronald L. *Anton Chekhov* . . . , 44, 62.

"A Trifle from Life" [same as "A Trifling Occurrence"]
Johnson, Ronald L. *Anton Chekhov* . . . , 29.

"A Trivial Incident"
Johnson, Ronald L. *Anton Chekhov* . . . , 48–49.

"Typhus"
Johnson, Ronald L. *Anton Chekhov* . . . , 22–23.

"An Upheaval"
Johnson, Ronald L. *Anton Chekhov* . . . , 23–24.

"Uprooted—An Incident of My Travels" [same as "The Rolling Stone—A Traveller's Sketch"; "Thistledown"]
Johnson, Ronald L. *Anton Chekhov* . . . , 44.

"Vanka"
Johnson, Ronald L. *Anton Chekhov* . . . , 37–38.

"Verotchka"
Johnson, Ronald L. *Anton Chekhov* . . . , 25–26.

"Volodya"
Johnson, Ronald L. *Anton Chekhov* . . . , 22.

"Ward Number Six"
Johnson, Ronald L. *Anton Chekhov* . . . , 64–66.
Knapp, Liza. "Fear and Pity in 'Ward Six': Chekhovian Catharsis," in Jackson, Robert L., Ed. *Reading Chekhov's Text*, 145–154.
Peace, Richard. " 'In Exile' and Russian Fatalism," in Jackson, Robert L., Ed. *Reading Chekhov's Text*, 142–143.

"The Witch"
Johnson, Ronald L. *Anton Chekhov* . . . , 30.

"The Woman Who Had No Prejudices—A Romance" [same as "An Unprejudiced Girl—A Love Story"]
Johnson, Ronald L. *Anton Chekhov* . . . , 12–13.

"A Woman's Kingdom"
Johnson, Ronald L. *Anton Chekhov* . . . , 59–61.

"Worse and Worse"
Johnson, Ronald L. *Anton Chekhov* . . . , 14.

KELLY CHERRY

"What I Don't Tell People"
Wear, Delese, and Lois L. Nixon. *Literary Anatomies* . . . , 31–33.

CHARLES W. CHESNUTT

"Baxter's Procrustes"
Werner, Craig H. *Playing the Changes* . . . , 5–7.

"The Conjurer's Revenge"
Molyneaux, Sandra. "Expanding the Collective Memory: Charles W. Chesnutt's *The Conjure Woman* Tales," in Singh, Amritjit, Joseph T. Skerrett, and Robert E. Hogan, Eds. *Memory, Narrative* . . . , 169–171.
Sundquist, Eric J. *To Wake the Nations* . . . , 369, 373–375, 391.
White, Jeannette S. "Baring Slavery's Darkest Secrets: Charles Chesnutt's *Conjure Tales* as Masks of Truth," *Southern Lit J*, 27, i (1994), 97–98.

"Dave's Neckliss"
Sundquist, Eric J. *To Wake the Nations* . . . , 285, 363, 378–380, 381–383, 391.

"The Doll"
Sundquist, Eric J. *To Wake the Nations* . . . , 450–453.

"The Dumb Witness"
Sundquist, Eric J. *To Wake the Nations* . . . , 389–392, 396, 404.

"The Goophered Grapevine"
Bodie, Edward H. "Chesnutt's 'The Goophered Grapevine,' " *Explicator*, 51 (1992), 28–29.
Kulii, Elon A. "Poetic License and Chesnutt's Use of Folklore," *Coll Lang Assoc J*, 38 (1994), 247–253.
Slote, Ben. "Listening to 'The Goophered Grapevine,' and Hearing Raisins Sing," *Am Lit Hist*, 6 (1994), 684–694.
Sundquist, Eric J. *To Wake the Nations* . . . , 361–364.
Werner, Craig H. *Playing the Changes* . . . , 18–19, 22.
White, Jeannette S. "Baring Slavery's . . . ," 90–93.

"The Gray Wolf's Ha'nt"
Molyneaux, Sandra. "Expanding . . . ," 171–173.
White, Jeannette S. "Baring Slavery's . . . ," 99.

"Her Virginia Mammy"
Sundquist, Eric J. *To Wake the Nations* . . . , 400–402.

"Hot-Foot Hannibal"
Molyneaux, Sandra. "Expanding . . . ," 173.
White, Jeannette S. "Baring Slavery's . . . ," 96.

"Lonesome Ben"
Sundquist, Eric J. *To Wake the Nations* . . . , 404–406.

"The Marked Tree"
Sundquist, Eric J. *To Wake the Nations* . . . , 377–378.

"Mars Jeems's Nightmare"
Sundquist, Eric J. *To Wake the Nations* . . . , 327–334, 371–372.
Werner, Craig H. *Playing the Changes* . . . , 19, 22, 23.
White, Jeannette S. "Baring Slavery's . . . ," 100.

"Po' Sandy"
Sundquist, Eric J. *To Wake the Nations* . . . , 375–377, 384, 391.
White, Jeannette S. "Baring Slavery's . . . ," 93–94.

"Sis' Becky's Pickaninny"
Molyneaux, Sandra. "Expanding . . . ," 171–172.
White, Jeannette S. "Baring Slavery's . . . ," 94.

"Tobe's Tribulations"
Sundquist, Eric J. *To Wake the Nations* . . . , 313–318, 323, 384–385, 386–388.

"Uncle Wellington's Wives"
Hurd, Myles R. "Booker T., Blacks, and Brogues: Chesnutt's Sociohistorical Links to Realism in 'Uncle Wellington's Wives,' " *Am Lit Realism*, 26, ii (1994), 19–31.

"White Weeds"
Sundquist, Eric J. *To Wake the Nations* . . . , 402–403, 404.

"The Wife of His Youth"
Sundquist, Eric J. *To Wake the Nations* . . . , 298–301, 364, 387, 391.

GILBERT KEITH CHESTERTON

"The Man in the Passage"
Raubicheck, Walter. "Father Brown and the 'Performance' of Crime," *Chesterton R*, 19, i (1993), 41–42.

"The Paradise of Thieves"
Raubicheck, Walter. "Father Brown . . . ," 40–41.

"The Wrong Shape"
Sage, Victor. "Empire Gothic: Explanation and Epiphany in Conan Doyle, Kipling, and Chesterton," in Bloom, Clive, Ed. *Creepers* . . . , 16–22.

LYDIA MARIA CHILD

"The Children of Mt. Ida"
Mills, Bruce. *Cultural Reformations* . . . , 95–98.

"Hilda Silfvering"

Kostova, Ludmila K. "'Hilda Silfvering': Lydia Maria Child and the Convention of the Idyllic Retreat," *Swansea R*, [n.v.] (1994), 343–357.

"The Quadroons"

Roberts, Diane. *The Myth of Aunt Jemima* . . . , 136–137.

"Slavery's Pleasant Home"

Roberts, Diane. *The Myth of Aunt Jemima* . . . , 137–138.

"Thot and Freia"

Mills, Bruce. *Cultural Reformations* . . . , 104–106, 107–108.

FRANK CHIN

"The Eat and Run Midnight People"

Wong, Sau-ling C. *Reading Asian American Literature* . . . , 150–153.

"Food for All His Dead"

Wong, Sau-ling C. *Reading Asian American Literature* . . . , 35–37, 41–42.

KATE CHOPIN

"At the 'Cadian Ball"

Charters, Ann. *Resources* . . . , 41–42.

Cutter, Martha J. "Losing the Battle but Winning the War: Resistance to Patriarchal Discourse in Kate Chopin's Short Fiction," *Legacy*, 11 (1994), 19–20.

"Athénaïse"

Cutter, Martha J. "Losing the Battle . . . ," 21–22.

Goodwyn, Janet. " 'Dah you is, settin' down, lookin' jis' like w'ite folks!': Ethnicity Enacted in Kate Chopin's Short Fiction," *Yearbook Engl Stud*, 24 (1994), 6–7.

Loving, Jerome. *Lost in the Customhouse* . . . , 187–188, 189–190.

"Azelie"

Shurbutt, Sylvia B. "The Cane River Characters and Revisionist Mythmaking in the Work of Kate Chopin," *Southern Lit J*, 25, ii (1993), 20–21.

"La Belle Zoaïde"

Bryan, Violet H. *The Myth of New Orleans* . . . , 55.

Cothern Lynn. "Speech and Authorship in Kate Chopin's 'La Belle Zoraïde,' " *Louisiana Lit*, 11, i (1994), 118–125.

Goodwyn, Janet. " 'Dah you is . . . ," 3–4.

Lundie, Catherine. "Doubly Dispossessed: Kate Chopin's Women of Color," *Louisiana Lit*, 11, i (1994), 134–139.

"Charlie"

Cutter, Martha J. "Losing the Battle . . . ," 32–33.

Fusco, Richard. *Maupassant* . . . , 169–170.
Shurbutt, Sylvia B. ''The Cane . . . ,'' 21–22.

''Désirée's Baby''
Charters, Ann. *Resources* . . . , 43–44.
Fusco, Richard. *Maupassant* . . . , 150–152.
Goodwyn, Janet. '' 'Dah you is . . . ,'' 10–11.
Lundie, Catherine. ''Doubly Dispossessed . . . ,'' 129–134.

''A Dresden Lady in Dixie''
Goodwyn, Janet. '' 'Dah you is . . . ,'' 7–10.

''An Egyptian Cigarette''
Cutter, Martha J. ''Losing the Battle . . . ,'' 24–25.
Day, Karen. ''The 'Elsewhere' of Female Sexuality and Desire in Kate Chopin's 'A Vocation and a Voice,' '' *Louisiana Lit*, 11, i (1994), 109–111.

''Elizabeth Stock's One Story''
Cutter, Martha J. ''Losing the Battle . . . ,'' 27–31.

''Fedora''
Day, Karen. ''The 'Elsewhere' . . . ,'' 115–116.

''A Gentleman of Bayou Teche''
Steiling, David. ''Multi-Cultural Aesthetic in Kate Chopin's 'A Gentleman of Bayou Teche,' '' *Mississippi Q*, 47 (1994), 197–200.

''The Gentleman from New Orleans''
Cutter, Martha J. ''Losing the Battle . . . ,'' 31–32.

''The Godmother''
Fusco, Richard. *Maupassant* . . . , 163–166.

''Her Letters''
Cutter, Martha J. ''Losing the Battle . . . ,'' 25–27.

''In and Out of Old Natchitoches''
Bryan, Violet H. *The Myth of New Orleans* . . . , 61–62.

''In Sabine''
Fusco, Richard. *Maupassant* . . . , 147–148.

''A Lady of Bayou St. John''
Shurbutt, Sylvia B. ''The Cane . . . ,'' 19–20.

''Lilacs''
Padgett, Jacqueline O. ''Kate Chopin and the Literature of the Annunciation, with a Reading of 'Lilacs,' '' *Louisiana Lit*, 11, i (1994), 97–107.

''Loka''
Saar, Doreen A. ''The Failure and the Triumph of 'The Maid of Saint Phillippe': Chopin Rewrites American Literature for American Women,'' *Louisiana Lit*, 11, i (1994), 68–69.

''Madame Celestin's Divorce''
Shurbutt, Sylvia B. ''The Cane . . . ,'' 21.

''Madame Martel's Christmas Eve''
Fusco, Richard. *Maupassant* . . . , 167–168.

"The Maid of Saint Phillippe"
Saar, Doreen A. "The Failure . . . ," 59–72.

"A Matter of Prejudice"
Goodwyn, Janet. " 'Dah you is . . . ," 5–6.

"Mrs. Mobry's Reason"
Cutter, Martha J. "Losing the Battle . . . ," 22–24.

"A Night in Acadie"
Cutter, Martha J. "Losing the Battle . . . ," 20.

"Nég Créol"
Byran, Violet H. *The Myth of New Orleans* . . . , 55–58.

"Ripe Figs"
Branscomb, Jack. "Chopin's 'Ripe Figs,' " *Explicator*, 52 (1994), 165–167.

"The Storm"
Baker, Christopher. "Chopin's 'The Storm,' " *Explicator*, 52 (1994), 225–226.
Birkle, Carmen. "Kate Chopin: 'The Storm'—Die Geburt der 'New Woman' aus dem Geiste des Regionalismus," in Lubbers, Klaus, Ed. *Die Englische* . . . , 110–119.
Charters, Ann. *Resources* . . . , 45–46.
Pickering, James H., and Jeffrey D. Hoeper. *Instructor's Manual* . . . , 37–38.

"The Story of an Hour"
+Bohner, Charles H. *Instructor's Manual* . . . , 3rd ed., 30–31.
Day, Karen. "The 'Elsewhere' . . . ," 112–113.
Fusco, Richard. *Maupassant* . . . , 153–154.
Padgett, Jacqueline O. "Kate Chopin . . . ," 101.

"Two Portraits"
Day, Karen. "The 'Elsewhere' . . . ," 114–115.

"Vagabonds"
Dyer, Joyce. " 'Vagabonds': A Story without a Home," *Louisiana Lit*, 11, i (1994), 74–82.

"A Visit to Avoyelles"
Shurbutt, Sylvia B. "The Cane . . . ," 20.

"A Vocation and a Voice"
Fusco, Richard. *Maupassant* . . . , 160–163.

"The White Eagle"
Day, Karen. "The 'Elsewhere' . . . ," 112.

"Wiser than a God"
Cutter, Martha J. "Losing the Battle . . . ," 20–21.
Ellis, Nancy S. "Sonata No. 1 in Prose, the 'Von Stoltz': Musical Structure in an Early Work by Kate Chopin," *Louisiana Lit*, 11, i (1994), 147–153.

AGATHA CHRISTIE

"The Witness for the Prosecution"
Pickering, James H., and Jeffrey D. Hoeper. *Instructor's Manual* . . . , 56–57.

CHU T'IEN-WEN

"*Fin-de-siècle* Splendor"
Wang, David Der-wei. "*Fin-de-siècle* Splendor: Contemporary Women Writers' Vision of Taiwan," *Mod Chinese Lit*, 6, i–ii (1992), 42–47.

LEILA S. CHUDORI

"About Malin Kundang"
Hellwig, Tineke. "Leila S. Chudori and Women in Contemporary Fiction Writing," *Tenggara*, 31 (1993), 83–84.

"Adila"
Hellwig, Tineke. "Leila S. Chudori . . . ," 81–82.

"Home from America"
Hellwig, Tineke. "Leila S. Chudori . . . ," 83.

"Ilona"
Hellwig, Tineke. "Leila S. Chudori . . . ," 82, 85.

"Keats"
Hellwig, Tineke. "Leila S. Chudori . . . ," 82.

"The Purification of Sita"
Hellwig, Tineke. "Leila S. Chudori . . . ," 83.

SANDRA CISNEROS

"Barbie-Q"
Thomson, Jeff. " 'What Is Called Heaven': Identity in Sandra Cisneros's *Woman Hollering Creek*," *Stud Short Fiction*, 31 (1994), 417.

"*Bien* Pretty"
Lewis, L. M. "Ethnic and Gender Identity: Parallel Growth in Sandra Cisneros's *Woman Hollering Creek*," *Short Story* 2, ii, N.S. (1994), 71–73, 76–77.
Thomson, Jeff. " 'What Is Called . . . ," 421–423.

"Eyes of Zapata"
Lewis, L. M. "Ethnic and . . . ," 75–76.
Thomson, Jeff. " 'What Is Called . . . ," 415–416, 421.

"The House on Mango Street"
Gibson, Michelle. "The 'Unreliable' Narrator in 'The House on Mango Street,' " *San Jose Stud*, 19, ii (1993), 40–44.

Gutiérrez-Jones, Leslie S. "Different Voices: The Re-*Bildung* of the Barrio in Sandra Cisneros's 'The House on Mango Street,' " in Singley, Carol J., and Susan E. Sweeney, Eds. *Anxious Power*. . . , 295–314.

"Mexican Movies"
Thomson, Jeff. " 'What Is Called . . . ,'' 417.

"My Tocaya"
Thomson, Jeff. " 'What Is Called . . . ,'' 419.

"Never Marry a Mexican"
Lewis, L. M. "Ethnic and . . . ," 70–71, 75.
Thomson, Jeff. " 'What Is Called . . . ,'' 420–421.

"One Holy Night"
Thomson, Jeff. " 'What Is Called . . . ,'' 418–419.

"Salvador Late or Early"
Thomson, Jeff. " 'What Is Called . . . ,'' 418.

"There Was a Man, There Was a Woman"
Thomson, Jeff. " 'What Is Called . . . ,'' 419–420.

"Woman Hollering Creek"
Lewis, L. M. "Ethnic and . . . ," 74–75.

CLARÍN [LEOPOLDO ALAS]

"La tara"
Tibbits, Mercedes Vidal. "Un cuento absurdo de Clarín: 'La tara,' " in Paolini, Gilbert, Ed. *La Chispa* . . . , 248–253.

UVA A. CLAVIJO

"La leyenda del aula"
Leeder, Ellen L. "Acercamiento a los cuentos de Uva Clavijo," *Círculo*, 22 (1993), 144.

"No puedo más"
Leeder, Ellen L. "Acercamiento . . . ," 145.

"Y de pronto un viernes"
Leeder, Ellen L. "Acercamiento . . . ," 146.

J. M. COETZEE

"In the Heart of the Country"
Briganti, Chiara. "A Bored Spinster with a Locked Diary: The Politics of Hysteria in 'In the Heart of the Country,' " *Research African Lit*, 25, iv (1994), 33–49.
Gitzen, Julian. "The Voice of History in the Novels of J. M. Coetzee," *Critique*, 35 (1993), 5–7.

Macaskill, Brian. "Charting J. M. Coetzee's Middle Voice," *Contemp Lit*, 35 (1994), 456–471.
Wohlpart, James. "A (Sub)Version of the Language of Power: Narrative and Narrative Technique in J. M. Coetzee's 'In the Heart of the Country,' " *Critique*, 35 (1994), 219–228.

"The Narrative of Jacobus Coetzee"
Gitzen, Julian. "The Voice of History . . . ," 4–6.
Marais, Mike. " 'Omnipotent Fantasies' of a Solitary Self: J. M. Coetzee's 'The Narrative of Jacobus Coetzee,' " *J Commonwealth Lit*, 28, ii (1993), 48–65.

SIDONIE-GABRIELLE COLETTE

"The Other Wife"
+Bohner, Charles H. *Instructor's Manual* . . . , 3rd ed., 33–34.

"The Tender-Shoot"
Ketchum, Anne D. "Defining an Ethics from a Later Short Story by Colette," in Myers, Eunice, and Ginette Adamson, Eds. *Continental, Latin-American* . . . , 71–77.

[WILLIAM] WILKIE COLLINS

"The Dream Woman"
Andriano, Joseph. *Our Ladies* . . . , 152–153.

JOSEPH CONRAD

"Amy Foster"
Carrabine, Keith. " 'Irreconcilable Differences': England as an 'Undiscovered Country' in Conrad's 'Amy Foster,' " in Gatrell, Simon, Ed. *The Ends of the Earth* . . . , 187–204.
Kurczaba, Alex. "Witold Gombrowicz' *Princess Ivona* and Joseph Conrad's 'Amy Foster,' " *L'Epoque Conradienne*, 19 (1993), 94–101.

"An Anarchist"
Shaddock, Jennifer. "Hanging a Dog: The Politics of Naming in 'An Anarchist,' " *Conradiana*, 26 (1994), 56–69.

"The Black Mate"
White, Andrea. *Joseph Conrad* . . . , 111–113.

"Freya of the Seven Isles"
Elbert, Monika M. " 'Freya of the Seven Isles' and the Heart of Male Darkness," *Conradiana*, 26 (1994), 35–55.
———. "Possession and Self-Possession: The 'Dialectic of Desire' in *Twixt Land and Sea*," *Conradian*, 17, ii (1993), 133–140.

"Heart of Darkness"
Andrade, Susan. "Upending the River: Surface Equanimity,

Submerged Ideology,'' in Harrow, Kenneth, Jonathan Ngaté, and Clarisse Zimra, Eds. *Crisscrossing . . .* , 142–145.

Bode, Rita. '' 'They . . . should be out of it': The Women of 'Heart of Darkness,' '' *Conradiana*, 26 (1994), 20–34.

Booker, M. Keith. ''The Horror of Mortality: Conrad's Dialogue with Mastery in 'Heart of Darkness,' '' *Arkansas Q*, 2, i (1993), 1–29.

Galef, David. ''On the Margin: The Peripheral Characters in Conrad's 'Heart of Darkness,' '' *J Mod Lit*, 17 (1990), 117–138.

———. *The Supporting Cast . . .* , 27–63.

Elbarbary, Samir. '' 'Heart of Darkness' and Late-Victorian Fascination with the Primitive and the Double,'' *Twentieth Century Lit*, 39 (1993), 113–128.

Fayad, Mona. ''The Problem of the Subject in Africanist Discourse: Conrad's 'Heart of Darkness' and Camus's 'The Renegade,' '' *Comp Lit Stud*, 27 (1990), 298–307, 309–312.

Fothergill, Anthony. ''The Poetics of Particulars: Pronouns, Punctuation, and Ideology in 'Heart of Darkness,' '' in Carabine, Keith, Owen Knowles, and Wiesław Krajka, Eds. *Conrad's Literary . . .* , 60–72.

Foulke, Robert. ''From the Center to the Dangerous Hemisphere: 'Heart of Darkness' and 'Typhoon,' '' in Carabine, Keith, Owen Knowles, and Wiesław Krajka, Eds. *Conrad's Literary . . .* , 128.

Guetti, James. ''Wittgenstein, Conrad, and the Darkness,'' *Symplokē*, 2, i (1994), 1–27.

Hawthorn, Jeremy. ''Joseph Conrad's Theory of Reading,'' in Kennedy, Andrew, and Orm Øverland, Eds. *Excursions in Fiction . . .* , 98–99.

Hooper, Myrtle J. ''The Heart of Light: Silence in Conrad's 'Heart of Darkness,' '' *Conradiana*, 25 (1993), 69–76.

Humphries, Reynold. ''Language and 'Adjectival Insistence' in 'Heart of Darkness,' '' *Conradiana*, 26 (1994), 119–134.

———. ''Taking the Figural Literally: Language and 'Heart of Darkness,' '' *Études Anglaises*, 46, i (1993), 19–31.

Jackson, Tony E. *The Subject of Modernism . . .* , 101–109.

Knowles, Owen. '' 'Whose Afraid of Arthur Schopenhauer?': A New Context for Conrad's 'Heart of Darkness,' '' *Nineteenth-Century Lit*, 49 (1994), 75–106.

Kuchta, Todd M. ''Framing 'the Horror': Voice and Voice-Over in 'Heart of Darkness' and *Apocalypse Now*,'' *Stud Hum*, 21, i (1994), 47–49.

Milton, Colin. ''Region, Nation—and Empire in 'Heart of Darkness,' '' *Swansea R*, [n.v.] (1994), 408–426.

Mongia, Padmini. ''Empire, Narrative and the Feminine in *Lord Jim* and 'Heart of Darkness,' '' in Carabine, Keith, Owen Knowles, and Wieslaw Krajka, Eds. *Contexts for Conrad*, 135–150.

Navarette, Susan J. ''The Anatomy of Failure in Joseph Conrad's 'Heart of Darkness,' '' *Texas Stud Lit & Lang*, 35 (1993), 279–315.

Paris, Bernard J. ''Marlow's Transformation,'' *Aligarh J Engl Stud*, 15, i–ii (1993), 65–72.

Putnam, Walter. "Marlow, Michel et le silence des sirènes," *Bull des Amis d'André Gide*, 21 (1993), 613–629.
Reilly, Jim. *Shadowtime* . . . , 20–21, 42, 141–143, 166.
Sarvan, Charles P., and Paul Balles. "Buddhism, Hinduism, and the Conradian Darkness," *Conradiana*, 26 (1994), 70–75.
Shaffer, Brian W. *The Blinding Torch* . . . , 47–57.
Shillock, Larry T. "Primitivism and its 'Heart of Darkness,' " *West Virginia Univ Philol Papers*, 38 (1992), 76–82.
Vidan, Ivo. "Conrad and Thomas Mann," in Carabine, Keith, Owen Knowles, and Wiesław Krajka, Eds. *Contexts for Conrad*, 266–276.
Watson, Wallace S. " 'A Howl and a Dance': Conrad's Congo as European Theater," in Lucente, Carla E., Ed. *The Western Pennsylvania* . . . , 139–143.
White, Andrea. *Joseph Conrad* . . . , 167–192.

"The Informer"
Erdinast-Vulcan, Daphna. "Where Does the Joke Come in?: Ethics and Aesthetics in Conrad's 'The Informer,' " *L'Epoque Conradienne*, 19 (1993), 38–46.

"Karain"
Conroy, Mark. "Ghostwriting (in) 'Karain,' " *Conradian*, 18, ii (1994), 1–16.
Krajka, Wiesław. "Betrayal, Self-Exile, and Language Registers. The Case of 'Karain: A Memory,' " *L'Epoque Conradienne*, 19 (1993), 47–69.

"The Lagoon"
Rising, Catharine. "Conrad and Kohut: The Fortunate Oedipal Fall," *Psycho & Contemp Thought*, 17, i (1994), 107–120.
Ruppel, Richard. " 'The Lagoon' and the Popular Exotic Tradition," in Carabine, Keith, Owen Knowles, and Wiesław Krajka, Eds. *Contexts for Conrad*, 177–187.

"An Outpost of Progress"
White, Andrea. *Joseph Conrad* . . . , 151–166.

"The Planter of Malta"
Erdinast-Vulcan, Daphna. " 'The Planter of Malta': A Case of Creative Pathology," *Conradiana*, 26 (1994), 187–200.

"The Secret Sharer"
+Bohner, Charles H. *Instructor's Manual* . . . , 3rd ed., 34–35.
Charters, Ann. *Resources* . . . , 47–48.
Elbert, Monika M. " 'Freya . . . ," 35, 36, 37–38.
———. "Possession . . . ," 138, 143–145.
Pickering, James H., and Jeffrey D. Hoeper. *Instructor's Manual* . . . , 43–44.

"A Smile of Fortune"
Elbert, Monika M. "Possession . . . ," 140–143.

"Typhoon"
Caminero-Santangelo, Byron. "Testing for Truth: Joseph Conrad and the Ideology of the Examination," *Clio*, 23 (1994), 275–284.

Foulke, Robert. "From the Center . . . ," 128–150.
Hansford, James. "Money, Language, and the Body in 'Typhoon,' " *Conradiana*, 26 (1994), 135–155.

"Youth"
Charters, Ann. *Resources* . . . , 49–50.
Woolf, Leonard. "Conrad's Vision: The Illumination of Romance," *Engl Lit Transition*, 36 (1993), 292–295, 298.

BENJAMIN CONSTANT

"Adolphe"
Waller, Margaret. *The Male Malady* . . . , 93–113.

ROSE TERRY COOKE

"Miss Beulah's Bonnet"
Fetterly, Judith. " 'Not in the Least American': Nineteenth-Century Literary Realism," *Coll Engl*, 56 (1994), 885–886.

ROBERT COOVER

"The Babysitter"
Weinstein, Arnold. *Nobody's Home* . . . , 237.

"Charlie in the House of Rue"
Pughe, Thomas. *Comic Sense* . . . , 47–52.
Weinstein, Arnold. *Nobody's Home* . . . , 261–262.

"The Door: A Prologue of Sorts"
Hansen, Arlen J. "Robert Coover: 'The Door: A Prologue of Sorts,' " in Lubbers, Klaus, Ed. *Die Englische* . . . , 421–426.

"The Hat Act"
Pughe, Thomas. *Comic Sense* . . . , 52–54.

"The Magic Poker"
+Bohner, Charles H. *Instructor's Manual* . . . , 3rd ed., 35–37.

"Panel Game"
Pughe, Thomas. *Comic Sense* . . . , 44–47.

"Whatever Happened to Gloomy Gus of the Chicago Bears?"
Frick, Daniel E. "The Prison House of Art: Aesthetics vs. Politics in Robert Coover's 'Whatever Happened to Gloomy Gus of the Chicago Bears?' " *Stud Short Fiction*, 31 (1994), 217–223.
Pughe, Thomas. *Comic Sense* . . . , 13–19.

"You Must Remember This"
Weinstein, Arnold. *Nobody's Home* . . . , 262–264.

FÉLIX CÓRDOVA ITURREGUI

"El momento divino de Caruso Llompart"
Vázquez Arce, Carmen. "Los desastres de la guerra: sobre la

articulación de la ironía en los cuentos: 'La recién nacida sangre,' de Luis Rafael Sánchez y 'El momento divino de Caruso Llompart,' de Félix Córdova Iturregui,'' *Revista Iberoamericana*, 59 (1993), 196–199, 200.

JOHN WILLIAM CORRINGTON

''The Actes and Monuments''
Domnarski, William. ''Corrington's Lawyer as Moralist,'' in Mills, William, Ed. *John William Corrington* . . . , 148–149.
Heilman, Robert B. ''Scene, Tradition, and the Unresolved,'' in Mills, William, Ed. *John William Corrington* . . . , 86–89.
Preston, Tom. ''Anchorites in Sodom: John William Corrington's Secular Urbanism and the Transcendent in These Latter and Perilous Days,'' in Mills, William, Ed. *John William Corrington* . . . , 42–44.

''The Arrangement''
Heilman, Robert B. ''Scene, Tradition . . . ,'' 63.

''The Dark Corner''
Heilman, Robert B. ''Scene, Tradition . . . ,'' 63–65.
Willingham, John R. ''The South Within: Believing and Seeing,'' in Mills, William, Ed. *John William Corrington* . . . , 8–9, 14–17, 18.

''A Day in Thy Court''
Heilman, Robert B. ''Scene, Tradition . . . ,'' 95–98.

''Every Act Whatever of Man''
Heilman, Robert B. ''Scene, Tradition . . . ,'' 93–95.

''The Great Pumpkin''
Heilman, Robert B. ''Scene, Tradition . . . ,'' 73.

''Heroic Measures/Vital Signs''
Heilman, Robert B. ''Scene, Tradition . . . ,'' 65–68.

''If Time Were Not / A Moving Thing''
Heilman, Robert B. ''Scene, Tradition . . . ,'' 77–80.

''Keep Them Cards and Letters Coming In''
Heilman, Robert B. ''Scene, Tradition . . . ,'' 74–75.

''The Lonesome Traveler''
Heilman, Robert B. ''Scene, Tradition . . . ,'' 80–85.

''The Man Who Slept with Women''
Heilman, Robert B. ''Scene, Tradition . . . ,'' 62–63.

''The Night School''
Heilman, Robert B. ''Scene, Tradition . . . ,'' 73–74.

''Nothing Succeeds''
Heilman, Robert B. ''Scene, Tradition . . . ,'' 89–92.

''Old Men Dream Dreams, Young Men See Visions''
Heilman, Robert B. ''Scene, Tradition . . . ,'' 61–62.

"Pleadings"
Domnarski, William. "Corrington's Lawyer . . . ," 147, 150.
Heilman, Robert B. "Scene, Tradition . . . ," 85–86.

"The Retrievers"
Heilman, Robert B. "Scene, Tradition . . . ," 61.

"Reunion"
Heilman, Robert B. "Scene, Tradition . . . ," 75–76.
Willingham, John R. "The South Within . . . ," 8–9, 10–12.

"The Southern Reporter"
Heilman, Robert B. "Scene, Tradition . . . ," 70–73.

"A Time to Embrace"
Heilman, Robert B. "Scene, Tradition . . . ," 68–70.
Willingham, John R. "The South Within . . . ," 8–9, 12–13.

JULIO CORTÁZAR

"Apocalypse in Solentiname"
Sugano, Marian Z. "Beyond What Meets the Eye: The Photographic Analogy in Cortázar's Short Stories," *Style*, 27 (1993), 344–348.
Zamora, Lois P. "The Politics of Torture and Julio Cortázar's Literature of Embodiment," in Gallagher, Susan V., Ed. *Postcolonial Literature* . . . , 104, 106–109.

"Axolotl"
Capacci di Giovanni, Graciela. " 'Axototl' de Julio Cortázar: un reclamo desde el silencio (intextualidad social en la literatura del exilio)," in Arancibia, Juana Alcira, Ed. *Literatura como* . . . , 193–204.
Natarajan, Nalini. "Man into Beast: Representations of Metamorphosis," *Bestia*, 5 (1993), 119, 120–121.

"Las babas del diablo"
Báez Báez, Edith M. "Versiones de la realidad en 'Las babas del diablo' de Cortázar," *Hispanic J*, 14, i (1993), 47–61.
Beardsell, Peter. "Introduction," *Siete cuentos* [by Julio Cortázar], 17–22.

"Blow-up"
Sugano, Marian Z. "Beyond What . . . ," 340–344.

"Botella al mar"
Beardsell, Peter, "Introduction," 32–34.

"Clone"
Carmosino, Roger B. "El 'doble manifiesto' y el 'doble implícito' en cuatro relatos de Julio Cortázar," *So Eastern Latin Amer*, 37, iii (1994), 7–8.

"Continuidad de los parques"
Duncan, Cynthia K. "Hacia una interpretación de lo fantástico en el contexto de la literatura hispanoamericana," *Texto Crítico*, 16 (1990), 56.

"La escuela de la noche"
Kason, Nancy M. "El compromiso político en 'La escuela de noche,' de Julio Cortázar," in Arancibia, Juana Alcira, Ed. *Literatura como . . .*, 184–192.

"Final del juego"
Beardsell, Peter, "Introduction," 13–17.
Bernal, A. Alejandro. "Búsqueda a bordo de lo desconocido: 'Final del juego'/'La isla a mediodía' de Julio Cortázar," in Martín, Gregorio C., Ed. *Selected Proceedings . . .*, 29–31.

"Una flor amarilla"
Carmosino, Roger B. "El 'doble . . . ," 2–4.

"Graffiti"
Tyler, Joseph. "Repression and Violence in Selected Contemporary Argentine Stories," *Discurso*, 9, ii (1992), 92–93.

"La isla a mediodía"
Beardsell, Peter, "Introduction," 22–25.
Bernal, A. Alejandro. "Búsqueda . . . ," 29–31.
Carmosino, Roger B. "El 'doble . . . ," 4–5.

"Lugar Llamado Kindberg"
Young, Richard A. "La lectura intertextual y 'Lugar llamado Kindberg,' de Julio Cortázar," in *Coloquio Internacional . . .*, II, 201–211.

"La noche boca arriba"
Beardsell, Peter, "Introduction," 8–13.

"Los pasos en las huellas"
Carmosino, Roger B. "El 'doble . . . ," 5–6.

"Press Clippings"
Beardsell, Peter, "Introduction," 25–30.
Zamora, Lois P. "The Politics of Torture . . . ," 94–99.

"The Pursuer"
Domínguez de Rodríguez Pasques, Mignon. "Montaje intertextual en 'El perseguidor' de Julio Cortázar," in Arancibia, Juana Alcira, Ed. *Literatura como . . .*, 172–183.
Lindstrom, Naomi. *Twentieth-Century . . .*, 169–170.

"Queremos tanto a Glenda"
Beardsell, Peter, "Introduction," 30–32.

"Second Time Around"
Tyler, Joseph. "Repression . . . ," 89–92.

"Verano"
Young, Richard A. " 'Verano,' de Julio Cortázar, 'The Nightmare,' de John Henry Fuseli, y 'The judicious adoption of figures of art,' " *Revista Canadiense*, 17 (1993), 373–382.

MARY ELIZABETH COUNSELMAN

"Twister"
Burleson, Donald R. "On Mary Elizabeth Counselman's 'Twister,' " *Stud Weird Fiction*, 15 (1994), 16–18.

JUAN DÍAZ COVARRUBIAS

"La sensitiva"
Vargas, Margarita. "Romanticism," in Foster, David W., Ed. *Mexican Literature* . . . , 91.

HEINZ VON CRAMER

"Aufzeichnungen eines ordentlichen Menschen"
Haynes, Roslynn D. *From Faust* . . . , 225–226.

STEPHEN CRANE

"The Blue Hotel"
+Bohner, Charles H. *Instructor's Manual* . . . , 3rd ed., 37–38.
Charters, Ann. *Resources* . . . , 51.
Dooley, Patrick K. *The Pluralistic* . . . , 90–92.
Kowalewski, Michael. *Deadly Musings* . . . , 123–129.
Pickering, James H., and Jeffrey D. Hoeper. *Instructor's Manual* . . . , 42.

"The Carriage-Lamps"
Jacobson, Marcia. *Being a Boy* . . . , 126–127, 129.

"A Dark-Brown Dog"
Dooley, Patrick K. *The Pluralistic* . . . , 81–83.

"Death and the Child"
Dooley, Patrick K. *The Pluralistic* . . . , 28–29.

"An Episode of War"
Dooley, Patrick K. *The Pluralistic* . . . , 27–28.

"The Five White Mice"
Dooley, Patrick K. *The Pluralistic* . . . , 61–62.

"Killing His Bear"
Kowalewski, Michael. *Deadly Musings* . . . , 113–118.

"Lynx-Hunting"
Jacobson, Marcia. *Being a Boy* . . . , 121–122, 123–124, 125–126, 129.

"Maggie, A Girl of the Streets"
Gandal, Keith. "Stephen Crane's 'Maggie' and the Modern Soul," *ELH*, 60 (1993), 759–785.
Irving, Katrina. "Gendered Space, Racialized Space: Nativism, the Immigrant Woman, and Stephen Crane's 'Maggie,' " *Coll Lit*, 20, iii (1993), 30–43.
Kowalewski, Michael. *Deadly Musings* . . . , 118–122.
Pizer, Donald. *The Theory and Practice* . . . , 40–44, 124–132.

"One Dash—Horses"
Dooley, Patrick K. *The Pluralistic* . . . , 59–60.

"The Open Boat"
Billingslea, Oliver. "Why Does the Oiler 'Drown'? Perception and

Cosmic Chill in 'The Open Boat,' " *Am Lit Realism*, 27, i (1994), 23–41.
+Bohner, Charles H. *Instructor's Manual* . . . , 3rd ed., 38–39.
Charters, Ann. *Resources* . . . , 52–53.
Dooley, Patrick K. *The Pluralistic* . . . , 63–66.
Frus, Phyllis. *The Politics and Poetics* . . . , 23–27, 31, 36–41, 45–46, 48.
Kowalewski, Michael. *Deadly Musings* . . . , 107–112.

"The Upturned Face"
Charters, Ann. *Resources* . . . , 54–55.

DORTHEA DAHL

"Christmas Song"
Øverland, Orm. "Dorthea Dahl: Fiction from the Margin of the Margin," in Kennedy, Andrew, and Orm Øverland, Eds. *Excursions in Fiction* . . . , 165–166.

"The Commandment of Love"
Øverland, Orm. "Dorthea Dahl . . . ," 160.

"The Old Bookcase"
Øverland, Orm. "Dorthea Dahl . . . ," 164–165.

ROALD DAHL

"The Fox"
Treglown, Jeremy. *Roald Dahl: A Biography*, 194–197.

"The Gremlins"
Treglown, Jeremy. *Roald Dahl: A Biography*, 62–63.

"Katina"
Treglown, Jeremy. *Roald Dahl: A Biography*, 71–72.

"Nunc Dimittis"
Treglown, Jeremy. *Roald Dahl: A Biography*, 112–113.

"Poison"
Treglown, Jeremy. *Roald Dahl: A Biography*, 39–40.

"The Soldier"
Treglown, Jeremy. *Roald Dahl: A Biography*, 86–87.

"Taste"
Treglown, Jeremy. *Roald Dahl: A Biography*, 105–106.

"They Shall Not Grow Old"
Treglown, Jeremy. *Roald Dahl: A Biography*, 50–51.

"The Way Up to Heaven"
+Bohner, Charles H. *Instructor's Manual* . . . , 3rd ed., 40–41.

"William and Mary"
Treglown, Jeremy. *Roald Dahl: A Biography*, 122–123.

ELLA D'ARCY

"The Elegie"
Maier, Sarah E. "Subverting the Ideal: The New Woman and the Battle of the Sexes in the Short Fiction of Ella D'Arcy," *Victorian R*, 20, i (1994), 37–39, 45.

"Irremediable"
Maier, Sarah E. "Subverting . . . ," 43–44.

"A Marriage"
Maier, Sarah E. "Subverting . . . ," 41–42.

"The Pleasure Pilgrim"
Maier, Sarah E. "Subverting . . . ," 39–40, 43, 45–46.

RUBÉN DARÍO

"El rubí"
Holland, Norman S. " 'Doctoring' in Quiroga," *Confluencia*, 9, ii (1994), 69–70.

REBECCA HARDING DAVIS

"Blind Tom"
Pfaelzer, Jean. "Domesticity and the Discourse of Slavery: 'John Lamar' and 'Blind Tom' by Rebecca Harding Davis," *ESQ: J Am Renaissance*, 38, i (1992), 45–51.

"John Lamar"
Pfaelzer, Jean. "Domesticity . . . ," 37–45, 50–51.

"Life in the Iron-Mills"
Scheiber, Andrew J. "An Unknown Infrastructure: Gender, Production, and Aesthetic Exchange in Rebecca Harding Davis's 'Life in the Iron-Mills,' " *Legacy*, 11 (1994), 101–117.

L. SPRAGUE DE CAMP

"Judgement Day"
Haynes, Roslynn D. *From Faust . . .* , 198–199.

JOSÉ DE LA CUADRA

"P'al caso"
Ibáñez Pastor de Ehrlich, María-Teresa. "El diálogo como marco de historias contadas en tres cuentos del Grupo de Guayaquil," *Iberoromania*, 39 (1994), 72–74.

"Los Sangurimas"
Lindstrom, Naomi. *Twentieth-Century . . .* , 116–117.

LESTER DEL REY

"Helen O'Loy"
Grace, Dominick M. "Rereading Lester del Rey's 'Helen O' Loy,' " *Sci-Fiction Stud*, 20 (1993), 45–51.

FLOYD DELL

"Ex-Villager's Confession"
Clayton, Douglas. *Floyd Dell* . . . , 230–231.

"Hallelujah, I'm a Bum!"
Clayton, Douglas. *Floyd Dell* . . . , 230.

"Jessica Screams"
Clayton, Douglas. *Floyd Dell* . . . , 83–85.

"Mothers and Daughters"
Clayton, Douglas. *Floyd Dell* . . . , 82–83.

"Phantom Adventure"
Clayton, Douglas. *Floyd Dell* . . . , 231–232.

"Portrait of Murray Swift"
Clayton, Douglas. *Floyd Dell* . . . , 96–98.

RICK DE MARINIS

"Under the Wheat"
Anisfield, Nancy. " 'Under the Wheat': An Analysis of Options and Ethical Components," in Anisfield, Nancy, Ed. *The Nightmare* . . . , 143–145.

RENÉ DEPESTRE

"Alléluia pour une femme-jardin"
Lapaire, Pierre G. "L'Erotisme baroque, le *télédiol* et les femmes-jardins de René Depestre," *Essays French Lit*, 27 (November, 1990), 93–95.

"De l'eau fraîche pour Georgina"
Lapaire, Pierre G. "L'Erotisme baroque . . . ," 95–97.

"Un Nègre à l'ombre blanche"
Lapaire, Pierre G. "L'Erotisme baroque . . . ," 97.

"Un Retour à Jacmel"
Lapaire, Pierre G. "L'Erotisme baroque . . . ," 98–99.

"Roséna dans la montagne"
Lapaire, Pierre G. "L'Erotisme baroque . . . ," 92–93.

ALINA DIACONÚ

"El cajón"
Marbán, Jorge. "Visión de lo cotidiano y perspectiva existencial en la cuentística de Alina Diaconú," in Gimbernat González, Ester, and Cynthia Tompkins, Eds. *Utopías, ojos azules* . . . , 25–27.

"Mamaya"
Marbán, Jorge. "Visión . . . ," 30.

"Otros paisajes, otras gentes"
Marbán, Jorge. "Visión . . . ," 29.

"El pintor"
Marbán, Jorge. "Visión . . . ," 27–28.

"La pluma"
Marbán, Jorge. "Visión . . . ," 29–30.

"¿Qué nos pasa, Nicolás?"
Marbán, Jorge. "Visión . . . ," 28–29.

"Tarde en Praga"
Marbán, Jorge. "Visión . . . ," 24.

JUAN DÍAZ COVARRUBIAS

"La sensitiva"
Vargas, Margarita. "Romanticism," in Foster, David W., Ed. *Mexican Literature* . . . , 91.

GUSTAVO DÍAZ SOLÍS

"Arco secreto"
Mandrillo, Cósimo. "Acercamiento múltiple a los cuentos de Gustavo Díaz Solís," *Revista Iberoamericana*, 60 (1994), 479–480.

"La efigie"
Mandrillo, Cósimo. "Acercamiento . . . ," 482–483, 484, 485.

"Llueve sobre el mar"
Mandrillo, Cósimo. "Acercamiento . . . ," 485.

"El niño y el mar"
Mandrillo, Cósimo. "Acercamiento . . . ," 479.

"Ophidia"
Mandrillo, Cósimo. "Acercamiento . . . ," 481–482, 483–484.

"El punto"
Mandrillo, Cósimo. "Acercamiento . . . ," 484, 486.

CHARLES DICKENS

"The Chimes"
Allingham, Philip V. "Dickens' Christmas Books: Names and Motifs," *Engl Lang Notes*, 29, 4 (1992), 59–63.

"A Christmas Carol"
Butterworth, R. D. " 'A Christmas Carol' and the Masque," *Stud Short Fiction*, 30 (1993), 63–69.
Jaffe, Audrey. "Spectacular Sympathy: Visuality and Ideology in Dickens's 'A Christmas Carol,' " *PMLA*, 109 (1994), 254–265.
Miller, J. Hillis. "The Genres of 'A Christmas Carol,' " *Dickensian*, 89 (1993), 193–206.
Slater, Michael. "The Triumph of Humour: The *Carol* Revisited," *Dickensian*, 89 (1993), 184–192.
"The Cricket on the Hearth"
Allingham, Philip V. "Dickens' Christmas . . . ," 63–67.
"The Haunted Man"
Allingham, Philip V. "Dickens' Christmas . . . ," 67–68.

JOAN DIDION

"Los Angeles Notebook"
Wells, Walter. "Didion's 'Los Angeles Notebook,' " *Explicator*, 52 (1994), 181–182.

ISAK DINESEN [BARONESS KAREN BLIXEN]

"Alkmene"
Henriksen, Aage. "Karen Blixen and Marionettes," in *Isak Dinesen/Karen Blixen* . . . , 33–37; rpt. Pelensky, Olga A., Ed. *Isak Dinesen* . . . , 12–15.
"The Blank Page"
Kaplan, Carla. "Reading Feminist Readings: Recuperative Reading and the Silent Heroine of Feminist Criticism," in Hedges, Elaine, and Shelley F. Fishkin, Eds. *Listening to Silences* . . . , 182–183, 185–186.
"The Blue Jar"
+Bohner, Charles H. *Instructor's Manual* . . . , 3rd ed., 41–42.
"Carnival"
+Greene-Gantzberg, Vivian, and Arthur R. Gantzberg. "Karen Blixen's 'Carnival,' " in Pelensky, Olga A., Ed. *Isak Dinesen* . . . , 123–137.
"The Deluge at Norderney"
+Johannesson, Eric O. "The Mask in Isak Dinesen's Tales," in Pelensky, Olga A., Ed. *Isak Dinesen* . . . , 31–35.
"The Dreamers"
+Hannah, Donald. "Art and Dream in 'The Dreaming Child' and 'The Dreamers,' " in Pelensky, Olga A., Ed. *Isak Dinesen* . . . , 59–62.
+Johannesson, Eric O. "The Mask . . . ," 35–37.
Scholtz, Antonine M. L. M. "Africa and Creative Fantasy:

Archetypes in Three of Isak Dinesen's Tales,'' in Houe, Poul, and Donna Dacus, Eds. *Karen Blixen/Isak Dinesen . . .*, 91–92; rpt. Pelensky, Olga A., Ed. *Isak Dinesen . . .*, 285–287.

''The Dreaming Child''
+Hannah, Donald. ''Art and Dream . . . ,'' 55–57.
Henriksen, Aage. ''Karen Blixen and Marionettes,'' in *Isak Dinesen/Karen Blixen . . .*, 29–33; rpt. Pelensky, Olga A., Ed. *Isak Dinesen . . .*, 9–12.

''Eneboerne''
Black, Casey Bjerregaard. ''The Fantastic in Karen Blixen's *Osceola* Production,'' *Scandinavian Stud*, 57 (1985), 383–384; rpt. Pelensky, Olga A., Ed. *Isak Dinesen . . .*, 218–219.

''Familien de Cats''
Black, Casey Bjerregaard. ''The Fantastic . . . ,'' 387–388; rpt. Pelensky, Olga A., Ed. *Isak Dinesen . . .*, 221–223.

''The Monkey''
+Mishler, William. ''Parents and Children, Brothers and Sisters in Isak Dinesen's 'The Monkey,' '' in Pelensky, Olga A., Ed. *Isak Dinesen . . .*, 225–249.
Scholtz, Antonine M. L. M. ''Africa and Creative . . . ,'' 92–93; rpt. Pelensky, Olga A., Ed. *Isak Dinesen . . .*, 287–289.

''The Old Chevalier''
+Stambaugh, Sara. ''Imagery of Entrapment in the Fiction of Isak Dinesen,'' in Pelensky, Olga A., Ed. *Isak Dinesen . . .*, 158–162.

''Pløjeren''
Black, Casey Bjerregaard. ''The Fantastic . . .'', 384–387; rpt. Pelensky, Olga A., Ed. *Isak Dinesen . . .*, 219–221.

''The Poet''
Henriksen, Aage. ''Karen Blixen and Marionettes,'' in *Isak Dinesen/Karen Blixen . . .*, 24–27; rpt. Pelensky, Olga A., Ed. *Isak Dinesen . . .*, 6–8.

''The Roads of Life''
Henriksen, Aage. ''Karen Blixen and Marionettes,'' in *Isak Dinesen/Karen Blixen . . .*, 27–29; rpt. Pelensky, Olga A., Ed. *Isak Dinesen . . .*, 8–9.

''The Roads Round Pisa''
Henriksen, Aage. ''Karen Blixen and Marionettes,'' in *Isak Dinesen/Karen Blixen . . .*, 21–24; rpt. Pelensky, Olga A., Ed. *Isak Dinesen . . .*, 3–6.
+Høyrup, Helene. ''The Arabesque of Existence: Existential Focus and Aesthetic Form in Isak Dinesen's 'The Roads Round Pisa,' '' in Pelensky, Olga A., Ed. *Isak Dinesen . . .*, 250–265.
Kyndrup, Morten. ''Objective Relativity of Absolute Authority,'' *Framing and Fiction . . .*, 297–318; rpt., altered, as ''The Vertigo of Staging: Authority and Narration in Isak Dinesen's 'The Roads Round Pisa,' '' Pelensky, Olga A., Ed. *Isak Dinesen . . .*, 333–345.

"The Sailor-Boy's Tale"
Kullmann, Thomas. "Exotic Landscapes and Borderline Experiences in Twentieth Century Fiction: D. H. Lawrence, Karen Blixen, and Malcolm Lawry," in Seeber, Hans U., and Walter Göbel, Eds. *Anglistentag 1992* . . . , 383.
Scholtz, Antonine M. L. M. "Africa and Creative . . . ," 93–94; rpt. Pelensky, Olga A., Ed. *Isak Dinesen* . . . , 289–292.

"Sorrow-Acre"
Aiken, Susan H. "Dinesen's 'Sorrow-Acre': Tracing the Woman's Line," *Contemp Lit*, 25 (1984), 156–186; rpt. Pelensky, Olga A., Ed. *Isak Dinesen* . . . , 174–198.
Richter, David H. "Covert Plot in Isak Dinesen's 'Sorrow-Acre,' " *J Narrative Technique*, 15 (1985), 82–90; rpt. Pelensky, Olga A., Ed. *Isak Dinesen* . . . , 295–303.

"The Supper at Elsinore"
+ Stambaugh, Sara. "Imagery of Entrapment . . . ," 163–170.

DING LING

"When I Was in Xiacun Village"
Słupski, Zbigniew. "The New and the Traditional in Modern Chinese Literature—Reflections on the Short Story 'When I Was in Xiacun Village' by Ding Ling," *Rocznik Orientalistyczny*, 47, ii (1991), 125–130.

BIRAGO DIOP

"Les Mamelles"
Harrow, Kenneth W. "Bessie Head's 'The Collector of Treasures': Change on the Margins," *Callaloo*, 16 (1993), 176–177.
———. *Thresholds of Change* . . . , 204–206.

ASSIA DJEBAR

"The Dead Speak"
Zimra, Clarisse. "Afterword," *Women of Algiers* . . . [Assia Djebar], 207–208.

"Women of Algiers in their Apartment"
Zimra, Clarisse. "Afterword," 198–200, 204–207.

VALENTINA DMITRIEVA

"The Turkish Soldier's Wife"
Kelly, Catriona. *A History of Russian* . . . , 146–147.

ANATOLY DNEPROV

"Formula for Immortality"
Haynes, Roslynn D. *From Faust* . . . , 245–256.

"S*T*A*P*L*E Farm"
Haynes, Roslynn D. *From Faust* . . . , 272–273.

ALFRED DÖBLIN

"Die Ermordung einer Butterblume"
Sheppard, Richard. "Insanity, Violence and Cultural Criticism: Some Further Thoughts on Four Expressionist Short Stories," *Forum Mod Lang Stud*, 30, ii (1994), 152–162.

E. L. DOCTOROW

"Willi"
Miller, Ann V. "Through a Glass Clearly: Vision as Structure in E. L. Doctorow's 'Willi,' " *Stud Short Fiction,* 30 (1993), 337–342.

JOSÉ DONOSO

"Chattanooga Choo-choo"
Ballesteros, Isolina. "La función de las máscaras en *Tres novelitas burguesas* de José Donoso," *Revista Iberoamericana*, 60 (1994), 982–985.
Magnarelli, Sharon. *Understanding José Donoso*, 5, 120–124, 127, 128, 129–130.

"Gaspard de la nuit"
Ballesteros, Isolina. "La función . . . ," 989–991.
Magnarelli, Sharon. *Understanding José Donoso*, 124–126, 127–128, 130–131.

"Green Atom Number Five"
Ballesteros, Isolina. "La función . . . ," 985–988.
Magnarelli, Sharon. *Understanding José Donoso*, 123–124, 127, 130.

"Santelices"
Magnarelli, Sharon. *Understanding José Donoso*, 18–22.

"Veraneo"
Callan, Richard J. "José Donoso's Story 'Veraneo': A Treasure at the Beach," in Paolini, Gilbert, Ed. *La Chispa* . . . , 32–37.

"The Walk"
Lindstrom, Naomi. *Twentieth-Century* . . . , 177–178.
Magnarelli, Sharon. *Understanding José Donoso*, 5, 9–11, 14–19.

FYODOR DOSTOEVSKY

"Another Man's Wife"
Amoia, Alba. *Feodor Dostoevsky*, 201–204.

"Because of Little Apples"
Jackson, Robert L. *Dialogues* . . . , 8–9, 83–90, 92–94, 98–99, 102–103.

"Bobok"
Amoia, Alba. *Feodor Dostoevsky*, 215–217.

"A Christmas Tree and a Wedding"
Amoia, Alba. *Feodor Dostoevsky*, 197–199.
Jackson, Robert L. *Dialogues* . . . , 94–103.

"The Crocodile"
Amoia, Alba. *Feodor Dostoevsky*, 212–215.

"The Double"
Amoia, Alba. *Feodor Dostoevsky*, 149–156.

"The Dream of a Ridiculous Man"
Amoia, Alba. *Feodor Dostoevsky*, 220–223.

"The Eternal Husband"
Amoia, Alba. *Feodor Dostoevsky*, 179–183.

"The Gambler"
Amoia, Alba. *Feodor Dostoevsky*, 175–178.
Frank, Joseph. " 'The Gambler': A Study in Ethnopsychology," *Hudson R*, 46 (1993), 301–322.

"A Gentle Creature"
Amoia, Alba. *Feodor Dostoevsky*, 217–220.
Isenberg, Charles. *Telling Silence* . . . , 50–78.

"An Honest Thief"
Amoia, Alba. *Feodor Dostoevsky*, 196–197.

"The Landlady"
Amoia, Alba. *Feodor Dostoevsky*, 190–193.

"A Little Hero"
Amoia, Alba. *Feodor Dostoevsky*, 204–207.

"Mr. Prokharchin"
Amoia, Alba. *Feodor Dostoevsky*, 188–189.

"A Nasty Tale"
Amoia, Alba. *Feodor Dostoevsky*, 209–212.

"Notes from Underground"
Amoia, Alba. *Feodor Dostoevsky*, 167–174.
Briggs, A. D. P. "Introduction," in Briggs, A. D. P., Ed. *Notes from Underground* . . . , xv–xxi, xxiv–xxvii.
Flath, Carol A. "Fear of Faith: The Hidden Religious Message of 'Notes from Underground,' " *Slavic & East European J*, 37, iv (1993), 510–529.
Jackson, Robert L. *Dialogues* . . . , 16, 117–118, 209, 217–223, 225–227.

"A Novel in Nine Letters"
Amoia, Alba. *Feodor Dostoevsky*, 189–190.

"The Peasant Marey"
Jackson, Robert L. *Dialogues* . . . , 239–241.

"Polzunkov"
Amoia, Alba. *Feodor Dostoevsky*, 195–196.

"Uncle's Dream"
Amoia, Alba. *Feodor Dostoevsky*, 157–161.

"A Weak Heart"
Amoia, Alba. *Feodor Dostoevsky*, 193–195.

"White Nights"
Amoia, Alba. *Feodor Dostoevsky*, 199–201.

FREDERICK DOUGLASS

"The Heroic Slave"
Sundquist, Eric J. *To Wake the Nations* . . . , 115–124.

ARTHUR CONAN DOYLE

"The Adventure of the Cardboard Box"
Thomas, Ronald R. "The Fingerprint of the Foreigner: Colonizing the Criminal Body in 1890s Detective Fiction and Criminal Anthropology," *ELH*, 61 (1994), 670–676.

"The Adventure of the Copper Beeches"
Duyfhuizen, Bernard. "The Case of Sherlock Homes and Jane Eyre," *Baker Street J*, 43, iii (1993), 135–145.

"The Adventure of the Engineer's Thumb"
Kimball, Miles A. " 'A benefactor of the race': Sherlock Holmes, Voyeurism, and Victorian Readers," *Kentucky Philol R*, 9 (1994), 19–20.

"The Adventure of the Speckled Band"
Hodgson, John A. "The Recoil of 'The Speckled Band': Detective Story and Detective Discourse," *Poetics Today*, 13, ii (1992), 309–324.
Nicholson, Mervyn. "Peripety Cues in Short Fiction," *CEA Critic*, 56, ii (1994), 48–49.
Sage, Victor. "Empire Gothic: Explanation and Epiphany in Conan Doyle, Kipling, and Chesterton," in Bloom, Clive, Ed. *Creepers* . . . , 4–12.
Trotter, David. *The English Novel* . . . , 81–82.

"The Adventure of the Yellow Face"
Thomas, Ronald R. "The Fingerprint . . . ," 676–679.

"The Final Problem"
Kimball, Miles A. " 'A benefactor . . . ," 20–21.

"The Five Orange Pips"
Kimball, Miles A. " 'A benefactor . . . ,'' 16–17.

"The Red-Headed League"
+Bohner, Charles H. *Instructor's Manual* . . . , 3rd ed., 43.

"A Scandal in Bohemia"
Pickering, James H., and Jeffrey D. Hoeper. *Instructor's Manual* . . . , 31–33.

"The Second Strain"
Metress, Christopher. "Diplomacy and Detection in Conan Doyle's 'The Second Strain,' " *Engl Lit Transition*, 37 (1993), 39–51.

THEODORE DREISER

"Second Choice"
Harris, Susan K. "Vicious Binaries: Gender and Authorial Paranoia in Dreiser's 'Second Choice,' Howells' 'Editha,' and Hemingway's 'The Short Happy Life of Francis Macomber,' " *Coll Lit*, 20, ii (1993), 72–74, 79–80.

ANNETTE VON DROSTE-HÜLSHOFF

"Die Judenbuche"
Nollendorfs, Cora L. " '. . . kein Zeugnis ablegen': Woman's Voice in Droste-Hülshoff's 'Judenbuche,' " *Germ Q*, 67 (1994), 325–334.
Pickar, Gertrud B. "The Battering and Meta-Battering of Droste's Margreth: Covert Misogyny in 'Die Judenbuche's' Critical Reception," *Women Germ Yearbook*, 9 (1993), 71–90.

ANDRE DUBUS

"The Curse"
Miner, Madonne M. " 'The Seirênês will sing his mind away': Andre Dubus's 'The Curse,' " *Stud Short Fiction*, 31 (1994), 397–406.

"The Doctor"
+Bohner, Charles H. *Instructor's Manual* . . . , 3rd ed., 43–45.

GUADALUPE DUEÑAS

"Tiene la noche un árbol"
Mine, Rose S. "Guadalupe Dueñas: La obsesiva e implacable búsqueda de la realidad," *Foro Lit*, 2, iv (1978), 41–47.

ALICE DUNBAR-NELSON

"Little Miss Sophie"
Bryan, Violet H. *The Myth of New Orleans* . . . , 70–71.

"Sister Josepha"
Byran, Violet H. *The Myth of New Orleans* . . . , 71–72.

"Stones of the Village"
Bryan, Violet H. *The Myth of New Orleans* . . . , 75–76.

ASHLEY SHEUN DUNN

"No Man's Land"
Wong, Sau-ling C. *Reading Asian American Literature* . . . , 25, 102–106, 111.

MARGUERITE DURAS

"L'Amant"
Diego, Rosa de. "Marguerite Duras: Más allá de la realidad o la invención de la literatura," in *Actas del IV simposio* . . . , 605–613.
Hill, Leslie. *Marguerite Duras* . . . , 78–80, 118, 119–123, 124.
Hulley, Kathleen. "Contaminated Narratives: The Politics of Form and Subjectivity in Marguerite Duras's 'The Lover,' " *Discourse*, 15, ii (1992–1993), 38–47.
Martin, Graham D. "The Drive for Power in Marguerite Duras's 'L'Amant,' " *Forum Mod Lang Stud*, 30, iii (1994), 204–218.
Medcalf, Anne-Marie C. "Blurring the Boundaries? The Sense of Time and Place in Marguerite Duras's 'L'Amant,' " *SPAN*, 36 (1993), 220–229.
Peeters, I., and P. Swiggers. "La Narration décentrée chez Marguerite Duras," in Marotin, François, and Jacques-Philippe Saint-Gérand, Eds. *Poétique et narration* . . . , 545–556.
Schuster, Marilyn R. *Marguerite Duras* . . . , 116–124.
Suárez, Ramón M. " 'El Amante' de Marguerite Duras," *Revista Chilena*, 45 (1994), 115–119.
Thormann, Janet. "Feminine Masquerade in 'L'Amant': Duras with Lacan," *Lit & Psych*, 40, iv (1994), 28–39.

"The Boa"
Schuster, Marilyn R. *Marguerite Duras* . . . , 21–27.

"L'Homme assis dans le couloir"
Chalongue, Florence de. "Des Rencontres élémentaires: Personnage et décor dans deux textes de Marguerite Duras," *Sémiotiques*, 4 (June, 1993), 94–106.
Hill, Leslie. *Marguerite Duras* . . . , 57–63.

"Moderato cantabile"
Hill, Leslie. *Marguerite Duras* . . . , 50–56.
Reid. James H. "The Café Duras: Mourning Descriptive Space," *French Forum*, 19 (1994), 45–46, 48–54.
Schuster, Marilyn R. *Marguerite Duras* . . . , 38–41.

"The Seated Man in the Passage"
Schuster, Marilyn R. *Marguerite Duras* . . . , 107–110.

MARIE VON EBNER-ESCHENBACK

"Die Prinzessin von Banalien"
Steiner, Carl. *Of Reason and Love* . . . , 105–106.

"Prometheus"
Steiner, Carl. *Of Reason and Love* . . . , 193–194.

"Rittmeister Brand"
Steiner, Carl. *Of Reason and Love* . . . , 131–133.

"Das Schädliche"
Steiner, Carl. *Of Reason and Love* . . . , 49, 129–130.

"Die Spitzin"
Steiner, Carl. *Of Reason and Love* . . . , 52, 119–121.

"Die Totenwacht"
Steiner, Carl. *Of Reason and Love* . . . , 130–131.

"Unverbesserlich"
Steiner, Carl. *Of Reason and Love* . . . , 142–143.

"Verschollen"
Steiner, Carl. *Of Reason and Love* . . . , 107.

"De Vorzugsschüler"
Steiner, Carl. *Of Reason and Love* . . . , 137–139.

"Wieder die Alte"
Steiner, Carl. *Of Reason and Love* . . . , 127.

ESTEBAN ECHEVERRÍA

"El matadero"
Agresti, Mabel S. "Una lectura de 'El Matadero,' de Esteban Echeverría," *Revista de Lit Modernas*, 24 (1991), 137–156.
Briesemeister, Dietrich. "Esteban Echeverría: 'El matadero,' " in Roloff, Volker, and Harald Wentzlaff-Eggebert, Eds. *Der Hispanoamerikanische* . . . , 44–51.

MARIA EDGEWORTH

"The Bee & the Cow"
Myers, Mitzi. "Reading Rosamond Reading: Maria Edgeworth's 'Wee-Wee Stories' Interrogate the Canon," in Goodenough, Elizabeth, Mark A. Heberle, and Naomi Sokoloff, Eds. *Infant Tongues* . . . , 63–65.

JORGE EDWARDS

"El amigo Juan"
Noguerol Jiménez, Francisca. "Fantasmas de carne y hueso: La última narrativa de Jorge Edwards," *Quaderni Ibero-Americani*, 76 (1994), 61–62.

"Cumpleaños feliz"
Noguerol Jiménez, Francisca. "Fantasmas . . . ," 59–61.
"In memoriam"
Noguerol Jiménez, Francisca. "Fantasmas . . . ," 62.
"El pie de Irene"
Noguerol Jiménez, Francisca. "Fantasmas . . . ," 54, 57–58.
"La sombra de Huelquiñur"
Noguerol Jiménez, Francisca. "Fantasmas . . . ," 54–56.

GEORGE EGERTON [MARY CHAVELITA DUNNE BRIGHT]

"A Cross Line"
Showalter, Elaine. "Introduction," in Showalter, Elaine, Ed. *Daughters of Decadence* . . . , xiii–xiv.

JOSEPH VON EICHENDORFF

"Aus dem Leben eines Taugenichts"
Eberhardt, Otto. "Kritik an Loeben in Eichendorffs 'Taugenichts,' " *Aurora*, 52 (1992), 101–110.
Mehigan, Tim. "Eichendorff's 'Taugenichts'; or, The Social Education of a Private Man," *Germ Q*, 66 (1993), 60–70.

GEORGE ELIOT [MARY ANN EVANS]

"Amos Barton" [same as 'The Sad Fortunes of Amos Barton]
Heyns, Michiel. *Expulsion* . . . , 146–147.
Martin, Carol A. *George Eliot's Serial* . . . , 46–49, 50–52.
Sorensen, Katherine. "Conventions of Realism and the Absence of Color in George Eliot's 'The Sad Fortunes of the Reverend Amos Barton,' " *Victorians Institute J*, 22 (1994), 15–31.
Winnifrith, T. J. " 'Subtle Shadowy Suggestions': Fact and Fiction in *Scenes of Clerical Life*," *George Eliot-George Henry Lewes Stud*, 24–25 (September, 1993), 65–67.
"Hester Benfield"
Martin, Carol A. *George Eliot's Serial* . . . , 53–56.
"Janet's Repentance"
Bailin, Miriam. *The Sickroom in Victorian Fiction*, 111–115, 115–118, 120–123.
Demetrakopoulos, Stephanie. "George Eliot's 'Janet's Repentance': The First Literary Portrait of a Woman Addict and Her Recovery," *Midwest Q*, 35 (1993), 95–108.
Martin, Carol A. *George Eliot's Serial* . . . , 78–84, 85–92.
Winnifrith, T. J. " 'Subtle Shadowy . . . ," 69–73.
"The Lifted Veil"
Ashby, Kevin. "The Centre and the Margins in 'The Lifted Veil' and

Blackwood's *Edinburgh Magazine*," *George Eliot-George Henry Lewes Stud*, 24–25 (September, 1993), 132–146.
Bailin, Miriam. *The Sickroom in Victorian Fiction*, 115.

"Mr. Gilfil's Love Story"
Heyns, Michiel. *Expulsion . . .*, 147–148.
Martin, Carol A. *George Eliot's Serial . . .*, 53–59.
Winnifrith, T. J. " 'Subtle Shadowy . . .,' " 67–69.

STANLEY ELKIN

"A Poetic for Bullies"
Pughe, Thomas. *Comic Sense . . .*, 126–133.

RALPH ELLISON

"Flying Home"
O'Meally, Robert G. "On Burke and the Vernacular: Ralph Ellison's Boomerang of History," in Fabre, Geneviève, and Robert O'Meally, Eds. *History . . .*, 250–253.

"King of the Bingo Game"
+Bohner, Charles H. *Instructor's Manual . . .*, 3rd ed., 45–46.
Pickering, James H., and Jeffrey D. Hoeper. *Instructor's Manual . . .*, 76–77.

ENCHI FUMIKO

"Blind Man's Bluff"
Hulvey, S. Yumiko. "Enchi Fumiko (1905–1986)," in Mulhern, Chieko I., Ed. *Japanese . . .*, 58.

"Bond for Two Lifetimes—Gleanings"
Hulvey, S. Yumiko. "Enchi Fumiko . . .," 54.

"Boxcar of Chrysanthemums"
Hulvey, S. Yumiko. "Enchi Fumiko . . .," 54–55.

"Enchantress"
Hulvey, S. Yumiko. "Enchi Fumiko . . .," 53–54.

"Skeletons of Men"
Hulvey, S. Yumiko. "Enchi Fumiko . . .," 53.

SOFIA ENGEL'GARDT

"Fate or Character?"
Zirin, Mary F. "Women's Prose Fiction in the Age of Realism," in Clyman, Toby W., and Diana Greene, Eds. *Women Writers . . .*, 84–85.

"The Touchstone"
Zirin, Mary F. "Women's Prose . . . ," 85–86.

LOUISE ERDRICH

"Mauser"
Pickering, James H., and Jeffrey D. Hoeper. *Instructor's Manual* . . . , 128–130.

OLEG ERMAKOV

"Baptism"
Brown, Deming. *The Last Years* . . . , 172–173.

VIKTOR EROFEEV

"Berdyaev"
Porter, Robert. *Russia's Alternative Prose*, 145–146.

"The Half-mast Orgasm of the Century"
Porter, Robert. *Russia's Alternative Prose*, 141–142.

"Life with an Idiot"
Kustanovich, Konstantin. "Erotic Glasnost: Sexuality in Recent Russian Literature," *World Lit Today*, 67 (1993), 143.

"The Parakeet"
Brown, Deming. *The Last Years* . . . , 167–168.

"Piss Off"
Porter, Robert. *Russia's Alternative Prose*, 140–141.

"The Three-Headed Brain Child"
Porter, Robert. *Russia's Alternative Prose*, 143–145.

JULIO ESCOTO

"Resistir. No resistir. La resistencia. ¿Y por qué la resistencia?"
Salinas Paguada, Manuel. "El cuento hondureño contemporáneo," in Róman-Lagunas, Jorge, Ed. *La literatura centroamericana* . . . , 89.

TATYANA ESENINA

"Zhenya, the Wonder of the Twentieth Century"
Kelly, Catriona. *A History of Russian* . . . , 354.

AMINATA SOW FALL

"La Grève des Bàttu"
Bangura, Ahmed S. " 'Translating' Islam: Islam and Linguistic

Differentiation in the Narratives of Aminata Sow Fall,'' *Yearbook Comp Gen Lit*, 41 (1993), 27, 29–33.

''Le Revenant''

Bangura, Ahmed S. '' 'Translating' Islam . . . ,'' 24–27, 28.

WILLIAM FAULKNER

''Ad Astra''

Martin, Reginald. ''Faulkner's Southern Reflections: The Black on the Back of the Mirror in 'Ad Astra,' '' *African Am R*, 27 (1993), 53–57.

''Barn Burning''

Pickering, James H., and Jeffrey D. Hoeper. *Instructor's Manual* . . . , 64–65.

Rio-Jelliffe, R. ''The Language of Time in Fiction: A Model in Faulkner's 'Barn Burning,' '' *J Narrative Technique*, 24 (1994), 103–110.

Yunis, Susan S. ''The Narrator of Faulkner's 'Barn Burning,' '' *Faulkner J*, 6, ii (1991), 23–31.

''The Bear''

Ford, Dan. '' 'He Was Talking About Truth': Faulkner in Pursuit of the Old Verities,'' in Hönnighausen, Lothar, and Valeria G. Lerda, Eds. *Rewriting the South* . . . , 318–323.

Kowalewski, Michael. *Deadly Musings* . . . , 177–180.

Scholtmeijer, Marian. *Animal Victims* . . . , 249–256.

''Delta Autumn''

Whitt, Jan. *Allegory and the Modern* . . . , 106–108.

''Dry September''

+Bohner, Charles H. *Instructor's Manual* . . . , 3rd ed., 46–47.

''Evangeline''

Simpson, Lewis P. *The Fable of the Southern Writer*, 90–93.

''Honor''

Wagner, Vivian. ''Gender, Technology, and Utopia in Faulkner's Airplane Tales,'' *Arizona Q*, 49, iv (1994), 83–87, 94.

''Old Man''

Kowalewski, Michael. *Deadly Musings* . . . , 170–174.

''Red Leaves''

Hoffmann, Gerhard and Gisela. ''William Faulkner: 'Red Leaves,' '' in Lubbers, Klaus, Ed. *Die Englische* . . . , 231–254.

Watkins, Floyd C. ''Sacrificial Rituals and Anguish in the Victim's Heart in 'Red Leaves,' '' *Stud Short Fiction*, 30 (1993), 71–78.

''A Rose for Emily''

+Bohner, Charles H. *Instructor's Manual* . . . , 3rd ed., 47–48.

Charters, Ann. *Resources* . . . , 56–57.

Curry, Renée R. ''Gender and Authorial Limitation in Faulkner's 'A Rose for Emily,' '' *Mississippi Q*, 47 (1994), 391–402.

Pickering, James H., and Jeffrey D. Hoeper. *Instructor's Manual* . . . , 60–62.
Rodman, Isaac. "Irony and Isolation: Narrative Distance in Faulkner's 'A Rose for Emily,' " *Faulkner J*, 8, ii (1993), 3–12.

"Smoke"
Lahey, Michael E. "Trying Emotions: Unpredictable Justice in Faulkner's 'Smoke' and 'Tomorrow,' " *Mississippi Q*, 46 (1993), 447–454.

"That Evening Sun"
+Bohner, Charles H. *Instructor's Manual* . . . , 3rd ed., 49–50.
Charters, Ann. *Resources* . . . , 58–59.

"Tomorrow"
Lahey, Michael E. "Trying Emotions . . . ," 454–462.

"Was"
Kleppe, Sandra L. "Elements of the Carnivalesque in Faulkner's 'Was,' " *Mississippi Q*, 46 (1993), 437–445.
Wall, Carey. "*Go Down, Moses*: The Collective Action of Redress," *Faulkner J*, 7, i–ii (1991), 168.

MORDECAI ZEV FEIERBERG

"Whither?"
Steinhardt, Deborah. "Figures of Thought: Psycho-Narration in the Fiction of Berdichewsky, Bershadsky, and Feierberg," *Prooftexts*, 8, ii (1988), 211–214.

LAURA FEIXAS

"Final Absurdo"
Villalba Álvarez, Marina. "Vida vs. muerte en la narrativa de Laura Feixas: *El asesino en la muñeca* o la inútil medición del tiempo," in Romera Castillo, José, Ed. *Actas del IV simposio* . . . , 850–851.

"Isla en Babia"
Villalba Álvarez, Marina. "Vida vs. muerte . . . ," 848.

"Joven Promesa"
Villalba Álvarez, Marina. "Vida vs. muerte . . . ," 849–850.

"Memoria en venta"
Villalba Álvarez, Marina. "Vida vs. muerte . . . ," 846–847.

"Miss Hyde y el dragón"
Villalba Álvarez, Marina. "Vida vs. muerte . . . ," 847–848.

"La octava plaga"
Villalba Álvarez, Marina. "Vida vs. muerte . . . ," 846.

CRISTINA FERNÁNDEZ CUBAS

"La ventana del jardín"
Valls, Fernando. "De las certezas del amigo a las dudas del héroe:

Sobre 'La ventana del jardín,' de Cristina Fernández Cubas,'' *Insula*, 568 (April, 1994), 18–19.

ROSARIO FERRÉ

''Cuando las mujeres quieren a los hombres''
Roses, Lorraine E. ''Las esperanzas de Pandora: prototipos femeninos en la obra de Rosario Ferré,'' *Revista Iberoamericana*, 59 (1993), 281–282, 284–285.
Vega Carney, Carmen. '' 'Cuando las mujeres quieren a los hombres,' '' in Myers, Eunice, and Ginette Adamson, Eds. *Continental, Latin-American . . .*, 183–193.

''El cuento envenenado''
Francescato, Martha P. ''Un cuento de hadas contemporáneo (envenenado) de Rosario Ferré,'' *Revista de Crítica*, 20 (1994), 177–181.

''Maldito amor''
Acosta Cruz, María I. ''Historia y escritura femenina en Olga Nolla, Magali García Ramis, Rosario Ferré y Ana Lydia Vega,'' *Revista Iberoamericana*, 59 (1993), 271–273.

''Marina and the Lion''
Lindstrom, Naomi. *Twentieth-Century . . .*, 214.

''La muñeca menor''
Bilbija, Ksenija. ''Rosario Ferré's 'The Youngest Doll': On Women, Dolls, Golems, and Cyborgs,'' *Callaloo*, 17 (1994), 878–888.
Roses, Lorraine E. ''Las esperanzas de Pandora . . . ,'' 281, 283–284, 285.
Zee, Linda S. ''Rosario Ferré's 'La muñeca menor' and Caribbean Myth,'' *Chasqui*, 23, ii (1994), 102–110.

''El regalo''
Gosser-Esquilín, Mary A. ''Textualidad y sensualidad compartidas en 'El regalo' de Rosario Ferré,'' *Alba de América*, 11 (1993), 199–210.

IDA FINK

''The Garden That Floated Away''
Wilczynski, Marek. ''Trusting the Words: Paradoxes of Ida Fink,'' *Mod Lang Stud*, 24, iv (1994), 26–27.

''Inspector von Galoshinsky''
Wilczynski, Marek. ''Trusting . . . ,'' 31–32.

CHARLES G. FINNEY

''The Circus of Dr. Lao''
Whyde, Janet M. ''Fantastic Disillusionment: Rupturing Narrative

and Rewriting Reality in 'The Circus of Dr. Lao,' " *Extrapolation*, 35 (1994), 230–240.

GUÐRÚN FINNSDÓTTIR

"Traustirmáttarviðir"

Wolf, Kirsten. "Western Icelandic Women Writers: Their Contribution to the Literary Canon," *Scandinavian Stud*, 66 (1994), 179–180.

RUDOLPH FISHER

"Miss Cynthie"

Andrews, William L. "Rudolph Fisher," in Andrews, William L., Ed. *Classic Fiction* . . . , 240.

F. SCOTT FITZGERALD

"Babylon Revisited"

+Bohner, Charles H. *Instructor's Manual* . . . , 3rd ed., 50–51.

"May Day"

Ickstadt, Heinz. "F. Scott Fitzgerald: 'May Day,' " in Lubbers, Klaus, Ed. *Die Englische* . . . , 255–264.

"One Trip Abroad"

Baldwin, Marc. "F. Scott Fitzgerald's 'One Trip Abroad': A Metafantasy of the Divided Self," *J Fantastic Arts*, 4, iii (1991), 69–78.

"The Scandal Detectives"

Minter, David. *A Cultural History* . . . , 107–109.

GUSTAVE FLAUBERT

"Hérodias"

Hollard, T. L. "Flaubert's 'Herodias' and Massenet's *Herodiade*," *New Zealand J French Stud*, 13, ii (1992), 18, 19–20, 21, 23–24, 25, 27.

Killick, Rachel. " 'The Power and the Glory'? Discourses of Authority and Tricks of Speech in *Trois Contes*," *Mod Lang R*, 88 (1993), 315–319.

"Saint Julien"

Killick, Rachel. " 'The Power . . . ," 313–315.

Scholtmeijer, Marian. *Animal Victims* . . . , 241–243.

"A Simple Heart"

Brombert, Victor. "La chambre de Félicité: bazar ou chapelle?" in Mosele, Elio, Ed. *George Sand* . . . , 73–86.

Gallagher, Edward J. "Heavenly Bodies: Dogmatic Parody in Flaubert's 'Un coeur simple,' " *New Zealand J French Stud*, 12, ii (1991), 16–23.
Haig, Stirling. "Parrot and Parody: Flaubert," in Mickel, Emanuel J., Ed. *The Shaping of the Text* . . . , 105–112.
Killick, Rachel. " 'The Power . . . ," 308–313.
Stipa, Ingrid. "Desire, Repetition and the Imaginary in Flaubert's 'Un Coeur simple,' " *Stud Short Fiction*, 31 (1994), 617–626.
Wing, Nathaniel. "Reading Simplicity: Flaubert's 'Un coeur simple,' " *Nineteenth-Century French Stud*, 21 (1992–1993), 88–101.

RICHARD FORD

"Empire"
Trussler, Michael. " 'Famous Times': Historicity in the Short Fiction of Richard Ford and Raymond Carver," *Wascana R*, 28, ii (1994), 38.

"Rock Springs"
Trussler, Michael. " 'Famous Times' . . . ," 36–37.

E. M. FORSTER

"The Eternal Moment"
Buzard, James. *The Beaten Track* . . . , 305–308.

"The Road from Colonus"
Buzard, James. *The Beaten Track* . . . , 300–303.

"The Story of a Panic"
Buzard, James. *The Beaten Track* . . . , 293–296.

JOHN FOWLES

"The Cloud"
Foster, Thomas C. *Understanding John Fowles*, 7–8, 106–111.

"The Ebony Tower"
Foster, Thomas C. *Understanding John Fowles*, 91–98.

"The Enigma"
Broich, Ulrich. "Muted Postmodernism: The Contemporary British Short Story," *Zeitschrift für Anglistik und Amerikanistik*, 41 (1993), 36–37.
Foster, Thomas C. *Understanding John Fowles*, 102–106.

MARY E. WILKINS FREEMAN

"Arethusa"
Meese, Elizabeth. "Signs of Undecidability: Reconsidering the

Stories of Mary Wilkins Freeman,'' in *Crossing the Double-cross . . .* , 32–34; rpt. Marchalonis, Shirley, Ed. *Critical Essays . . .* , 168–170.
+Toth, Susan A. ''Defiant Light: A Positive View of Mary Wilkins Freeman,'' in Marchalonis, Shirley, Ed. *Critical Essays . . .* , 128–129.

''The Balking of Christopher''
Fisken, Beth W. '' 'Unusual' People in a 'Usual Place': 'The Balking of Christopher' by Mary Wilkins Freeman,'' *Colby Lib Q*, 21 (1985), 99–103; rpt. Marchalonis, Shirley, Ed. *Critical Essays . . .* , 146–150.

''A Church Mouse''
Daniel, Janice B. ''Freeman's 'A Church Mouse,' '' *Explicator*, 53 (1994), 43–44.
Pryse, Marjorie. '' 'Distilling Essences': Regionalism and 'Women's Culture,' '' *Am Lit Realism*, 25, ii (1993), 6–8.
+Toth, Susan A. ''Defiant Light . . . ,'' 126–127.

''A Conflict Ended''
Meese, Elizabeth. ''Signs of . . . ,'' 166–168.

''The Conquest of Humility''
Pennell, Melissa M. ''The Liberating Will: Freedom of Choice in the Fiction of Mary Wilkins Freeman,'' in Marchalonis, Shirley, Ed. *Critical Essays . . .* , 208–210.

''Eglantina''
Getz, John. '' 'Eglantina': Freeman's Revision of Hawthorne's 'The Birth-mark,' '' in Marchalonis, Shirley, Ed. *Critical Essays . . .* , 180–184.

''Evelina's Garden''
+Donovan, Josephine. ''Silence or Capitulation: Prepatriarchal 'Mother's Gardens' in Jewett and Freeman,'' in Marchalonis, Shirley, Ed. *Critical Essays . . .* , 153–154.

''The Givers''
Marchalonis, Shirley. ''The Sharp-edged Humor of Mary Wilkins Freeman: *The Jamesons*—and Other Stories,'' in Marchalonis, Shirley, Ed. *Critical Essays . . .* , 230–231, 232–233.

''An Honest Soul''
Johnsen, Norma. ''Pieces: Artist and Audience in Three Mary Wilkins Freeman Stories,'' *Colby Q*, 29, i (1993), 45–47.

''An Independent Thinker''
+Toth, Susan A. ''Defiant Light . . . ,'' 127–128.

''Louisa''
Pennell, Melissa M. ''The Liberating Will . . . ,'' 210–212.

''A New England Nun''
Getz, John. ''Mary Wilkins Freeman and Sherwood Anderson: Confluence or Influence,'' *Midamerica*, 19 (1992), 79–83.
+Hirsch, David H. ''Subdued Meaning in 'A New England Nun,' '' in Marchalonis, Shirley, Ed. *Critical Essays . . .* , 106–117.

Lutwack, Leonard. *Birds in Literature*, 295.
Meese, Elizabeth. "Signs of . . . ," 162–165.
Pennell, Melissa M. "The Liberating Will . . . ," 212–213.
Pryse, Marjorie. " 'Distilling Essences' . . . ," 3–6.
+Pryse, Marjorie. "An Uncloistered 'New England Nun,' " in Marchalonis, Shirley, Ed. *Critical Essays* . . . , 139–145.

"Old Woman Magoun"
Karpinski, Joanne B. "The Gothic Underpinnings of Realism in the Local Colorists' No Man's Land," in Mogen, David, Scott P. Sanders, and Joanne B. Karpinski, Eds. *Frontier Gothic* . . . , 148–154.

"On the Walpole Road"
Johnsen, Norma. "Pieces: Artist . . . ," 47–52.

"The Poetess"
Grasso, Linda. " 'Thwarted Life, Mighty Hunger, Unfinished Work': The Legacy of Nineteenth-Century Women Writing in America," *ATQ*, 8, N.S. (1994), 97–106, 114–117.

"The Revolt of Mother"
+McElrath, Joseph R. "The Artistry of Mary E. Wilkins Freeman's 'The Revolt,' " in Marchalonis, Shirley, Ed. *Critical Essays* . . . , 132–138.
Meese, Elizabeth. "Signs of . . . ," 170–173.

"Sister Liddy"
Johnsen, Norma. "Pieces: Artist . . . ," 52–54.

"Sour Sweetings"
Getz, John. "Mary Wilkins Freeman . . . ," 83–84.

"A Village Singer"
+Toth, Susan A. "Defiant Light . . . ," 124–126.

BRIAN FRIEL

"Among the Ruins"
Cronin, John. " ' "Donging the Tower"—The Past Did Have Meaning': The Short Stories of Brian Friel," in Peacock, Alan J., Ed. *The Achievement* . . . , 3–6.
Heaney, Seamus. "For Liberation: Brian Friel and the Use of Memory," in Peacock, Alan J., Ed. *The Achievement* . . . , 233–234.
Welch, Robert. " 'Isn't This Your Job?—To Translate?': Brian Friel's Languages," in Peacock, Alan J., Ed. *The Achievement* . . . , 136.

"Foundry House"
Cronin, John. " ' "Donging . . . ," 9–10.

MAX FRISCH

"Der Mensch erscheint im Holozän"
Pender, Malcolm. " 'Du mußt das Haus abtragen': The Motif of the

House in Recent German-Swiss Fiction,'' *Mod Lang R*, 88 (1993), 692–695.

CARLOS FUENTES

''Aura''

Frenk, Susan F. ''Rewriting History: Carlos Fuentes' 'Aura,' '' *Forum Mod Lang Stud*, 30, iii (1994), 256–276.

Gómez Carro, Carlos. ''Carlos Fuentes, narrador (1954–1967),'' in Mata, Oscar, Ed. *En torna* . . . , 115–118.

''El día de las madres''

Birckel, Maurice. ''Sauveurs, substituts, vicaires: à propos de deux rècits de Carlos Fuentes, dans *Agua quemada*,'' *Bulletin Hispanique*, 95, i (1993), 31–38.

Van Delden, Maarten. ''Carlos Fuentes' *Agua Quemada*: The Nation as Unimaginable Community,'' *Latin Am Lit R*, 21 (July–December, 1993), 61–66, 67.

''Estos fueron los palacios''

Birckel, Maurice. ''Sauveurs, substituts . . . ,'' 38–56.

FUKAZAWA SHICHIRŌ

''The Story of a Dream of Courtly Elegance''

Treat, John W. ''Beheaded Emperors and the Absent Figure in Contemporary Japanese Literature,'' *PMLA*, 109 (1994), 100–115.

ERNEST J. GAINES

''Bloodline''

Luscher, Robert M. ''The Pulse of *Bloodline*,'' in Estes, David C., Ed. *Critical* . . . , 69, 71, 72–73, 76–77, 82–83.

Shannon, Sandra G. ''Strong Men Getting Stronger: Gaines's Defense of the Elderly Black Male in *A Gathering of Old Men*,'' in Estes, David C., Ed. *Critical* . . . , 199, 201, 203–204.

Smith, David L. ''Bloodlines and Patriarchs: *Of Love and Dust* and Its Revisions of Faulkner,'' in Estes, David C., Ed. *Critical* . . . , 54.

TuSmith, Bonnie. *All My Relatives* . . . . 95–97.

''Just Like a Tree''

Gaudet, Marcia. ''Black Women: Race, Gender, and Culture in Gaines's Fiction,'' in Estes, David C., Ed. *Critical* . . . , 141–142.

———. ''Images of Old Age in Three Louisiana Short Stories,'' *Louisiana Engl J*, 1, i (1993), 63–64.

Luscher, Robert M. ''The Pulse . . . ,'' 73, 77, 79, 83–85.

Shelton, Frank W. ''Of Machines and Men: Pastoralism in Gaines's Fiction,'' in Estes, David C., Ed. *Critical* . . . , 22, 25.

"A Long Day in November"
Estes, David C. "Gaines's Humor: Race and Laughter," in Estes, David C., Ed. *Critical* . . . , 230–231.
Gaudet Marcia. "Black Women: Race . . . ," 144, 146–147, 149, 153–154.
Luscher, Robert M. "The Pulse . . . ," 74–75, 78, 80–81.
Shelton, Frank W. "Of Machines . . . ," 22.

"The Sky Is Gray"
Charney, Mark J. "Voice and Perspective in the Film Adaptations of Gaines's Fiction," in Estes, David C., Ed. *Critical* . . . , 126–129.
Gaudet Marcia. "Black Women: Race . . . ," 144–145.
Luscher, Robert M. "The Pulse . . . ," 71, 75, 81–82.
White, Daniel. " 'Haunted by the Idea': Fathers and Sons in *In My Father's House* and *A Gathering of Old Men*," in Estes, David C., Ed. *Critical* . . . , 160, 173.

"Three Men"
Luscher, Robert M. "The Pulse . . . ," 72, 75–76, 82.
Rickels, Milton, and Patricia Rickels. " 'The Sound of My People Talking': Folk Humor in *A Gathering of Old Men*," in Estes, David C., Ed. *Critical* . . . , 223–224.

MAVIS GALLANT

"About Geneva"
Schaub, Danielle. "Structural Patterns of Alienation and Disjunction," *Canadian Lit*, 136 (1993), 46–48.

"The Ice Wagon Going Down the Street"
Masel, Carolyn. "Reflections on Belatedness in Australian and Canadian Literature," in White, Jonathan, Ed. *Recasting the World* . . . , 167–169.

"Its Image on the Mirror"
Irvine, Lorna. "Mirroring the Canadas: Mavis Gallant's Fiction," *Colby Q*, 29, ii (1993), 119–125.

"My Heart Is Broken"
Schaub, Danielle. "Structural . . . ," 53–55.

"Orphan's Progress"
Schaub, Danielle. "Structural . . . ," 49–53.

JOAQUÍN GALLEGOS LARA

"Hambrientería"
Ibáñez Pastor de Ehrlich, María-Teresa. "El diálogo como marco de historias contadas en tres cuentos del Grupo de Guayaquil," *Iberoromania*, 39 (1994), 76–77.

JANICE GALLOWAY

"Blood"

Metzstein, Margery. "Of Myths and Men: Aspects of Gender in the Fiction of Janice Galloway," in Wallace, Gavin, and Randall Stevenson, Eds. *The Scottish Novel* . . . , 142–144.

"David"

Metzstein, Margery. "Of Myths . . . ," 144–145.

ELENA GAN

"Recollections of Zheleznozavodsk"

Kelly, Catriona. *A History of Russian* . . . , 112, 117.

"Theophania Abbiagio"

Kelly, Catriona. *A History of Russian* . . . , 113–114.

JUAN GARCÍA HORTELANO

"Los archivos secretos"

Percival, Anthony. "A Contemporary Spanish Inter-National-Textual Story: Juan García Hortelano's 'Los archivos secretos,' " *Revista Canadiense*, 18 (1994), 316–321.

GABRIEL GARCÍA MÁRQUEZ

"Balthazar's Marvelous Afternoon"

Oberhelman, Harley D. *The Presence of Hemingway* . . . , 37.

"Chronicle of a Death Foretold"

Bell, Michael. *Gabriel García Márquez* . . . , 84–105.

Del-Río, Marcela. "El epígrafe revelador: Clave para acercarse a la parábola de la 'Crónica de una muerte anunciada,' " *Confluencia*, 8, i (1992), 81–99.

Eyzaguirre, Luis. "Rito y sacrificio en 'Crónica de una muerte anunciada,' " *Revista Chilena*, 42 (1993), 81–87.

Hart, Stephen M. *Gabriel García Márquez* . . . , 18–56.

Lopez, François. " 'Crónica de una muerte anunciada' de Gabriel García Márquez ou le crime était presque partait," *Bull Hispanique*, 96 (1994), 545–561.

"The Handsomest Drowned Man in the World"

Charters, Ann. *Resources* . . . , 60.

Romeo, Gabriela María. " 'El ahogado más hermoso del mundo,' de Gabriel García Márquez," in Arancibia, Juana Alcira, Ed. *Literatura como* . . . , 443–456.

"The Incredible and Sad Tale of Innocent Eréndira and Her Heartless Grandmother"

Jaeck, Lois M. " 'The Incredibly Sad Tale of Eréndira . . .': A New

Look at Female Suppression," *Canadian R Comp Lit*, 20 (1993), 381–393.
Penuel, Arnold M. *Intertextuality* . . . , 88–106.

"Last Voyage of the Ghost Ship"
Oberhelman, Harley D. *The Presence of Hemingway* . . . , 38.

"María dos Prazeres"
R-Vergara, Isabel. "Escritura, creación y destrucción en *Doce cuentos peregrinos* de Gabriel García Márquez," *Hispanic J*, 15, ii (1994), 356–357.

"Me alquilo para soñar"
R-Vergara, Isabel. "Escritura . . . ," 350–352.

"Montiel's Widow"
Oberhelman, Harley D. *The Presence of Hemingway* . . . , 37–38.

"Nabo: The Black Man Who Made the Angels Wait"
Carvalho, Susan de. "The Fusion of the Subjective and Objective Realities in Gabriel García Márquez's 'Nabo: The Black Man Who Made the Angels Wait,' " *Int'l Fiction R*, 20 (1993), 133–137.

"One of These Days"
Oberhelman, Harley D. *The Presence of Hemingway* . . . , 36.

"Sólo vine a hablar por teléfono"
R-Vergara, Isabel. "Escritura . . . ," 352–356.

"The Story of a Shipwrecked Sailor"
Oberhelman, Harley. "Hemingway and García Márquez: Two Shipwreck Narratives," *Int'l Fiction R*, 21 (1994), 4–6.
———. *The Presence of Hemingway* . . . , 27–28.

"Tuesday Siesta"
+Bohner, Charles H. *Instructor's Manual* . . . , 3rd ed., 52.
Oberhelman, Harley D. *The Presence of Hemingway* . . . , 34–36.

"A Very Old Man with Enormous Wings"
Charters, Ann. *Resources* . . . , 61–62.
Pickering, James H., and Jeffrey D. Hoeper. *Instructor's Manual* . . . , 107–108.

"The Woman Who Came at Six O'Clock"
Oberhelman, Harley D. *The Presence of Hemingway* . . . , 23–24.

JOHN GARDNER

"John Napper Sailing Through the Universe"
Howell, John M. *Understanding John Gardner*, 101–103.

"King Gregor and the Fool"
Howell, John M. *Understanding* . . . , 105–106.

"The King's Indian"
Howell, John M. *Understanding* . . . , 107–120.

"Muriel"
Howell, John M. *Understanding* . . . , 106–107.

"Pastoral Care"
Howell, John M. *Understanding . . .*, 92–94.

"Queen Louisa"
Howell, John M. *Understanding . . .*, 104–105.

"The Ravages of Spring"
Fenlon, Katherine F. "John Gardner's 'The Ravages of Spring' as Re-creation of 'The Fall of the House of Usher,' " *Stud Short Fiction*, 31 (1994), 481–487.
Howell, John M. *Understanding . . .*, 94–97.

"The Temptation of St. Ivo"
Howell, John M. *Understanding . . .*, 97–99.

"The Warden"
Howell, John M. *Understanding . . .*, 99–101.

ZUFAR GAREEV

"On Holiday"
Brown, Deming. *The Last Years . . .*, 184.

"The Park"
Brown, Deming. *The Last Years . . .*, 184–185.

"When Other Birds Call"
Brown, Deming. *The Last Years . . .*, 183–184.

HAMLIN GARLAND

"God's Ravens"
MacDonald, Bonney. "Eastern Imaginings of the West in Hamlin Garland's 'Up the Coolly' and 'God's Ravens,' " *Western Am Lit*, 28 (1993), 209–215, 223–228.

"A Prairie Heroine"
Newlin, Keith. "Melodramatist of the Middle Border: Hamlin Garland's Early Work Reconsidered," *Stud Am Fiction*, 21 (1993), 165–166, 167.

"Under the Lion's Paw"
Newlin, Keith. "Melodramatist . . .," 166.

"Up the Coolly"
MacDonald, Bonney. "Eastern Imaginings . . .," 209–223.

JULIO GARMENDIA

"El cuarto de los duendes"
Barrera Linares, Luis. "Julio Garmendia: Mito y realidad/ambigüedad e ironía," *Escritura*, 17 (1992), 28, 29.

"El cuento ficticio"
Barrera Linares, Luis. "Julio Garmendia . . .," 35–39.

"Guachirongo"
Barrera Linares, Luis. "Julio Garmendia . . . ," 43–44.

"La tienda de muñecos"
Barrera Linares, Luis. "Julio Garmendia . . . ," 39–43.

ELENA GARRO

"La culpa es de los tlaxcaltecas"
Glantz, Margo. "Las hijas de la malinche," *Debate Feminista* (September, 1992), [n.p.]; rpt. *Esguince de cintura* . . . , 190–192.
Rojas-Trempe, Lady. "Historia narrativa de la conquista de los indígenas mexicanos: Elena Garro," *Lit Mexicana*, 3, i (1992), 157–168.

"El zapaterito de Guanajuato"
Rojas-Trempe, Lady. "Las peripecias de la mirada del zapaterito de Guanajuato," *Alba de América*, 11 (1993), 303–310.

ELIZABETH CLEGHORN GASKELL

"My Lady Ludlow"
Krueger, Christine L. "The 'female paternalist' as historian: Elizabeth Gaskell's 'My Lady Ludlow,' " in Shires, Linda M., Ed. *Rewriting the Victorians* . . . , 166–182.

"Lizzie Leigh"
Fitzwilliam, Marie. "The Politics behind the Angel: Separate Spheres in Elizabeth Gaskell's 'Lizzie Leigh,' " *Gaskell Soc J*, 8 (1994), 15–27.

WILLIAM GASS

"Icicles"
Díaz Sánchez, Mª Eugenia. " 'You have Fallen into Art—Return to Life': *In the Heart of the Heart of the Country* de William Gass," *Atlantis*, 12, ii (1991), 115–116.

"In the Heart of the Heart of the Country"
Díaz Sánchez, Mª Eugenia. " 'You have Fallen . . . ," 118–120.
Truchlar, Leo. "William Gass: 'In the Heart of the Heart of the Country,' " in Lubbers, Klaus, Ed. *Die Englische* . . . , 399–408.

"Mrs. Mean"
Díaz Sánchez, Mª Eugenia. " 'You have Fallen . . . ," 114–115.

"Order of Insects"
Díaz Sánchez, Mª Eugenia. " 'You have Fallen . . . ," 117–118.

"The Pedersen Kid"
Díaz Sánchez, Mª Eugenia. " 'You have Fallen . . . ," 111–114.

THÉOPHILE GAUTIER

"La Morte amoureuse"
Andriano, Joseph. *Our Ladies . . .*, 76–84.

MEMPO GIARDINELLI

"La entrevista"
Stone, Kenton V. "Mempo Giardinelli and the Anxiety of Borges's Influence," *Chasqui*, 23, i (1994), 83–84, 85–87.

WILLIAM GIBSON

"Hinterlands"
Yule, Jeffrey. "The Marginalized Short Stories of William Gibson: 'Hinterlands' and 'The Winter Market,' " *Foundation*, 58 (1993), 76–84.

"The Winter Market"
Delany, Paul. " 'Hardly the Center of the World': Vancouver in William Gibson's 'The Winter Market,' " in Delany, Paul, Ed. *Vancouver . . .*, 179–192.
Yule, Jeffrey. "The Marginalized . . . ," 76–84.

ANDRÉ GIDE

"El Hadj"
Benmerad, Saïd, and Simone Rezzoug. "Le Désert inversé," *Bull Amis d'André Gide*, 22 (April, 1994), 227–233.

ENRIQUE GIL GILBERT

"La blanca de los ojos de luna"
Ibáñez Pastor de Ehrlich, María-Teresa. "El diálogo como marco de historias contadas en tres cuentos del Grupo de Guayaquil," *Iberoromania*, 39 (1994), 74–75.

ELLEN GILCHRIST

"Some Blue Hills at Sundown"
Larue, Dorie. "Progress and Prescription: Ellen Gilchrist's Southern Belles," *Southern Q*, 31, iii (1993), 71–72.

CHARLOTTE PERKINS GILMAN

"The Giant Wistaria"
Scharnhorst, Gary. "Charlotte Perkins Gilman's 'The Giant

Wistaria': A Hieroglyph of the Female Frontier Gothic,'' in Mogan, David, Scott P. Sanders, and Joanne B. Karpinski, Eds. *Frontier Gothic* . . . , 156–164.

''The Yellow Wallpaper''

Bak, John S. ''Escaping the Jaundiced Eye: Foucauldian Panopticism in Charlotte Perkins Gilman's 'The Yellow Wallpaper,' '' *Stud Short Fiction*, 31 (1994), 39–46.

+Bohner, Charles H. *Instructor's Manual* . . . , 3rd ed., 53–54.

DeKoven, Marianne. ''Gendered Doubleness and the 'Origins' of Modernist Form,'' *Tulsa Stud Women's Lit*, 8, i (1989), 28–35; rpt. Erskine, Thomas L., and Connie L. Richards, Eds. *Charlotte Perkins Gilman* . . . , 212–223.

Fetterley, Judith. ''Reading about Reading: 'The Yellow Wallpaper,' '' in Flynn, Elizabeth A., and Patrocinio P. Schweickart, Eds. *Gender and Reading* . . . , 158–164; rpt. Erskine, Thomas L., and Connie L. Richards, Eds. *Charlotte Perkins Gilman* . . . , 181–189.

+Fleenor, Juliann E. ''The Gothic Prism: Charlotte Perkins Gilman's Gothic Stories and Her Autobiography,'' in Erskine, Thomas L., and Connie L. Richards, Eds. *Charlotte Perkins Gilman* . . . , 139–158.

Golden, Catherine. '' 'Overwriting' the Rest Cure: Charlotte Perkins Gilman's Literary Escape from S. Weir Mitchell's Fictionalization of Women,'' in Karpinski, Joanne B., Ed. *Critical Essays* . . . , 153–154.

+Haney-Peritz, Janice. ''Monumental Feminism and Literature's Ancestral House: Another Look at 'The Yellow Wallpaper,' '' in Erskine, Thomas L., and Connie L. Richards, Eds. *Charlotte Perkins Gilman* . . . , 191–208.

Hedges, Elaine R. '' 'Out at Last'? 'The Yellow Wallpaper' after Two Decades of Feminist Criticism,'' in Golden Catherine, Ed. *The Captive Imagination* . . . , 319–338; rpt. Karpinski, Joanne B., Ed. *Critical Essays* . . . , 222–233.

Herndl, Diane P. *Invalid Women* . . . , 112–113, 129–133, 141–149.

Lanser, Susan S. ''Feminist Criticism, 'The Yellow Wallpaper,' and the Politics of Color in America,'' *Feminist Stud*, 15 (1989), 415–441; rpt. Erskine, Thomas L., and Connie L. Richards, Eds. *Charlotte Perkins Gilman* . . . , 225–256.

Kaplan, Carla. ''Reading Feminist Readings: Recuperative Reading and the Silent Heroine of Feminist Criticism,'' in Hedges, Elaine, and Shelley F. Fishkin, Eds. *Listening to Silences* . . . , 177–180, 183–184.

Kolodny, Annette. ''A Map for Rereading: Or, Gender and the Interpretation of Literary Texts,'' *New Lit His*, 11 (1980), 451–467; rpt. Erskine, Thomas L., and Connie L. Richards, Eds. *Charlotte Perkins Gilman* . . . , 159–180.

Pickering, James H., and Jeffrey D. Hoeper. *Instructor's Manual* . . . , 35.

Shumaker, Conrad. '' 'Too Terribly Good to Be Printed': Charlotte

Gilman's 'The Yellow Wallpaper,' " *Am Lit*, 57 (1985), 588–599; rpt. Erskine, Thomas L., and Connie L. Richards, Eds. *Charlotte Perkins Gilman* . . . , 125–137.

Tallack, Douglas. *The Nineteenth-Century American Short Story* . . . , 218–241.

MARIANNE GINGHER

"Camouflage"

Cosslett, Tess. *Women Writing Childbirth* . . . , 121–132, 151.

NATALIA GINZBURG

"La madre"

Giorgio, Adalgisa. "Natalia Ginzburg's 'La madre': Exposing Patriarchy's Erasure of the Mother," *Mod Lang R,* 88 (1993), 864–880.

ELLEN GLASGOW

"Dare's Gift"

Matthews, Pamela R. *Ellen Glasgow* . . . , 115, 124–129.

"Jordan's End"

Matthews, Pamela R. *Ellen Glasgow* . . . , 144–149.

"The Past"

Matthews, Pamela R. *Ellen Glasgow* . . . , 130–136.

"A Point in Morals"

Scheick, William J. "The Narrative Ethos of Glasgow's 'A Point in Morals,' " *Ellen Glasgow News*, 30 (Spring, 1993), 2–4.

"The Shadowy Third"

Matthews, Pamela R. *Ellen Glasgow* . . . , 115–124.

"Whispering Leaves"

Matthews, Pamela R. *Ellen Glasgow* . . . , 136–144.

"A Woman of To-morrow"

Matthews, Pamela R. *Ellen Glasgow* . . . , 26–29.

SUSAN GLASPELL

"Contrary to Precedent"

Makowsky, Veronica. *Susan Glaspell's Century* . . . , 31–33.

"The Faithless Shepherd"

Makowsky, Veronica. *Susan Glaspell's Century* . . . , 90–91.

"From A to Z"

Makowsky, Veronica. *Susan Glaspell's Century* . . . , 34–36.

"A Jury of Her Peers"
Kaplan, Carla. "Reading Feminist Readings: Recuperative Reading and the Silent Heroine of Feminist Criticism," in Hedges, Elaine, and Shelley F. Fishkin, Eds. *Listening to Silences* . . . , 180–183, 184–185.
Pickering, James H., and Jeffrey D. Hoeper. *Instructor's Manual* . . . , 52.

NORA GLICKMAN

"One of Her Johns"
Baumgarten, Murray. "Urban Life and Jewish Memory in the Tales of Moacyr Scliar and Nora Glickman," in DiAntonio, Robert, and Nora Glickman, Eds. *Tradition and Innovation* . . . , 64–66.

"Puesto Vacante"
Baumgarten, Murray. "Urban Life . . . ," 68.

"U.S.A. Musa S.A."
Baumgarten, Murray. "Urban Life . . . ," 67–68.

NIKOLAI GOGOL

"The Diary of a Madman"
Ernst, Charles A. " 'I Am That King'—Disordered History and Delusional Writing: The Artful Derangements of Gogol's 'Diary,' " *Cithara*, 32, ii (1993), 40–45.
Fusso, Susanne. *Designing* . . . , 107–109.
Maguire, Robert A. *Exploring Gogol*, 48–66.

"Ivan Fedorovich Shponka and His Aunt"
Fusso, Susanne. *Designing* . . . , 105–106.

"Nevsky Prospect"
Hart, Pierre R. "Narrative Oscillation in Gogol's 'Nevsky Prospect,' " *Stud Short Fiction*, 31 (1994), 639–645.
Swensen, Andrew. "Vampirism in Gogol's Short Fiction," *Slavic & East European J*, 37, iv (1993), 500–502.

"The Nose"
Seifrid, Thomas. "Suspicion toward Narrative: The Nose and the Problem of Autonomy in Gogol's 'Nos,' " *Russian R*, 52 (1993), 384–392.

"Old World Landowners"
Maguire, Robert A. *Exploring Gogol*, 22–34, 258–264.

"The Overcoat"
+Bohner, Charles H. *Instructor's Manual* . . . , 3rd ed., 54–55.
Howe, Irving. . . . *A Critic's Notebook*, 137–143.
Jackson, Robert L. *Dialogues* . . . , 200–203.

"The Portrait"
Basom, Ann M. "The Fantastic in Gogol's Two Versions of 'Portret,' " *Slavic & East European J*, 38 (1994), 419–437.
Maguire, Robert A. *Exploring Gogol*, 143–173.
Swensen, Andrew. "Vampirism . . . ," 502–505.

"Rome"
Fusso, Susanne. *Designing . . .* , 110–114.

"The Tale of How Ivan Ivanovich Quarreled with Ivan Nikiforovich"
Maguire, Robert A. *Exploring Gogol*, 35–48.

"Taras Bulba"
Maguire, Robert A. *Exploring Gogol*, 273–282.

"A Terrible Vengeance"
Maguire, Robert A. *Exploring Gogol*, 5–18.
Swensen, Andrew. "Vampirism . . . ," 495–497.

"Viy"
Maguire, Robert A. *Exploring Gogol*, 182–189.
Swensen, Andrew. "Vampirism . . . ," 497–499.

WILLIAM GOLDING

"Clonk, Clonk"
D'Amelio, Nadia. "Equivocation in *The Scorpion God*," in Delbaere, Jeanne, Ed. *William Golding . . .* , 116, 120–121.
Friedman, Lawrence S. *William Golding*, 117–119.

"Envoy Extraordinary"
D'Amelio, Nadia. "Equivocation . . . ," 116–117, 121–122.
Friedman, Lawrence S. *William Golding*, 119–121.

"The Inheritors"
Friedman, Lawrence S. *William Golding*, 33–50.

"The Scorpion God"
D'Amelio, Nadia. "Equivocation . . . ," 116, 117–120.
Friedman, Lawrence S. *William Golding*, 115–117.

JOSÉ JUSTO GÓMEZ DE LA CORTINA

"Euclea, o La griega de Trieste"
Vargas, Margarita. "Romanticism," in Foster, David W., Ed. *Mexican Literature . . .* , 95–97.

JOSÉ LUIS GONZÁLEZ

"En el fondo del caño hay un negrito"
Díaz, Luis F. " 'En el fondo del caño hay un negrito' de José Luis González: Estructura y discursos narcisistas," *Revista Iberoamericana*, 59 (1993), 127–143.

NADINE GORDIMER

"A Bit of Young Life"
Ettin, Andrew V. *Betrayals* . . . , 107–108.

"Blinder"
Ettin, Andrew V. *Betrayals* . . . , 97.
Lazar, Karen. "Feminism as 'Piffling'? Ambiguities in Gordimer's Short Stories," in King, Bruce, Ed. *The Later Short Fiction* . . . , 221–222.
Lomberg, Alan R. "Once More into the Burrows: Gordimer's Later Short Fiction," in King, Bruce, Ed. *The Later Short Fiction* . . . , 234–235.

"A Chip of Glass Ruby"
Kinkead-Weekes, Mark. "Sharp Knowing in Apartheid?: The Shorter Fiction of Nadine Gordimer and Doris Lessing," in Gurnah, Abdulrazak, Ed. *Essays* . . . , 97–98.

"A City of the Dead, A City of the Living"
Ettin, Andrew V. *Betrayals* . . . , 97–99.
Lomberg, Alan R. "Once More . . . ," 229–230.

"A Company of Laughing Faces"
Huggan, Graham. "Echoes from Elsewhere: Gordimer's Short Fiction as Social Critique," *Research African Lit*, 25, i (1994), 68–69.

"Crimes of Conscience"
Ettin, Andrew V. *Betrayals* . . . , 108–109.
Lomberg, Alan R. "Once More . . . ," 233–234.

"The Defeated"
Wade, Michael. "*A Sport of Nature*: Identity and Repression of the Jewish Subject," in King, Bruce, Ed. *The Later Short Fiction* . . . , 157–160.

"Face from Atlantis"
Ettin, Andrew V. *Betrayals* . . . , 114–115.

"Good Climate, Friendly Inhabitants"
Lazar, Karen. "Feminism . . . ," 218–220.

"Harry's Presence"
Wade, Michael. "*A Sport of Nature* . . . ," 160–162.

"Home"
Ettin, Andrew V. *Betrayals* . . . , 109–111.

"An Intruder"
Lazar, Karen. "Feminism . . . ," 222–225.

"Is There Nowhere Else We Can Meet?"
Kinkead-Weekes, Mark. "Sharp Knowing . . . ," 90–91.

"Keeping Fit"
Ettin, Andrew V. *Betrayals* . . . , 26–27, 63.
Huggan, Graham. "Echoes . . . ," 70–71.

"Letter from His Father"
Ettin, Andrew V. *Betrayals . . .* , 132–134.

"The Life of the Imagination"
+Bohner, Charles H. *Instructor's Manual . . .* , 3rd ed., 56–57.

"A Lion on the Freeway"
Lomberg, Alan R. "Once More . . . ," 228–229.

"Livingstone's Companions"
Huggan, Graham. "Echoes . . . ," 69–70.

"Not for Publication"
Kinkead-Weekes, Mark. "Sharp Knowing . . . ," 95–96.

"Oral History"
Lomberg, Alan R. "Once More . . . ," 228.

"Rags and Bones"
Ettin, Andrew V. *Betrayals . . .* , 112–114.

"Safe Houses"
Ettin, Andrew V. *Betrayals . . .* , 124–126.

"Siblings"
Charters, Ann. *Resources . . .* , 63–64.

"Sins of the Third Age"
Lomberg, Alan R. "Once More . . . ," 233.

"Six Feet of the Country"
Huggan, Graham. "Echoes . . . ," 64–68.

"The Smell of Death and Flowers"
Ettin, Andrew V. *Betrayals . . .* , 67–68.

"Some are Born to Sweet Delight"
Ettin, Andrew V. *Betrayals . . .* , 117–118.

"Some Monday for Sure"
Kinkead-Weekes, Mark. "Sharp Knowing . . . ," 101–105.

"Something Out There"
Ettin, Andrew V. *Betrayals . . .* , 89–95, 100–104.
Lomberg, Alan R. "Once More . . . ," 230–231.

"Teraloyna"
Colleran, Jeanne. "Archive of Apartheid: Nadine Gordimer's Short Fiction at the End of the Interregnum," in King, Bruce, Ed. *The Later Short Fiction . . .* , 238–239.

"The Termitary"
Lazar, Karen. "Feminism . . . ," 225–226.

"The Third Presence"
Lazar, Karen. "Feminism . . . ," 216–217.

"Time Did"
Lomberg, Alan R. "Once More . . . ," 232–233.

"Town and Country Lovers"
Charters, Ann. *Resources . . .* , 65–66.

Lomberg, Alan R. "Once More . . . ," 235.
Wade, Michael. "*A Sport of Nature* . . . ," 163–164.

"Train from Rhodesia"
Nicholson, Mervyn. "Peripety Cues in Short Fiction," *CEA Critic*, 56, ii (1994), 51–52.

"The Ultimate Safari"
Ettin, Andrew V. *Betrayals* . . . , 126–127.

"What Were You Dreaming?"
Ettin, Andrew V. *Betrayals* . . . , 47–48.

CAROLINE GORDON

"The Brilliant Leaves"
Hersh, Allison. "Representations of Temporal Liminality in Caroline Gordon's 'The Brilliant Leaves' and Robert Penn Warren's *Meet Me in the Green Glen*," *Southern Q*, 32, ii (1994), 83–88.

"The Captive"
Fritz-Piggott, Jill. "The Dominant Chord and the Different Voice: The Sexes in Gordon's Stories," in Manning, Carol S., Ed. *The Female Tradition* . . . , 209–210, 211–214.

"Old Red"
Brown, Ashley. "Caroline Gordon: 'Old Red,' " in Lubbers, Klaus, Ed. *Die Englische* . . . , 222–230.

"The Petrified Woman"
Fritz-Piggott, Jill. "The Dominant Chord . . . ," 212–214.

"Tom Rivers"
Fritz-Piggott, Jill. "The Dominant Chord . . . ," 214–216.

ANGÉLICA GORODISCHER

"Los embriones del violeta"
Juzyn-Amestoy, Olga. "La narrativa fantástica de Angélica Gorodischer: la mirada 'femenina' y los límites del desea," *Letras Femeninas*, Número Extraordinario Conmemorativo: 1974–1994 (1994), 87–93.

JUANA MANUELA GORRITI

"El emparedado"
Terrón de Bellomo, Herminia. "Literatura fantástica y denuncia social: Juana Manuela Gorriti," *Letras Femeninas*, 19, i–ii (1993), 114.

JEREMIAS GOTTHELF

"Die Schwarze Spinne"
Donahue, William C. "The Kiss of the Spider Woman: Gotthelf's

'Matricentric' Pedagogy and Its (Post)war Reception,'' *German Q*, 67 (1994), 304–324.

ALAIN GRANDBOIS

''Illusions''

Bouillaguet, Annick. ''Brefs aperçus sur quelques faits d'intertextualité dans *Avant le chaos*,'' *Etudes Française*, 30, ii (1994), 21–22.

''Le rire''

Bouillaguet, Annick. ''Brefs aperçus . . . ,'' 22–23.

''Le 13''

Bouillaguet, Annick. ''Brefs aperçus . . . ,'' 18–19, 20.

JULIAN GREEN

''Léviathan ou la Traversée inutile''

Filipczak, Dorota. '' 'Léviathan ou la Traversée inutile' and the Death of the Old Self in 'Through the Panama,' '' *Malcolm Lowry R*, 31–32 (Fall–Spring, 1992–1993), 47–53.

GRAHAM GREENE

''The Lieutenant Died Last''

Shelden, Michael. . . . *The Enemy Within*, 240–241.

''May We Borrow Your Husband''

Shelden, Michael. . . . *The Enemy Within*, 62–63.

''Two Gentle People''

+Bohner, Charles H. *Instructor's Manual* . . . , 3rd ed., 57–58.

''Under the Garden''

Böker, Uwe. ''Graham Greene: 'Under the Garden,' '' in Lubbers, Klaus, Ed. *Die Englische* . . . , 369–378.

Degan, James. ''Memory and Automythography in Graham Greene's 'Under the Garden,' '' *Lit & Psych*, 40, i–ii (1994), 87–106.

Shelden, Michael. . . . *The Enemy Within*, 42–45.

IRINA GREKOVA [ELENA SERGEEVNA VENCEL]

''Ladies' Hairdresser''

Aiken, Susan H. ''Stages of Dissent: Olsen, Grekova, and the Politics of Creativity,'' in Aiken, Susan H., Adele M. Barker, Maya Koreneva, and Ekaterina Stetsenko, Eds. *Dialogues/Dialogi* . . . , 124–132.

Stetsenko, Ekaterina. ''Revolutions from Within,'' in Aiken, Susan H., Adele M. Barker, Maya Koreneva, and Ekaterina Stetsenko, Eds. *Dialogues/Dialogi* . . . , 143–151.

"The Pheasant"
Brown, Deming. *The Last Years . . .*, 41.

"Without Smiles"
Brown, Deming. *The Last Years . . .*, 41–42.

ALEXANDR GRIN [ALEXANDER STEPANOVICH GRINEVSKY]

"Apel'siny"
Luker, Nicholas. "Tales of an Invisible Man: Aleksandr Grin's *Shapka-nevidimka* (1908)," *New Zealand Slavonic J*, [n.v.] (1994), 80–82.

"Gost' "
Luker, Nicholas. "Tales . . . ," 83–84.

"Karantin"
Luker, Nicholas. "Tales . . . ," 85–91.

"Kirpich i muzyka"
Luker, Nicholas. "Tales . . . ," 73–75.

"Luibimyi"
Luker, Nicholas. "Tales . . . ," 84–85.

"Marat"
Luker, Nicholas. "Tales . . . ," 72–73.

"Na dosuge"
Luker, Nicholas. "Tales . . . ," 82–83.

"Podzemnoe"
Luker, Nicholas. "Tales . . . ," 75–77.

"Sluchai"
Luker, Nicholas. "Tales . . . ," 78–80.

"V Italiiu"
Luker, Nicholas. "Tales . . . ," 77–78.

LUCÍA GUERRA-CUNNINGHAM

"Frutos extraños"
Gálvez-Carlisle, Gloria. "Si nos permiten hablar: Los espacios silenciados y la deconstrucción del discurso del silencio en la narrativa de Lucía Guerra," *Revista Iberoamericana*, 60 (1994), 1077–1078.

"Más allá de las máscaras"
Muñoz, Elías M. "La mujer y la historia en 'Más allá de las máscaras de Lucía Guerra," in Myers, Eunice, and Ginette Adamson, Eds. *Continental, Latin-American . . .*, 139–147.

"Travesías"
Gálvez-Carlisle, Gloria. "Si nos permiten . . . ," 1076–1077.

"The Virgin's Passion"
Ferris, Erin. "Le nom de la mère in Lucía Guerra's 'The Virgin's Passion,' " *Letras Femeninas*, 20, i–ii (1994), 117–129.

JOHN MALCOLM GUNN

"Ko-pot Ka-nat"
Nelson, Robert M. "He Said/She Said: Writing Oral Tradition in John Gunn's 'Ko-pot Ka-nat' and Leslie Silko's *Storyteller*," *Stud Am Indian Lit*, 5, i (1993), 32–39.

EDWARD EVERETT HALE

"The Man Without a Country"
Pearce, Colin D. "The Wisdom of Exile: Edward Everett Hale's 'The Man Without a Country,' " *Interpretation*, 22, i (1994), 91–109.

DONALD HALL

"Argument and Persuasion"
+Bohner, Charles H. *Instructor's Manual* . . . , 3rd ed., 59–60.

EDMOND HAMILTON

"Metal Giants"
Haynes, Roslynn D. *From Faust* . . . , 271.

DASHIELL HAMMETT

"They Can Only Hang You Once"
Nicholson, Mervyn. "Peripety Cues in Short Fiction," *CEA Critic*, 56, ii (1994), 48.

PETER HANDKE

"Der Chinese des Schmerzes"
Markolin, Caroline. " 'Schließ die Augen . . .': Die poetisierte Suche nach Schrift und Erzählung in Peter Handkes 'Der Chinese des Schmerzes,' " *Mod Austrian Lit*, 27, ii (1994), 113–127.

"Kindergeschichte"
Firda, Richard A. *Peter Handke*, 109–113.

"Der kurze Brief zum langen Abschied"
Firda, Richard A. *Peter Handke*, 67–76.
Schneilin, Gérard. "Les images de l'Amérique et leur fonction dans

le roman de Peter Handke: 'La Courte lettre pour un long adieu,' " in Meslin, Michel, Ed. *Regards européens . . .* , 191–206.

"Langsame Heimkehr"

Küchler, Tilman. "Kunst und Raum: Peter Handkes langsame Heimkehr ins Spiel," *New Germ R*, 8 (1992), 91–103.

"Die Linkshämdige Frau"

Firda, Richard A. *Peter Handke*, 91–98.

"Nachmittag eines Schriftstellers"

Firda, Richard A. *Peter Handke*, 132–136.

"Versuche über die Jukebox"

Moser, Samuel. "Das Glück des Erzählens ist das Erzählen des Glücks: Peter Handkes 'Versuche,' " in Fuchs, Gerhard, and Gerhard Melzer, Eds. *Peter Handke . . .* , 137–151.

"Wunschloses Unglück"

Firda, Richard A. *Peter Handke*, 77–85.

Kreyenberg, Regina, and Gudrun Lipjes-Türr. "Peter Handke: 'Wunschloses Unglück,' " in Kaiser, Herbert, and Gerhard Köpf, Eds. *Erzählen, Erinnern . . .* , 125–148.

MAURITS HANSEN

"Luren"

Sjaåvik, Jan. "Rhetorical Manipulation in Maurits Hansen's 'Luren,' " *Scandinavian Stud*, 66 (1994), 521–532.

YAHYA HAQQI

"The Saint's Lamp"

Badawi, M. M. *A Short History of Modern . . .* , 131–132.

THOMAS HARDY

"Barbara of the House of Grebe"

Marroni, Francesco. "The Negation of Eros in 'Barbara of the House of Grebe,' " *Thomas Hardy J*, 10, i (1994), 33–41.

"Destiny and a Blue Cloak"

Dalziel, Pamela. "Hapless 'Destiny': An Uncollected Story of Marginalised Lives," *Thomas Hardy J*, 8, ii (1992), 41–49.

"An Imaginative Woman"

Essex, Ruth. "Mrs. Marchmill, Mother and Poetess," *Thomas Hardy J*, 10, iii (1994), 64–66.

"Tony Kytes, the Arch-Deceiver"

+Bohner, Charles H. *Instructor's Manual . . .* , 3rd ed., 61–62.

"The Three Strangers"

Marroni, Francesco. " 'The Three Stranger' and the Verbal Representation of Wessex," *Thomas Hardy J*, 8, ii (1992), 26–39.

"A Tradition of Eighteen Hundred and Four"

King, Kathryn R. "Hardy's 'A Tradition of Eighteen Hundred and Four' and the Anxiety of Invention," *Thomas Hardy J*, 8, ii (1992), 23–24.

"The Withered Arm"

Ebbatson, Roger. " 'The Withered Arm' and History," *Critical S*, 5, ii (1993), 131–135.

SHULAMIT HAREVEN

"Twilight"

Brenner, Rachel F. "The Reception of Holocaust Testimony in Israeli Literature: Shulamit Hareven's 'The Witness' and 'Twilight,' " in Yudkin, Leon L., Ed. *Hebrew Literature* . . . , 109–113, 117–123.

"The Witness"

Brenner, Rachel F. "The Reception . . . ," 109–111, 113–117.

FRANCES ELLEN WATKINS HARPER

"The Two Offers"

Davis, Cynthia J. "Speaking the Body's Pain: Harriet Wilson's 'Our Nig,' " *African Am R*, 27 (1993), 395.

WILLIAM HARRISON

"Roller Ball Murder"

Vanderwerken, David L. "Roller Ball: Sport and Society in the Future," *Arete*, 2, ii (1985), 39–45.

BRET HARTE

"The Outcasts of Poker Flat"

Clark, Michael. "Bret Harte's 'The Outcasts of Poker Flat,' and the Donner Pass Tragedy," *Short Story*, 1, ii, N.S. (1993), 49–56.

GERHART HAUPTMANN

"Flagman Thiel" [same as "Signalman Thiel"]

Crosby, Donald H. "Nature's Nightmare: The Inner World of Hauptmann's 'Flagman Thiel,' " *J Fantastic Arts*, 1, ii (1988), 25–33.

NATHANIEL HAWTHORNE

"Alice Doane's Appeal"

Lee, Catherine C. "Silencing the Female in Hawthorne's 'Alice Doane's Appeal,' " *Mount Olive R*, 6 (Spring, 1992), 86–93.

Thompson, G. R. *The Art* . . . , 160–201.

"The Ambitious Guest"
Bunge, Nancy. *Nathaniel Hawthorne* . . . , 25–27.

"The Artist of the Beautiful"
Bromell, Nicholas K. *By the Sweat* . . . , 101–104, 111.
Bunge, Nancy. *Nathaniel Hawthorne* . . . , 36–38.
McKee, Kathryn B. " 'A Small Heap of Glittering Fragments': Hawthorne's Discontent with the Short Story Form," *ATQ*, 8, N.S. (1994), 140–142.

"The Birthmark"
+Bohner, Charles H. *Instructor's Manual* . . . , 3rd ed., 62–63.
Charters, Ann. *Resources* . . . , 68–69.
Bromell, Nicholas K. *By the Sweat* . . . , 101–105, 108–113.
Bunge, Nancy. *Nathaniel Hawthorne* . . . , 28–30.
Haynes, Roslynn D. *From Faust* . . . , 88–89.
Herndl, Diane P. *Invalid Women* . . . , 87–90.
Rosenberg, Liz. " 'The Best That Earth Could Offer': 'The Birthmark,' a Newlywed's Story," *Stud Short Fiction*, 30 (1993), 145–151.
Weinstein, Cindy. "The Invisible Hand Made Visible: 'The Birthmark,' " *Nineteenth-Century Lit*, 48 (1993), 44–73.

"The Celestial Railroad"
Bunge, Nancy. *Nathaniel Hawthorne* . . . , 61–62.
Cook, Jonathan A. "New Heavens, Poor Old Earth: Satirical Apocalypse in Hawthorne's *Mosses from an Old Manse*," *ESQ: J Am Renaissance*, 39 (1993), 211, 214–218.

"Chippings with a Chisel"
Bunge, Nancy. *Nathaniel Hawthorne* . . . , 43–48.

"The Christmas Banquet"
Wohlpart, A. James. "Allegories of Art, Allegories of Heart: Hawthorne's 'Egotism' and 'The Christmas Banquet,' " *Stud Short Fiction*, 31 (1994), 450–455.

"The Devil in Manuscript"
Thompson, G. R. *The Art* . . . , 210–212.

"Dr. Heidegger's Experiment"
Bunge, Nancy. *Nathaniel Hawthorne* . . . , 33–36.

"Drowne's Wooden Image"
Bromell, Nicholas K. *By the Sweat* . . . , 101–102, 105–112.
Bunge, Nancy. *Nathaniel Hawthorne* . . . , 48–51.
McKee, Kathryn B. " 'A Small . . . ,' " 142–144.

"Earth's Holocaust"
Bunge, Nancy. *Nathaniel Hawthorne* . . . , 24–25.
Cook, Jonathan A. "New Heavens . . . ," 219–222.

"Egotism; or, the Bosom Serpent"
Bunge, Nancy. *Nathaniel Hawthorne* . . . , 22–24.
Wohlpart, A. James. "Allegories of Art . . . ," 455–458.

"Endicott and the Red Cross"
Orton, Stephen. "De-centered Symbols in 'Endicott and the Red Cross,' " *Stud Short Fiction*, 30 (1993), 565–573.
Tallack, Douglas. *The Nineteenth-Century* . . . , 121–134.

"Ethan Brand"
Allen, Glen S. "Master Mechanics and Evil Wizards: Science and the American Imagination from Frankenstein to Sputnik," *Massachusetts R*, 33 (1993), 525–526.
Bunge, Nancy. *Nathaniel Hawthorne* . . . , 30–33.
Harris, Mark. "A New Reading of 'Ethan Brand': The Failed Quest," *Stud Short Fiction*, 31 (1994), 69–77.

"Feathertop"
Charters, Ann. *Resources* . . . , 69–70.
Voller, Jack G. *The Supernatural Sublime* . . . , 215.

"The Gentle Boy"
Thompson, G. R. *The Art* . . . , 102–119.

"The Gray Champion"
Thompson, G. R. *The Art* . . . , 85–94.

"The Great Carbuncle"
Bunge, Nancy. *Nathaniel Hawthorne* . . . , 73–75.
Zuppinger, Renaud. "*Vanitas Vanitatis* ou la gemme mal aimée: 'The Great Carbuncle' de Hawthorne," *Études Anglaises*, 46, i (1993), 10–18.

"The Great Stone Face"
Bunge, Nancy. *Nathaniel Hawthorne* . . . , 75–77.

"The Hall of Fantasy"
Bunge, Nancy. *Nathaniel Hawthorne* . . . , 55–58.
Cook, Jonathan A. "New Heavens . . . ," 227–233.

"The Haunted Mind"
Bunge, Nancy. *Nathaniel Hawthorne* . . . , 77–79.
Moore, Thomas R. " 'A Thick and Darksome Veil': The Rhetoric of Hawthorne's Sketches," *Nineteenth-Century Lit*, 48 (1993), 323–324.

"The Hollow of the Three Hills"
Thompson, G. R. *The Art* . . . , 58–66.
Voller, Jack G. *The Supernatural Sublime* . . . , 215–216.

"The Intelligence Office"
Cook, Jonathan A. "New Heavens . . . ," 234–235.

"Lady Eleanore's Mantle"
Bunge, Nancy. *Nathaniel Hawthorne* . . . , 16–18.

"The Man of Adamant"
Bunge, Nancy. *Nathaniel Hawthorne* . . . , 20–22.

"The Maypole of Merry Mount"
Bunge, Nancy. *Nathaniel Hawthorne* . . . , 72–73.
Taketani, Etsuko. "Re-narrativization of the Maypole Incident:

Hawthorne and His New England Annalists,'' *Stud Engl Lit*, 70 (1994), 239–256.

''The Minister's Black Veil''
Bunge, Nancy. *Nathaniel Hawthorne . . .*, 18–20.
Coale, Samuel. ''Hawthorne's Black Veil: From Image to Icon,'' *CEA Critic*, 55, iii (1993), 79–87.
Tallack, Douglas. *The Nineteenth-Century . . .*, 134–136.

''Monsieur du Miroir''
Moore, Thomas R. '' 'A Thick . . . ,'' 314–317.

''Mr. Higginbotham's Catastrophe''
Elbert, Monica. ''Nathaniel Hawthorne, *The Concord Freeman*, and the Irish 'Other,' '' *Éire*, 29, iii (1994), 66–68.

''My Kinsman, Major Molineux''
Abrams, Robert E. ''Critiquing Colonial American Geography: Hawthorne's Landscape of Bewilderment,'' *Texas Stud Lit & Lang*, 36 (1994), 371–373.
Budick, Emily M. ''American Literature's Declaration of In/dependence: Stanley Cavell, Nathaniel Hawthorne, and the Covenant of Consent,'' in Spolsky, Ellen, Ed. *Summoning: Ideas . . .*, 217–226.
Bunge, Nancy. *Nathaniel Hawthorne . . .*, 6–11.
Freese, Peter. ''Robin und seine vielen Verwandten: Zur Rezeptionsgeschichte von Nathaniel Hawthornes 'My Kinsman, Major Molineux,' '' in Lubbers, Klaus, Ed. *Die Englische . . .*, 12–27.
Pickering, James H., and Jeffrey D. Hoeper. *Instructor's Manual . . .*, 1–2.
Thompson, G. R. *The Art . . .*, 120–158.

''The New Adam and Eve''
Bunge, Nancy. *Nathaniel Hawthorne . . .*, 69–70.
Cook, Jonathan A. ''New Heavens . . . ,'' 222–227.

''The Old Apple Dealer''
Moore, Thomas R. '' 'A Thick . . . ,'' 313–314, 320–322.

''Old News''
Bunge, Nancy. *Nathaniel Hawthorne . . .*, 58–61.

''An Old Woman's Tale''
Thompson, G. R. *The Art . . .*, 76–82.

''The Pomegranate-Seeds''
Laffrado, Laura. ''The Persephone Myth in Hawthorne's *Tanglewood Tales*,'' in Hayes, Elizabeth T., Ed. *Images of Persephone . . .*, 75–82.

''The Procession of Life''
Cook, Jonathan A. ''New Heavens . . . ,'' 233–234.

''The Prophetic Pictures''
Bunge, Nancy. *Nathaniel Hawthorne . . .*, 41–43.

"Rappaccini's Daughter"
Bunge, Nancy. *Nathaniel Hawthorne . . .* , 67–71.
Haynes, Roslynn D. *From Faust . . .* , 89.
Herndl, Diane P. *Invalid Women . . .* , 94–99.

"A Rill from the Town Pump"
Moore, Thomas R. " 'A Thick . . . ,'' 318–319.

"Roger Malvin's Burial"
Bunge, Nancy. *Nathaniel Hawthorne . . .* , 14–16.
Thompson, G. R. *The Art . . .* , 94–102.

"A Select Party"
Cook, Jonathan A. "New Heavens . . . ,'' 235–237.

"Seven Vagabonds"
Thompson, G. R. *The Art . . .* , 215–216.

"Sights from a Steeple"
Bunge, Nancy. *Nathaniel Hawthorne . . .* , 62–65.

"The Snow-Image"
Bunge, Nancy. *Nathaniel Hawthorne . . .* , 51–55.
McKee, Kathryn B. " 'A Small . . . ,'' 144–145.
Voller, Jack G. *The Supernatural Sublime . . .* , 219.

"Sylph Etherege"
Bunge, Nancy. *Nathaniel Hawthorne . . .* , 65–67.

"Wakefield"
Bunge, Nancy. *Nathaniel Hawthorne . . .* , 38–41.
Kelsey, Angela M. "Mrs. Wakefield's Gaze: Femininity and Dominance in Nathaniel Hawthorne's 'Wakefield,' " *ATQ*, 8, N.S. (1994), 17–31.
Markus, Manfred. "Nathaniel Hawthorne: 'Wakefield,' " in Lubbers, Klaus, Ed. *Die Englische . . .* , 28–39.
Weinstein, Arnold. *Nobody's Home . . .* , 13–26.

"The Wives of the Dead"
Thompson, G. R. *The Art . . .* , 66–76.

"Young Goodman Brown"
Abrams, Robert E. "Critiquing Colonial . . . ,'' 362–364.
Benoit, Raymond. " 'Young Goodman Brown': The Second Time Around," *Nathaniel Hawthorne R*, 19, ii (1993), 18–21.
+Bohner, Charles H. *Instructor's Manual . . .* , 3rd ed., 63–64.
Bunge, Nancy. *Nathaniel Hawthorne . . .* , 11–14.
Charters, Ann. *Resources . . .* , 71–72.
Franklin, Benjamin V. "Goodman Brown and the Puritan Catechism," *ESQ: J Am Renaissance*, 40 (1994), 67–88.
Hale, John K. "The Serpentine Staff in 'Young Goodman Brown,' " *Nathaniel Hawthorne R*, 19, ii (1993), 17–18.
Pickering, James H., and Jeffrey D. Hoeper. *Instructor's Manual . . .* , 4–5.
Voller, Jack G. *The Supernatural Sublime . . .* , 216–218.

HAIM [HAYIM] HAZAZ

"Drabkin"

Gertz, Nurit. "To Caesar What Is Caesar's: Ideology Versus Literature in the Stories of Hazaz," *Prooftexts*, 8, ii (1988), 185–190.

BESSIE HEAD

"The Cardinals"

Daymond, M. J. "Introduction," *The Cardinals* . . . [by Bessie Head], vii–xvi.

"The Collector of Treasures"

Driver, Dorothy. "Reconstructing the Past, Shaping the Future: Bessie Head and the Question of Feminism in a New South Africa," in Wisker, Gina, Ed. *Black Women's Writing*, 178–180.

Harrow, Kenneth W. "Bessie Head's 'The Collector of Treasures': Change on the Margins," *Callaloo*, 16 (1993), 177–178.

———. *Thresholds of Change* . . . , 206–208.

Lionnet, Françoise, "Geographies of Pain: Captive Bodies and Violent Acts in the Fictions of Myriam Warner-Vieyre, Gayl Jones, and Bessie Head," *Callaloo*, 16 (1993), 148–150.

"The Deep River"

Driver, Dorothy. "Reconstructing . . . ," 173–175.

"Heaven Is Not Closed"

Harrow, Kenneth W. "Bessie Head's . . ." 170–173.

———. *Thresholds of Change* . . . , 195–201.

"Kgotla"

Driver, Dorothy. "Reconstructing . . . ," 173.

"Life"

Driver, Dorothy. "Reconstructing . . . ," 162–164.

Harrow, Kenneth W. "Bessie Head's . . . ," 174–175.

———. *Thresholds of Change* . . . , 201–203.

Lionnet, Françoise, "Geographies . . . ," 147–148.

"Looking for a Rain God"

+Bohner, Charles H. *Instructor's Manual* . . . , 3rd ed., 64–65.

"Maru"

Olaogun, Modupe. "Irony and Schizophrenia in Bessie Head's 'Maru,' " *Research African Lit*, 25, iv (1994), 69–87.

Phillips, Maggi. "Engaging Dreams: Alternative Perspectives on Flora Nwapa, Buchi Emecheta, Ama Ata Aidoo, Bessie Head, and Tsitsi Dangarembga's Writing," *Research African Lit*, 25, iv (1994), 97.

"Snapshots of a Wedding"

Driver, Dorothy. "Reconstructing . . . ," 162, 163, 164.

Harrow, Kenneth W. "Bessie Head's . . . ," 176.

———. *Thresholds of Change* . . . , 204.

"The Wind and a Boy"
Driver, Dorothy. "Reconstructing . . . ," 172–73.

LAFCADIO HEARN

"Yuki-Onna"
Makino, Yoko. "Lafcadio Hearn's 'Yuki-Onna' and Baudelaire's 'Les Bienfaits de la lune,' " *Comp Lit Stud*, 28 (1991), 234–243.

CHRISTOPH HEIN

"Die Vergewaltigung"
McKnight, Phillip. *Understanding Christoph Hein*, 31.

"Einladung zum Lever Bourgeois"
McKnight, Phillip. *Understanding Christoph Hein*, 161–163.

"Der fremde Freund"
Kaufmann, Hans. "Herzloses Pathos. Christoph Hein: 'Der fremde Freund,' " in Deiritz, Karl, and Hannes Krauss, Eds. *Verrat an der Kunst? . . .* , 152–156.
Pfeiffer, Peter C. "Tote und Geschichte(n): Christoph Heins *Drachenblut* und *Horns Ende*," *Germ Stud R*, 16, i (1993), 23–31.

"Der neuere (glücklichere) Kohlhaas"
McKnight, Phillip. *Understanding Christoph Hein*, 163–165.

"Kein Seeweg nach Indien"
McKnight, Phillip. *Understanding Christoph Hein*, 166–167.

HEINRICH HEINE

"The Rabbi of Bacherach"
Krobb, Florian. " 'Mach die Augen zu, schöne Sara': Zur Gestaltung der Judischen Assimilationsproblematik in Heines 'Der Rabbi von Bacherach,' " *Germ Life & Letters*, 47 (1994), 167–181.

LILIANA HEKER

"Los primeros principios o arte poética"
Corpa Vargas, Mirta. " 'Los primeros principios o arte poética' de Liliana Heker: Narrativa del proceso: Resistencias y reflexiones en un discurso autobiográfico," *Alba de América*, 12 (1994), 417–424.

MARK HELPRIN

"A Vermont Tale"
+Bohner, Charles H. *Instructor's Manual . . .* , 3rd ed., 65–67.

ERNEST HEMINGWAY

"After the Storm"

Philbrick, Nathaniel. "A Window on the Prey: The Hunter Sees a Human Face in Hemingway's 'After the Storm' and Melville's 'The Grand Armada,' " *Hemingway R*, 14, i (1994), 25–35.

Plath, James. " 'After the Denim' and 'After the Storm': Raymond Carver Comes to Terms with the Hemingway Influence," *Hemingway R*, 13, ii (1994), 43–49.

"Banal Story"

Fleming, Robert E. *The Face* . . . , 25–30.

"Big Two-Hearted River"

Adair, William. " 'Big Two-Hearted River': Why the Swamp Is Tragic," *J Mod Lit*, 17 (1994), 584–588.

Charters, Ann. *Resources* . . . , 73–75.

Civello, Paul. "Hemingway's 'Primitivism': Archetypal Patterns in 'Big Two-Hearted River,' " *Hemingway R*, 13, i (1993), 1–16.

Hurm, Gerd. " 'I Made It All Up': Die gestaltete Natur in Hemingways 'Big Two-Hearted River,' " in Groß, Konrad, Kurt Müller, and Meinhard Winkgens, Eds. *Das Natur/Kultur-Paradigma* . . . , 288–303.

Kowalewski, Michael. *Deadly Musings* . . . , 141–147.

Phillips, Dana. "Is Nature Necessary?" *Raritan*, 13, iii (1993), 78–80.

"Black Ass at the Crossroads"

Fleming, Robert E. *The Face* . . . , 99–100.

"The Butterfly and the Tank"

Fleming, Robert E. *The Face* . . . , 91–93.

"A Canary for One"

Oberhelman, Harley D. *The Presence* . . . , 35–36.

"Cat in the Rain"

Barton, Edwin J. "The Story as It Should Be: Epistemological Uncertainty in Hemingway's 'Cat in the Rain,' " *Hemingway R*, 14, i (1994), 72–78.

Devost, Nadine. "Hemingway's Girls: Unnaming and renaming Hemingway's Female Characters," *Hemingway R*, 14, i (1994), 51–53.

"A Clean, Well-Lighted Place"

Leonard, John. " 'A Man of the World' and 'A Clean, Well-Lighted Place': Hemingway's Unified View of Old Age," *Hemingway R*, 13, ii (1994), 62–73.

Oberhelman, Harley D. *The Presence* . . . , 36–37.

"A Day's Wait"

Beegel, Susan F. "*Howard Pyle's Book of Pirates* and Male Taciturnity in Hemingway's 'A Day's Wait,' " *Stud Short Fiction*, 30 (1993), 535–541.

"The Denunciation"

Fleming, Robert E. *The Face* . . . , 89–91.

"Fathers and Sons"
Fleming, Robert E. *The Face . . .*, 61–66.

"Fifty Grand"
Thoreen, David. "Poor Ernest's Almanac: The Petty Economies of 'Fifty Grand's' Jack Brennan," *Hemingway R*, 13, ii (1994), 24–36.

"The Gambler, the Nun, and the Radio"
Fleming, Robert E. *The Face . . .*, 53–61.

"Get a Seeing-Eyed Dog"
Fleming, Robert E. *The Face . . .*, 146–147.

"God Rest You Merry, Gentlemen"
Harrington, Gary. "Hemingway's 'God Rest You Merry, Gentlemen,' " *Explicator*, 52 (1993), 51–53.

"Great News from the Mainland"
Fleming, Robert E. *The Face . . .*, 127–128.

"Hills Like White Elephants"
+Bohner, Charles H. *Instructor's Manual . . .*, 3rd ed., 67–68.
Hardy, Donald E. and Heather K. "Metaphorical Interaction in Hemingway's 'Hills Like White Elephants,' " *Language and Lit*, 15 (1990), 1–56.
Kozikowski, Stanley. "Hemingway's 'Hills Like White Elephants,' " *Explicator*, 52 (1994), 107–109.
Lansky, Ellen. "Two Unfinished Beers: A Note on Drinking in Hemingway's 'Hills Like White Elephants,' " *Dionysos*, 5, ii (1993), 28–30.
Pickering, James H., and Jeffrey D. Hoeper. *Instructor's Manual . . .*, 58–59.

"I Guess Everything Reminds You of Something"
Fleming, Robert E. *The Face . . .*, 125–127.

"In Another Country"
Soens, A. L. "Hemingway and Hawks: The Hierarchy of Heroism in 'In Another Country,' " *Engl Lang Notes*, 28, ii (1990), 62–79.

"Indian Camp"
Wolter, Jürgen C. "Caesareans in an Indian Camp," *Hemingway R*, 13, i (1993), 92–94.

"The Killers"
Martin, Quentin E. "Hemingway's 'The Killers,' " *Explicator*, 52 (1993), 53–57.
Oberhelman, Harley D. *The Presence . . .*, 22, 23–24.

"Landscape with Figures"
Fleming, Robert E. *The Face . . .*, 96–98.

"The Light of the World"
Jobst, Jack W., and W. J. Williamson. "Hemingway and Maupassant: More Light on 'The Light of the World,' " *Hemingway R*, 13, ii (1994), 54–59.

"A Man of the World"
Leonard, John. "'A Man of the World' . . .," 62–73.

"Mr. and Mrs. Elliot"
Fleming, Robert E. *The Face* . . . , 18–25.

"My Old Man"
Phelan, James. "Present Tense Narration, Mimesis, the Narrative Norm, and the Positioning of the Reader in *Waiting for the Barbarians*," in Phelan, James, and Peter J. Rabinowitz, Eds. *Understanding Narrative*, 227–230.

"Night Before Battle"
Fleming, Robert E. *The Face* . . . , 94–96.

"The Old Man and the Sea"
Oberhelman, Harley. "Hemingway and García Márquez: Two Shipwreck Narratives," *Int'l Fiction R*, 21 (1994), 3–4.

"The Old Man at the Bridge"
Frus, Phyllis. *The Politics and Poetics* . . . , 80, 82–83, 87–89.
———. *The Presence* . . . , 25–27.

"On the Quai at Smyrna"
Kowalewski, Michael. *Deadly Musings* . . . , 136–137.

"The Revolutionist"
Montgomery, Martin. "Language, Character and Action: A Linguistic Approach to the Analysis of Character in a Hemingway Short Story," in Sinclair, John M., Michael Hoey, and Gwyneth Fox, Eds. *Techniques of Description* . . . , 127–142.

"A Room on the Garden Side"
Beegel, Susan F. " 'A Room on the Garden Side': Hemingway's Unpublished Liberation of Paris," *Stud Short Fiction*, 31 (1994), 627–637.

"The Sea Change"
Fleming, Robert E. *The Face* . . . , 48–53.

"The Short Happy Life of Francis Macomber"
Breuer, Horst, and Dieter Ohlmeier. "Reise ins finsterste Afrika: Psychoanalytische Bemerkungen zu Ernest Hemingways Erzählung 'The Short Happy Life of Francis Macomber,' " *Amerikastudien*, 30, i (1985), 47–57.
Eby, Cecil D. "Hemingway's 'The Short Happy Life of Francis Macomber,' " *Explicator*, 51 (1992), 48.
Harris, Susan K. "Vicious Binaries: Gender and Authorial Paranoia in Dreiser's 'Second Choice,' Howells' 'Editha,' and Hemingway's 'The Short Happy Life of Francis Macomber,' " *Coll Lit*, 20, ii (1993), 76–78.
Kowalewski, Michael. *Deadly Musings* . . . , 154–158.
Kozikowski, S., S. Adriaansen, D. Moruzzi, and C. Prokop. "Hemingway's 'The Short Happy Life of Francis Macomber,' " *Explicator*, 51 (1993), 239–241.

"The Snows of Kilimanjaro"
Fleming, Robert E. *The Face* . . . , 76–83.

"Soldier's Home"
Fleissner, R. F. "Krebs, Cancer, Crab(s): Homing in on Hemingway's 'Soldier's Home,' " *Germ Notes & R*, 25, ii (1994), 7.

Kobler, J. F. " 'Soldier's Home' Revisited: A Hemingway *Mea Culpa*," *Stud Short Fiction*, 30 (1993), 377–385.

"The Three-Day Blow"

Summerlin, Tim. "Baseball and Hemingway's 'The Three-Day Blow,' " *Arete*, 4, ii (1987), 99–102.

"Today Is Friday"

Flora, Joseph. " 'Today Is Friday' and the Pattern of *Men Without Women*," *Hemingway R*, 13, i (1993), 17–35.

"The Undefeated"

Plath, James. "*Le Torero* and 'The Undefeated': Hemingway's Foray into Analytical Cubism," *Stud Short Fiction*, 30 (1993), 35–43.

"Under the Ridge"

Fleming, Robert E. *The Face . . .* , 98–99.

"Up in Michigan"

Tyler, Lisa. "Ernest Hemingway's Date Rape Story: Sexual Trauma in 'Up in Michigan,' " *Hemingway R*, 13, ii (1994), 1–11.

"A Way You'll Never Be"

Vaderbilt, Kermit. "Nick Adams Through the Looking Glass: 'A Way You'll Never Be,' " *Explicator*, 51 (1993), 104–110.

ZENNA HENDERSON

"Subcommittee"

Mendlesohn, Farah. "Gender, Power, and Conflict Resolution: 'Subcommittee' by Zenna Henderson," *Extrapolation*, 35 (1994), 120–129.

SAFIYA HENDERSON-HOLMES

"Snapshots of Grace"

Wear, Delese, and Lois L. Nixon. *Literary Anatomies . . .* , 75–77.

FELISBERTO HERNÁNDEZ

"El acomodador"

Correa, Rafael. " 'El acomodador' de F. Hernández o el espectaculo de la mirada," *Alba de América*, 6 (1988), 187–197.

"Las Hortensias"

Bilbija, Ksenija. "Rosario Ferré's 'The Youngest Doll': On Women, Dolls, Golems and Cyborgs," *Callaloo*, 17 (1994), 881.

"La mujer parecida a mí"

Chichester, Ana G. "Metamorphosis in Two Short Stories of the Fantastic by Virgilio Piñera and Felisberto Hernández," *Stud Short Fiction*, 31 (1994), 387–88, 390–394.

HERMANN HESSE

"Das erste Abenteuer"
Zepetnek, Steven Totosy de. "Hesse's 'Das erste Abenteuer': A Socio-literary Analysis," *Seminar*, 29 (1993), 255–260.

"Journey to the East"
Del Caro, Adrian. "A Hölderlinian Background to Hermann Hesse's 'Die Morgenlandfahrt,' " *Germ Life & Letters*, 46 (1993), 254–265.

GEORG HEYM

"Der Dieb"
Sheppard, Richard. "Insanity, Violence and Cultural Criticism: Some Further Thoughts on Four Expressionist Short Stories," *Forum Mod Lang Stud*, 30, ii (1994), 152–162.

"Der Irre"
Sheppard, Richard. "Insanity . . . ," 152–162.

WOLFGANG HILDESHEIMER

"Das Ende einer Welt"
Pérennec, Marie-Hélène. "Ironie et polyphonie dans la nouvelle de W. Hildesheimer 'Das Ende einer Welt,' " *Cahiers d'Etudes Germ*, 21 (1991), 137–147.

SUSAN HILL

"The Albatross"
Hofer, Ernest H. "Enclosed Structures, Disclosed Lives: The Fictions of Susan Hill," in Hosmer, Robert E., Ed. *Contemporary British . . .* , 139–140.

"A Bit of Singing and Dancing"
Hofer, Ernest H. "Enclosed Structures . . . ," 141–142.

E[RNEST] T[HEODOR] A[MADEUS] HOFFMANN

"Automata"
Willis, Martin T. "Scientific Portraits in Magical Frames: The Construction of Preternatural Narrative in the Works of E. T. A. Hoffmann and Arthur Machen," *Extrapolation*, 35 (1994), 186–193.

"Des Vetters Eckfenster"
Eicher, Thomas. " 'Mit einem Blick das ganze Panorama des grandiosen Platzes': Panoramatische Strukturen in 'Des Vetters Eckfenster,' von E. T. A. Hoffmann," *Poetica*, 25, iii–iv (1993), 360–377.

"Das Fräulein von Scuderi"

Dickson, Sheila. "Black, White and Shades of Grey: A Reassessment of Narrative Ambiguity in E. T. A. Hoffmann's 'Das Fräulein von Scuderi,' " *New Germ Stud*, 17, ii (1992–1993), 133–157.

———. "Devil's Advocate? The Artistic Detective in E. T. A. Hoffmann's 'Das Fräulein von Scuderi,' " *Forum Mod Lang Stud*, 29, iii (1993), 246–256.

Lee, Christopher A. "E. T. A. Hoffmann's 'Mademoiselle de Scudery' as a Forerunner of the Detective Story," *Clues*, 15, ii (1994), 63–74.

"The Golden Pot"

Crisman, William. "Registrator Heerbrand, Fantasy Broker and Forgotten Figure in Hoffmann's 'Goldne Topf,' " *Germ Notes & R*, 25, ii (1994), 8–10.

"Das Majorat"

Riedl, Peter P. "Die Zeichen der Krise: Erbe und Eigentum in Achim von Arnims 'Die Majoratsherren' und E. T. A. Hoffmanns 'Das Majorat,' " *Aurora*, 52 (1992), 39–50.

Stiffler, Muriel W. *The German Ghost Story* . . . , 51–66.

"The Mines at Falun"

Andriano, Joseph. *Our Ladies* . . . , 59–68.

"Das öde Haus"

Sato, Kazue. "Anführungszeichen und Erzählkomplexe in E. T. A. Hoffmanns 'Das öde Haus,' " in Takahashi, Teruaki, Ed. *Literarische* . . . , 137–146.

"The Sandman"

Andriano, Joseph. *Our Ladies* . . . , 49–59.

Haynes, Roslynn D. *From Faust* . . . , 87–88.

Huet, Marie-Hélène. *Monstrous Imagination*, 233–236.

Kohlenbach, Margarete. "Women and Artists: E. T. A. Hoffmann's Implicit Critique of Early Romanticism," *Mod Lang R*, 89 (1994), 664–671.

HUGO VON HOFMANNSTHAL

"Reitergeschichte"

Wilpert, Gero von. "Anton Lerch—geduppelt? Zum sogenannten 'Doppelgänger' in Hofmannsthals 'Reitergeschichte,' " *Seminar*, 29 (1993), 125–137.

ANDREW HOLLERAN

"Friends at Evening"

Cady, Joseph. "Immersive and Counterimmersive Writing About AIDS: The Achievement of Paul Monette's *Love Alone*," in Murphy, Timothy F., and Suzanne Poirier, Eds. *Writing AIDS* . . . , 253–255, 256–258.

Jones, James W. "Refusing the Name: The Absence of AIDS in Recent American Gay Male Fiction," in Murphy, Timothy F., and Suzanne Poirier, Eds. *Writing AIDS* . . . , 229–231.

CHENJERAI HOVE

"Bones"

Boehmer, Elleke. "The Nation as Metaphor in Contemporary African Literature," in Clark, Robert, and Piero Boitani, Eds. *English Studies in Transition* . . . , 323–326.

WILLIAM DEAN HOWELLS

"A Difficult Case"

Berkove, Lawrence I. " 'A Difficult Case': W. D. Howells's Impression of Mark Twain," *Stud Short Fiction*, 31 (1994), 609–612.

"Editha"

Harris, Susan K. "Vicious Binaries: Gender and Authorial Paranoia in Dreiser's 'Second Choice,' Howells' 'Editha,' and Hemingway's 'The Short Happy Life of Francis Macomber,' " *Coll Lit*, 20, ii (1993), 74–76.

HSIAO YEH

"The Town of Olive in 1994"

Xiaobing Tang. "The Mirror of History and History as Spectacle: Reflections on Hsiao Yeh and Su T'ung," *Mod Chinese Lit*, 6, i–ii (1992), 204–210.

LANGSTON HUGHES

"Big Meeting"

Emanuel, James A. "The Christ and the Killers," in Gates, Henry L., and K. A. Appiah, Eds. *Langston Hughes* . . . , 179–182.

"Blessed Assurance"

Borden, Anne. "Heroic 'Hussies' and 'Brilliant Queers': Genderracial Resistance in the Works of Langston Hughes," *African Am R*, 28 (1994), 339.

"The Blues I'm Playing"

Tracy, Steven C. "Blues to Live By: Langston Hughes's 'The Blues I'm Playing,' " *Langston Hughes R*, 12, i (1993), 12–18.

"Father and Son"

Borden, Anne. "Heroic . . . ," 336–337.

Emanuel, James A. "The Christ . . . ," 191–196.

"Home" [Originally "The Folks at Home"]
Emanuel, James A. "The Christ . . . ," 183–187.

"On the Road"
Emanuel, James A. "The Christ . . . ," 175–178.

T. A. G. HUNGERFORD

"Of Biddy and My Dad"
+Bohner, Charles H. *Instructor's Manual* . . . , 3rd ed., 69–70.

THOMAS HÜRLIMANN

"Das Gartenhaus"
Pender, Malcolm. " 'Du mußt das Haus abtragen': The Motif of the House in Recent German-Swiss Fiction," *Mod Lang R*, 88 (1993), 699–701.

ZORA NEALE HURSTON

"The Gilded Six-Bits"
Charters, Ann. *Resources* . . . , 76–77.

"John Redding Goes to Sea"
Thompson, Gordon E. "Projecting Gender: Personification in the Works of Zora Neale Hurston," *Am Lit*, 66 (1994), 750–751, 752, 753.

"Spunk"
+Bohner, Charles H. *Instructor's Manual* . . . , 3rd ed., 70–72.

"Sweat"
Andrews, William L. "Zora Neale Hurston," in Andrews, William L., Ed. *Classic Fiction* . . . , 76.
Charters, Ann. *Resources* . . . , 78.
Hurd, Myles R. "What Goes Around Comes Around: Characterization, Climax, and Closure in Hurston's 'Sweat,' " *Langston Hughes R*, 12, ii (1993), 7–15.
Thompson, Gordon E. "Projecting Gender . . . ," 745–746.

JORGE IBARGÜENGOITIA

"Cuento para el niño revolucionario"
González, Alfonso. "La sátira en los escritos breves de Jorge Ibargüengoitia," *La Palabra y el Hombre*, 87 (1993), 138.

"El lenguaje de las piedras"
González, Alfonso. "La sátira . . . ," 140.

"La ley de Herodes"
González, Alfonso. "La sátira . . . ," 138.

"Manos muertas"
González, Alfonso. "La sátira . . . ," 139.

"La mujer que no"
González, Alfonso. "La sátira . . . ," 137–138.

"What Became of Pampa Hash?"
González, Alfonso. "La sátira . . . ," 136, 137.

YUSUF IDRIS

"Ahmad of the Local Council"
Kurpershoek, P. M. "The Later Stories," in Allen, Roger, Ed. *Critical Perspectives* . . . , 32–33.

"The Aorta"
Allen, Roger. "Yusuf Idris's Short Stories: Themes and Techniques," in Allen, Roger, Ed. *Critical Perspectives* . . . , 23.
Hafez, Sabry. "Questions on the World of Yusuf Idris's Short Stories," in Allen, Roger, Ed. *Critical Perspectives* . . . , 59.
Kurpershoek, P. M. "The Later Stories," 38–39.

"The Black Soldier"
Allen, Roger. "Yusuf Idris's . . . ," 21.
Somekh, Sasson. "The Function of Sound in the Stories of Yusuf Idris," in Allen, Roger, Ed. *Critical Perspectives* . . . , 109–110.

"Camel Corps"
Hafez, Sabry. "Questions . . . ," 54.

"Caught Napping"
Hafez, Sabry. "Questions . . . ," 62.

"The Chair Bearer"
Allen, Roger. "Yusuf Idris's . . . ," 27.
Kurpershoek, P. M. "The Later Stories," 39–40.

"City Dregs"
Somekh, Sasson. "The Function . . . ," 110–112.

"The Deception"
Kurpershoek, P. M. "The Later Stories," 43.

"Heart of the City"
Cobham, Catherine. "Sex and Society in Yusuf Idris: 'Qa' al-Madina,' " in Allen, Roger, Ed. *Critical Perspectives* . . . , 77–84.
Mikhail, Mona N. "The Search for the Authentic Self Within Idris's City," in Allen, Roger, Ed. *Critical Perspectives* . . . , 65–69.

"His Mother"
Abu al-Naja, Abu al-Ma'ati. "The Short Story Collection, *Vision at Fault*," in Allen, Roger, Ed. *Critical Perspectives* . . . , 100–101.

"House of Flesh"
Allen, Roger. "Yusuf Idris's . . . ," 24.
Malti-Douglas, Fedwa. "Blindness and Sexuality: Traditional Mentalities in Yusuf Idris' 'House of Flesh,' " in Allen, Roger, Ed. *Critical Perspectives* . . . , 89–96.

Somekh, Sasson. "Structure of Silence: A Reading of Yûsuf Idrîs's 'Bayt min Lahm' (House of Flesh)," in Elad, Ami, Ed. *Writer* . . . , 56–61.

"In Cellophane Wrapping"
Allen, Roger. "Yusuf Idris's . . . ," 24–25.

"The Incident"
Hafez, Sabry. "Questions . . . ," 56–57.

"The Journey"
Kurpershoek, P. M. "The Later Stories," 43–44.

"Language of Pain"
Mikhail, Mona N. "The Search . . . ," 73–75.
Sherif, Nur. " 'The Language of Pain' by Youssef Idris," in Allen, Roger, Ed. *Critical Perspectives* . . . , 85–88.

"Leader of Men"
Abu al-Naja, Abu al-Ma'ati. "The Short . . . ," 101–104.

"Lily, Did You Have to Put the Light On?"
Allen, Roger. "Yusuf Idris's . . . ," 25–26.

"The Little Bird on the Telephone Wire"
Allen, Roger. "Yusuf Idris's . . . ," 26.

"The Master of Egypt"
Kurpershoek, P. M. "The Later Stories," 33–35.

"The Miracle of Our Time"
Kurpershoek, P. M. "The Later Stories," 36–38.

"The Omitted Letter"
Allen, Roger. "Yusuf Idris's . . . ," 20.

"Peace with Honor"
Allen, Roger. "Yusuf Idris's . . . ," 18–19.

"The Siren"
Mikhail, Mona N. "The Search . . . ," 69–73.

"A Story with a Thin Voice"
Kurpershoek, P. M. "The Later Stories," 35–36.

"Summer Night"
Hafez, Sabry. "Questions . . . ," 51–52.

"Sunset March"
Somekh, Sasson. "The Function . . . ," 106–109.

"To Asyut"
Kurpershoek, P. M. "The Later Stories," 32–33.

"Vision at Fault"
Abu al-Naja, Abu al-Ma'ati. "The Short . . . ," 99–100.

"The Wallet"
Allen, Roger. "Yusuf Idris's . . . ," 17–18.

"Way Out"
Abu al-Naja, Abu al-Ma'ati. "The Short . . . ," 98–99.

WITI IHIMAERA

"Cat and Mouse"
Potter, Tiffany. "A View of Strategies of Assimilation and Resistance in Witi Ihimaera's *Dear Miss Mansfield*," *World Lit Written Engl*, 33, ii & 34, i (1993–1994), 63–64.

"A Contemporary Kezia"
Potter, Tiffany. "A View . . . ," 70–71.

"The Halcyon Summer"
Potter, Tiffany. "A View . . . ," 69–70.

"Her First Ball"
Potter, Tiffany. "A View . . . ," 64–68.

"On a Train"
Potter, Tiffany. "A View . . . ," 71–72.

WASHINGTON IRVING

"Adventure of the German Student"
Andriano, Joseph. *Our Ladies* . . . , 70–75.

"The Legend of Sleepy Hollow"
Achilles, Von Jochen. "Washington Irving: 'The Legend of Sleepy Hollow'—Ein prekärer amerikanischer Traum vom guten Leben," in Lubbers, Klaus, Ed. *Die Englische* . . . , 1–11.
Loving, Jerome. *Lost in the Customhouse* . . . , 16–17.
Plummer, Laura, and Michael Nelson. " 'Girls can take care of themselves': Gender and Storytelling in Washington Irving's 'The Legend of Sleepy Hollow,' " *Stud Short Fiction*, 30 (1993), 175–185.

"Rip Van Winkle"
Hulpke, Erika. "Elemente im Zusammenwirken: Ein Fall von Unterdrückung des politisch Fremden," in Frank, Armin P., Ed. *Die literarische Übersetzung* . . . , 245–253.
———. "Übersetzer als Landschaftsgestalter, 1819–1978: Die Catskill-Berge im Dreieck von Werkstruktur, sprachlichen Zwängen und literarischen Konventionen," in Frank, Armin P., Ed. *Die literarische Übersetzung* . . . , 104–116.
Loving, Jerome. *Lost in the Customhouse* . . . , 10–13, 16–18.
Pearce, Colin D. "Changing Regimes: The Case of Rip Van Winkle," *Clio*, 22 (1993), 115–128.
Pickering, James H., and Jeffrey D. Hoeper. *Instructor's Manual* . . . , 7.

KAZUO ISHIGURO

"A Family Supper"
Broich, Ulrich. "Muted Postmodernism: The Contemporary British

Short Story,'' *Zeitschrift für Anglistik und Amerikanistik*, 41 (1993), 35.

ESTER DE IZAGUIRRE

''El castigo''
Galovic Norris, Nélida. ''*Ultimo domicilio conocido*: Linaje poético en la narrativa de Ester de Izaguirre,'' *Alba de América*, 12 (1994), 363–364.

''Cuando fui joven ya era viejo por dentro''
Galovic Norris, Nélida. ''*Ultimo* . . . ,'' 366–367.

''Entre dos homigas negras''
Galovic Norris, Nélida. ''*Ultimo* . . . ,'' 364.

''El gusto de la lluvia''
Galovic Norris, Nélida. ''*Ultimo* . . . ,'' 365–366.

''Los que no comprenden''
Galovic Norris, Nélida. ''*Ultimo* . . . ,'' 367–368.

''Tiempos impares''
Galovic Norris, Nélida. ''*Ultimo* . . . ,'' 364–365.

SHIRLEY JACKSON

''After You, My Dear Alphonse''
Hall, Joan W. *Shirley Jackson* . . . , 25–26.

''Afternoon in Linen''
Hall, Joan W. *Shirley Jackson* . . . , 28.

''The Beautiful Stranger''
Hall, Joan W. *Shirley Jackson* . . . , 62–63.

''Behold the Child Among His Newborn Blisses''
Hall, Joan W. *Shirley Jackson* . . . , 81–83.

''Charles''
Hall, Joan W. *Shirley Jackson* . . . , 27–28.

''Come Dance with Me in Ireland''
Hall, Joan W. *Shirley Jackson* . . . , 41–42.

''A Great Voice Stilled''
Hall, Joan W. *Shirley Jackson* . . . , 83–84.

''Home''
Hall, Joan W. *Shirley Jackson* . . . , 88–90.

''I Know Who I Love''
Hall, Joan W. *Shirley Jackson* . . . , 59–62.

''The Intoxicated''
Hall, Joan W. *Shirley Jackson* . . . , 9–10.

''Island''
Hall, Joan W. *Shirley Jackson* . . . , 72–73.

"Janice"
Hall, Joan W. *Shirley Jackson* . . . , 57–58.

"Journey with a Lady"
Hall, Joan W. *Shirley Jackson* . . . , 80–81.

"Like Mother Used to Make"
Hall, Joan W. *Shirley Jackson* . . . , 14–16.

"The Little House"
Hall, Joan W. *Shirley Jackson* . . . , 68–69.

"The Lottery"
+Bohner, Charles H. *Instructor's Manual* . . . , 3rd ed., 72–73.
Hall, Joan W. *Shirley Jackson* . . . , 48–53.
Kosenko, Peter. "A Marxist/Feminist Reading of Shirley Jackson's 'The Lottery,' " *New Orleans R*, 12 (1985), 27–31; rpt. Hall, Joan W., Ed. *Shirley Jackson* . . . , 179–183.
Nebeker, Helen E. " 'The Lottery': Symbolic Tour de Force," *Am Lit*, 46 (1974), 102–104, 106–107; rpt. Hall, Joan W., Ed. *Shirley Jackson* . . . , 171–174.
Oehlschlaeger, Fritz. "The Stoning of Mistress Hutchinson: Meaning and Context in 'The Lottery,' " *Essays Lit*, 15 (1988), 259–260, 262–263; rpt. Hall, Joan W., Ed. *Shirley Jackson* . . . , 175–177.
Pickering, James H., and Jeffrey D. Hoeper. *Instructor's Manual* . . . , 78–79.
Stark, Jack. "Shirley Jackson's 'The Lottery,' " in Karolides, Nicholas J., Lee Burress, and John M. Kean, Eds. *Censored Books* . . . , 358–362.
Yarmove, Jay A. "Jackson's 'The Lottery,' " *Explicator*, 52 (1994), 242–245.

BÁRBARA JACOBS

"Carol dice"
Rojas-Trempe, Lady. "La iniciación y el discurso de dos adolescentes en 'Carol dice' de Bárbara Jacobs," in Pavón, Alfredo, Ed. *Cuento contigo* . . . , 117–127.

ANGELIKA JAKOB

"Flieg, Schwesterlein, flieg"
Braunbeck, Helga G. " 'Fly, little sister, fly': Sister Relationship and Identity in Three Contemporary German Stories," in Mink, JoAnna S., and Janet D. Ward, Eds. *The Significance of Sibling* . . . , 163–165.

HENRY JAMES

"Adina"
Fussell, Edwin S. *The Catholic Side* . . . , 70–71.

Geoffroy-Renoux, Sophie. "H. James et l'Italie: 'The Last of the Valerii' (Janv. 1874); 'Adina' (Mai-Juin 1874)," *Cahiers Victoriens et Edouardiens*, 39 (1994), 271–287.

"The Altar of the Dead"

Fussell, Edwin S. *The Catholic Side* . . . , 104–109.

"The Aspern Papers"

Perosa, Sergio. "Henry James: 'The Aspern Papers,' " in Lubbers, Klaus, Ed. *Die Englische* . . . , 60–69.

"At Isella"

Buzard, James. *The Beaten Track* . . . , 253–259.

Fussell, Edwin S. *The Catholic Side* . . . , 66–68.

"The Author of Beltraffio"

Person, Leland S. "James's Homo-Aesthetics: Deploying Desire in the Tales of Writers and Artists," *Henry James R*, 14 (1993), 190–193.

"The Beast in the Jungle"

Bar'am, Ilana. "Bodily Movement as Narrative Strategy in 'The Beast in the Jungle,' " *Henry James R*, 15 (1994), 170–178.

Griffiths, James. "James's Stories and His Characters: A Reading of 'The Beast in the Jungle' and 'The Bench of Desolation,' " *Cambridge Q*, 22 (1993), 54–59.

Sedgwick, Eve K. "Das Tier in der Kammer: Henry James und das Schreiben homosexueller Angst," in Vinken, Barbara, Ed. *Dekonstruktiver* . . . , 254–274.

Trotter, David. *The English Novel* . . . , 270–272.

"The Bench of Desolation"

Griffiths, James. "James's Stories . . . ," 46–53.

"The Birthplace"

Frye, Northrop. *The Eternal Act* . . . , 112–113.

Fussell, Edwin S. *The Catholic Side* . . . , 112–114.

"Broken Wings"

Golumbia, David. "Toward an Ethics of Cultural Acts: The Jamesian Dialectic in 'Broken Wings,' " *Henry James R*, 15 (1994), 152–169.

"The Chaperon"

Tintner, Adeline R. . . . *Lust of the Eyes*, 3, 70–71, 74–77.

"Crapy Cornelia"

Aziz, Maqbool. "How Long Is Long; How Short Short! Henry James and the Small Circular Frame," in Fogel, Daniel M., Ed. *A Companion* . . . , 229–233.

"Daisy Miller"

Graham, Kenneth. " 'Daisy Miller': Dynamics of an Enigma," in Pollak, Vivian R., Ed. *New Essays on* . . . , 35–63.

Pollak, Vivian R. "Introduction," in Pollak, Vivian R., Ed. *New Essays on* . . . , 6–8.

Tintner, Adeline R. " 'Daisy Miller' and Chaucer's 'Daisy' Poem: *The Prologue to the Legend of Good Women*," *Henry James R*, 15 (1994), 10–12, 16–22.

Weisbuch, Robert. ''Winterbourne and the Doom of Manhood in 'Daisy Miller,' '' in Pollak, Vivian R., Ed. *New Essays on . . .*, 65–89.

''The Death of the Lion''
Person, Leland S. ''James's . . . ,'' 196–200.

''De Grey''
Fussell, Edwin S. *The Catholic Side . . .*, 115–119.
Lustig, T. J. *Henry James and the Ghostly*, 66–67.

''The Figure in the Carpet''
Smith, Virginia L. *Henry James . . .*, 5–6.

''Four Meetings''
Pickering, James H., and Jeffrey D. Hoeper. *Instructor's Manual . . .*, 19–21.

''Gabrielle de Bergerac''
Fussell, Edwin S. *The Catholic Side . . .*, 102–104.
Lustig, T. J. *Henry James and the Ghostly*, 109–111.

''The Ghostly Rental''
Lustig, T. J. *Henry James and the Ghostly*, 70–74.

''The Great Good Place''
Fussell, Edwin S. *The Catholic Side . . .*, 109–112.

''Hugh Merrow''
Stafford, Norman E. ''Rediscovering Henry James's 'Hugh Merrow,' '' *CEA Critic*, 56, ii (1994), 61–68.

''In the Cage''
Aziz, Maqbool. ''How Long . . . ,'' 216–225.
Lustig, T. J. *Henry James and the Ghostly*, 191–194.
Smith, Virginia L. *Henry James . . .*, 48–49.
Trotter, David. *The English Novel . . .*, 243–244.
Veeder, William. ''Toxic Mothers, Cultural Criticism: 'In the Cage' and Elsewhere,'' *Henry James R*, 14 (1993), 264–272.

''The Jolly Corner''
Brown, Chris. ''Henry James and the Passage's End,'' *Kipling J*, 68 (June, 1994), 36–40.
Charters, Ann. *Resources . . .*, 80–81.
Cramer, Kathryn. ''Possession and 'The Jolly Corner,' '' *New York R Sci Fiction*, 65 (January, 1994), 19–22.
Lustig, T. J. *Henry James and the Ghostly*, 216–228.
Warren, Kenneth W. *Black and White . . .*, 124–129.

''A Landscape Painter''
Tallack, Douglas. *The Nineteenth-Century . . .*, 202–205.

''The Last of the Valerii''
Andriano, Joseph. *Our Ladies . . .*, 126–133.
Fussell, Edwin S. *The Catholic Side . . .*, 69–70.
Geoffroy-Renoux, Sophie. ''H. James et l'Italie . . . ,'' 271–279.
Naiburg, Suzi. ''Archaic Depths in Henry James's 'The Last of the Valerii,' '' *Henry James R*, 14 (1993), 151–165.

"The Liar"

Lane, Christopher. "Framing Fears, Reading Designs: The Homosexual Art of Painting in James, Wilde, and Beerbohm," *ELH*, 61 (1994), 924–936.

"A London Life"

Tintner, Adeline R. . . . *Lust of the Eyes*, 43–55.

"The Madonna of the Future"

Andriano, Joseph. *Our Ladies* . . . , 118–126.
Fussell, Edwin S. *The Catholic Side* . . . , 68–69.

"Maud-Evelyn"

Griffiths, James. "James's Stories . . . ," 53–54.

"The Middle Years"

Person, Leland S. "James's . . . ," 193–196.

"Owen Wingrave"

Lustig, T. J. *Henry James and the Ghostly*, 100–103.

"A Passionate Pilgrim"

Buzard, James. *The Beaten Track* . . . , 259–270.
Lustig, T. J. *Henry James and the Ghostly*, 69–70.

"Paste"

Charters, Ann. *Resources* . . . , 81–82.
Fusco, Richard. *Maupassant* . . . , 199–202.

"The Private Life"

Bresnick, Adam. "The Artist That Was Used Up: Henry James's 'Private Life,' " *Henry James R*, 14 (1993), 87–98.
Calinescu, Matei. *Rereading*, 227–238.
Tallack, Douglas. *The Nineteenth-Century* . . . , 187–189, 191.
Tintner, Adeline R. . . . *Lust of the Eyes*, 79–86.

"The Pupil"

Hoy, Helen. "Homotextual Duplicity in Henry James's 'The Pupil,' " *Henry James R*, 14 (1993), 34–42.

"The Real Thing"

Fusco, Richard. *Maupassant* . . . , 190–193.
+Bohner, Charles H. *Instructor's Manual* . . . , 3rd ed., 73–74.
Smith, Virginia L. *Henry James* . . . , 1–5.

"The Romance of Certain Old Clothes"

Lustig, T. J. *Henry James and the Ghostly*, 52–54.

"The Siege of London"

Aziz, Maqbool. "How Long . . . ," 225–229.
Tintner, Adeline R. . . . *Lust of the Eyes*, 10–21.

"Sir Edmund Orme"

Fusco, Richard. *Maupassant* . . . , 206–209.
Lustig, T. J. *Henry James and the Ghostly*, 97–100, 101–102.

"The Story in It"

Griffiths, James. "James's Stories . . . ," 43–44.

"Travelling Companions"
Buzard, James. *The Beaten Track . . .*, 237–247.
Fussell, Edwin S. *The Catholic Side . . .*, 65–66.
Lustig, T. J. *Henry James and the Ghostly*, 68–70.

"The Tree of Knowledge"
Fusco, Richard. *Maupassant . . .*, 203–204.
Hagberg, Garry. "Wittgenstein, Henry James, and Epistemological Fiction," *Philosophy & Lit*, 13 (1989), 75–95.

"The Turn of the Screw"
Bell, Millicent. "Class, Sex, and the Victorian Governess: James's 'The Turn of the Screw,' " in Pollak, Vivian R., Ed. *New Essays on . . .*, 91–119.
Calinescu, Matei. *Rereading*, 193–205.
Chinitz, Lisa G. "Fairy Tale Turned Ghost Story: James's 'The Turn of the Screw,' " *Henry James R*, 15 (1994), 264–285.
Currie, Gregory. "Interpreting Fictions," in Freadman, Richard, and Lloyd Reinhardt, Eds. *On Literary . . .*, 96–101.
Frye, Northrop. *The Eternal Act . . .*, 119–120.
Fusco, Richard. *Maupassant . . .*, 211–214.
Fussell, Edwin S. *The Catholic Side . . .*, 93–101.
Glasser, William A. *Reclaiming Literature . . .*, 135–149.
Ludwig, Sämi, "Metaphors, Cognition and Behavior: The Reality of Sexual Puns in 'The Turn of the Screw,' " *Mosaic*, 27, i (1994), 33–53.
Lustig, T. J. *Henry James and the Ghostly*, 111–192.
McWhirter, David. "In the 'Other House' of Fiction: Writing, Authority, and Femininity in 'The Turn of the Screw,' " in Pollak, Vivian R., Ed. *New Essays on . . .*, 121–148.
Munich, Adrienne A. "What Lily Knew: Virginity in the 1890s," in Davis, Lloyd, Ed. *Virginal . . .*, 155–157.
Pollak, Vivian R. "Introduction," 11–14.
Renaux, Sigrid. *. . . A Semiotic Reading*, 39–278.
Rio-Jelliffe, R. "The Language of Time in Fiction: A Model in Faulkner's 'Barn Burning,' " *J Narrative Technique*, 24 (1994), 99–100.
Sawyer, Richard. " 'What's Your Title?'—'The Turn of the Screw,' " *Stud Short Fiction*, 30 (1993), 53–61.
Smith, Allan L. "A Word Kept Back in 'The Turn of the Screw,' " in Bloom, Clive, Ed. *Creepers . . .*, 47–63.
Trotter, David. *The English Novel . . .*, 235–238.

"The Way It Came"
Lustig, T. J. *Henry James and the Ghostly*, 102–104.

M[ONTAGUE] R[HODES] JAMES

"Mr. Humphreys and His Inheritance"
Hughes, Martin. "A Maze of Secrets in a Story by M. R. James," *Durham Univ J*, 85, i (January, 1993), 81–93.

SARAH ORNE JEWETT

"An Autumn Holiday"
Charters, Ann. *Resources* . . . , 83–84.

"A Bit of Shore Life"
Silverthorne, Elizabeth. *Sarah Orne Jewett* . . . , 88–89.

"The Foreigner"
Fetterly, Judith. " 'Not in the Least American': Nineteenth-Century Literary Realism," *Coll Engl*, 56 (1994), 892–893.
Silverthorne, Elizabeth. *Sarah Orne Jewett* . . . , 173.

"The Girl with the Cannon Dresses"
Silverthorne, Elizabeth. *Sarah Orne Jewett* . . . , 66.

"The Guests of Miss Timms"
Silverthorne, Elizabeth. *Sarah Orne Jewett* . . . , 160–162.

"Jenny Garrow's Lovers"
Silverthorne, Elizabeth. *Sarah Orne Jewett* . . . , 40, 47.

"A Late Supper"
Silverthorne, Elizabeth. *Sarah Orne Jewett* . . . , 89.

"The Luck of the Bogans"
Silverthorne, Elizabeth. *Sarah Orne Jewett* . . . , 144.

"Miss Tempy's Watchers"
Silverthorne, Elizabeth. *Sarah Orne Jewett* . . . , 136.

"Mr. Bruce"
Silverthorne, Elizabeth. *Sarah Orne Jewett* . . . , 55.

"A Native of Winby"
Silverthorne, Elizabeth. *Sarah Orne Jewett* . . . , 154.

"Tom's Husband"
Maik, Thomas A. "Reclaiming Paradise: Role Reversal as Liberation in Sarah Orne Jewett's 'Tom's Husband,' " *Legacy*, 7 (1990), 23–29.
Silverthorne, Elizabeth. *Sarah Orne Jewett* . . . , 110–111.

"The Town Poor"
Silverthorne, Elizabeth. *Sarah Orne Jewett* . . . , 144–145.

"A White Heron"
Bell, Michael D. *The Problem* . . . , 188–192.
+Bohner, Charles H. *Instructor's Manual* . . . , 3rd ed., 74–75.
Charters, Ann. *Resources* . . . , 85–86.
+Donovan, Josephine. "Silence or Capitulation: Prepatriarchal 'Mother's Gardens' in Jewett and Freeman," in Marchalonis, Shirley, Ed. *Critical Essays* . . . , 153–154.
Lutwack, Leonard. *Birds in Literature*, 205–207.
Pickering, James H., and Jeffrey D. Hoeper. *Instructor's Manual* . . . , 29–30.
Tripathi, Vanashree. "Initiation—Male/Female: Volitional Consciousness in Nineteenth Century American Fiction with

Reference to Sarah Orne Jewett's 'A White Heron,' " in Rao, E. Nageswara, Ed. *Mark Twain* . . . , 114–119.

"William's Wedding"
Silverthorne, Elizabeth. *Sarah Orne Jewett* . . . , 172–173.

"A Winter Courtship"
Silverthorne, Elizabeth. *Sarah Orne Jewett* . . . , 39–40.

GAYL JONES

"Veronica"
Ash, Susan. " 'All the Fraught Politics': Race, Gender and the Female Traveller," *SPAN*, 36 (1993), 349–355.

GABRIEL JOSIPOVICI

"Mobius the Stripper"
Broich, Ulrich. "Muted Postmodernism: The Contemporary British Short Story," *Zeitschrift für Anglistik und Amerikanistik*, 41 (1993), 35–36.

JAMES JOYCE

"After the Race"
Kelly, John S. "Afterword," *Dubliners* [by James Joyce], 257–258.
Leonard, Garry M. *Reading "Dubliners"* . . . , 113–117.
Mosher, Harold F. "The Narrated and Its Negatives: The Nonnarrated and the Disnarrated in Joyce's *Dubliners*," *Style*, 27 (1993), 410–411, 419.

"Araby"
+Bohner, Charles H. *Instructor's Manual* . . . , 3rd ed., 75–76.
Charters, Ann. *Resources* . . . , 87–88.
Blythe, Hal, and Charlie Sweet. "Diptych in 'Araby': The Key to Understanding the Boy's 'Anguish and Anger,' " *Notes Mod Irish Lit*, 6 (1994), 16–18.
Coulthard, A. R. "Joyce's 'Araby,' " *Explicator*, 52 (1994), 97–99.
Leonard, Garry M. *Reading "Dubliners"* . . . , 73–94.
Mosher, Harold F. "The Narrated . . . ," 415–416, 419.
Pickering, James H., and Jeffrey D. Hoeper. *Instructor's Manual* . . . , 46–47.
Schöneich, Christoph. "Perspektive und Erkenntnis in James Joyces 'Araby,' " *Literatur in Wissenschaft und Unterricht*, 21, iii (1988), 216–229.
Slack, John S. "*Dubliners* as Playful (Pre)Text: Role-Playing, Pretending and Deceiving Games," *Aethlon*, 10, ii (1993), 38.

"The Boarding House"
Ingersoll, Earl G. "The Stigma of Femininity in James Joyce's

'Eveline' and 'The Boarding House,' " *Stud Short Fiction*, 30 (1993), 506–510.
Kelly, John S. "Afterword," 260–262.
Laroque, François. " 'The Boarding House' as an Archetypal Story," *Mythes*, 4 (1986), 70–97.
Leonard, Garry M. *Reading "Dubliners"* . . . , 132–148.
Mosher, Harold F. "The Narrated . . . ," 413–415, 419.

"Clay"
Charters, Ann. *Resources* . . . , 89–90.
Kelly, John S. "Afterword," 263–264.
Leonard, Garry M. *Reading "Dubliners"* . . . , 184–209.
Mosher, Harold F. "The Narrated . . . ," 408–409, 419.

"Counterparts"
Leonard, Garry M. *Reading "Dubliners"* . . . , 170–183.
Slack, John S. "*Dubliners* as Playful . . . ," 39–40.

"The Dead"
Anspaugh, Kelly. " 'Three Mortal Hour[i]s': Female Gothic in Joyce's 'The Dead,' " *Stud Short Fiction*, 31 (1994), 1–12.
Brunsdale, Mitzi M. *James Joyce* . . . , 36–47.
Charters, Ann. *Resources* . . . , 91–92.
Gottfried, Roy. " 'Scrupulous meanness' reconsidered: *Dubliners* as stylistic parody," in Cheng, Vincent J., and Timothy Martin, Eds. *Joyce in Context* . . . , 167–168.
Harman, Mark. "Joyce and Kafka," *Sewanee R*, 101 (1993), 75–76.
Ingersoll, Earl G. "The Gender of Travel in 'The Dead,' " *James Joyce Q*, 30 (1993), 41–50.
Kelly, John S. "Afterword," 269–275.
Ledden, Patrick J. "Letter: Some Comments on Vincent Cheng's 'Empire and Patriarchy in "The Dead," ' " *Joyce Stud Annual*, 5 (1994), 202–207.
Leonard, Garry M. *Reading "Dubliners"* . . . , 289–308.
Levenson, Michael. "Living History in 'The Dead,' " in Schwarz, Daniel R., Ed. *James Joyce* . . . , 163–177.
Mosher, Harold F. "The Narrated . . . ," 421–424.
Mosley, David L. "Music and Language in Joyce's 'The Dead,' " in Tymieniecka, Anna-Teresa, Ed. *Allegory* . . . , 191–199.
Norris, Margot. "Not the Girl She Was at All: Women in 'The Dead,' " in Schwarz, Daniel R., Ed. *James Joyce* . . . , 190–205.
Pickering, James H., and Jeffrey D. Hoeper. *Instructor's Manual* . . . , 48–49.
Pier, John. "Dimensions de la parodie dans 'Les morts' de James Joyce," in Bourquin, Jacques, and Daniel Jacobi, Eds. *Mélanges* . . . , 203–210.
Rabinowitz, Peter J. " 'A Symbol of Something': Interpretive Vertigo in 'The Dead,' " in Schwarz, Daniel R., Ed. *James Joyce* . . . , 137–149.
Rice, Thomas J. "Dante . . . Browning. Gabriel . . . Joyce: Allusion and Structure in 'The Dead,' " *James Joyce Q*, 30 (1993), 29–40.
Riquelme, John P. "For Whom the Snow Taps: Style and Repetition

in 'The Dead,' " in Schwarz, Daniel R., Ed. *James Joyce . . .* , 219–233.
Schwarz, Daniel R. "Gabriel Conroy's Psyche: Character as Concept in Joyce's 'The Dead,' " in Schwarz, Daniel R., Ed. *James Joyce . . .* , 102–124.
Spoo, Robert. "Uncanny Returns in 'The Dead': Ibsenian Intertexts and the Estranged Infant," in Friedman, Susan S., Ed. *Joyce . . .* , 89–113.

"An Encounter"
Kelly, John S. "Afterword," 255–256.
Leonard, Garry M. *Reading "Dubliners" . . .* , 56–72.
Norris, David. "The 'unhappy mania' and Mr. Bloom's Cigar: Homosexuality in the Works of James Joyce," *James Joyce Q*, 31 (1994), 362–364.
Slack, John S. "*Dubliners* as Playful . . . ," 37, 39.

"Eveline"
Charters, Ann. *Resources . . .* , 93–94.
Florio, Joseph. "Joyce's 'Eveline,' " *Explicator*, 51 (1993), 181–185.
Ingersoll, Earl G. "The Stigma . . . ," 503–506.
Kelly, John S. "Afterword," 256–257.
Leonard, Garry M. *Reading "Dubliners" . . .* , 95–112.
Mosher, Harold F. "The Narrated . . . ," 419–420.

"Grace"
Gottfried, Roy. " 'Scrupulous meanness' . . . ," 162–163.
Kelly, John S. "Afterword," 268–269.
Leonard, Garry M. *Reading "Dubliners" . . .* , 272–288.

"Ivy Day in the Committee Room"
Brunsdale, Mitzi M. *James Joyce . . .* , 20–27.
Kelly, John S. "Afterword," 266–267.
Leonard, Garry M. *Reading "Dubliners" . . .* , 228–255.
Mosher, Harold F. "The Narrated . . . ," 420–421.
Slack, John S. "*Dubliners* as Playful . . . ," 41–42.

"A Little Cloud"
Brunsdale, Mitzi M. *James Joyce . . .* , 27–36.
Eicher, Thomas. "Augenblicke in James Joyces 'A Little Cloud': Ein Nachtrag zur Epiphanie-Diskussion," *Anglia*, 112 (1994), 75–89.
Kelly, John S. "Afterword," 262–263.
Leonard, Garry M. *Reading "Dubliners" . . .* , 149–169.
Romine, Scott. "Poetry and Parody: James Joyce and His 'Little Cloud,' " *Notes Mod Irish Lit*, 5 (1993), 5–12.

"A Mother"
Kelly, John S. "Afterword," 267–268.
Leonard, Garry M. *Reading "Dubliners" . . .* , 256–271.
Mosher, Harold F. "The Narrated . . . ," 410.

"A Painful Case"
Kelly, John S. "Afterword," 264–265.
Leonard, Garry M. *Reading "Dubliners" . . .* , 210–227.
Mosher, Harold F. "The Narrated . . . ," 421.

Norris, David. "The 'unhappy mania' . . . ," 364–365.
Slack, John S. "*Dubliners* as Playful . . . ," 40–41.

"The Sisters"
Brunsdale, Mitzi M. *James Joyce: A Study* . . . , 7–14.
Dilworth, Thomas. "Not 'too much noise': Joyce's 'The Sisters' in Irish Catholic Perspective," *Twentieth Century Lit*, 39 (1993), 99–112.
Kelly, John S. "Afterword," 251–255.
Leonard, Garry M. *Reading "Dubliners"* . . . , 24–55.
McDermott, John V. "Joyce's 'The Sisters,' " *Explicator*, 51 (1993), 236–237.
Norris, David. "The 'unhappy mania' . . . ," 360–362.
Rabaté, Jean-Michel. "On Joyce and Wildean Sodomy," *James Joyce Q*, 31 (1994),160.
Wohlpart, A. James. "Laughing in the Confession-Box: Vows of Silence in Joyce's 'The Sisters,' " *James Joyce Q*, 30 (1993), 409–417.

"Two Gallants"
Brunsdale, Mitzi M. *James Joyce: A Study* . . . , 14–20.
Kelly, John S. "Afterword," 258–260.
Leonard, Garry M. *Reading "Dubliners"* . . . , 118–131.
Mosher, Harold F. "The Narrated . . . ," 411–412, 415, 419.

FRANZ JUNG

"Der Fall Gross"
Sheppard, Richard. "Insanity, Violence and Cultural Criticism: Some Further Thoughts on Four Expressionist Short Stories," *Forum Mod Lang Stud*, 30, ii (1994), 152–162.

FRANZ KAFKA

"Before the Law"
Heidsieck, Arnold. *The Intellectual Contexts* . . . , 125–129.
Kluback, William. *Franz Kafka* . . . , 77–82.

"The Bucket Rider"
Kluback, William. *Franz Kafka* . . . , 72–75.

"The Burrow"
Fickert, Kurt. *End of a Mission* . . . , 69, 75–76, 77–85, 96–98.
Gichter, Gerhard. "Difficile Dwellings: Kafka's 'The Burrow,' " in Timm, Eitel, and Kenneth Mendoza, Eds. *The Poetics* . . . , 5–18.
Kluback, William. *Franz Kafka* . . . , 25–38.

"The Cares of a Family Man"
Kluback, William. *Franz Kafka* . . . , 69–71.

"A Country Doctor"
Bloom, Harold. *The Western Canon* . . . , 457–459.

Fickert, Kurt. *End of a Mission* . . . , 13–22, 92–93.
———. "The Triadic Structure of 'Ein Landarzt,' " *Germ Notes & R*, 24, i (1993), 16–18.
Heidsieck, Arnold. *The Intellectual Contexts* . . . , 142–145.

"Description of a Struggle"
Heidsieck, Arnold. *The Intellectual Contexts* . . . , 21–22, 24–25.

"Excursion into the Mountains"
Heidsieck, Arnold. *The Intellectual Contexts* . . . , 60.

"First Sorrow"
Fickert, Kurt. *End of a Mission* . . . , 24–26.

"The Giant Mole"
Fickert, Kurt. *End of a Mission* . . . , 70–75.

"The Great Wall of China"
Beckmann, Martin. "Franz Kafkas Erzählung 'Beim Bau der Chinesischen Mauer': Selbsterfahrung als Existenzproblem," *Neophilologus*, 77 (1993), 433–445.
Hartley, George. "Althusser Metonymy China Wall," *J Kafka Soc Am*, 16, i (1992), 40–45.
Heidsieck, Arnold. *The Intellectual Contexts* . . . , 76–77, 146–147.

"The Hunger Artist"
+Bohner, Charles H. *Instructor's Manual* . . . , 3rd ed., 77–78.
Charters, Ann. *Resources* . . . , 95–96.
Fickert, Kurt. *End of a Mission* . . . , 45–54, 93–94.
Heidsieck, Arnold. *The Intellectual Contexts* . . . , 172–173.
Kluback, William. *Franz Kafka* . . . , 2–12.
Pickering, James H., and Jeffrey D. Hoeper. *Instructor's Manual* . . . , 53–54.
Vulpi, Frank. "Kafka's 'A Hunger Artist': A Cautionary Tale for Faustian Man Caught Between Creativity and Communion," *Germ Notes & R*, 24, i (1993), 9–12.

"The Hunter Gracchus"
Heidsieck, Arnold. *The Intellectual Contexts* . . . , 61–62, 76, 146.
Kluback, William. *Franz Kafka* . . . , 83–85.

"An Imperial Message"
Beckmann, Martin. "Franz Kafkas Erzählung . . . ," 424–432.

"In the Penal Colony"
Beckmann, Martin. "Zeitverfallenheit und Existenzerfahrung: Franz Kafka's Erzählung 'In der Strafkolonie,' " *Seminar*, 30 (1994), 286–302.
Brooks, Peter. *Body Work* . . . , 283–286.
Charters, Ann. *Resources* . . . , 97–98.
Fickert, Kurt. *End of a Mission* . . . , 48–49, 91–92.
Heidsieck, Arnold. *The Intellectual Contexts* . . . , 130–132.
Kipniss, Marc. "The Threat of the (Marginal) Feminine: Decolonizing Kafka's 'Strafkolonie,' " *J Kafka Soc Am*, 16, i (1992), 46–51.
Kluback, William. *Franz Kafka* . . . , 39–50.

Rey-Flaud, Henry. ''A corps et à écrits 'La Colonie pénitenciaire,' '' *Bull des Etudes Valéryennes*, 21 (March–June, 1994), 139–146.

''In the Theater-Gallery''

Fickert, Kurt. *End of a Mission . . .*, 26.

''Investigations of a Dog''

Bruce, Iris. '' 'Aggadah Raises Its Paw Against Halakha': Kafka's Zionist Critique in 'Forschungen eines Hundes,' '' *J Kafka Soc Am*, 16, i (1992), 4–18.

Fickert, Kurt. *End of a Mission . . .*, 31–41, 95–96.

———. ''Kafka's Search for Truth in 'Forschungen eines Hundes,' '' *Monatshefte*, 85 (1993), 189–196.

Kluback, William. *Franz Kafka . . .*, 52–63.

Leadbeater, Lewis W. ''The Sophistic Nature of Kafka's 'Forschungen eines Hundes,' '' *Germ Life & Letters*, 46 (1993), 148–155.

''Jackals and Arabs''

Heidsieck, Arnold. *The Intellectual Contexts . . .*, 163.

''Josephine the Singer''

Fickert, Kurt. *End of a Mission . . .*, 58–66, 96.

Harman, Mark. ''Joyce and Kafka,'' *Sewanne R*, 101 (1993), 81–82.

Vitzthum, Thomas. ''A Revolution in Writing: The Overthrow of Epic Storytelling by Written Narrative in Kafka's 'Josefine, Die Sängerin,' '' *Symposium*, 47, iv (1993), 269–278.

''The Judgment''

Harman, Mark. ''Joyce and Kafka,'' *Sewanee R*, 101 (1993), 76–77.

Heidsieck, Arnold. *The Intellectual Contexts . . .*, 92–97.

Kluback, William. *Franz Kafka . . .*, 117–127.

''A Little Woman''

Fickert, Kurt. *End of a Mission . . .*, 29–31.

''A Message from the Emperor''

Fickert, Kurt. *End of a Mission . . .*, 26–28.

''Metamorphosis''

Ben-Ephraim, Gavriel. ''The Anxiety of History: Kafka's Allegory of the Oedipal Scapegoat,'' *J Kafka Soc Am*, 16, ii (1992), 6–19.

———. ''Making and Breaking Meaning: Deconstruction, Four-Level Allegory and 'The Metamorphosis,' '' *Midwest Q*, 35 (1994), 450–467.

Hagel, Jaime. ''La metamorfosis,'' *Taller de Letras*, 22 (November, 1994), 79–88.

Heidsieck, Arnold. *The Intellectual Contexts . . .*, 97–100.

Kluback, William. *Franz Kafka . . .*, 89–101.

Levine, Michael G. *Writing Through Repression . . .*, 159–167, 170–177.

Munk, Linda. ''What Does Hegel Make of the Jews?: A Scato-Logical Reading of Kafka's '*Die Verwandlung*,' '' *Hist European Ideas*, 18, vi (1994), 913–925.

Natarajan, Nalini. ''Man into Beast: Representations of Metamorphosis,'' *Bestia*, 5 (1993), 119, 120–121.

Weninger, Robert. ''Sounding Out the Silence of Gregor Samsa: Kafka's Rhetoric of Dys-Communication,'' *Stud Twentieth-Century Lit*, 17 (1993), 263–286.

''A Report to an Academy''

Fickert, Kurt. *End of a Mission . . .*, 20–22.

Heidsieck, Arnold. *The Intellectual Contexts . . .*, 147–149.

''Unhappiness''

Heidsieck, Arnold. *The Intellectual Contexts . . .*, 55.

''Up in the Gallery'' [Same as ''In the Gallery'']

Heidsieck, Arnold. *The Intellectual Contexts . . .*, 84–85.

''The Vulture''

Faure, Alain. ''Le Père-vautour: Essai d'interprétation de 'Der Geier' de Franz Kafka,'' *Cahiers d'Etudes Germ*, 21 (1991), 61, 64–73.

LAURA KALPAKIAN

''Veteran's Day''

Ryan, Maureen. ''The Other Side of Grief: American Women Writers and the Vietnam War,'' *Critique*, 36 (1994), 48.

ANATOLY KAMENSKY

''The Four''

Kustanovich, Konstantin. ''Erotic Glasnost: Sexuality in Recent Russian Literature,'' *World Lit Today*, 67 (1993), 140.

KANAI MIEKO

''The Child of Nature''

Yoshida, Sanroku. ''Kanai Mieko (1947—),'' in Mulhern, Chieko I., Ed. *Japanese . . .*, 179–180.

''Platonic Love''

Yoshida, Sanroku. ''Kanai Mieko . . .,'' 183.

''Rabbits''

Yoshida, Sanroku. ''Kanai Mieko . . .,'' 182–183.

''Things That Are''

Yoshida, Sanroku. ''Kanai Mieko . . .,'' 180.

LONNY KANEKO

''The Shoyu Kid''

Wong, Sau-ling C. *Reading Asian American Literature . . .*, 47–49, 99–102.

NIKOLAY KARAMZIN

"Martha the Posadnik"
Wachtel, Andrew B. *An Obsession . . .*, 38–39, 48–55.

MARIE LUISE KASCHNITZ

"Das dicke Kind"
Braunbeck, Helga G. " 'Fly, little sister, fly': Sister Relationship and Identity in Three Contemporary German Stories," in Mink, JoAnna S., and Janet D. Ward, Eds. *The Significance of Sibling . . .*, 159–161.

"Gespenster"
Stiffler, Muriel W. *The German Ghost Story . . .*, 115–124.

GARRISON KEILLOR

"The Tip-Top Club"
Pickering, James H., and Jeffrey D. Hoeper. *Instructor's Manual . . .*, 115–117.

GOTTFRIED KELLER

"Kleider machen Leute"
Widdig, Bernd. "Mode und Moderne: Gottfried Kellers 'Kleider machen Leute,' " *Merkur*, 48, ii (1994), 109–123.

"Pankraz, der Schmoller"
Boomers, Jost. "Realismus versus Romantik. Kellers 'Pankraz' als realistischer 'Anti-Taugenichts," *Wirkendes Wort*, 42 (1993), 197–199, 203–209.

NADEZHDA KHVOSHCHINSKAIA [V. KRESTOVSKY]

"The Boarding School Girl"
Costlow, Jane. "Love, Work, and the Woman Question in Mid Nineteenth-Century Women's Writing," in Clyman, Toby W., and Diana Greene, Eds. *Women Writers . . .*, 65–67.

"The Meeting"
Costlow, Jane. "Love, Work . . .," 70–71.

ANATOLY KIM

"The Herb Gatherers"
Rollberg, Peter. "Man Between Beast and God: Anatoly Kim's Apocalyptic Visions," *World Lit Today*, 67 (1993), 104.

"Myoko's Eglantine"
Rollberg, Peter. "Man Between Beast . . . ," 102–103.

"The Smile of the Fox"
Rollberg, Peter. "Man Between Beast . . . ," 103.

JAMAICA KINCAID

"Annie John"
Simmons, Diane. "The Mother Mirror in Jamaica Kincaid's 'Annie John' and Gertrude Stein's 'The Good Anna,' " in Pearlman, Mickey, Ed. *The Anna Book* . . . , 101–104.
Yeoh, Gilbert. "From Caliban to Sycorax: Revisions of *The Tempest* in Jamaica Kincaid's 'Annie John,' " *World Lit Written Engl*, 33 ii–34, i (1993–1994), 103–116.

"At the Bottom of the River"
Simmons, Diane. "The Rhythm of Reality in the Works of Jamaica Kincaid," *World Lit Today*, 68 (1994), 469.

"The Circling Hand"
+Bohner, Charles H. *Instructor's Manual* . . . , 3rd ed., 78–79.

"Girl"
Simmons, Diane. "The Rhythm . . . ," 467–468.

"In the Night"
Simmons, Diane. "The Rhythm . . . ," 468.

"Ovando"
Ferguson, Moira. *Jamaica Kincaid* . . . , 132–135, 139–160, 165.
Simmons, Diane. "The Rhythm . . . ," 471.

"Wingless"
Wallace, Jo-Ann. "De-scribing *The Water-Babies*: 'The Child' in Post-Colonial Theory," in Tiffin, Chris, and Alan Lawson, Eds. *De-scribing* . . . , 171, 173, 176–177, 182–183.

GRACE KING

"Bonne Maman"
Bryan, Violet H. *The Myth of New Orleans* . . . , 47–50.

"The Little Convent Girl"
Bryan, Violet H. *The Myth of New Orleans* . . . , 52–53.

"Madrilène; or, the Festival of the Dead"
Bryan, Violet H. *The Myth of New Orleans* . . . , 50–52.

STEPHEN KING

"Apt Pupil"
Reesman, Jeanne C. "Riddle Game: Stephen King's Metafictive

Dialogue,'' in Magistrale, Tony, Ed. *The Dark Descent . . .*, 158–161.

''The Monkey''
Doty, Gene. ''A Clockwork Evil: Guilt and Coincidence in 'The Monkey,' '' in Magistrale, Tony, Ed. *The Dark Descent . . .*, 129–136.

RUDYARD KIPLING

''Arrest of Lieutenant Golightly''
Bauer, Helen P. *Rudyard Kipling . . .*, 38.

''At the End of the Passage''
Bauer, Helen P. *Rudyard Kipling . . .*, 4–5.
Brown, Chris. ''Henry James and the Passage's End,'' *Kipling J*, 68 (June, 1994), 37–40.
Mallett, Phillip. ''Rudyard Kipling: Narrating India,'' *Swansea R*, [n.v.] (1994), 364.

''At the Pit's Mouth''
Bauer, Helen P. *Rudyard Kipling . . .*, 15.

''Baa, Baa, Black Sheep''
Bauer, Helen P. *Rudyard Kipling . . .*, 11–13.

''A Bank Fraud''
Bauer, Helen P. *Rudyard Kipling . . .*, 31–32.

''Beyond the Pale''
Bauer, Helen P. *Rudyard Kipling . . .*, 45–47.
Mallett, Phillip. ''Rudyard Kipling . . . ,'' 363–364, 365.

''Bread upon the Waters''
Bauer, Helen P. *Rudyard Kipling . . .*, 22–23.

''The Bridge-Builders''
Bauer, Helen P. *Rudyard Kipling . . .*, 19–21.
Mallett, Phillip. ''Rudyard Kipling . . . ,'' 359–362.

''Brother Square-Toes''
Bauer, Helen P. *Rudyard Kipling . . .*, 95.

''The Brushwood Boy''
Bauer, Helen P. *Rudyard Kipling . . .*, 76–77.

''The Bull that Thought''
Bauer, Helen P. *Rudyard Kipling . . .*, 99–100.

''The Children of the Zodiac''
Bauer, Helen P. *Rudyard Kipling . . .*, 100–102.

''The City of Dreadful Night''
Bauer, Helen P. *Rudyard Kipling . . .*, 90.

''Cold Iron''
Bauer, Helen P. *Rudyard Kipling . . .*, 19.
Mason, Philip. '' 'Cold Iron,' '' *Kipling J*, 68 (December, 1994), 22–28.

"The Crab that Played with the Sea"
Bauer, Helen P. *Rudyard Kipling* . . . , 53–54.

"The Daughter of the Regiment"
Bauer, Helen P. *Rudyard Kipling* . . . , 18–19.

"Dayspring Mishandled"
+Hanson, Clare. *Short Stories and Short Fictions, 1880–1980*, in Bauer, Helen P. *Rudyard Kipling* . . . , 143–144.

"A Doctor of Medicine"
Bauer, Helen P. *Rudyard Kipling* . . . , 24–25.

"The Drums of the Fore and Aft"
Bauer, Helen P. *Rudyard Kipling* . . . , 38.

"The Education of Otis Yeere"
Bauer, Helen P. *Rudyard Kipling* . . . , 16.

"A Friend of the Family"
Bauer, Helen P. *Rudyard Kipling* . . . , 9.

"The Gardener"
Bauer, Helen P. *Rudyard Kipling* . . . , 84–85.

"An Habitation Enforced"
Trotter, David. *The English Novel* . . . , 161.

"Haunted Subalterns"
Bauer, Helen P. *Rudyard Kipling* . . . , 72–73.

"The Hill of Illusion"
Bauer, Helen P. *Rudyard Kipling* . . . , 14.

"His Chance of Life"
Arata, Stephen D. "A Universal Foreignness: Kipling in the Fin-de-Siècle," *Engl Lit Transition*, 36 (1993), 18–19.
Bauer, Helen P. *Rudyard Kipling* . . . , 41–42.

"The House Surgeon"
Bauer, Helen P. *Rudyard Kipling* . . . , 79–80.

"How Fear Came"
Bauer, Helen P. *Rudyard Kipling* . . . , 58–59.
McBratney, John. "Imperial Subjects, Imperial Space in Kipling's *Jungle Book*," *Victorian Stud*, 35 (1992), 284.

"How the Rhinoceros Got His Skin"
Bauer, Helen P. *Rudyard Kipling* . . . , 52–53.

"How the Whale Got His Throat"
Bauer, Helen P. *Rudyard Kipling* . . . , 52.

"In the Pride of His Youth"
Bauer, Helen P. *Rudyard Kipling* . . . , 36.

"In the Rukh"
McBratney, John. "Imperial Subjects . . . ," 288–289.
Newton, Michael. "Kipling and the Savage Child," *Commonwealth Essays & Studs*, 15, i (1992), 12–19.

"Kaa's Hunting"
Bauer, Helen P. *Rudyard Kipling* . . . , 60–61, 93–94.

"Kidnapped"
Bauer, Helen P. *Rudyard Kipling* . . . , 43–44.

"The King's Ankus"
Flint, M. "Kipling's Mowgli and Human Focalization," *Studia Neophilologica*, 65, i (1993), 73–76.

"The Knife and the Naked Chalk"
Bauer, Helen P. *Rudyard Kipling* . . . , 67–68.

"Letting in the Jungle"
McBratney, John. "Imperial Subjects . . . ," 286–287.

"Lispeth"
Bauer, Helen P. *Rudyard Kipling* . . . , 44.
Verch, Maria. "Rudyard Kipling: 'Lispeth,' " in Lubbers, Klaus, Ed. *Die Englische* . . . , 141–155.

"A Maddona of the Trenches"
Bauer, Helen P. *Rudyard Kipling* . . . , 10–11.

"The Man Who Would Be King"
Bauer, Helen P. *Rudyard Kipling* . . . , 39–41.

"The Mark of the Beast"
Arata, Stephen D. "A Universal . . . ," 26–27.
Bauer, Helen P. *Rudyard Kipling* . . . , 73–75.
Sage, Victor. "Empire Gothic: Explanation and Epiphany in Conan Doyle, Kipling, and Chesterton," in Bloom, Clive, Ed. *Creepers* . . . , 12–16.
Trotter, David. *The English Novel* . . . , 248–250.

"Mary Postgate"
+Bohner, Charles H. *Instructor's Manual* . . . , 3rd ed., 79–81.
Trotter, David. *The English Novel* . . . , 250–251.

"The Miracle of Purun Bhagat"
Bauer, Helen P. *Rudyard Kipling* . . . , 91–93.

"The Miracle of Saint Jubanus"
Bauer, Helen P. *Rudyard Kipling* . . . , 81–82.

"Mowgli's Brothers"
Bauer, Helen P. *Rudyard Kipling* . . . , 55, 56.
McBratney, John. "Imperial Subjects . . . ," 284–285.

"Mrs. Bathurst"
Bauer, Helen P. *Rudyard Kipling* . . . , 77–79.
Trotter, David. *The English Novel* . . . , 245–256.

"My Own True Ghost Story"
Bauer, Helen P. *Rudyard Kipling* . . . , 72.

"My Son's Wife"
+Hanson, Clare. *Short Stories and Short Fictions, 1880–1980*, in Bauer, Helen P. *Rudyard Kipling* . . . , 137–138.

"Old Men at Pevensey"
Bauer, Helen P. *Rudyard Kipling* . . . , 65.

"Only a Subaltern"
Bauer, Helen P. *Rudyard Kipling* . . . , 18.

"The Phantom Rickshaw"
Bauer, Helen P. *Rudyard Kipling* . . . , 75–76.

"The Rescue of Pluffles"
Bauer, Helen P. *Rudyard Kipling* . . . , 29.

"The Return of Imray"
+McClure, John A. *Kipling and Conrad: The Colonial Fiction*, in Bauer, Helen P. *Rudyard Kipling* . . . , 131–135.

"A Sahibs' War"
Havely, Cicely P. " 'A Sahibs' War': Reflections on Kipling's 'Compellingly Unpleasant Story,' " *Kipling J*, 68 (December, 1994), 12–22.

"The Spring Running"
Flint, M. "Kipling's Mowgli . . . ," 76–78.

"The Story of Muhammad Din"
Mallett, Phillip. "Rudyand Kipling . . . ," 366–367.

"The Strange Ride of Morrowbie Jukes"
Bauer, Helen P. *Rudyard Kipling* . . . , 6–8.

"They"
Bauer, Helen P. *Rudyard Kipling* . . . , 82–84, 95–96.
+Hanson, Clare. *Short Stories and Short Fictions, 1880–1980*, in Bauer, Helen P. *Rudyard Kipling* . . . , 138–139.

"Three and—an Extra"
Bauer, Helen P. *Rudyard Kipling* . . . , 16.

"The Three Musketeers"
Bauer, Helen P. *Rudyard Kipling* . . . , 30–31.

"Thrown Away"
Bauer, Helen P. *Rudyard Kipling* . . . , 5–6.
Reilly, Jim. *Shadowtime* . . . , 141–143.

"Tiger, Tiger"
McBratney, John. "Imperial Subjects . . . ," 286.

"To Be Filed for Reference"
Arata, Stephen D. "A Universal . . . , " 22–25.

"Tod's Amendment"
Bauer, Helen P. *Rudyard Kipling* . . . , 38–39.

"The Tomb of His Ancestors"
Bauer, Helen P. *Rudyard Kipling* . . . , 33.

"Uncovenanted Mercies"
Bauer, Helen P. *Rudyard Kipling* . . . , 82.

"Unprofessional"
Bauer, Helen P. *Rudyard Kipling* . . . , 26–27.

"Venus Annodomini"
Bauer, Helen P. *Rudyard Kipling* . . . , 30.

"A Walking Delegate"
Bauer, Helen P. *Rudyard Kipling* . . . , 21–22.

"A Wayside Comedy"
Bauer, Helen P. *Rudyard Kipling* . . . , 13–14.

"Wee Willie Winkie"
Bauer, Helen P. *Rudyard Kipling* . . . , 42–43.

"William the Conqueror"
Bauer, Helen P. *Rudyard Kipling* . . . , 33–35.

"Wireless"
Bauer, Helen P. *Rudyard Kipling* . . . , 97–99.
Stamers-Smith, Eileen. "Kipling's 'Wireless' and the Nature of Poetic Inspiration," *Kipling J*, 68 (December, 1994), 29–30.

"The Wish House"
Bauer, Helen P. *Rudyard Kipling* . . . , 85–87.
+Hanson, Clare. *Short Stories and Short Fictions, 1880–1980*, in Bauer, Helen P. *Rudyard Kipling* . . . , 140–143.

"Without Benefit of Clergy"
Bauer, Helen P. *Rudyard Kipling* . . . , 47–49.

CAROLINE KIRKLAND

"Comfort"
Merish, Lori. " 'The Hand of Refined Taste' in the Frontier Landscape: Caroline Kirkland's *A New Home, Who'll Follow?* and the Feminization of American Consumerism," *Am Q*, 45 (1993), 500–501.

PERRI KLASS

"Not a Good Girl"
+Bohner, Charles H. *Instructor's Manual* . . . , 3rd ed., 81–82.

HEINRICH VON KLEIST

"Bettelweib von Locarno"
Furst, Lilian R. "Begging an Answer: Kleist's 'The Beggarwoman of Locarno,' " in Prier, Raymond A., Ed. *Countercurrents* . . . , 104–111.
Stephens, Anthony. *Heinrich von Kleist* . . . , 272–275.
Stiffler, Muriel W. *The German Ghost Story* . . . , 39–50.

"Das Erdbeben in Chili"
Gelus, Marjorie. "Birth as Metaphor in Kleist's 'Das Erdbeben in Chili': A Comparison of Critical Methodologies," *Women Germ Yearbook*, 8 (1993), 1–20.
Stephens, Anthony. *Heinrich von Kleist* . . . , 194–206.

"Der Findling"
Stephens, Anthony. *Heinrich von Kleist . . .*, 224–235.

"Die Marquise von O——"
Dutoit, Thomas. "Rape, Crypt, and Fantasm: Kleist's 'The Marquise of O— . . .,' " *Mosaic*, 27, iii (1994), 45–64.
Stephens, Anthony. *Heinrich von Kleist . . .*, 212–225.

"Michael Kohlhaas"
Horst, Falk. "Kleists Kohlhaas: Ueber die Taeuschbarkeit von Beweggruenden," *Wirkendes Wort*, 44 (1994), 47–66.
Klemm, László. "Heinrich von Kleist: Michael Kohlhaas—Maximalismus des Ausdrucks und biblische Bezüge," *Acta Litteraria*, 33, i–iv (1991), 37–46.
Kuchinke-Bach, Anneliese. "Heinrich von Kleists 'Michael Kohlhass': Anmerkungen zum Zigeuner-Motiv,"*Germanisch-Romanische Monatsschrift*, 43, ii (1993), 167–179.
Pugmire, Troy A. "Ein Vergleich: Heinrich von Kleists 'Michael Kohlhaas' und die 'Rote Armee Fraktion,' " *Utah Foreign Lang R*, [n.v.] (1993–1994), 124–126.
Stephens, Anthony. *Heinrich von Kleist . . .*, 244–261.
Sterne, Richard C. *Dark Mirror . . .*, 55–57, 59–60.

"St. Cecilia or the Power of Music"
Boehringer, Michael. "Of Meaning and Truth: Narrative Ambiguity in Kleist's 'Die heilige Cäcilie oder die Gewalt der Musik. Eine Legende,' " *Frontenac R*, 10–11 (1993–1994), 103–128.

"Über das Marionettentheater"
Stephens, Anthony. *Heinrich von Kleist . . .*, 277–291.

"Die Verlobung in St. Domingo"
Stephens, Anthony. *Heinrich von Kleist . . .*, 206–211.

"Der Zweikampf"
Stephens, Anthony. *Heinrich von Kleist . . .*, 236–244.

KOMETANI FUMIKO

"A Visitor from Afar"
Samuel, Yoshiko Y. "Kometani Fumiko (1930—)," in Mulhern, Chieko I., Ed. *Japanese . . .*, 193–194.

S. KON

"The Morning Expedition"
Jarrett, Mary. "Teachers and Servants: Colliding Worlds in Short Stories by Malaysia-Singapore Women Writers," in Thumboo, Edwin, Ed. *Perceiving . . .*, 68.

HELGA KÖNIGSDORF

"Liriodendron tulipifera"
Lawson, Ursula D. " 'So, We Are Condemned.' Cancer in the GDR

Short Story Written by Women,'' in Adamson, Ginette, and Eunice Myers, Eds. *Continental, Latin-American . . .*, 83–89.

CYRIL M. KORNBLUTH

''The Altar at Midnight''
Haynes, Roslynn D. *From Faust . . .*, 276.

''Gomez''
Haynes, Roslynn D. *From Faust . . .*, 306–307.

VLADIMIR GALAKTIONOVICH KOROLENKO

''The Strange One''
Balasubramanian, Radha. ''Spatial Form and Character Revelations: Korolenko's Siberian Stories,'' *Canadian Slavonic Papers*, 35 (1994), 253–254, 256, 258–259.

ETHEL KRAUZE

''Al teléfono''
Neate, Wilson. ''La inscripción del sujeto femenino en la narrativa de Ethel Krauze,'' *Crítica Hispánica*, 16, ii (1994), 361.

''El lunes te amaré''
Neate, Wilson. ''La inscripción . . .,'' 361.

''El monstruo''
Neate, Wilson. ''La inscripción . . .,'' 360.

''La mula en la noria''
Neate, Wilson. ''La inscripción . . .,'' 362.

''Pin pong''
Neate, Wilson. ''La inscripción . . .,'' 363–364.

MARYA KRESTOVSKAYA

''The Wail''
Kelly, Catriona. *A History of Russian . . .*, 138–139.

MILAN KUNDERA

''Dr. Havel After Twenty Years''
Misurella, Fred. *Understanding Milan . . .*, 182–183.

''Edward and God''
Misurella, Fred. *Understanding Milan . . .*, 183–189.

''The Golden Apples of Desire''
Misurella, Fred. *Understanding Milan . . .*, 170–172.

"The Hitchhiking Game"
Misurella, Fred. *Understanding Milan* . . . , 172–174.

"Let the Old Dead Make Room for the Young Dead"
Misurella, Fred. *Understanding Milan* . . . , 179–181.

"Nobody Will Laugh"
Misurella, Fred. *Understanding Milan* . . . , 167, 168–170, 191.

"Symposium"
Misurella, Fred. *Understanding Milan* . . . , 174–179.

KURAHASHI YUMIKO

"The Monastery"
Yamamoto, Fumiko. "Kurahashi Yumiko (1935–)," in Mulhern, Chieko I., Ed. *Japanese* . . . , 201–202.

"Party"
Yamamoto, Fumiko. "Kurahashi Yumiko . . . ," 200–201.

"To Die at the Estuary"
Yamamoto, Fumiko. "Kurahashi Yumiko . . . ," 203–204.

ENRIQUE LABRADOR RUIZ

"Conejito Ulán"
Herrera, Roberto. "Innovación técnica y originalidad de estilo en un cuento de Enrique Labrador Ruiz," *Círculo*, 23 (1994), 132–136.

SELMA LAGERLÖF

"Astrid"
Forsaås-Scott, Helena. "Selma Lagerlöf's 'Astrid': Textual Strategy and Feminine Identity," in Death, Sarah, and Helena Forsaås-Scott, Eds. *A Century of Swedish* . . . , 63–74.

"Herr Arnes Hoard"
Green, Brita. "The Warp and Weft of Selma Lagerlöf's Narrative Fabric," in Death, Sarah, and Helena Forsaås-Scott, Eds. *A Century of Swedish* . . . , 76–81.

"The Outlaws"
Graves, Peter. "Selma Lagerlöf's 'De faågelfrie': The Divide between the Seen and the Spoken," in Death, Sarah, and Helena Forsaås-Scott, Eds. *A Century of Swedish* . . . , 51–62.

"Tales of a Manor"
Green, Brita. "The Warp and Weft . . . ," 76–81.

ALEX LA GUMA

"A Walk in the Night"
Povey, John F. "English-language Fiction from South Africa," in Owomoyela, Oyekan, Ed. *A History* . . . , 95–96.

OSVALDO LAMBORGHINI

"El niño proletario"

Fernández, Nancy P. "Violencia, risa y parodia: 'El niño proletario' de O. Lamborghini y *Sin rumbo* de E. Cambaceres," *Escritura*, 17 (1992), 159–163; rpt. *Revista Interamericana*, 43 (1993), 413–415.

HERNÁN LARA ZAVALA

"De Zitilchén"

Rudoy, Myriam. "De la literatura, el realismo y la verosimilitud. Viaje por la narrativa de Hernán Lara Zavala," in Mata, Oscar, Ed. *En torna* . . . , 181–186.

RING LARDNER

"The Golden Honeymoon"

Cowlishaw, Brian T. "The Reader's Role in Ring Lardner's Rhetoric," *Stud Short Fiction*, 31 (1994), 213–214.

"Haircut"

+Bohner, Charles H. *Instructor's Manual* . . . , 3rd ed., 82–83.

Cowlishaw, Brian T. "The Reader's Role . . . ," 212–213.

"Zone of Quiet"

Cowlishaw, Brian T. "The Reader's Role . . . ," 209–212.

NELLA LARSEN

"Freedom"

Davis, Thadious M. *Nella Larsen, Novelist* . . . , 179–181.

"Sanctuary"

Davis, Thadious M. *Nella Larsen, Novelist* . . . , 346–353.

"The Wrong Man"

Davis, Thadious M. *Nella Larsen, Novelist* . . . , 175–179.

NORMAN LAVERS

"The Telegraph Relay Station"

Pickering, James H., and Jeffrey D. Hoeper. *Instructor's Manual* . . . , 126–128.

MARY LAVIN

"Happiness"

Hawthorne, Mark D. "Words That Do Not Speak Themselves: Mary Lavin's 'Happiness,' " *Stud Short Fiction*, 31 (1994), 683–688.

"My Vocation"
+Bohner, Charles H. *Instructor's Manual* . . . , 3rd ed., 83–84.

D. H. LAWRENCE

"The Blind Man"
Charters, Ann. *Resources* . . . , 99–100.
Sasaki, Toru. "Towards a Systematic Description of Narrative 'Point of View': An Examination of Chatman's Theory with an Analysis of 'The Blind Man' by D. H. Lawrence," *Lang & Lit*, 3, ii (1994), 125–138.
Thornton, Weldon. *D. H. Lawrence* . . . , 15–16, 50–55.

"England, My England"
Thornton, Weldon. *D. H. Lawrence* . . . , 43–50.

"The Fox"
Charters, Ann. *Resources* . . . , 100–102.

"The Horse Dealer's Daughter"
Charters, Ann. *Resources* . . . , 103–104.

"The Man Who Died"
Kennedy, Andrew. "The Myth of Rebirth in D. H. Lawrence's 'The Man Who Died,' " in Kennedy, Andrew, and Orm Øverland, Eds. *Excursions in Fiction* . . . , 124–130.

"The Man Who Loved Islands"
Doherty, Gerald. "The Art of Survival: Narrating the Nonnarratable in D. H. Lawrence's 'The Man Who Loved Islands,' " *D. H. Lawrence R*, 24 (1992), 117–126.
Link, Viktor. "D. H. Lawrence: 'The Man Who Loved Islands'—Anatomie eines Idealisten," in Lubbers, Klaus, Ed. *Die Englische* . . . , 176–185.

"New Eve and Old Adam"
Thornton, Weldon. *D. H. Lawrence* . . . , 16–18.

"The Odour of Chrysanthemums"
Thornton, Weldon. *D. H. Lawrence* . . . , 29–35.
Trotter, David. *The English Novel* . . . , 75–76.

"The Princess"
Kinkead-Weekes, Mark. "Re-placing the Imagination: D. H. Lawrence and Bessie Head," *World Lit Written Engl*, 33, ii & 34, i (1993–1994), 40.

"The Prussian Officer"
Thornton, Weldon. *D. H. Lawrence* . . . , 21–22.

"The Rocking Horse Winner"
+Bohner, Charles H. *Instructor's Manual* . . . , 3rd ed., 84–85.
Pickering, James H., and Jeffrey D. Hoeper. *Instructor's Manual* . . . , 67–68.
Sklenicka, Carol, and Mark Spilka. "A Womb of His Own: Lawrence's Passional/Parental View of Childhood," in

Goodenough, Elizabeth, Mark A. Heberle, and Naomi Sokoloff, Eds. *Infant Tongues . . .* , 179–180.
Thornton, Weldon. *D. H. Lawrence . . .* , 72–77.

"The Shadow in the Rose Garden"
Thornton, Weldon. *D. H. Lawrence . . .* , 35–42.

"St. Mawr"
Kinkead-Weekes, Mark. "Re-placing . . . ," 38–39.

"Two Blue Birds"
Thornton, Weldon. *D. H. Lawrence . . .* , 66–72.

"The Virgin and the Gipsy"
Lally, M. M. " 'The Virgin and the Gipsy': Rewriting the Pain," in Wyatt-Brown, Anne M., and Janice Rossen, Eds. *Aging and Gender . . .* , 129–135.

"Wintry Peacock"
Thornton, Weldon. *D. H. Lawrence . . .* , 55–60.

"The Woman Who Rode Away"
Hyde, Virginia. " 'Lost' Girls: D. H. Lawrence's Versions of Persephone," in Hayes, Elizabeth T., Ed., *Images of Persephone . . .* , 114–116.
Kullmann, Thomas. "Exotic Landscapes and Borderline Experiences in Twentieth Century Fiction: D. H. Lawrence, Karen Blixen and Malcolm Lowry," in Seeber, Hans U., and Walter Göbel, Eds. *Anglistentag 1992 . . .* , 380–382.
Thornton, Weldon. *D. H. Lawrence . . .* , 77–86.

"You Touched Me"
Thornton, Weldon. *D. H. Lawrence . . .* , 60–66.

HENRY LAWSON

"The Bush Undertaker"
Lee, Christopher. "The National Myth and the Stereotype: 'The Bush Undertaker' goes to the Bhabha," *Australian-Canadian Stud*, 10, ii (1992), 136–141.
O'Neill, Phillip. "Aborigines and Women in Lawson's 'The Bush Undertaker,' " *Australian & New Zealand Stud*, 8 (1992), 59–70.

JOSEPH SHERIDAN LE FANU

"Carmilla"
Andriano, Joseph. " 'Our Dual Existence': Archetypes of Love and Death in Le Fanu's 'Carmilla,' " in Langford, Michele K., Ed. *Contours of the Fantastic . . .* , 49–55.
———. *Our Ladies . . .* , 98–105.
Gelder, Ken. *Reading the Vampire*, 44–46, 49–50, 53–54, 55–56, 60–62, 64.
Tracy, Robert. "Introduction," *In a Glass Darkly* [by Sheridan Le Fanu], xix–xxvii.

"Green Tea"
Tracy, Robert. "Introduction," xvii–xix.

"The Mysterious Lodger"
Sanders, Joe. " 'My God, No!': The Varieties of Christian Horror Fiction," in Langford, Michele K., Ed. *Contours of the Fantastic* . . . , 135–136.

"A Strange Event in the Life of Schalken the Painter"
McCormack, W. J. *Dissolute Characters* . . . , 123–127, 129–132.

URSULA K. LE GUIN

"Horse Camp"
Pickering, James H., and Jeffrey D. Hoeper. *Instructor's Manual* . . . , 125.

"The Professor's Houses"
+Bohner, Charles H. *Instructor's Manual* . . . , 3rd ed., 85–86.

MURRAY LEINSTER

"The Man Who Put Out the Sun"
Haynes, Roslynn D. *From Faust* . . . , 195–196.

"The Storm That Had to Be Stopped"
Haynes, Roslynn D. *From Faust* . . . , 195–196.

DORIS LESSING

"Among the Roses"
Tyler, Lisa. "Our Mothers' Gardens: Doris Lessing's 'Among the Roses,' " *Stud Short Fiction*, 31 (1994), 163–173.

"The Ant Heap"
Kinkead-Weekes, Mark. "Sharp Knowing in Apartheid?: The Shorter Fiction of Nadine Gordimer and Doris Lessing," in Gurnah, Abdulrazak, Ed. *Essays* . . . , 99–101.

"The De Wets Come to Kloof Grange"
Kinkead-Weekes, Mark. "Sharp Knowing . . . ," 98–99.

"Dialogue"
Burgan, Mary. "The 'Feminine' Short Story: Recuperating the Moment," *Style*, 27 (1993), 384–385.

"A Mild Attack of Locusts"
Michel-Michot, Paulette. "Doris Lessing: 'A Mild Attack of Locusts,' " in Lubbers, Klaus, Ed. *Die Englische* . . . , 379–389.

"The Old Chief Mshlanga"
Charters, Ann. *Resources* . . . , 106–107.
Kinkead-Weekes, Mark. "Sharp Knowing . . . ," 91–94.

"One Off the Short List"
+Bohner, Charles H. *Instructor's Manual* . . . , 3rd ed., 86–87.
Harvey, Stephanie. "Doris Lessing's 'One Off the Short List' and Leo Bellingham's 'In for the Kill,' " *Critical S*, 5, i (1993), 66–67, 69–71, 72–75.

"A Sunrise on the Veld"
+Bohner, Charles H. *Instructor's Manual* . . . , 3rd ed., 87–88.
Charters, Ann. *Resources* . . . , 108.

"Wine"
Pickering, James H., and Jeffrey D. Hoeper. *Instructor's Manual* . . . , 86–87.

EKATERINA LETKOVA(-SULTANOVA)

"The Holiday"
Kelly, Catriona. *A History of Russian* . . . , 143–144, 145–146.

NORMAN LEVINE

"Something Happened Here"
Vauthier, Simone. "What Happens Here: A Reading of Norman Levine's 'Something Happened Here,' " in D'haen, Theo, and Hans Bertens, Eds. *Postmodern Fiction* . . . , 201–221.

ALUN LEWIS

"Night Journey"
Bergonzi, Bernard. *Wartime* . . . , 42.

LI ANG

"The Butcher's Wife"
Chien, Ying-Ying. "From Utopian to Dystopian World: Two Faces of Feminism in Contemporary Taiwanese Women's Fiction," *World Lit Today*, 68 (1994), 38–41.

ENRIQUE LIHN

"Huacho y Pochocha"
Gomes, Miguel. "Enrique Lihn, cuentista," *Revista Iberoamericana*, 60 (1994), 1017–1018, 1019.

"Para Eva"
Gomes, Miguel. "Enrique Lihn . . . ," 1021–1022.

"Retrato de un poeta"
Gomes, Miguel. "Enrique Lihn . . . ," 1018–1019.

BALDOMERO LILLO

"Invalido"
Lindstrom, Naomi. *Twentieth-Century* . . . , 40–41.

SHIRLEY LIM

"A Pot of Rice"
Jarrett, Mary. "Teachers and Servants: Colliding Worlds in Short Stories by Malaysia-Singapore Women Writers," in Thumboo, Edwin, Ed. *Perceiving* . . . , 73.

"Transportation to Westchester"
Jarrett, Mary. "Teachers . . . ," 73–74.

CLARICE LISPECTOR

"The Buffalo"
Peixoto, Marta. *Passionate Fictions* . . . , 29, 30–31.

"A Chicken"
Peixoto, Marta. *Passionate Fictions* . . . , 33, 34, 36.

"The Crime of the Mathematics Teacher"
Peixoto, Marta. *Passionate Fictions* . . . , 34.

"The Dinner"
Peixoto, Marta. *Passionate Fictions* . . . , 34–35.

"Os desastres de Sofia"
Andrade, Ana L. "In the Inter(t)sex(t) of Clarice Lispector and Nelson Rodigues: From Drama to Language," in Johnson, Randal, Ed. *Tropical Paths* . . . , 143–144.

"The Egg and the Chicken"
Peixoto, Marta. *Passionate Fictions* . . . , 53–58.

"Explanation"
Peixoto, Marta. *Passionate Fictions* . . . , 80.

"Family Ties"
Peixoto, Marta. *Passionate Fictions* . . . , 27–28, 33.

"Happy Birthday"
Peixoto, Marta. *Passionate Fictions* . . . , 29, 31–33.

"The Hour of the Star"
Archer, Deborah J. "Receiving the Other: The Feminine Economy of Clarice Lispector's 'The Hour of the Star,' " in Singley, Carol J., and Susan E. Sweeney, Eds. *Anxious Power*. . . , 253–264.
Peixoto, Marta. *Passionate Fictions* . . . , 89–99.
Tiago Jones, Haydn. "The Quest in Lispector's *A paixão segundo G. H.* and 'A hora da Estrela,' " *Romance Lang Annual*, 4 (1992), 617–619.

"The Imitation of the Rose"
Andrade, Ana L. "In the Inter(t)sex(t) . . . ," 143.
Peixoto, Marta. *Passionate Fictions* . . . , 29, 30, 33.

"Love"
Peixoto, Marta. *Passionate Fictions* . . . , 28–30, 33.

"The Man Who Appeared"
Peixoto, Marta. *Passionate Fictions* . . . , 77.

"The Misfortunes of Sofia"
Peixoto, Marta. *Passionate Fictions* . . . , 18–23.

"Miss Algrave"
Peixoto, Marta. *Passionate Fictions* . . . , 73–74.

"Mystery in São Cristóvão"
Peixoto, Marta. *Passionate Fictions* . . . , 26, 83–84.

"Pig Latin"
Peixoto, Marta. *Passionate Fictions* . . . , 87–89.

"Preciousness"
Andrade, Ana L. "In the Inter(t)sex(t) . . . ," 140–141.

"The Smallest Woman in the World"
Peixoto, Marta. *Passionate Fictions* . . . , 37–38.

"The Way of the Cross"
Peixoto, Marta. *Passionate Fictions* . . . , 78.

LIU HENG

"Fuxi Fuxi"
Huot, Marie-Claire. "Liu Heng's 'Fuxi Fuxi': What about Nüwa?" in Lu, Tonglin, Ed. *Gender and Sexuality* . . . , 85–105.

CAROLINE CAMERON LOCKHART

"Child of Nature"
Furman, Necah S. *Caroline Lockhart* . . . , 25, 26–27.

"His Own Medicine"
Furman, Necah S. *Caroline Lockhart* . . . , 35.

"The Qualities of Leadership"
Furman, Necah S. *Caroline Lockhart* . . . , 34–35.

"The Sign That Failed"
Furman, Necah S. *Caroline Lockhart* . . . , 28.

"The Tango Lizard"
Furman, Necah S. *Caroline Lockhart* . . . , 35–36.

"The Woman Who Gave No Quarter"
Furman, Necah S. *Caroline Lockhart* . . . , 33–34.

JACK LONDON

"The Call of the Wild"
Tavernier-Courbin, Jacqueline. *The Call . . .*, 20–22, 44–46, 56–109.

"The Pearls of Parlay"
Pache, Walter. "Jack London: 'The Pearls of Parlay,' " in Lubbers, Klaus, Ed. *Die Englische . . .*, 196–208.

"South of the Slot"
Gair, Christopher. "Hegemony, Metaphor, and Structural Difference: The 'Strange Dualism' of 'South of the Slot,' " *Arizona Q*, 49, i (1993), 73–97.

"To Build a Fire"
+Bohner, Charles H. *Instructor's Manual . . .*, 3rd ed., 88–89.
Nicholson, Mervyn. "Peripety Cues in Short Fiction," *CEA Critic*, 56, ii (1994), 46–47.

"White Silence"
Woodward, Servanne. "Sympathy and Indifference as Opposing Principles in the Society of Jack London's 'The Son of the Wolf,' " *Excavatio*, 2 (1993), 124–131.

AUGUSTUS BALDWIN LONGSTREET

"Darby, the Politician"
Watson, Ritchie D. *Yeoman Versus Cavalier . . .*, 59–60.

JEAN LORRAIN

"Sonyeuse"
Ziegler, Robert. "The Dynamics of Decadent Narrative in Jean Lorrain's 'Sonyeuse,' " *Stud Short Fiction*, 31 (1994), 99–107.

DAVID WONG LOUIE

"Displacement"
Wong, Sau-ling C. *Reading Asian American Literature . . .*, 154–157, 160.

H[OWARD] P. LOVECRAFT

"The Colour Out of Space"
Burleson, Donald R. "Lovecraft's 'The Colour Out of Space,' " *Explicator*, 52 (1993), 48–50.

"Dreams in the Witch House"
Ringel, Faye. " 'Diabolists and Decadents': Lovecraft's Gothic Puritans," *Lit Int Theory*, 5, i (1994), 49–50.

"The Night Ocean" [in collaboration with Robert H. Barlow]
Humphreys, Brian. " 'The Night Ocean' and the Subtleties of Cosmicism," *Lovecraft Stud*, 30 (Spring, 1994), 14–21.

"The Terrible Old Man"
Buchanan, Carl. " 'The Terrible Old Man': A Myth of the Devouring Father," *Lovecraft Stud*, 29 (Fall, 1993), 19–31.

"The Unnamable"
Ringel, Faye. " 'Diabolists and Decadents . . . ," 47, 48–49.

MALCOLM LOWRY

"Through the Panama"
Filipczak, Dorota. " 'Léviathan ou la Traversée inutile' and the Death of the Old Self in 'Through the Panama,' " *Malcolm Lowry R*, 31–32 (Fall–Spring, 1992–1993), 47–49, 53–55.

LU XIULIAN [HSIU-LIEN, LU]

"These Three Women"
Chien, Ying-Ying. "From Utopian to Dystopian World: Two Faces of Feminism in Contemporary Taiwanese Women's Fiction," *World Lit Today*, 68 (1994), 36–38.

LU XÜN

"Kong Yuji"
Wong, Yoon Wan. "A Journey to the Heart of Darkness: The Mode of Travel Literature in Lu Xün's Fiction," *Tamkang R*, 23, i–iv (1992–1993), 685.

LU YIN

"Lishi's Diary"
Larson, Wendy. "Female Subjectivity and Gender Relations: The Early Stories of Lu Yin and Bing Xin," in Liu Kang and Xiaobing Tang, Eds. *Politics, Ideology . . .*, 134–135.

"Someone's Tragedy"
Larson, Wendy. "Female Subjectivity . . . ," 131–132.

CARMEN LUGO FILIPPI

"Milagros, Calle Mercurio"
Handelsman, Michael. "El espacio afirmativo del salón de belleza: Un análisis de dos cuentos de Carmen Lugo Filippi," *SECOLAS Annals*, 25 (1994), 27–29.

Umpierre, Luz M. ''Incitaciones lesbianas en 'Milagros, Calle Mercurio' de Carmen Lugo Filippi,'' *Revista Iberoamericana*, 59 (1993), 309–316.

''Pilar, tus rizos''
Handelsman, Michael. ''El espacio afirmativo . . . ,'' 26–27.

LEOPOLDO LUGONES

''La fuerza Omega''
Naharro-Calderón, José M. ''Escritura fantástica y destrucción realista en *Las fuerzas extrañas* de Leopoldo Lugones,'' *Hispanic R*, 62, i (1994), 25–32.

''La metamúsica''
Naharro-Calderón, José M. ''Escritura . . . ,'' 25–28, 29–32.

''El psychon''
Naharro-Calderón, José M. ''Escritura . . . ,'' 25–28, 29–32.

''Yzur''
Jitrik, Noé, ''Cuentos fatales,'' *Las fuerzas extrañas: Cuentos fatales* [by Leopoldo Lugones], 38–39, 41–42.
Marini Palmieri, Enrique. ''Yzur, mono sabio: Sobre un cuento de Leopoldo Lugones,'' *Alba de América*, 12 (1994), 245–256.

DARRELL LUM

''Yahk Fahn, Auntie''
Wong, Sau-ling C. *Reading Asian American Literature* . . . , 72–73.

LINDIWE MABUZA

''Wake''
Viola, André. ''Children of Soweto: Lindiwe Mabuza's Short Story 'Wake,' '' *Commonwealth Essays & Studs*, 15, i (1992), 39–44.

MARY McCARTHY

''Cruel and Barbarous Treatment''
Schmidt, Rita T. ''Un juego de máscaras: Nelida Piñon y Mary McCarthy,'' *Escritura*, 16 (1991), 261–263, 265–267, 269–270.

CARSON McCULLERS

''The Ballad of the Sad Café''
Kieft, Ruth M. ''The Love Ethos of Porter, Welty, and McCullers,'' in Manning, Carol S., Ed. *The Female Tradition* . . . , 253, 254–255.

"A Tree, A Rock, A Cloud"
+Bohner, Charles H. *Instructor's Manual* . . . , 3rd ed., 95.

IAN McEWAN

"Solid Geometry"
Brown, Richard. "Postmodern Americas in the Fiction of Angela Carter, Martin Amis and Ian McEwan," in Massa, Ann, and Alistair Stead, Eds. *Forked Tongues* . . . , 104–105.

JOHN McGAHERN

"All Sorts of Impossible Things"
Sampson, Denis. *Outstaring Nature's Eye* . . . , 171.

"Along the Edges"
Sampson, Denis. *Outstaring Nature's Eye* . . . , 179–180.

"A Ballad"
Sampson, Denis. *Outstaring Nature's Eye* . . . , 204–205.

"The Beginning of an Idea"
Sampson, Denis. *Outstaring Nature's Eye* . . . , 165–170.

"The Conversion of William Kirkwood"
Sampson, Denis. *Outstaring Nature's Eye* . . . , 200–202.

"Crossing the Line"
Sampson, Denis. *Outstaring Nature's Eye* . . . , 203–204.

"Doorways"
Sampson, Denis. *Outstaring Nature's Eye* . . . , 176–179.

"Eddie Mac"
Sampson, Denis. *Outstaring Nature's Eye* . . . , 179–200.

"Gold Watch"
Sampson, Denis. *Outstaring Nature's Eye* . . . , 182–187.

"High Ground"
Sampson, Denis. *Outstaring Nature's Eye* . . . , 203.

"Korea"
Sampson, Denis. *Outstaring Nature's Eye* . . . , 94–99.

"Like All Other Men"
Sampson, Denis. *Outstaring Nature's Eye* . . . , 205–206.

"My Love, My Umbrella"
Sampson, Denis. *Outstaring Nature's Eye* . . . , 99–102.

"Oldfashioned"
Sampson, Denis. *Outstaring Nature's Eye* . . . , 192–197.

"Parachutes"
Sampson, Denis. *Outstaring Nature's Eye* . . . , 207–214.

"The Recruiting Officer"
Sampson, Denis. *Outstaring Nature's Eye* . . . , 102–108.

"Sierra Leone"
Sampson, Denis. *Outstaring Nature's Eye* . . . , 180–182.

"Swallows"
Sampson, Denis. *Outstaring Nature's Eye* . . . , 173–174.

"Wheels"
Sampson, Denis. *Outstaring Nature's Eye* . . . , 89–94.

"The Wine Breath"
Sampson, Denis. *Outstaring Nature's Eye* . . . , 174–176.

THOMAS McGUANE

"Flight"
Cook, Nancy S. "Investment in Place: Thomas McGuane in Montana," in Meldrum, Barbara H., Ed. *Old West—New West* . . . , 221–222.

"Like a Leaf"
Cook, Nancy S. "Investment . . . ," 222–226.

JOHN HENRY MacKAY

"A Farewell: A Late Letter"
Kennedy, Hubert. "Hiding in the Open: John Henry MacKay's 'A Farewell,' " *Paidika*, 2, iii (1991), 53–56.

REGINALD McKNIGHT

"Into Night"
Megan, Carolyn E. "New Perceptions on Rhythm in Reginald McKnight's Fiction," *Kenyon R*, 16, ii (1994), 58–62.

"The Kind of Light that Shines on Texas"
Megan, Carolyn E. "New Perceptions . . . ," 57–58.

MICHAEL McLAVERTY

"Pigeons"
Lubbers, Klaus. "Michael McLaverty: 'Pigeons,' " in Lubbers, Klaus, Ed. *Die Englische* . . . , 315–323.

NORMAN MacLEAN

"A River Runs Through It"
Ford, James E. "When 'life . . . becomes literature': The Neo-Aristotelian Poetics of Norman Maclean's 'A River Runs Through It,' " *Stud Short Fiction*, 30 (1993), 525–534.

REBECA MACTAS

"Simple Heart"
Glickman, Nora. "Jewish Women Writers in Latin America," in Baskin, Judith R., Ed. *Women of the Word . . .* , 302–303.

"Springs"
Glickman, Nora. "Jewish Women Writers . . . ," 303.

NAGUIB MAHFOUZ

"The Ambergris Pearl"
'Atiyya, Ahmad Muhammad. "Naguib Mahfouz and the Short Story," in Le Gassick, Trevor, Ed., *Critical Perspectives . . .* , 22–23.

"The Bartender"
'Atiyya, Ahmad Muhammad. "Naguib Mahfouz . . . ," 19.

"Beneath the Shelter"
'Atiyya, Ahmad Muhammad. "Naguib Mahfouz . . . ," 20.

"Closeness to God"
'Atiyya, Ahmad Muhammad. "Naguib Mahfouz . . . ," 14–16.

"A Cup of Tea"
'Atiyya, Ahmad Muhammad. "Naguib Mahfouz . . . ," 24–25.

"The Echo"
'Atiyya, Ahmad Muhammad. "Naguib Mahfouz . . . ," 19.

"Lover's Lane"
'Atiyya, Ahmad Muhammad. "Naguib Mahfouz . . . ," 22.

"The Mosque down the Lane"
'Atiyya, Ahmad Muhammad. "Naguib Mahfouz . . . ," 16.

"Under the Bus Shelter"
Snir, Reuven. "The 'World Upsidedown' in Modern Arabic Literature: New Literary Renditions of an Antique Religious Topos," *Edebiyât*, 5, i (1994), 57–60.

"A Word Misunderstood"
'Atiyya, Ahmad Muhammad. "Naguib Mahfouz . . . ," 18–19.

VLADIMIR MAKANIN

"A Story About a Story"
Isenberg, Charles. *Telling Silence . . .* , 136–142.

ELENA GRIGOR'EVNA MAKAROVA

"Needlefish"
Barker, Adele M. "The World of Our Mothers," in Aiken, Susan H.,

Adele M. Barker, Maya Koreneva, and Ekaterina Stetsenko, Eds. *Dialogues/Dialogi* . . . , 258–264.

Koreneva, Maya. "Hopes and Nightmares of the Young," in Aiken, Susan H., Adele M. Barker, Maya Koreneva, and Ekaterina Stetsenko, Eds. *Dialogues/Dialogi* . . . , 273–278.

BERNARD MALAMUD

"The Girl of My Dreams"

Salzberg, Joel. "The 'Loathly Landlady,' Chagallian Unions, and Malamudian Parody: 'The Girl of My Dreams' Revisited," *Stud Short Fiction*, 30 (1993), 543–554.

"The Jewbird"

Hanson, Philip. "Horror and Ethnic Identity in 'The Jewbird,' " *Stud Short Fiction*, 30 (1993), 359–366.

"The Letter"

Lasher, Lawrence M. "Plenty of News: Bernard Malamud's 'The Letter,' " *Stud Short Fiction*, 31 (1994), 657–666.

"The Magic Barrel"

+Bohner, Charles H. *Instructor's Manual* . . . , 3rd ed., 89–90.

"The Mourners"

Baris, Sharon D. "Intertextuality and Reader Responsibility: Living On in Malamud's 'The Mourners,' " Spolsky, Ellen, Ed. *Summoning: Ideas* . . . , 229–249.

MARILÚ MALLET

"Affaire classée"

Hazelton, Hugh. "Quebec Hispánico: Themes of Exile and Integration in the Writing of Latin Americans Living in Quebec," *Canadian Lit*, 142–143 (1994), 130.

"La mutation"

Hazelton, Hugh. "Quebec Hispánico . . . ," 130–131.

IVÁN MÁNDY

"Crossing"

Erdódy, Edit. "Symbolic Transsubstantiation and Autobiographical References in Iván Mándy's Short Stories: On the Volumes 'Crossings' and 'Autobiography,' " *Acta Litteraria*, 33, i–iv (1991), 336–339.

K. S. MANIAM

"Ratnamuni"

Lowenberg, Peter H. "Language Transfer and Levels of Meaning

Potential in Malaysian English,'' *Georgetown Univ. Round Table*, [n.v.] (1992), 50–51.

THOMAS MANN

"Death in Venice"

Vidan, Ivo. "Conrad and Thomas Mann," in Carabine, Keith, Owen Knowles, and Wieslaw Krajka, Eds. *Contexts* . . . , 266–276.

"Gefallen"

Kamla, Thomas A. "Thomas Mann's 'Gefallen': États d'âme and the Bahrian New Psychology," *Germ Q*, 66 (1993), 513–523.

"Das Gesetz"

Japp, Uwe. "Menschliche Annäherung an das Göttliche: Thomas Manns Erzählung 'Das Gesetz,' " in Hahn, Gerhard, and Ernst Weber, Eds. *Zwischen* . . . , 181–188.

"Herr und Hund"

Orlik, Franz. "'Wildfremd und sonderbar': Thomas Manns 'Idyll' 'Herr und Hund' aus dem Jahr 1918," *Wirkendes Wort*, 43 (1993), 597–607.

"Schwere Stunde"

Sandberg, Hans-Joachim. "Glück und Größe: Schattenspiele brüderlich geteilt," *Thomas Mann Jahrbuch*, 5 (1992), 80–96.

"Tobias Mindernickel"

Scholtmeijer, Marian. *Animal Victims* . . . , 159–164.

KATHERINE MANSFIELD

"At the Bay"

Boddy, Gillian. " 'Finding the Treasure,' Coming Home: Katherine Mansfield in 1921–1922," in Robinson, Roger, Ed. *Katherine Mansfield* . . . , 182–186.

+Hankin, C. A. "Katherine Mansfield and Her Confessional Stories," in Nathan, Rhoda B. *Critical Essays* . . . , 26–36.

Chakravarty, Radharani. "'Like a Child with a Box of Bricks': Katherine Mansfield's New Zealand Stories," in Dhawan, R. K., and William Tonetto, Eds. *New Zealand Literature Today*, 50–51.

"Bliss"

Dunbar, Pamela. "What Does Bertha Want?: A Re-reading of Katherine Mansfield's 'Bliss,' " *Women's Stud*, 4, ii (1988), 18–31; rpt. Nathan, Rhoda B., Ed. *Critical Essays* . . . , 128–139.

McFall, Gardner. "Poetry and Performance in Katherine Mansfield's 'Bliss,' " in Nathan, Rhoda B., Ed. *Critical Essays* . . . , 140–150.

Meisel, Perry. "What the Reader Knows; or the French One," in Robinson, Roger, Ed. *Katherine Mansfield* . . . , 115–116.

Mortimer, Armine K. "Fortifications of Desire: Reading the Second

Story in Katherine Mansfield's 'Bliss,' " *Narrative*, 2, i (1994), 41–52.
Wheeler, Kathleen. *'Modernist' Women* . . . , 121–140.

"A Cup of Tea"
Chakravarty, Radharani. " 'Like a Child . . . ,' " 44.

"A Dill Pickle"
+Bohner, Charles H. *Instructor's Manual* . . . , 3rd ed., 90–91.

"The Doll's House"
Mukherjee, Indibar. "Katherine Mansfield as a Short-Story Writer," in Dhawan, R. K., and William Tonetto, Eds. *New Zealand Literature Today*, 41–42.

"The Escape"
New, W. H. "Reading 'The Escape,' " in Robinson, Roger, Ed. *Katherine Mansfield* . . . , 90–111.

"Feuille d'Album"
Bonheim, Helmut. "Katherine Mansfield: 'Feuille d'Album,' " in Lubbers, Klaus, Ed. *Die Englische* . . . , 186–195.

"The Fly"
Mukherjee, Indibar. "Katherine Mansfield . . . ," 42–43.
O'Sullivan, Vincent. "'Finding the Pattern, Solving the Problem': Katherine Mansfield and the New Zealand European," in Robinson, Roger, Ed. *Katherine Mansfield* . . . , 19–20.
Pickering, James H., and Jeffrey D. Hoeper. *Instructor's Manual* . . . , 55–56.
Scholtmeijer, Marian. *Animal Victims* . . . , 164–169.

"The Garden Party"
Charters, Ann. *Resources* . . . , 110–111.
Nownes, Nicholas L. " 'The Garden Party': Responding to Katherine Mansfield's Invitation," *World Lit Written Engl*, 33, ii & 34, i (1993–1994), 49–57.

"Je ne parle pas français"
Meisel, Perry. "What the Reader . . . ," 113–115, 116–118.
Ramaswamy, S. "Katherine Mansfield: A Study," in Dhawan, R. K., and William Tonetto, Eds. *New Zealand Literature Today*, 32–37.

"Kezia and Tui"
Orr, Bridget. "Reading with the Taint of the Pioneer: Katherine Mansfield and Settler Criticism," *Landfall*, 43, iv (1989), 457–459; rpt. Nathan, Rhoda B., Ed. *Critical Essays* . . . , 56–58.

"A Married Man's Story"
Calder, Alex. "My Katherine Mansfield," in Robinson, Roger, Ed. *Katherine Mansfield* . . . , 125–133.

"Millie"
Wevers, Lydia. "How Kathleen Beauchamp Was Kidnapped," *Women's Studies Journal*, 4, ii (1988), 15–16; rpt. Nathan, Rhoda B., Ed. *Critical Essays* . . . , 45–46.

"Miss Brill"
+Bohner, Charles H. *Instructor's Manual* . . . , 3rd ed., 91–92.

"Poison"
Calder, Alex. "My Katherine . . . ," 122–124.

"Prelude" [previously "The Aloe" but originally "Mary"]
Chakravarty, Radharani. "'Like a Child . . . ," 48–50.
+Hankin, C. A. "Katherine Mansfield and Her Confessional Stories," in Nathan, Rhoda B. *Critical Essays* . . . , 12–26.
Parkin-Gounelas, Ruth. "Katherine Mansfield Reading Other Women: The Personality of the Text," in Robinson, Roger, Ed. *Katherine Mansfield* . . . , 50–51.

"Sun and Moon"
Bardolph, Jacqueline. "The French Connection: Bardol," in Robinson, Roger, Ed. *Katherine Mansfield* . . . , 165–170.

"The Woman at the Store"
Charters, Ann. *Resources* . . . , 111–113.
Wevers, Lydia. "How Kathleen . . . ," 12–15; rpt. Nathan, Rhoda B., Ed. *Critical Essays* . . . , 43–45.

VLADIMIR MARAMZIN

"The Two-Toned Blond"
Lowe, David. "Maramzin's 'Two-Toned Blond' and Nabokov's *Lolita*," *Int'l Fiction R*, 21 (1994), 85–89.

PIERRE MARCELLE

"La Démolition"
Cook, Margaret. " 'La démolition' de Pierre Marcelle ou le crime du signe," *Tangence*, 38 (1992), 55–64.

ANASTASIIA MARCHENKO

"Hills"
Zirin, Mary F. "Women's Prose Fiction in the Age of Realism," in Clyman, Toby W., and Diana Greene, Eds. *Women Writers* . . . , 81.

"A Near Miss"
Zirin, Mary F. "Women's Prose . . . ," 81.

"Too Late!"
Zirin, Mary F. "Women's Prose . . . ," 80–81.

JAVIER MARÍAS

"Mientras ellas duermen"
Izquierdo, Luis. "Una approximación a los relatos de Javier Marías," *Insula*, 568 (April, 1994), 21.

RENÉ MARQUÉS

"El juramento"
Cabellero Wangüemert, María A. "Discurso histórico y carnavalización de la historia: 'El juramento' de René Marqués," *Revista Iberoamericana*, 59 (1993), 145–156.

PAULA MARSHALL

"To Da-Duh in Memoriam"
Davies, Carole B. *Black Women . . .*, 117–118.

VALERIE MARTIN

"Sea Lovers"
Smith, R. McClure. "Valerie Martin's Re-visionary Gothic: The Example of 'Sea Lovers,' " *Critique*, 34 (1993), 171–181.

CARMEN MARTÍN GAITE

"El pastel del diablo"
Jiménez, Mercedes. " 'El pastel del diablo': Un juego alegórico sobre la iniciación literaria de Carmen Martín Gaite," *Letras Femeninas*, 18, i–ii (1992), 83–90.

LUIS MARTÍN SANTOS

"Historia de amor"
Molinaro, Nina L. "The Rhetoric of Silence in Luis Martín-Santos's *Apólogos*," *J Interdisciplinary Lit Stud*, 5, ii (1993), 226–228.

"El muchacho del fusil de goma"
Molinaro, Nina L. "The Rhetoric . . . ," 229–232.

"Razonamiento"
Molinaro, Nina L. "The Rhetoric . . . ," 228–229.

BOBBY ANN MASON

"Shiloh"
Cooke, Steward J. "Mason's 'Shiloh,' " *Explicator*, 51 (1993), 196–199.
Levy, Andrew. *The Culture . . .*, 113–117, 118–119.
Lohafer, Susan. "Stops on the Way to 'Shiloh': A Special Case for Literary Empiricism," *Style*, 27 (1993), 395–406.
Pickering, James H., and Jeffrey D. Hoeper. *Instructor's Manual . . .*, 117–119.

JAMES MATTHEWS

"The Park"
Povey, John F. "English-language Fiction from South Africa," in Owomoyela, Oyekan, Ed. *A History* . . . , 94.

"The Party"
Povey, John F. "English-language . . . ," 94–95.

ANA MARÍA MATUTE

"El incendio"
Nichols, Geraldine C. "Limits Unlimited: The Strategic Use of Fantasy in Contemporary Women's Fiction of Spain," in Vidal, Hernán, Ed. *Cultural and Historical* . . . , 115.

"Pecado de omisión"
Pennington, Eric. "Matute's 'Pecado de omisión,' " *Letras Femeninas*, 20, i–ii (1994), 141–148.

W. SOMERSET MAUGHAM

"The Ant and the Grasshopper"
Sopher, H. "Somerset Maugham's 'The Ant and the Grasshopper'—The Literary Implications of Its Multilayered Structure," *Stud Short Fiction*, 31 (1994), 109–114.

"The Luncheon"
Nischik, Reingard M. "W. Somerset Maugham: 'The Luncheon,' " in Lubbers, Klaus, Ed. *Die Englische* . . . , 156–175.

"The Outstation"
+Bohner, Charles H. *Instructor's Manual* . . . , 3rd ed., 92–94.

"The Pool"
Holtsmark, Erling B. "Maugham's 'The Pool': The Classical Influence," *Classical & Mod Lit*, 13 (1993), 217–227.

"Sanatorium"
Costa, Richard H. *An Appointment with* . . . , 21–24.

GUY DE MAUPASSANT

"Allouma"
Fusco, Richard. *Maupassant* . . . , 61–63.
Stivale, Charles J. *The Art* . . . , 139–140.
———. "Guy de Maupassant and Narrative Strategies of 'Othering,' " *Australian J of French Stud*, 30 (1993), 246, 247–248.

"L'Armoire"
Stivale, Charles J. *The Art* . . . , 128.

"Au bois"
Shryock, Richard. *Tales of Storytelling* . . . , 10–11.

"Autres temps"
Stivale, Charles J. *The Art* . . . , 46–47, 49.

"Aux champs"
Fusco, Richard. *Maupassant* . . . , 67–70.

"L'Aventure de Walter Schnaffs"
Fusco, Richard. *Maupassant* . . . , 19–20.

"Une aventure parisienne"
Stivale, Charles J. *The Art* . . . , 158–159.

"Beside a Dead Man"
Knowles, Owen. " 'Whose Afraid of Arthur Schopenhauer?': A New Context for Conrad's 'Heart of Darkness,' " *Nineteenth-Century Lit*, 49 (1994), 83–86.

"Boule de Suif" ["Tallow Ball"]
Fusco, Richard. *Maupassant* . . . , 85–88.
Stivale, Charles J. *The Art* . . . , 106–110, 119–120.

"Ça Ira"
Stivale, Charles J. *The Art* . . . , 130–131.

"Les Caresses"
Stivale, Charles J. *The Art* . . . , 35–36.

"Le Cas de Mme Luneau"
Stivale, Charles J. *The Art* . . . , 46–49.

"La Confidence"
Stivale, Charles J. *The Art* . . . , 153–155.

"A Coward"
Fusco, Richard. *Maupassant* . . . , 30–31, 54, 56.

"Cri d'alarme"
Stivale, Charles J. *The Art* . . . , 31–33.

"Le Donneur d'eau bénite"
Fusco, Richard. *Maupassant* . . . , 11–12.

"Les Épingles"
Stivale, Charles J. *The Art* . . . , 151–152.

"Étrennes"
Stivale, Charles J. *The Art* . . . , 150–151.

"Fou?"
Fusco, Richard. *Maupassant* . . . , 37–38.

"Le Gâteau"
Stivale, Charles J. *The Art* . . . , 160–161.

"Le Horla"
Fonyi, Antonia. "La Limite: Garantie précaire de l'identité," *Revue d'Histoire Littéraire*, 94, v (1994), 757–764.
Fusco, Richard. *Maupassant* . . . , 57–61.
Prince, Gerald. " 'Le Horla,' Sex, and Colonization," in Motte, Warren, and Gerald Prince, Eds. *Alteratives*, 181–188.
Shryock, Richard. *Tales of Storytelling* . . . , 32–33.
Stivale, Charles J. *The Art* . . . , 178–179, 188–194, 200–201.

"Les Idées du colonel"
Stivale, Charles J. *The Art* . . . , 90–98, 123.

"L'Inconnue"
Stivale, Charles J. *The Art* . . . , 136–137.

"The Jewels"
Fusco, Richard. *Maupassant* . . . , 69–70.

"The Jewels of M. Lantin"
Charters, Ann. *Resources* . . . , 114–115.

"Joseph"
Stivale, Charles J. *The Art* . . . , 42–44.

"The Kiss"
Fusco, Richard. *Maupassant* . . . , 80–81.
Stivale, Charles J. *The Art* . . . , 37–38.

"Letters"
Fusco, Richard. *Maupassant* . . . , 79–80.

"Le Lit"
Stivale, Charles J. *The Art* . . . , 33–35.

"The Little Soldier"
Charters, Ann. *Resources* . . . , 116.

"A Mad Man"
Fusco, Richard. *Maupassant* . . . , 56–57.

"Madame Tellier's Establishment"
Jobst, Jack W., and W. J. Williamson. "Hemingway and Maupassant: More Light on 'The Light of the World,' " *Hemingway R*, 13, ii (1994), 54–57.
Morrison, Ian R. "La Religion dans 'la Maison Tellier,' " *Neophilologus*, 78, iv (1994), 521–528.
Stivale, Charles J. *The Art* . . . , 114–120, 134, 135.

"Mademoiselle Fifi"
Stivale, Charles J. *The Art* . . . , 99–105, 113–114.

"Le Mariage du lieutenant Laré"
Stivale, Charles J. *The Art* . . . , 90–98.

"Marroca"
Stivale, Charles J. *The Art* . . . , 137, 138, 139.

"La Mère aux monstres"
Stivale, Charles J. *The Art* . . . , 165–166, 167.

"Misti"
Stivale, Charles J. *The Art* . . . , 149–150.

"Monsieur Parent"
Stivale, Charles J. *The Art* . . . , 181.

"Mots d'amour"
Stivale, Charles J. *The Art* . . . , 36–37.

"Mouche"
Stivale, Charles J. *The Art* . . . , 131.

"La Moustache"
Stivale, Charles J. *The Art* . . . , 38–39.

"The Necklace"
+Bohner, Charles H. *Instructor's Manual* . . . , 3rd ed., 94.
Charters, Ann. *Resources* . . . , 117–118.
Fusco, Richard. *Maupassant* . . . , 27–30.
Nicholson, Mervyn. "Peripety Cues in Short Fiction," *CEA Critic*, 56, ii (1994), 44–45.
Pickering, James H., and Jeffrey D. Hoeper. *Instructor's Manual* . . . , 24–25.

"L'Odysée d'une fille"
Stivale, Charles J. *The Art* . . . , 128–129.

"The Olive Orchard"
Fusco, Richard. *Maupassant* . . . , 31–32.
Stivale, Charles J. *The Art* . . . , 181–188.

"Une Partie de campagne"
Fusco, Richard. *Maupassant* . . . , 14–15.

"Paul's Woman"
Fusco, Richard. *Maupassant* . . . , 51–54.
Stivale, Charles J. *The Art* . . . , 132–134.
———. "Guy de Maupassant . . . ," 444–446.

"La Petite Roque"
Stivale, Charles J. *The Art* . . . , 53–83, 87.

"Pétition d'un viveur malgré lui"
Stivale, Charles J. *The Art* . . . , 163–164.

"Les Prisonniers"
Fusco, Richard. *Maupassant* . . . , 20–21.

"Promenade"
Fusco, Richard. *Maupassant* . . . , 76–77.

"Regret"
Fusco, Richard. *Maupassant* . . . , 73–76.

"Rencontre"
Stivale, Charles J. *The Art* . . . , 166–167.

"Le Rendez-vous"
Fusco, Richard. *Maupassant* . . . , 82–83.
Stivale, Charles J. *The Art* . . . , 152.

"Rose"
Stivale, Charles J. *The Art* . . . , 41–42.

"Rouerie"
Stivale, Charles J. *The Art* . . . , 152–153.

"Un sage"
Stivale, Charles J. *The Art* . . . , 162–163.

"Le Signe"
Shryock, Richard. *Tales of Storytelling* . . . , 132–133.
Stivale, Charles J. *The Art* . . . , 43–46.

"Simon's Papa"
Fusco, Richard. *Maupassant* . . . , 12–14.

"Les Soeurs Rondoli"
Stivale, Charles J. *The Art* . . . , 124–126.

"Souvenir"
Stivale, Charles J. *The Art* . . . , 90–98.

"Suicides"
Fusco, Richard. *Maupassant* . . . , 36–38.

"Sur l'eau"
Fusco, Richard. *Maupassant* . . . , 23–26.

"Tribunaux rustiques"
Stivale, Charles J. *The Art* . . . , 49–51.

"Two Friends"
Fusco, Richard. *Maupassant* . . . , 71–73.

"Useless Beauty"
Fusco, Richard. *Maupassant* . . . , 91–96.
Stivale, Charles J. *The Art* . . . , 168–175, 179–180.

"Le Vieux"
Roy, Alain. "Le Thème de la pomme dans 'Le Vieux' de Maupassant ou l'ombilic du texte," *R Histoire Lit*, 94, v (1994), 742–756.

"The Wolf"
Fusco, Richard. *Maupassant* . . . , 40–41.

"Yveline Samouris"
Stivale, Charles J. *The Art* . . . , 126–127.

"Yvette"
Fusco, Richard. *Maupassant* . . . , 88–91.
Stivale, Charles J. *The Art* . . . , 126–128.

DAPHNE DU MAURIER

"The Birds"
Rance, Nicholas. "Not like Men in Books, Murdering Women: Daphne du Maurier and the Infernal World of Popular Fiction," in Bloom, Clive, Ed. *Creepers* . . . , 95–96.

MARINA MAYORAL

"Al otro lado"
Camino Noia, María. "Claves de la narrativa de Marina Mayoral," *Letras Femeninas*, 19, i–ii (1993), 34–35.

"Unha árbore, un adeus"
Camino Noia, María. "Claves . . . ," 38.

"La única libertad"
Camino Noia, María. "Claves . . . ," 35–37.

HERMAN MELVILLE

"Bartleby the Scrivener"
Barnett, Louise K. *Authority and Speech* . . . , 77–87.
+Bohner, Charles H. *Instructor's Manual* . . . , 3rd ed., 96–97.
Charolles, Michel. "Bartleby le magnifique," in Bourquin, Jacques, and Daniel Jacobi, Eds. *Mélanges* . . . , 211–222.
Charters, Ann. *Resources* . . . , 119.
Hoag, Ronald W. "The Corpse in the Office: Mortality, Mutability and Salvation in 'Bartleby, the Scrivener,' " *ESQ: J Am Renaissance*, 38 (1992), 119–142.
Kiely, Robert. *Reverse Tradition* . . . , 79–80.
Morgan, Winifred. " 'Bartleby' and the Failure of Conventional Virtue," *Renascence*, 45 (1993), 257–271.
Piastrellini de Cuadrado, Beatriz G. " 'Bartleby, el escribiente. Una historia de Wall Street,' " *Revista Lit Modernas*, 24 (1991), 47–57.
Pickering, James H., and Jeffrey D. Hoeper. *Instructor's Manual* . . . , 15–16.
Post-Lauria, Sheila. "Canonical Texts and Context: The Example of Herman Meville's 'Bartleby, the Scrivener: A Story of Wall Street,' " *Coll Lit*, 20, ii (1993), 196–205.
Ruttenburg, Nancy. "Melville's Handsome Sailor: The Anxiety of Innocence," *Am Lit*, 66 (1994), 83–103.
Tallack, Douglas. *The Nineteenth-Century American Short Story* . . . , 148–180.
Vogel, Dan. "Bartleby / Job / America," *Midwest Q*, 35 (1994), 151–161.
Weiner, Susan. " 'Bartleby': Representation, Reproduction and the Law," *J Am Culture*, 17, ii (1994), 65–73.
Weinstein, Arnold. *Nobody's Home* . . . , 25–34, 37–43.

"The Bell-Tower"
Castronovo, Russ. "Radical Configurations of History in the Era of American Slavery," *Amer Lit*, 65 (1993), 534–543.

"Benito Cereno"
Barnett, Louise K. *Authority and Speech* . . . , 75–77.
Bloch, Bernard B. "Babo and Babeuf: Melville's 'Benito Cereno,' " *Melville Soc Extracts*, 96 (March, 1994), 9–12.
Charters, Ann. *Resources* . . . , 120–122.

Colatrella, Carol. "The Significant Silence of Race: *La Cousine Bette* and 'Benito Cereno,' " *Comp Lit*, 46 (1994), 241, 243–244, 251–258, 260–262.
Haegert, John. "Voicing Slavery Through Silence: Narrative Mutiny in Melville's 'Benito Cereno,' " *Mosaic*, 26, ii (1993), 21–38.
Horsley-Meacham, Gloria. "The Johnsonian Jest in 'Benito Cereno,' " *ANQ*, 6, i, N.S. (1993), 17–18.
Kiely, Robert. *Reverse Tradition* . . . , 61–80.
Martin, Terry J. "The Idea of Nature in 'Benito Cereno,' " *Stud Short Fiction*, 30 (1993), 161–168.
Sundquist, Eric. J. *To Wake the Nations* . . . , 22–23, 135–184.

"Billy Budd"
Barnett, Louise K. *Authority and Speech* . . . , 96–98.
Bartley, William. " 'Measured Forms' and Orphic Eloquence: The Style of Herman Melville's 'Billy Budd,' " *Univ Toronto Q*, 59 (1990), 516–534.
Brentano, Alisa von. "Herman Melville and 'The Sane Madness of Vital Truth," in Rieger, Branimir M., Ed. *Dionysus in Literature* . . . , 160–166.
Douglas, Lawrence. "Discursive Limits: Narrative and Judgment in 'Billy Budd,' " *Mosaic*, 27, iv (1994), 141–160.
Hocks, Richard A. "Melville and 'The Rise of Realism': The Dilemma of History in 'Billy Budd,' " *Am Lit Realism*, 26, ii (1994), 60–81.
Michael, Colette. " 'Billy Budd': An Allegory on the Rights of Man," in Kronegger, Marlies, and Anna-Teresa Tymieniecka, Eds. *Allegory Old* . . . , 251–258.
Mutalik Desai, A. A. "Innocence and Tragedy in Melville's 'Billy Budd,' " *Indian Scholar*, 13, i (1991), 47–53.
Phillips, Kathy J. " 'Billy Budd' as Anti-Homophobic Text," *Coll Engl*, 56 (1994), 896–909.
Ruttenberg. Nancy. "Melville's Handsome Sailor: The Anxiety of Innocence," *Am Lit*, 66 (1994), 83–103.
Shaw, Peter. "The Fate of a Story," *Am Scholar*, 62 (1993), 591–600.
———. *Recovering American Literature*, 75–99.
Smith, Stephanie A. *Conceived by Liberty* . . . , 184–188.
Sterne, Richard C. *Dark Mirror* . . . , 168–180.
Yoder, Jonathan A. "The Protagonists' Rainbow in 'Billy Budd': Critical Trimming of Truth's Ragged Edge," *ATQ*, 7, N.S. (1993), 97–113.

"Cock-a-Doodle-Doo"
Lutwack, Leonard. *Birds in Literature*, 92–94, 95.
Young, Philip. *The Private Melville*, 87–98.

"Daniel Orme"
Young, Philip. *The Private Melville*, 145–158.

"The Encantadas"
Barnett, Louise K. *Authority and Speech* . . . , 74–75.

"Fragment 2"
Obuchowski, Peter A. "Melville's First Short Story: A Parody of Poe," *Stud Am Fiction*, 21 (1993), 97–102.

"I and My Chimney"
Young, Philip. *The Private Melville*, 99–107.

"The Lightning-Rod Man"
Baldwin, Marc D. "Herman Melville's 'The Lightning-Rod Man': Discourse of the Deal," *Cahiers de la Nouvelle*, 21 (1993), 9–17.
Young, Philip. *The Private Melville*, 75–85.

"The Paradise of Bachelors and the Tartarus of Maids"
Bromell, Nicholas K. *By the Sweat* . . . , 72–74.
Durand, Régis. "Herman Melville: 'The Paradise of Bachelors and the Tartarus of Maids'—The Signs of Origin," in Lubbers, Klaus, Ed. *Die Englische* . . . , 52–59.
Weyler, Karen A. "Melville's 'The Paradise of Bachelors and the Tartarus of Maids': A Dialogue about Experience, Understanding, and Truth," *Stud Short Fiction*, 31 (1994), 461–469.
Young, Philip. *The Private Melville*, 111–125.

PAULINE MELVILLE

"The Conversion of Millicent Vernon"
Morris, Mervyn. "Cross-Cultural . . . ," 83.

"Eat Labba and Drink Creek Water"
Morris, Mervyn. "Cross-Cultural Impersonations: Pauline Melville's 'Shape-shifter,' " *Ariel*, 24, i (1993), 80–82.

"The Girl with the Celestial Limb"
Morris, Mervyn. "Cross-Cultural . . . ," 86, 87.

"The Iron and the Radio Have Gone"
Morris, Mervyn. "Cross-Cultural . . . ," 83–84.

"McGregor's Journey"
Morris, Mervyn. "Cross-Cultural . . . ," 84–86.

"A Quarrelsome Man"
Morris, Mervyn. "Cross-Cultural . . . ," 86.

"The Truth Is in the Clothes"
Morris, Mervyn. "Cross-Cultural . . . ," 86, 87–88.

"You Left the Door Open"
Morris, Mervyn. "Cross-Cultural . . . ," 88.

LAURA MÉNDEZ DE CUENCA

"Rosas muertas"
Vargas, Margarita. "Romanticism," in Foster, David W., Ed. *Mexican Literature* . . . , 155.

GUILLERMO MENESE

"Adolescencia"
Sifontes Greco, Lourdes C. "Guillermo Meneses: Del cuento al cuaderno metaficcional," *Revista Iberoamericana*, 60 (1994), 170–171.

"Borrachera"
Sifontes Greco, Lourdes C. "Guillermo Meneses . . . ," 171–172.

"El duque"
Sifontes Greco, Lourdes C. "Guillermo Meneses . . . ," 172–173.

"La mano junto al muro"
Sifontes Greco, Lourdes C. "Guillermo Meneses . . . ," 175–177.

"Tardío regreso a través de un espejo"
Sifontes Greco, Lourdes C. "Guillermo Meneses . . . ," 174–175.

MARTHA MERCADER

"Los astros decían que justo en La Habana"
Fares, Gustavo, and Eliana Hermann. "Exilios internos: El viaje en cinco escritoras," *Hispanic J*, 15, i (1994), 26.

JOSÉ MARÍA MERINO

"Del libro de Naufragios"
Glenn, Kathleen M. "Border Crossings, Re-encounters, and Recuperations in José María Merino's *El viajero perdido*," *Hispanic J*, 15, ii (1994), 315–317.

"Oaxacoalco"
Glenn, Kathleen M. "Border Crossings . . . ," 312–313.

"Las palabras del mundo"
Glenn, Kathleen M. "Border Crossings . . . ," 315.

"Un personaje absorto"
Glenn, Kathleen M. "Border Crossings . . . ," 311–312.

"La última tonada"
Glenn, Kathleen M. "Border Crossings . . . ," 313–314.

"El viajero"
Glenn, Kathleen M. "Border Crossings . . . ," 309–311.

CHARLOTTE MEWS

"A White Night"
Showalter, Elaine. "Introduction," in Showalter, Elaine, Ed. *Daughters of Decadence* . . . , xvii–xviii.

CONRAD FERDINAND MEYER

"Gustav Adolfs Page"
Gerlach, U. Henry. "Gustav Adolfs Page—Der unzulänglich vekappte Feigling? Eine Neuinterpretation von C. F. Meyers Novelle," *Wirkendes Wort*, 43 (1993), 212–225.

"Der Heilige"
Pizer, John. "Double and Other: C. F. Meyer's 'Der Heilige,' " *Seminar*, 30 (1994), 347–359.

"Plautus im Nonnenkloster"
Gerlach, U. Henry. "Doppelkreuz und Doppelspiel in C. F. Meyers 'Plautus im Nonnenkloster,' " *Germ Q*, 67 (1994), 338–346.

LEONIE MEYERHOF

"Die drei Nixen"
Hempen, Daniela. "Das Bild der Wasserfrau bei Meyerhof, Bachmann und Röhner," *Seminar*, 30 (1994), 383–386.

GUSTAV MEYRINK

"Das Geheimnis des Schlosses Hathaway"
Stiffler, Muriel W. *The German Ghost Story* . . . , 103–105.

"Der Kardinal Napellus"
Stiffler, Muriel W. *The German Ghost Story* . . . , 105–110.

"Die Pflanzen des Dr. Cinderella"
Stiffler, Muriel W. *The German Ghost Story* . . . , 95–102.

HENRI MICHAUX

"Un Certain Plume—Plume au restaurant"
Shryock, Richard. *Tales of Storytelling* . . . , 33–35.

SUSAN MINOT

"Lust"
Pickering, James H., and Jeffrey D. Hoeper. *Instructor's Manual* . . . , 120–121.

MISHIMA YUKIO

"Patriotism"
+Bohner, Charles H. *Instructor's Manual* . . . , 3rd ed., 97–98.

ROHINTON MISTRY

"Lend Me Your Light"
Heble, Ajay. " 'A Foreign Presence in the Stall': Towards a Poetics of Cultural Hybridity in Rohinton Mistry's Migration Stories," *Canadian Lit*, 137 (1993), 56–60.

"Squatter"
Heble, Ajay. " 'A Foreign . . . ," 51–56.

ANA MARÍA MOIX

"Ella comía cardos"
Cook, Beverly R. "Madness as Metaphor in Two Short Stories by Ana María Moix," in Adamson, Ginette, and Eunice Myers, Eds. *Continental, Latin-American . . .* , 23, 26–29.

"Ese chico pelirrojo a quien veo cada día"
Cook, Beverly R. "Madness as Metaphor . . . ," 23–26.

PAUL MONETTE

"Part One: *Halfway Home*"
Warner, Sharon O. "The Way We Write Now: The Reality of AIDS in Contemporary Short Fiction," *Stud Short Fiction*, 30 (1993), 496–497.

ALEKSANDRA MONTVID

"The Master of Arts and Frosia: Their First Steps in Life"
Zirin, Mary F. "Women's Prose Fiction in the Age of Realism," in Clyman, Toby W., and Diana Greene, Eds. *Women Writers . . .* , 89.

GEORGE MOORE

"Almsgiving"
Welch, Robert. *Changing States . . .* , 43–44.

"The Exile"
Welch, Robert. *Changing States . . .* , 42–43.

"Home Sickness"
Riedel, Wolfgang. "George Moore: 'Home Sickness'—Die Geschichte vom langen Abschied," in Lubbers, Klaus, Ed. *Die Englische . . .* , 279–292.

LORRIE MOORE

"You're Ugly, Too"
+Bohner, Charles H. *Instructor's Manual . . .* , 3rd ed., 98–100.

PAUL MORAND

"La Nuit hongroise"
Bonou, Marie. "Historie d'un crime: 'Le Nuit hongroise,' " *Roman 20–50*, 17 (1994), 197–205.

ALBERTO MORAVIA

"Il Pensatore"
LeBlanc, James D. " 'La Faccia da cameriere': An Existential Glance at Two of Moravia's Waiters," in Capozzi, Rocco, and Mario B. Mignone, Eds. *Homage to Moravia*, 98–106.

"Seduta spiritica"
Moss, Howard K. "Moravia and the Middle Class: The Case of 'Seduta spiritica,' " in Capozzi, Rocco, and Mario B. Mignone, Eds. *Homage to Moravia*, 145–148.

"Le Sue giornate"
LeBlanc, James D. " 'La Faccia . . . ," 106–110.

MORI MICHIYO

"Rain Falls in Shinjuku"
Morita, James R. "Mori Michiyo (1901–1977)," in Mulhern, Chieko I., Ed. *Japanese* . . . , 235.

"Youthful Wandering"
Morita, James R. "Mori Michiyo . . . ," 234–235.

TOSHIO MORI

"Toshio Mori"
Mayer, David R. "Toshio Mori and Loneliness," *Nanzan R Am Stud*, 15 (1993), 26–28.

"The Trees"
Mayer, David R. "Toshio Mori . . . ," 30.

MORI YŌKO

"Two Bedtime Stories: Be It Ever So Humble"
Samuel, Yoshiko Y. "Mori Yōko (1940–1993)," in Mulhern, Chieko I., Ed. *Japanese* . . . , 247–248.

"Two Bedtime Stories: Spring Storm"
Samuel, Yoshiko Y. "Mori Yōko . . . ," 248.

EDUARD FRIEDRICH MÖRIKE

"Stuttgarter Hutzelmännlein"

Futterknecht, Franz. "Eduard Mörikes 'Stuttgarter Hutzelmännlein': Versuch einer Interpretation," *Jahrbuch der Jean-Paul-Gesellschaft*, 28 (1993), 115–134.

TONI MORRISON

"Recitatif"

Abel, Elizabeth. "Black Writing, White Reading: Race and the Politics of Feminist Interpretation," *Critical Inquiry*, 19 (1993), 470–479.

"Sula"

Carmean, Karen. *Toni Morrison's World* . . . , 31–44.

Coleman, Alisha R. "One and One Make One: A Metacritical and Psychoanalytic Reading of Friendship in Toni Morrison's 'Sula,' " *Coll Lang Assoc J*, 37 (1993), 145–155.

Dubey, Madhu, *Black Women Novelists* . . . , 51–71.

Heinze, Denise. *The Dilemma* . . . , 78–82, 121–128, 160–164.

Hunt, Patricia. "War and Peace: Transfigured Categories and the Politics of 'Sula,' " *African Am R*, 27 (1993), 443–459.

Johnson, Barbara. " 'Aesthetic' and 'rapport' in Toni Morrison's 'Sula,' " *Textual Practice*, 7 (1993), 165–172.

Jones, Carolyn M. " 'Sula' and *Beloved*: Images of Cain in the Novels of Toni Morrison," *African Am R*, 27 (1993), 620–625.

Lee, Rachel. "Missing Peace in Toni Morrison's 'Sula' and *Beloved*," *African Am R*, 28 (1994), 571–577, 582.

Petrič, Jerneja. "Up and Down in the World of War and Peace: Toni Morrison's Use of Tropes in 'Sula' and *Song of Solomon*," in Jurak, Mirko, Ed. *Literature, Culture* . . . , 142–143.

Ramey, Deanna. "A Comparison of the Triads of Women in Toni Morrison's 'Sula' and *Song of Solomon*," *Mount Olive R*, 6 (Spring, 1992), 106–108.

Schramm, Margaret. "The Quest for the Perfect Mother in Toni Morrison's 'Sula,' " in Pearlman, Mickey, Ed. *The Anna Book* . . . , 167–176.

Seidel, Kathryn L. "The Lilith Figure in Toni Morrison's 'Sula' and Alice Walker's *The Color Purple*," *Weber Stud*, 10, ii (Spring-Summer, 1993), 90–91, 92–93.

KOSTIANTYN MOSKALETS

"Where Should I Go?"

Shkandrij, Myroslav. "Polarities in Contemporary Ukrainian Literature," *Dalhousie R*, 72 (1992), 245–246.

EZEKIEL MPHAHLELE

"Mrs. Plum"
Povey, John F. "English-language Fiction from South Africa," in Owomoyela, Oyekan, Ed. *A History* . . . , 93–94.

MANUEL MÚJICA LÁINEZ

"La Adoración de los Reyes Magos"
Ferrari, Alcira Raquel. "Un cuento de Manuel Mújica Láinez de *Misteriosa Buenos Aires* (1952). Análisis de la operatoria de los intertextos en la creación narrativa," *Incipit*, 13 (1993), 97–122.

BHARATI MUKHERJEE

"Buried Lives"
Sengupta, C. "Asian Protagonists in Bharati Mukherjee's *The Middleman and Other Stories*," *Lang Forum*, 18, i–ii (1992), 153–154.

"Danny's Girls
Sengupta, C. "Asian Protagonists . . . ," 151–153.

"The Tenant"
Sengupta, C. "Asian Protagonists . . . ," 154–156.

"A Wife's Story"
Sengupta, C. "Asian Protagonists . . . ," 149–151.

ANTONIO MUÑOZ MOLINA

"Nada del otro mundo"
Rodríguez-Fischer, Ana. "Materia y forma en los relatos de Antonio Muñoz Molina," *Insula*, 568 (April, 1994), 22.

ALICE MUNRO

"Accident"
Carscallen, James. *The Other Country* . . . , 28–29, 311, 320–321, 323, 328–329.
Heble, Ajay. *The Tumble of Reason* . . . , 136–138.

"Age of Faith"
Carscallen, James. *The Other Country* . . . , 126, 137–138, 204–205.
Heble, Ajay. *The Tumble of Reason* . . . , 59–60.

"Baptizing"
Carscallen, James. *The Other Country* . . . , 171–172, 381, 390, 391, 395–396, 397, 406, 413.
Heble, Ajay. *The Tumble of Reason* . . . , 66–68.

"Bardon Bus"
Carscallen, James. *The Other Country* . . . , 133–134, 150–151.
Heble, Ajay. *The Tumble of Reason* . . . , 138–139.

"The Beggar Maid"
Charters, Ann. *Resources* . . . , 123–125.
Heble, Ajay. *The Tumble of Reason* . . . , 111–112.

"Boys and Girls"
+Bohner, Charles H. *Instructor's Manual* . . . , 3rd ed., 100–101.
Carscallen, James. *The Other Country* . . . , 221, 222.
Charters, Ann. *Resources* . . . , 125–126.
Heble, Ajay. *The Tumble of Reason* . . . , 33–40.
Ventura, Héliane. "Alice Munro's 'Boys and Girls': Mapping Out Boundaries," *Commonwealth Essays & Stud*, 15, i (1992), 80–87.

"Carried Away"
Carrington, Ildikó de Papp. "What's in a Title?: Alice Munro's 'Carried Away,' " *Stud Short Fiction*, 30 (1993), 555–564.
Heble, Ajay. *The Tumble of Reason* . . . , 185–187.

"Changes and Ceremonies"
Carscallen, James. *The Other Country* . . . , 263–264, 269–270, 271–274.
Heble, Ajay. *The Tumble of Reason* . . . , 60–64.

"Characters"
Carscallen, James. *The Other Country* . . . , 37–39.

"Circle of Prayer"
Carscallen, James. *The Other Country* . . . , 492–493.

"Connection"
Heble, Ajay. *The Tumble of Reason* . . . , 122–125.

"Dance of the Happy Shades"
Carscallen, James. *The Other Country* . . . , 497, 498.

"The Dangerous One"
Carscallen, James. *The Other Country* . . . , 52.

"Day of the Butterfly"
Carscallen, James. *The Other Country* . . . , 51–52, 59, 67, 85.

"Deadeye Dick"
Carscallen, James. *The Other Country* . . . , 246–247.

"Dulse"
Carscallen, James. *The Other Country* . . . , 366, 370, 371, 374.
Heble, Ajay. *The Tumble of Reason* . . . , 130–134.

"Eskimo"
Carscallen, James. *The Other Country* . . . , 383–384, 499–501, 508.

"Executioners"
Carscallen, James. *The Other Country* . . . , 419–420, 421–422, 423, 424–425, 426–427, 428, 429–431, 432–433, 436, 522.

"Fits"
Carscallen, James. *The Other Country* . . . , 149–150, 210, 215, 219–220, 237.
Heble, Ajay. *The Tumble of Reason* . . . , 152–154.

Pickering, James H., and Jeffrey D. Hoeper. *Instructor's Manual* . . . , 95–96.

"Miles City, Montana"
Carscallen, James. *The Other Country* . . . , 221.
Heble, Ajay. *The Tumble of Reason* . . . , 149–152.

"Mischief"
Carscallen, James. *The Other Country* . . . , 305.
Heble, Ajay. *The Tumble of Reason* . . . , 112–114.

"Monsieur les Deux Chapeaux"
Carscallen, James. *The Other Country* . . . , 112–115, 223–224.

"The Moon in the Orange Street Skating Rink"
Carscallen, James. *The Other Country* . . . , 292–294, 321.

"The Moons of Jupiter"
Carscallen, James. *The Other Country* . . . , 517, 522.
Heble, Ajay. *The Tumble of Reason* . . . , 127–130.

"Mrs. Cross and Mrs. Kidd"
Carscallen, James. *The Other Country* . . . , 394–395.

"The Office"
Pickering, James H., and Jeffrey D. Hoeper. *Instructor's Manual* . . . , 93–94.

"Open Secrets"
Carrington, Ildikó de Papp. "Talking Dirty: Alice Munro's 'Open Secrets' and John Steinbeck's *Of Mice and Men*," *Stud Short Fiction*, 31 (1994), 595–606.

"The Ottawa Valley"
Carscallen, James. *The Other Country* . . . , 88, 467, 469–470, 473, 475, 476, 477, 486–487, 490, 501, 508–509, 514, 519–520.
Heble, Ajay. *The Tumble of Reason* . . . , 86–89.

"The Peace of Utrecht"
Carscallen, James. *The Other Country* . . . , 84–85, 147–148, 474, 482–483, 510.
Heble, Ajay. *The Tumble of Reason* . . . , 41–42.

"The Photographer"
Carscallen, James. *The Other Country* . . . , 496.

"Pictures of the Ice"
Carscallen, James. *The Other Country* . . . , 326–327.
Heble, Ajay. *The Tumble of Reason* . . . , 179–184.

"Postcard"
Carscallen, James. *The Other Country* . . . , 334.

"Princess Ida"
Carscallen, James. *The Other Country* . . . , 351–352, 354, 359, 365.
Heble, Ajay. *The Tumble of Reason* . . . , 56–59.

"Privilege"
Heble, Ajay. *The Tumble of Reason* . . . , 104–107.

"The Progress of Love"
Heble, Ajay. *The Tumble of Reason* . . . , 143–147.

"A Queer Streak"
Carscallen, James. *The Other Country* . . . , 396, 414–416, 421, 431–432, 440–443, 506, 521.
Heble, Ajay. *The Tumble of Reason* . . . , 155–158.

"Red Dress—1946"
Carscallen, James. *The Other Country* . . . , 83, 437.
Goodman, Charlotte. "Cinderella in the Classroom: (Mis)Reading Alice Munro's 'Red Dress—1946,' " *Reader*, 30 (1993), 49–64.

"Royal Beatings"
Carscallen, James. *The Other Country* . . . , 189, 190, 332–333.
Heble, Ajay. *The Tumble of Reason* . . . , 96–104.

"The Shining Houses"
Carscallen, James. *The Other Country* . . . , 310, 312, 323.

"Simon's Luck"
Carscallen, James. *The Other Country* . . . , 390–391, 418–419, 422, 426, 446–447, 501–502.
Heble, Ajay. *The Tumble of Reason* . . . , 114–117.

"Something I've Been Meaning to Tell You"
Heble, Ajay. *The Tumble of Reason* . . . , 75–81.

"The Spanish Lady"
Carscallen, James. *The Other Country* . . . , 502–503.

"Spelling"
Carscallen, James. *The Other Country* . . . , 516–517, 534.
Heble, Ajay. *The Tumble of Reason* . . . , 118–119.

"The Stone in the Field"
Carscallen, James. *The Other Country* . . . , 279–280, 310.
Heble, Ajay. *The Tumble of Reason* . . . , 125–127.

"Sunday Afternoon"
Carscallen, James. *The Other Country* . . . , 383.

"Tell Me Yes or No"
Carscallen, James. *The Other Country* . . . , 334–335, 512.
Heble, Ajay. *The Tumble of Reason* . . . , 80–83.
Ventura, Héliane. "The Setting Up of Unsettlement in Alice Munro's 'Tell Me Yes or No,' " in D'haen, Theo, and Hans Bertens, Eds. *Postmodern Fiction* . . . , 105–123.

"Teresa"
Carscallen, James. *The Other Country* . . . , 364.

"The Time of Death"
Carscallen, James. *The Other Country* . . . , 138–139, 223.

"A Trip to the Coast"
Carscallen, James. *The Other Country* . . . , 309, 388, 426, 427.

"The Turkey Season"
Carscallen, James. *The Other Country* . . . , 215, 217, 285–286.
Heble, Ajay. *The Tumble of Reason* . . . , 134–136.

"Visitors"
Carscallen, James. *The Other Country* . . . , 479.
Heble, Ajay. *The Tumble of Reason* . . . , 139–142.

"Walker Brothers Cowboy"
Carscallen, James. *The Other Country* . . . , 184, 185, 187.
Heble, Ajay. *The Tumble of Reason* . . . , 20–25.

"Walking on Water"
Carscallen, James. *The Other Country* . . . , 239, 405–406, 527–529.
Heble, Ajay. *The Tumble of Reason* . . . , 89–93.

"White Dump"
Carscallen, James. *The Other Country* . . . , 21–22, 27, 34–36, 290, 470, 495, 508–510.
Heble, Ajay. *The Tumble of Reason* . . . , 158–168.

"Who Do You Think You Are?"
Carscallen, James. *The Other Country* . . . , 469, 510, 517–518, 530.
Heble, Ajay. *The Tumble of Reason* . . . , 119–121.

"The Widower"
Carscallen, James. *The Other Country* . . . , 470, 471.

"Wild Swans"
Carscallen, James. *The Other Country* . . . , 208.
Heble, Ajay. *The Tumble of Reason* . . . , 107–110.

"Winter Wind"
Carscallen, James. *The Other Country* . . . , 31–32, 91, 236–237, 479, 481.

"Working for a Living"
Carscallen, James. *The Other Country* . . . , 145.

ROBERT MUSIL

"The Blackbird"
Rogowski, Christian. *Distinguished Outsider* . . . , 131–138, 140, 142, 143, 144–145.

"Grigia"
Rogowski, Christian. *Distinguished Outsider* . . . , 116–118, 121, 122, 126–127, 127–128.

"The Perfection of Love"
Rogowski, Christian. *Distinguished Outsider* . . . , 72–78, 79–81, 83–86, 87–88.

"The Portuguese Lady"
Kuzniar, Alice. "Inside Out: Robert Musil's 'Die Portugiesin,' " *Mod Austrian Lit*, 26, ii (1993), 91–106.
Rogowski, Christian. *Distinguished Outsider* . . . , 120, 124, 125, 127, 128–129.

"The Temptation of Silent Veronica"
Rogowski, Christian. *Distinguished Outsider* . . . , 72–74, 75–77, 78–80, 81–83, 86–88.

"Tonka"
Haynes, Roslynn D. *From Faust . . .*, 228–229.
Rogowski, Christian. *Distinguished Outsider . . .*, 113–129.

ÁLVARO MUTIS

"El último rostro"
Menton, Seymour. *Latin America's New . . .*, 116–123.
———. " 'El último rostro': nada de fragmento," *Revista de Estudios Colombianos*, 12–13 (1994), 39–42.

VLADIMIR NABOKOV

"Assistant Professor"
Nicol, Charles. "Finding the 'Assistant Professor,' " in Nicol, Charles, and Gennady Barabtarlo, Eds. *A Small . . .*, 155–165.

"A Busy Man"
Tolstaia, Natalia. "V. V. Nabokov Stages a Play: 'A Busy Man,' " in Nicol, Charles, and Gennady Barabtarlo, Eds. *A Small . . .*, 65–72.

"A Christmas Story"
Kuzmanovich, Zoran. " 'A Christmas Story': A Polemic with Ghosts," in Nicol, Charles, and Gennady Barabtarlo, Eds. *A Small . . .*, 81–97.

"The Circle"
Foster, John B. *Nabokov's Art . . .*, 85–86.

"The Defense"
Rampton, David. *Vladimir Nabokov*, 35–40.

"The Eye"
Rampton, David. *Vladimir Nabokov*, 40–45.

"The Fight"
Connolly, Julian W. "The Play of Light and Shadow in 'The Fight,' " in Nicol, Charles, and Gennady Barabtarlo, Eds. *A Small . . .*, 25–37.

"A Guide to Berlin"
Grossmith, Robert. "The Future Perfect of the Mind: 'Time and Ebb' and 'A Guide to Berlin,' " in Nicol, Charles, and Gennady Barabtarlo, Eds. *A Small . . .*, 152–153.

"Lance"
Howell, Yvonne. "Science and Gnosticism in 'Lance,' " in Nicol, Charles, and Gennady Barabtarlo, Eds. *A Small . . .*, 181–192.

"Mademoiselle O"
Feldman, Jessica R. *Gender on the Divide . . .*, 231–233.
Foster, John B. "An Archeology of 'Mademoiselle O': Narrative Between Art and Memory," in Nicol, Charles, and Gennady Barabtarlo, Eds. *A Small . . .*, 111–135.
———. *Nabokov's Art . . .*, 38–39, 110–129.

"The Passenger"
+Bohner, Charles H. *Instructor's Manual* . . . , 3rd ed., 101–102.

"Perfection"
Grossmith, Robert. " 'Perfection,' " in Nicol, Charles, and Gennady Barabtarlo, Eds. *A Small* . . . , 73–80.

"The Return of Chorb"
Larmour, David H. J. "Orpheus and Nabokov's 'Vozvraschchenie Chorba,' " *Studia Slavica*, 38, iii–iv (1993), 373–377.

"Reunion"
Foster, John B. *Nabokov's Art* . . . , 84–85.

"Revenge"
Barabtarlo, Gennady. "A Skeleton in Nabokov's Closet: 'Mest,' " in Nicol, Charles, and Gennady Barabtarlo, Eds. *A Small* . . . , 15–23.

"Scenes from the Life of a Double Monster"
Sweeney, Susan E. "The Small Furious Devil: Memory in 'Scenes from the Life of a Double Monster,' " in Nicol, Charles, and Gennady Barabtarlo, Eds. *A Small* . . . , 193–216.

"Signs and Symbols"
Toker, Leona. " 'Signs and Symbols' in and out of Contexts," in Nicol, Charles, and Gennady Barabtarlo, Eds. *A Small* . . . , 167–180.

"Spring in Fialta"
Feldman, Jessica R. *Gender on the Divide* . . . , 229–231.
Foster, John B. *Nabokov's Art* . . . , 130–146.
Matterson, Stephen. "Sprung from the Music Box of Memory: 'Spring in Fialta,' " in Nicol, Charles, and Gennady Barabtarlo, Eds. *A Small* . . . , 102–108.

"Terror"
Johnson, D. Barton. " 'Terror': Pre-texts and Post-texts," in Nicol, Charles, and Gennady Barabtarlo, Eds. *A Small* . . . , 39–45, 50–59.

"Time and Ebb"
Grossmith, Robert. "The Future Perfect . . . ," 149–152.

"The Visit to the Museum"
De Roeck, Galina L. " 'The Visit to the Museum': A Tour of Hell," in Nicol, Charles, and Gennady Barabtarlo, Eds. *A Small* . . . , 137–147.

V[IDIADHAR] S[URAJPASAD] NAIPAUL

"Flag on the Island"
King, Bruce. *V. S. Naipaul*, 65–66.

"In a Free State"
King, Bruce. *V. S. Naipaul*, 85–88, 89–91.

"Man-man"
King, Bruce. *V. S. Naipaul*, 19–24.

"My Aunt Gold Teeth"
King, Bruce. *V. S. Naipaul*, 65.

"One Out of Many"
King, Bruce. *V. S. Naipaul*, 87–88, 90, 91–92.

"Tell Me Who to Kill"
King, Bruce. *V. S. Naipaul*, 92–94.

"The Tramp at Piraeus"
King, Bruce. *V. S. Naipaul*, 94–97.

JUSUF NAOUM

"Der schwarze Schleier"
Khalil, Iman O. "Writing Civil War: The Lebanese Experience in Jusuf Naoum's German Short Stories," *Germ Q*, 67 (1994), 553–554.

"Schwarzer Samstag"
Khalil, Iman O. "Writing Civil War . . . ," 553–554.

R. K. NARAYAN

"Annamalai"
Lever, Susan. "The Comedy of Misreading in the Fiction of R. K. Narayan," in McLeod, A. L., Ed. *R. K. Narayan* . . . , 79.

"A Breath of Lucifer"
Lever, Susan. "The Comedy . . . ," 79–81.

"Fellow Feeling"
Shankar, D. A. "Caste in the Fiction of R. K. Narayan," in McLeod, A. L., Ed. *R. K. Narayan* . . . , 138–139.

"A Horse and Two Goats"
Lever, Susan. "The Comedy . . . ," 78.

"Naga"
Urstad, Tone S. "Symbolism in R. K. Narayan's 'Naga,' " *Stud Short Fiction*, 31 (1994), 425–432.

VALERIYA NARBIKOVA

"First Person. And Second Person"
Kelly, Catriona. *A History of Russian* . . . , 383, 384.

NJABULO NDEBELE

"The Music of the Violin"
Povey, John F. "English-language Fiction from South Africa," in Owomoyela, Oyekan, Ed. *A History* . . . , 98–99.

ANNA NERKAGI

"Aniko of the Nogo Tribe"
Barker, Adele M. "Crossings," in Aiken, Susan H., Adele M. Barker, Maya Koreneva, and Ekaterina Stetsenko, Eds. *Dialogues/Dialogi* . . . , 341–352.
Stetsenko, Ekaterina. "Retelling the Legends," in Aiken, Susan H., Adele M. Barker, Maya Koreneva, and Ekaterina Stetsenko, Eds. *Dialogues/Dialogi* . . . , 328–333.

FAE MYENNE NG

"A Red Sweater"
Wong, Sau-ling C. *Reading Asian American Literature* . . . , 25, 31–34, 71–72, 157.

IPPOLITO NIEVO

"Il Varmo"
Camerino, Marinella C. "The Journey in Ippolito Nievo's Narrative: Typologies," in Magliocchetti, Bruno, and Anthony Verna, Eds. *The Motif* . . . , 134–135.

NOGAMI YAEKO

"The Foxes"
Aoki, Michiko. "Nogami Yaeko (1885–1985)," in Mulhern, Chieko I., Ed. *Japanese* . . . , 281–282.
"The Full Moon"
Aoki, Michiko. "Nogami Yaeko . . . ," 281.

OLGA NOLLA

"Un corazón tierno"
Acosta Cruz, María I. "Historia y escritura femenina en Olga Nolla, Magali García Ramis, Rosario Ferré y Ana Lydia Vega," *Revista Iberoamericana*, 59 (1993), 267.
"El milagro de la calle del sol"
Acosta Cruz, María I. "Historia y escritura femenina . . . ," 267–268.

FRANK NORRIS

"Ambrosia Beer"
Berkove, Lawrence. "The Romantic Realism of Bierce and Norris," *Frank Norris Stud*, 15 (Spring, 1993), 13–17.

"A Deal in Wheat"
Marut, David. "Sam Lewiston's Bad Timing: A Note on the Economic Context of 'A Deal in Wheat,' " *Am Lit Realism*, 27, i (1994), 74–80.

"The Green Stone of Unrest"
Wertheim, Stanley. "Frank Norris's 'The Green Stone of Unrest,' " *Frank Norris Stud*, 15 (Spring, 1993), 5–8.

"The Hero of Tomato Can"
Scharnhorst, Gary. "Harte, Norris, and 'The Hero of Tomato Can,' " *Frank Norris Stud*, 15 (Spring, 1993), 8–10.

"I Call on Lady Dotty: From the Polly Parables"
Fisher, Benjamin F. "Frank Norris Parodies Anthony Hope," *Frank Norris Stud*, 15 (Spring, 1993), 17–20.

"The Puppets and the Puppy"
McElrath, Joseph R. "Frank Norris' 'The Puppets and the Puppy': LeContean Idealism or Naturalistic Skepticism?" *Am Lit Realism*, 26, i (1993), 50–59.

"The 'Ricksha That Happened"
McElrath, Joseph R. " 'The 'Ricksha That Happened': Norris's Parody of Rudyard Kipling," *Frank Norris Stud*, 15 (Spring, 1993), 1–4.

"Van Bubbles' Story"
Burgess, Douglas K. "Norris's 'Van Bubbles' Story': Bursting the Bubble of the Davis Mystique," *Frank Norris Stud*, 15 (Spring, 1993), 10–13.

LESLIE NORRIS

"Away, Away in China"
Sullivan, C. W. "Place as Theme: Wales in 'Away, Away in China' and 'A Roman Spring,' " in England, Eugene, and Peter Makuck, Eds. *An Open World* . . . , 142–145, 147–148.

"A Big Night"
Chappel, Fred. "Powers of Observation: The Stone, the Hawk, the Solitary I," in England, Eugene, and Peter Makuck, Eds. *An Open World* . . . , 189–190.

"A Flight of Geese"
Bennett, Bruce. "Intimations of Mortality: 'A Flight of Geese,' " in England, Eugene, and Peter Makuck, Eds. *An Open World* . . . , 113–121.
Curtis, Tony. "Norris's Birds," in England, Eugene, and Peter Makuck, Eds. *An Open World* . . . , 172–174.

"The Kingfisher"
Curtis, Tony. "Norris's Birds," 174–175.

"The Mallard"
Curtis, Tony. "Norris's Birds," 176.

"My Uncle's Story"
Jarman, Mark. "Painful Journeys, Many Happy Returns," in England, Eugene, and Peter Makuck, Eds. *An Open World* . . . , 139–140.

"Prey"
Chappel, Fred. "Powers . . . ," 186–188.
Curtis, Tony. "Norris's Birds," 175.

"A Roman Spring"
Chappel, Fred. "Powers . . . ," 182–185.
Sullivan, C. W. "Place as Theme . . . ," 145–148.

"A Seeing Eye"
Merrill, Christopher. "Norris's Book of Transformations," in England, Eugene, and Peter Makuck, Eds. *An Open World* . . . , 200–202.

"Shaving"
Drake, Barbara. "Out of Bounds with Leslie Norris," in England, Eugene, and Peter Makuck, Eds. *An Open World* . . . , 195–196.

"Sing It Again, Wordsworth"
Simpson, Richard. " 'Sing It Again, Wordsworth': English Romanticism, Music, and the Pleasure of the Phrase," in England, Eugene, and Peter Makuck, Eds. *An Open World* . . . , 152–154.

"Some Opposites of Good"
Rutsala, Vern. "Anecdote into Story: 'Some Opposites of Good,' " in England, Eugene, and Peter Makuck, Eds. *An Open World* . . . , 122–129.

JOYCE CAROL OATES

"The Abduction"
Schulz, Gretchen E. "*The Assignation* and *Where Is Here?*: What's Happening in the Miniature Narratives of Joyce Carol Oats," in Johnson, Greg. *Joyce Carol Oates* . . . , 205.

"Accomplished Desires"
Johnson, Greg. *Joyce Carol Oates* . . . , 47–49.

"All the Good People I've Left Behind"
McPhillips, Robert. "The Novellas of Joyce Carol Oates," in Johnson, Greg. *Joyce Carol Oates* . . . , 195–196.

"April"
Johnson, Greg. *Joyce Carol Oates* . . . , 95–96.

"Archways"
Johnson, Greg. *Joyce Carol Oates* . . . , 30–32.
———. "Out of Eden: Oates's *Upon the Sweeping Flood*," *Midwest Q*, 35 (1994), 439–440.

"At the Seminary"
Johnson, Greg. *Joyce Carol Oates* . . . , 29–30.
———. "Out of Eden . . . ," 437–438.

"Baby"
Johnson, Greg. *Joyce Carol Oates . . .*, 98–99.

"Blindfold"
Johnson, Greg. *Joyce Carol Oates . . .*, 57–58.

"Bodies"
Johnson, Greg. *Joyce Carol Oates . . .*, 53–54.

"The Boyfriend"
Johnson, Greg. *Joyce Carol Oates . . .*, 102–103.

"Boys at a Picnic"
Johnson, Greg. "A Barbarous Eden: Joyce Carol Oates's First Collection," *Stud Short Fiction*, 30 (1993), 6–7.
———. *Joyce Carol Oates . . .*, 20–21.

"By the North Gate"
Johnson, Greg. "A Barbarous Eden . . . ," 5, 6, 9.

"The Bystander"
Schulz, Gretchen E. "*The Assignation . . .*," 206–207.

"The Census Taker"
Johnson, Greg. *Joyce Carol Oates . . .*, 24.
Wesley, Marilyn C. *Refusal . . .*, 17–18.

"Ceremonies"
Johnson, Greg. "A Barbarous Eden . . . ," 5–6, 13.
———. *Joyce Carol Oates . . .*, 19–20.

"Customs"
Wesley, Marilyn C. "Love's Journey in *Crossing the Border*," in Johnson, Greg. *Joyce Carol Oates . . .*, 177–178.

"Daisy"
Johnson, Greg. *Joyce Carol Oates . . .*, 91.
Steiner, Dorothea. "Joyce Carol Oates: 'Daisy'—Woman as Prototype and Persona," in Lubbers, Klaus, Ed. *Die Englische . . .*, 436–449.

"The Dead"
Johnson, Greg. *Joyce Carol Oates . . .*, 79–81.
+Showalter, Elaine. "Joyce Carol Oates's 'The Dead' and Feminist Criticism," in Johnson, Greg. *Joyce Carol Oates . . .*, 168–170.

"The Death of Mrs. Sheer"
Johnson, Greg. *Joyce Carol Oates . . .*, 33–34.
———. "Out of Eden . . . ," 441–443.

"Détente"
Zins, Daniel L. "*Last Days* and New Opportunities: Joyce Carol Oates Writes the End of the Cold War," in Johnson, Greg. *Joyce Carol Oates . . .*, 188–189.

"Family"
Johnson, Greg. *Joyce Carol Oates . . .*, 105–106.

"Famine Country"
Johnson, Greg. *Joyce Carol Oates . . .*, 90–91.

"The Fine White Mist of Winter"
Johnson, Greg. "A Barbarous Eden . . . ," 8–9.
———. *Joyce Carol Oates . . .* , 22–23.

"First Views of the Enemy"
Johnson, Greg. *Joyce Carol Oates . . .* , 34–36.
———. "Out of Eden . . . ," 443–445.

"Four Summers"
Johnson, Greg. *Joyce Carol Oates . . .* , 54–55.
Pickering, James H., and Jeffrey D. Hoeper. *Instructor's Manual . . .* , 101–102.

"The Goddess"
Johnson, Greg. *Joyce Carol Oates . . .* , 65–66.

"Heat"
Johnson, Greg. *Joyce Carol Oates . . .* , 103–104.

"Hello Fine Day Isn't It"
Wesley, Marilyn C. "Love's Journey . . . ," 176–177.

"Hostage"
Johnson, Greg. *Joyce Carol Oates . . .* , 100–101.

"How I Contemplated the World from the Detroit House of Correction and Began My Life Over Again"
Charters, Ann. *Resources . . .* , 128–129.
Daly, Brenda O. " 'How Do We [Not] Become These People Who Victimize Us?': Anxious Authorship in the Early Fiction of Joyce Carol Oates," in Singley, Carol J., and Susan E. Sweeney, Eds. *Anxious Power . . .* , 235–236, 237–238, 246–248.
Johnson, Greg. *Joyce Carol Oates . . .* , 45–46.

"I Lock My Door Upon Myself"
McPhillips, Robert. "The Novellas . . . ," 198–199.

"I Must Have You"
Johnson, Greg. *Joyce Carol Oates . . .* , 60.

"I Was in Love"
Johnson, Greg. *Joyce Carol Oates . . .* , 50–51.

"Ich Bin Ein Berliner"
Zins, Daniel L. "*Last Days . . .* ," 185–186.

"In the Old World"
Johnson, Greg. *Joyce Carol Oates . . .* , 20, 22.

"In the Region of Ice"
Johnson, Greg. *Joyce Carol Oates . . .* , 52–53.

"In the Warehouse"
Johnson, Greg. *Joyce Carol Oates . . .* , 57.

"An Incident in the Park"
Wesley, Marilyn C. "Love's Journey . . . ," 178.

"Ladies and Gentlemen"
Johnson, Greg. *Joyce Carol Oates . . .* , 105.

"The Lady with the Pet Dog"
Johnson, Greg. *Joyce Carol Oates* . . . , 77–78.

"Last Days"
Zins, Daniel L. "*Last Days* . . . ," 182–183.

"Little Wife"
Johnson, Greg. *Joyce Carol Oates* . . . , 97–98.

"Loss"
Padgett, Jacqueline O. "The Portugal of Joyce Carol Oates," *Stud Short Fiction*, 31 (1994), 679–680.

"Magna Mater"
Johnson, Greg. *Joyce Carol Oates* . . . , 64.

"The Man That Turned into a Statue"
Johnson, Greg. *Joyce Carol Oates* . . . , 32–33.
———. "Out of Eden . . . ," 440–441.

"The Man Whom Women Adored"
Zins, Daniel L. "*Last Days* . . . ," 184.

"Matter and Energy"
Johnson, Greg. *Joyce Carol Oates* . . . , 46–47.

"The Metamorphosis"
Johnson, Greg. *Joyce Carol Oates* . . . , 78–79.

"The Molesters"
Wesley, Marilyn C. *Refusal* . . . , 112–115.

"My Warszawa"
Zins, Daniel L. "*Last Days* . . . ," 189–190.

"Nairobi"
Johnson, Greg. *Joyce Carol Oates* . . . , 96–97.

"Naked"
Johnson, Greg. *Joyce Carol Oates* . . . , 104–105.

"Night-Side"
Johnson, Greg. *Joyce Carol Oates* . . . , 85–87.

"Old Budapest"
Zins, Daniel L. "*Last Days* . . . ," 190–191.

"Our Lady of the Easy Death of Alferce"
Padgett, Jacqueline O. "The Portugal . . . ," 679.

"Our Wall"
Zins, Daniel L. "*Last Days* . . . ," 187–188.

"Pastoral Blood"
Johnson, Greg. "A Barbarous Eden . . . ," 11–12.
———. *Joyce Carol Oates* . . . , 26–27.

"Picnic"
Schulz, Gretchen E. "*The Assignation* . . . ," 204–205.

"The Rise of Life on Earth"
McPhillips, Robert. "The Novellas . . . ," 199–200.

"Unmailed, Unwritten Letters"
Johnson, Greg. *Joyce Carol Oates* . . . , 49–50.

"Upon the Sweeping Flood"
Johnson, Greg. *Joyce Carol Oates* . . . , 36–38.
———. "Out of Eden . . . ," 445–448.
Wesley, Marilyn C. *Refusal* . . . , 24–25.

"Where Are You Going, Where Have you Been?"
+Bohner, Charles H. *Instructor's Manual* . . . , 3rd ed., 103–104.
Dessommes, Nancy B. "O'Connor's Mrs. May and Oates's Connie: An Unlikely Pair of Religious Initiates," *Stud Short Fiction*, 31 (1994), 433–440.
+Gillis, Christina M. " 'Where Are You Going, Where Have You Been?': Seduction, Space, and a Fictional Mode," in Showalter, Elaine, Ed. *Joyce Carol Oates* . . . , 133–139.
Johnson, Greg. *Joyce Carol Oates* . . . , 44–45.
Kowalewski, Michael. *Deadly Musings* . . . , 27–29.
Pickering, James H., and Jeffrey D. Hoeper. *Instructor's Manual* . . . , 98–99.
+Rubin, Larry. "Oates's 'Where Are You Going, Where Have You Been?' " in Showalter, Elaine, Ed. *Joyce Carol Oates* . . . , 109–112.
+Schulz, Gretchen, and R. J. R. Rockwood. "In Fairyland, Without a Map: Connie's Exploration Inward in Joyce Carol Oates's 'Where Are You Going, Where Have You Been?' " in Showalter, Elaine, Ed. *Joyce Carol Oates* . . . , 113–130.
Showalter, Elaine, "Introduction," in Showalter, Elaine, Ed. *Joyce Carol Oates* . . . , 14–18.
+Urbanski, Marie M. O. "Existential Allegory: Joyce Carol Oates's 'Where Are You Going, Where Have You Been?' " in Showalter, Elaine, Ed. *Joyce Carol Oates* . . . , 75–79.
+Wegs, Joyce M. " 'Don't You Know Who I Am?' The Grotesque in Oates's 'Where Are You Going, Where Have You Been?' " in Showalter, Elaine, Ed. *Joyce Carol Oates* . . . , 99–107.
Wesley, Marilyn C. *Refusal* . . . , 145–146.
White, Terry. "Allegorical Evil, Existential Choice in O'Connor, Oates, and Styron," *Midwest Q*, 34 (1993), 389–392.
+Winslow, Joan D. "The Stranger Within: Two Stories by Oates and Hawthorne," in Showalter, Elaine, Ed. *Joyce Carol Oates* . . . , 91–98.

"Where *Is* Here?"
Schulz, Gretchen E. "*The Assignation* . . . ," 209–211.

"The Widows"
Johnson, Greg. *Joyce Carol Oates* . . . , 91.

"Yarrow"
Johnson, Greg. *Joyce Carol Oates* . . . , 99–100.

"You"
Fludernik, Monika. "Second Person Fiction: Narrative *You* as

Addressee and/or Protagonist,'' *Arbeiten aus Anglistik und Amerikanistik*, 18, ii (1993), 239–243.
Wesley, Marilyn C. *Refusal* . . . , 39–40.

ŌBA MINAKO

''The Smile of a Mountain Witch''
Wilson, Michiko N. ''Ōba Minako (1930–),'' in Mulhern, Chieko I., Ed. *Japanese* . . . , 292–293.

EDNA O'BRIEN

''Baby Blue''
O'Hara, Kiera. ''Love Objects: Love and Obsession in the Stories of Edna O'Brien,'' *Stud Short Fiction*, 30 (1993), 319–320.

''The Creature''
+Bohner, Charles H. *Instructor's Manual* . . . , 3rd ed., 104–105.

''Irish Revel''
O'Hara, Kiera. ''Love Objects . . . ,'' 317–318.

''Lantern Slides''
O'Hara, Kiera. ''Love Objects . . . ,'' 322–323.

''The Love Object''
O'Hara, Kiera. ''Love Objects . . . ,'' 318–319.

''No Place''
O'Hara, Kiera. ''Love Objects . . . ,'' 323–324.

''Ways''
O'Hara, Kiera. ''Love Objects . . . ,'' 320–322.

FITZ-JAMES O'BRIEN

''The Diamond Lens''
Haynes, Roslynn D. *From Faust* . . . , 86.

''The Wondersmith''
Hoppenstand, Gary. ''Robots of the Past: Fitz-James O'Brien's 'The Wondersmith,' '' *J Pop Culture*, 27, iv (1994), 16–29.

TIM O'BRIEN

''Field Trip''
Smith, Lorrie N. '' 'The Things Men Do': The Gendered Subtext in Tim O'Brien's *Esquire* Stories,'' *Critique*, 36 (1994), 21–22.

''How to Tell a True War Story''
Smith, Lorrie N. '' 'The Things . . . ,'' 29–31.

''The Lives of the Dead''
Smith, Lorrie N. '' 'The Things . . . ,'' 37–38.

"The Man I Killed"
Smith, Lorrie N. " 'The Things . . . ,'' 22–23.

"Speaking of Courage"
Smith, Lorrie N. " 'The Things . . . ,'' 22.

"Style"
Smith, Lorrie N. " 'The Things . . . ,'' 22.

"Sweetheart of the Song Tra Bong"
Smith, Lorrie N. " 'The Things . . . ,'' 31–36.

"The Things They Carried"
+Bohner, Charles H. *Instructor's Manual* . . . , 3rd ed., 105–106.
Smith, Lorrie N. " 'The Things . . . ,'' 24–27.

SILVINA OCAMPO

"El asco"
Mathieu, Corina S. "La subversión del orden en *La furia y otros cuentos* de Silvina Ocampo," *Alba de América*, 11 (1993), 265–266.

"Azabache"
Mathieu, Corina S. "La subversión . . . ," 266.

"La casa de azúcar"
Duncan, Cynthia K. "Hacia una interpretación de lo fantástico en el contexto de la literatura hispanoamericana," *Texto Crítico*, 16 (1990), 62.

"La continuación"
Mathieu, Corina S. "La subversión . . . ," 265.

"Cornelia frente al espejo"
Klingenberg, Patricia N. "Divising the Self: Mirrors in Silvina Ocampo's *Cornelia frente al espejo*," in Paolini, Gilbert, Ed. *La Chispa* . . . , 129–131.

"La liebre dorada"
Mathieu, Corina S. "La subversión . . . ," 265.

"El mal"
Mathieu, Corina S. "La subversión . . . ," 267.

"Mimoso"
Mathieu, Corina S. "La subversión . . . ," 267–268.

"Las ondas"
Mathieu, Corina S. "La subversión . . . ," 269–270.

"La sibila"
Mathieu, Corina S. "La subversión . . . ," 266–267.

"El vestido de terciopelo"
Duncan, Cynthia K. "Hacia una interpretación . . . ," 61–62.
Mathieu, Corina S. "La subversión . . . ," 268–269.

FLANNERY O'CONNOR

"The Artificial Nigger"
MacKethan, Lucinda H. "Redeeming Blackness: Urban Allegories of

O'Connor, Percy, and Toole," *Stud Lit Imagination*, 27, ii (1994), 29–33.

Schleifer, Ronald. "Rural Gothic: The Sublime Rhetoric of Flannery O'Connor," in Mogen, David, Scott P. Sanders, and Joanne B. Karpinski, Eds. *Frontier Gothic* . . . , 177, 181–184.

"The Barber"

Larsen, Val. "A Tale of Tongue and Pen: Orality and Literacy in 'The Barber,' " *Flannery O'Connor Bull*, 22 (1993–1994), 25–44.

"A Circle of Fire"

Reuman, Ann E. "Revolting Fictions: Flannery O'Connor's Letter to Her Mother," *Papers Lang & Lit*, 29 (1993), 212–214.

Smith, Peter A. "Flannery O'Connor's Empowered Women," *Southern Lit J*, 26, ii (1994), 36–38.

"The Displaced Person"

Smith, Peter A. "Flannery O'Connor's . . . ," 38–39.

Weinstein, Arnold. *Nobody's Home* . . . , 122–128.

"The Enduring Chill"

Folks, Jeffrey J. " 'The Enduring Chill': Physical Disability in Flannery O'Connor's *Everything That Rises Must Converge*," *Univ Dayton R*, 22, ii (1993–1994), 85–86.

Havird, David. "The Saving Rape: Flannery O'Connor and Patriarchal Religion," *Mississippi Q*, 47 (1993–94), 16–17.

Reuman, Ann E. "Revolting Fictions . . . ," 204–205, 206.

Smith, Peter A. "Flannery O'Connor's . . . ," 39.

"Everything That Rises Must Converge"

+Bohner, Charles H. *Instructor's Manual* . . . , 3rd ed., 106–107.

Charters, Ann. *Resources* . . . , 133.

Niland, Kurt R., and Robert C. Evans. "*A Memoir of Mary Ann* and 'Everything That Rises Must Converge,' " *Flannery O'Connor Bull*, 22 (1993–1994), 53–69.

Reuman, Ann E. "Revolting Fictions . . . ," 207, 208–209.

Smith, Peter A. "Flannery O'Connor's . . . ," 40–41.

"Good Country People"

Burke, William. "Fetishism in the Fiction of Flannery O'Connor," *Flannery O'Connor Bull*, 22 (1993–1994), 45–47.

Charters, Ann. *Resources* . . . , 134–135.

Havird, David. "The Saving Rape . . . ," 22–24.

Reuman, Ann E. "Revolting Fictions . . . ," 212–214.

Smith, Peter A. "Flannery O'Connor's . . . ," 41–42.

Weinstein, Arnold. *Nobody's Home* . . . , 119–122.

"A Good Man Is Hard to Find"

+Bellamy, Michael O. "Everything Off Balance: Protestant Election in Flannery O'Connor's 'A Good Man Is Hard to Find,' " in Asals, Frederick, Ed. *Flannery O'Connor* . . . , 103–111.

+Bohner, Charles H. *Instructor's Manual* . . . , 3rd ed., 107–109.

+Bryant, Hallman B. "Reading the Map in 'A Good Man Is Hard to Find,' " in Asals, Frederick, Ed. *Flannery O'Connor* . . . , 73–81.

Charters, Ann. *Resources* . . . , 136–137.

+Doxey, William S. "A Dissenting Opinion of Flannery O'Connor's 'A Good Man Is Hard to Find,' " in Asals, Frederick, Ed. *Flannery O'Connor . . .*, 95–102.

Dyson, J. Peter. "Cats, Crime, and Punishment: The *Mikado*'s Pitti-Sing in 'A Good Man Is Hard to Find,' " *Engl Stud Canada*, 14 (1988), 436–452; rpt. Asals, Frederick, Ed. *Flannery O'Connor . . .*, 139–163.

+Jones, Madison. "A Good Man's Predicament," in Asals, Frederick, Ed. *Flannery O'Connor . . .*, 119–126.

+Marks, W. S. "Advertisements for Grace: Flannery O'Connor's 'A Good Man Is Hard to Find,' " in Asals, Frederick, Ed. *Flannery O'Connor . . .*, 83–94.

Martin, Carter. "The Meanest of Them Sparkled': Beauty and Landscape in Flannery O'Connor's Fiction," in Westarp, Karl-Heinz, and Jan N. Gretlund, Eds. *Realist of Distances . . .*, 151–155; rpt. Asals, Frederick, Ed. *Flannery O'Connor . . .*, 132–136.

Pickering, James H., and Jeffrey D. Hoeper. *Instructor's Manual . . .*, 80–82.

+Schenck, Mary Jane. "Deconstructed Meaning in ['A Good Man Is Hard to Find']," in Asals, Frederick, Ed. *Flannery O'Connor . . .*, 165–174.

Weinstein, Arnold. *Nobody's Home . . .*, 115–119.

White, Terry. "Allegorical Evil, Existential Choice in O'Connor, Oates, and Styron," *Midwest Q*, 34 (1993), 383, 386–388.

"Greenleaf"

Dessommes, Nancy B. "O'Connor's Mrs. May and Oates's Connie: An Unlikely Pair of Religious Initiates," *Stud Short Fiction*, 31 (1994), 433–440.

Havird, David. "The Saving Rape . . . ," 17–20.

Kowalewski, Michael. *Deadly Musings . . .*, 204–213.

Smith, Peter A. "Flannery O'Connor's . . . ," 43–45.

"The Lame Shall Enter First"

Folks, Jeffrey J. " 'The Enduring Chill . . . ," 86.

Kowalewski, Michael. *Deadly Musings . . .*, 194–195.

Whitt, Jan. *Allegory and the Modern . . .*, 92–93.

"The Life You Save May Be Your Own"

Burke, William. "Fetishism . . . ," 49–50.

Charters, Ann. *Resources . . .*, 139.

Smith, Peter A. "Flannery O'Connor's . . . ," 46.

Weinstein, Arnold. *Nobody's Home . . .*, 113–115.

"Parker's Back"

Donahoo, Robert. "Tarwater's March Toward the Feminine: The Role of Gender in O'Connor's *The Violent Bear It Away*," *CEA Critic*, 56, i (1993), 104–105.

Schleifer, Ronald. "Rural Gothic . . . ," 179–180.

Streight, Irwin H. "Is There a Text in This Man? A Semiotic Reading of 'Parker's Back,' " *Flannery O'Conner Bull*, 22 (1993–1994), 1–10.

"Revelation"

Burke, William. "Fetishism . . . ," 48–49.

Hardy, Donald E. "Free Indirect Discourse, Irony, and Empathy in Flannery O'Connor's 'Revelation,' " *Lang & Lit*, 16 (1991), 37–53.

Havird, David. "The Saving Rape . . . ," 20–22.

Martin, Karl. "Flannery O'Connor's Prophetic Imagination," *Religion & Lit*, 26, iii (1994), 50–53.

Pepin, Ronald. "Latin Names and Images of Ugliness in Flannery O'Connor's 'Revelation,' " *ANQ*, 6, i, N.S. (1993), 25–27.

Reuman, Ann E. "Revolting Fictions . . . ," 211–212.

Rowley, Rebecca K. "Individuation and Religious Experience: A Jungian Approach to O'Connor's 'Revelation,' " *Southern Lit J*, 25, ii (1993), 92–102.

Schleifer, Ronald. "Rural Gothic . . . ," 181.

Smith, Peter A. "Flannery O'Connor's . . . ," 40.

"The River"

Weinstein, Arnold. *Nobody's Home* . . . , 111–113.

"The Turkey"

Monteiro, George. "The Great American Hunt in O'Connor's 'The Turkey,' " *Explicator*, 51 (1993), 118–121.

"A View of the Woods"

Burke, William. "Fetishism . . . ," 50–51.

FRANK O'CONNOR

"Bridal Night"

Neary, Michael. "The Inside-Out World in Frank O'Connor's Stories," *Stud Short Fiction*, 30 (1993), 333–334.

"Guests of the Nation"

+Bohner, Charles H. *Instructor's Manual* . . . , 3rd ed., 109–110.

Charters, Ann. *Resources* . . . , 141–142.

"My Oedipus Complex"

+Bohner, Charles H. *Instructor's Manual* . . . , 3rd ed., 110–111.

Charters, Ann. *Resources* . . . , 142–143.

"There Is a Lone House"

Neary, Michael. "The Inside-Out World . . . ," 334–335.

"The Man of the World"

Steinman, Michael. "Frank O'Connor's 'The Man of the World' and the Betrayed Reader," *Colby Q*, 30 (1994), 279–290.

SEAN O'FAOLAIN

"Admiring the Scenery"

Butler, Pierce. *Sean O'Faolain* . . . , 25–28.

"A Born Genius"

Butler, Pierce. *Sean O'Faolain* . . . , 21–23.

"Brainsy"
Butler, Pierce. *Sean O'Faolain . . .*, 95–97.

"Childybawn"
Butler, Pierce. *Sean O'Faolain . . .*, 66–68.

"Discord"
Butler, Pierce. *Sean O'Faolain . . .*, 24–25.

"The Faithless Wife"
Butler, Pierce. *Sean O'Faolain . . .*, 100–101.

"Foreign Affairs"
Butler, Pierce. *Sean O'Faolain . . .*, 102–104.

"Fugue"
Butler, Pierce. *Sean O'Faolain . . .*, 13–16.

"The Fur Coat"
Finn, James. "High Standards and High Achievements," *Commonweal*, 66 (1957), 429; rpt. Butler, Pierce. *Sean O'Faolain . . .*, 142–143.

"In the Bosom of the Country"
Butler, Pierce. *Sean O'Faolain . . .*, 79–83.

"Inside Outside Complex"
Butler, Pierce. *Sean O'Faolain . . .*, 105–109.

"The Kitchen"
Butler, Pierce. *Sean O'Faolain . . .*, 90–92.

"Kitty the Wren"
Butler, Pierce. *Sean O'Faolain . . .*, 31–33.

"Lady Lucifer"
Butler, Pierce. *Sean O'Faolain . . .*, 28–31.

"Lord and Master"
Butler, Pierce. *Sean O'Faolain . . .*, 68–72.

"Lovers of the Lake"
Butler, Pierce. *Sean O'Faolain . . .*, 61–65.

"The Man Who Invented Sin"
Butler, Pierce. *Sean O'Faolain . . .*, 60–61.
Harmon, Maurice. *Sean OFaolain . . .*, 95–100; rpt. Butler, Pierce. *Sean O'Faolain . . .*, 149–153.

"Marmalade"
Butler, Pierce. *Sean O'Faolain . . .*, 104–105.

"A Meeting"
Hanley, Katherine. "The Short Stories of Sean O'Faolain: Theory and Practice," in *Eire-Ireland*, 6, iii (Fall, 1971), 6–7; rpt. Butler, Pierce. *Sean O'Faolain . . .*, 156–157.

"Midsummer Night Madness"
Butler, Pierce. *Sean O'Faolain . . .*, 11–13.

"Mother Matilda's Book"
Butler, Pierce. *Sean O'Faolain . . .*, 42–45.

"Murder at Cobbler's Hulk"
Butler, Pierce. *Sean O'Faolain* . . . , 109–111.

"Of Sanctity and Whiskey"
Butler, Pierce. *Sean O'Faolain* . . . , 97–99.

"One Night in Turin"
Butler, Pierce. *Sean O'Faolain* . . . , 72–78.

"Passion"
Butler, Pierce. *Sean O'Faolain* . . . , 50–52.
Hanley, Katherine. "The Short Stories . . . ," 7–8; rpt. Butler, Pierce. *Sean O'Faolain* . . . , 157–158.

"The Patriot"
Butler, Pierce. *Sean O'Faolain* . . . , 16–19.

"A Present of Clonmacnois"
Butler, Pierce. *Sean O'Faolain* . . . , 112–113.

"Shades of the Prison House"
Butler, Pierce. *Sean O'Faolain* . . . , 48–50.

"The Silence of the Valley"
Butler, Pierce. *Sean O'Faolain* . . . , 57–60.
Hopkins, Robert H. "The Pastoral Mode of Sean O'Faolain's 'The Silence of the Valley,' " *Stud Short Fiction*, 1 (1963–1964), 93–98; rpt. Butler, Pierce. *Sean O'Faolain* . . . , 144–148.
Roskoski, Mark. "The Cycle of Time in Sean O'Faolain's 'The Silence of the Valley,' " *Notes Mod Irish Lit*, 6 (1994), 19–24.

"Sinners"
Butler, Pierce. *Sean O'Faolain* . . . , 41–42.

"The Sugawn Chair"
Butler, Pierce. *Sean O'Faolain* . . . , 84–86.

"Teresa"
Butler, Pierce. *Sean O'Faolain* . . . , 45–48.

"There's a Birdie in the Cage"
Butler, Pierce. *Sean O'Faolain* . . . , 34–37.

"A Touch of Autumn in the Air"
Butler, Pierce. *Sean O'Faolain* . . . , 86–87.
Hanley, Katherine. "The Short Stories . . . ," 9–10; rpt. Butler, Pierce. *Sean O'Faolain* . . . , 158–159.

"Unholy Living and Half Dying"
Achilles, Jochen. "Sean O'Faolains 'Unholy Living and Half Dying' im Lichte von James Joyces 'Grace,' " in Lubbers, Klaus, Ed. *Die Englische* . . . , 293–314.

"The Younger Generation"
Butler, Pierce. *Sean O'Faolain* . . . , 52–55.

LIAM O'FLAHERTY

"Desire"
Cahalan, James M. *Liam O'Flaherty* . . . , 22–27.

"The Ecstasy of Angus"
Cahalan, James M. *Liam O'Flaherty* . . . , 50–51.

"The Fairy Goose"
Cahalan, James M. *Liam O'Flaherty* . . . , 38.

"Going into Exile"
Cahalan, James M. *Liam O'Flaherty* . . . , 39, 62.

"The Hawk"
Cahalan, James M. *Liam O'Flaherty* . . . , 60.

"Indian Summer"
Cahalan, James M. *Liam O'Flaherty* . . . , 48.

"King of Inishcam"
Cahalan, James M. *Liam O'Flaherty* . . . , 71–72.

"Milking Time"
Cahalan, James M. *Liam O'Flaherty* . . . , 44–45.

"The Mirror"
Cahalan, James M. *Liam O'Flaherty* . . . , 46.

"The Old Woman"
Cahalan, James M. *Liam O'Flaherty* . . . , 50.

"Pasta, or the Belly of Gold"
Cahalan, James M. *Liam O'Flaherty* . . . , 69.

"The Post Office"
Cahalan, James M. *Liam O'Flaherty* . . . , 72–73.

"The Reaping Race"
Cahalan, James M. *Liam O'Flaherty* . . . , 45.

"Red Barbara"
Cahalan, James M. *Liam O'Flaherty* . . . , 49–50.

"Spring Sowing"
Cahalan, James M. *Liam O'Flaherty* . . . , 44.

"The Wounded Cormorant"
Cahalan, James M. *Liam O'Flaherty* . . . , 53.

JOHN O'HARA

"Do You Like It Here?"
+Bohner, Charles H. *Instructor's Manual* . . . , 3rd ed., 111–112.

"The Ideal Man"
Zachrau, Thekla. "John O'Hara: 'The Ideal Man,' " in Lubbers, Klaus, Ed. *Die Englische* . . . , 324–333.

O. HENRY [WILLIAM SYDNEY PORTER]

"According to Their Lights"
Current-Garcia, Eugene. *O. Henry* . . . , 77.

"Thimble, Thimble"
Current-Garcia, Eugene. *O. Henry* . . . , 17–18.

"To Him Who Waits"
Current-Garcia, Eugene. *O. Henry* . . . , 94.

"Transients in Arcadia"
Current-Garcia, Eugene. *O. Henry* . . . , 88–89.

"The Trimmed Lamp"
Current-Garcia, Eugene. *O. Henry* . . . , 69–70.

"An Unfinished Story"
Current-Garcia, Eugene. *O. Henry* . . . , 70–71.

"The Unknown Quantity"
Current-Garcia, Eugene. *O. Henry* . . . , 75.

"The Venturers"
Current-Garcia, Eugene. *O. Henry* . . . , 93–94.

"Vereton Villa"
Current-Garcia, Eugene. *O. Henry* . . . , 5–6.

"What You Want"
Current-Garcia, Eugene. *O. Henry* . . . , 75–76.

"While the Auto Waits"
Current-Garcia, Eugene. *O. Henry* . . . , 87–88.

"Witches Loaves"
Current-Garcia, Eugene. *O. Henry* . . . , 66–67.

"The World and the Door"
Current-Garcia, Eugene. *O. Henry* . . . , 51–52.

OKAMOTO KANOKO

"Legacy"
Copeland, Rebecca L. "Okamoto Kanoko (1889–1939)," in Mulhern, Chieko I., Ed. *Japanese* . . . , 298.

"The Old Geisha"
Copeland, Rebecca L. "Okamoto Kanoko . . . ," 300–301.

MANUEL ZAPATA OLIVELLA

"The Metamorphosis of Mr. 'Nearly Blind' "
Captain-Hidalgo, Yvonne. . . . *Manuel Zapata Olivella*, 83–86, 88–89.

"The Multi-colored Lenses"
Captain-Hidalgo, Yvonne. . . . *Manuel Zapata Olivella*, 86–88.

"A Stranger Under My Skin"
Captain-Hidalgo, Yvonne. . . . *Manuel Zapata Olivella*, 86, 90–91, 125.

"Who Passed the Gun to Oswald?"
Captain-Hidalgo, Yvonne. . . . *Manuel Zapata Olivella*, 91.

TILLIE OLSEN

"Hey Sailor, What Ship?"

+Coiner, Constance. " 'No One's Private Ground': A Bakhtinian Reading of Tillie Olsen's *Tell Me a Riddle*," in Hedges, Elaine, and Shelley F. Fishkin, Eds. *Listening to Silences* . . . , 79–81. [See also Nelson, Kay H., and Nancy Huse, Eds. *The Critical Response* . . . , 178–181.]

Faulkner, Mara. *Protest and Possibility* . . . , 73–76, 148.

Rosenfelt, Deborah S. "Rereading *Tell Me a Riddle* in the Age of Deconstruction," in Hedges, Elaine, and Shelley F. Fishkin, Eds. *Listening to Silences* . . . , 56–57.

"I Stand Here Ironing"

+Bohner, Charles H. *Instructor's Manual* . . . , 3rd ed., 112–113.

+Coiner, Constance. " 'No One's Private . . . ," 74–76 [*The Critical Response* . . . , 172–175].

Faulkner, Mara. *Protest and Possibility* . . . , 104, 105, 117–120, 136.

Frye, Joanne S. " 'I Stand Here Ironing': Motherhood as Experience in Metaphor," *Stud Short Fiction*, 18 (1981), 287–292; rpt. Nelson, Kay H., and Nancy Huse, Eds. *The Critical Response* . . . , 128–133.

Kloss, Robert J. "Balancing the Hurts and Needs: Olsen's 'I Stand Here Ironing,' " *J Evolutionary Psych*, 15, i–ii (1994), 78–86.

Lidoff, Joan. "Fluid Boundaries: The Mother-Daughter Story, the Story-Reader Matrix," *Texas Stud Lit & Lang*, 35 (1993), 410–411.

Pickering, James H., and Jeffrey D. Hoeper. *Instructor's Manual* . . . , 91–92.

Rosenfelt, Deborah S. "Rereading . . . ," 60–62.

"O Yes"

+Coiner, Constance. " 'No One's Private . . . ," 81–83, 90 [*The Critical Response* . . . , 181–187, 191].

Faulkner, Mara. *Protest and Possibility* . . . , 60, 95–96, 101–102, 148, 152.

Huse, Nancy. "Re-reading Tillie Olsen's 'O Yes,' " in Nelson, Kay H., and Nancy Huse, Eds. *The Critical Response* . . . , 196–205.

+Jacobs, Naomi. "Olsen's 'O Yes': Alv's Vision as Childbirth Account," in Nelson, Kay H., and Nancy Huse, Eds. *The Critical Response* . . . , 134–135.

Lidoff, Joan. "Fluid Boundaries . . . ," 405–407, 408, 417.

Rosenfelt, Deborah S. "Rereading . . . ," 62–68.

"Requa"

+Gelfant, Blanche H. "After Long Silence: Tillie Olsen's 'Requa,' " in Nelson, Kay H., and Nancy Huse, Eds. *The Critical Response* . . . , 206–215.

Faulkner, Mara. *Protest and Possibility* . . . , 65, 76–77, 79, 102–104, 122–123, 129–130, 134–135, 144–145, 146–147.

Orr, Elaine. "Rethinking the Father: Maternal Recursion in Tillie Olsen's 'Requa,' " in Nelson, Kay H., and Nancy Huse, Eds. *The Critical Response* . . . , 216–228.

"Tell Me a Riddle"

Aiken, Susan H. "Stages of Dissent: Olsen, Grekova, and the Politics of Creativity," in Aiken, Susan H., Adele M. Barker, Maya Koreneva, and Ekaterina Stetsenko, Eds. *Dialogues/Dialogi* . . . , 132–140.

+Coiner, Constance. " 'No One's Private . . . ," 76–78, 87–90 [*The Critical Response* . . . , 175–178, 187–190].

Faulkner, Mara. *Protest and Possibility* . . . , 44–46, 48–55, 58–59, 60–61, 72–73, 83–95, 101, 120–122, 134, 148, 149, 152, 154.

Lidoff, Joan. "Fluid Boundaries . . . ," 408–410, 417.

+Neihus, Edward L., and Teresa Jackson. "Polar Stars, Pyramids, and 'Tell Me a Riddle,' " in Nelson, Kay H., and Nancy Huse, Eds. *The Critical Response* . . . , 136–143.

Rosenfelt, Deborah S. "Rereading . . . ," 51–57.

Stetsenko, Ekaterina. "Revolutions from Within," in Aiken, Susan H., Adele M. Barker, Maya Koreneva, and Ekaterina Stetsenko, Eds. *Dialogues/Dialogi* . . . , 152–156.

JUAN CARLOS ONETTI

"La araucaria"

Tijeras, Eduardo. "Cuentos de Juan Carlos Onetti," *Cuadernos Hispanoamericanos*, 532 (October, 1994), 120–121.

"Bienvenido, Bob"

Turton, Peter. " 'Bienvenido, Bob,' " *'Esbjerg, en la costa' y otros cuentos* [by Juan Carlos Onetti], 10–17.

"La cara de la desgracia"

Tijeras, Eduardo. "Cuentos . . . ," 120.

Turton, Peter. " 'La cara de la desgracia,' " *'Esbjerg* . . . , 35–47.

"Esbjerg, en la costa"

Turton, Peter. " 'Esbjerg, en la costa,' " *'Esbjerg* . . . , 17–28.

"Goodbyes"

Sullivan, Mary-Lee. "Projection as a Narrative Technique in Juan Carlos Onetti's 'Goodbyes,' " *Stud Short Fiction*, 31 (1994), 441–447.

"El infierno tan temida"

Turton, Peter. " 'El infierno tan temida,' " *'Esbjerg* . . . , 28–35.

"La larga historia"

Tijeras, Eduardo. "Cuentos . . . ," 120.

"Mascarada"

Méndez-Clark, Ronald S. *Onetti y la (in)fidelidad* . . . , 156–157.

"El pozo"

Ainsa, Fernando. "Juan Carlos Onetti (1909–1994): An Existential Allegory of Contemporary Man," trans. David D. Clark, *World Lit Today*, 68 (1994), 501, 502.

"Tan triste como ella"

Tijeras, Eduardo. "Cuentos . . . ," 119–120.

PEDRO ORGAMBIDE

"Los otros"
Rodríguez Michemberg, Susana M. " 'Los otros' o el tercer hombre," *Alba de América*, 11 (1993), 189–198.

ANTONIO LÓPEZ ORTEGA

"Bajo los pinos"
Leáñez Aristimuño, Carlos. "Antonio López Ortega: hacia el cuento lírico," *Revista Iberoamericana*, 60 (1994), 359–360.

"De rodillas"
Aristimuño, Carlos L. "Antonio López Ortega . . . ," 360–362.

"En la palma de la mano"
Aristimuño, Carlos L. "Antonio López Ortega . . . ," 358–359.

"Los labios de Laura"
Aristimuño, Carlos L. "Antonio López Ortega . . . ," 357–358.

"La lengua"
Aristimuño, Carlos L. "Antonio López Ortega . . . ," 356–357.

"La nuez"
Aristimuño, Carlos L. "Antonio López Ortega . . . ," 353–355.

"Piraguas"
Aristimuño, Carlos L. "Antonio López Ortega . . . ," 362–363.

GEORGE ORWELL

"Animal Farm"
Bergonzi, Bernard. *Wartime* . . . , 97–100.
Letemendia, V. C. "Revolution on Animal Farm: Orwell's Neglected Commentary," *J Mod Lit*, 18 (1992), 129–137.

CYNTHIA OZICK

"At Fumicaro"
Strandberg, Victor. *Greek Mind* . . . , 108–111.

"Bloodshed"
Kauvar, Elaine M. *Cynthia Ozick's Fiction* . . . , 84–92.
Strandberg, Victor. *Greek Mind* . . . , 95–96.

"The Butterfly and the Traffic Light"
Kauvar, Elaine M. *Cynthia Ozick's Fiction* . . . , 40–41.
Strandberg, Victor. *Greek Mind* . . . , 84–85.

"The Dock-Witch"
Kauvar, Elaine M. *Cynthia Ozick's Fiction* . . . , 49–59.
Strandberg, Victor. *Greek Mind* . . . , 83.

"The Doctor's Wife"
Kauvar, Elaine M. *Cynthia Ozick's Fiction* . . . , 66–70.
Strandberg, Victor. *Greek Mind* . . . , 85–87.

"An Education"
Kauvar, Elaine M. *Cynthia Ozick's Fiction* . . . , 92–99.
Strandberg, Victor. *Greek Mind* . . . , 92.

"Envy; or, Yiddish in America"
Cohen, Sarah B. "Cynthia Ozick: Prophet for Parochialism," in Baskin, Judith R., Ed. *Women of the Word* . . . , 288–295.
———. *Cynthia Ozick's Comic Art* . . . , 48–62.
Kauvar, Elaine M. *Cynthia Ozick's Fiction* . . . , 53–62
Strandberg, Victor. *Greek Mind* . . . , 88–90.

"From a Refugee's Notebook"
Strandberg, Victor. *Greek Mind* . . . , 100, 101.

"Levitation"
Cohen, Sarah B. *Cynthia Ozick's Comic Art* . . . , 68–72.
Kauvar, Elaine M. *Cynthia Ozick's Fiction* . . . , 111–119.
Strandberg, Victor. *Greek Mind* . . . , 97–98.

"A Mercenary"
Friedman, Lawrence S. "A Postcolonial Jew: Cynthia Ozick's Holocaust Survivor," *SPAN*, 36 (1993), 436–443.
Kauvar, Elaine M. *Cynthia Ozick's Fiction* . . . , 75–84, 91–92.
Strandberg, Victor. *Greek Mind* . . . , 93–95.

"The Messiah of Stockholm"
Strandberg, Victor. *Greek Mind* . . . , 124–139.

"The Pagan Rabbi"
Cohen, Sarah B. "Cynthia Ozick . . . ," 285–288.
———. *Cynthia Ozick's Comic Art* . . . , 64–68.
Kauvar, Elaine M. *Cynthia Ozick's Fiction* . . . , 41–49.
Strandberg, Victor. *Greek Mind* . . . , 82–83.

"Puttermesser and Xanthippe"
Finkelstein, Norman. *The Ritual of New* . . . , 70–72.
Kauvar, Elaine M. *Cynthia Ozick's Fiction* . . . , 131–146.
Strandberg, Victor. *Greek Mind* . . . , 103–104, 155.

"Puttermesser: Her Work History, Her Ancestry, Her Afterlife"
Kauvar, Elaine M. *Cynthia Ozick's Fiction* . . . , 127–131.
Strandberg, Victor. *Greek Mind* . . . , 101.

"Puttermesser Paired"
Strandberg, Victor. *Greek Mind* . . . , 104–108.

"Rosa"
Kauvar, Elaine M. *Cynthia Ozick's Fiction* . . . , 184–202.

"The Sewing Harems"
Kauvar, Elaine M. *Cynthia Ozick's Fiction* . . . , 125–127.

"The Shawl"
Gordon, Andrew. "Cynthia Ozick's 'The Shawl' and the Transitional Object," *Lit & Psych*, 40, i–ii (1994), 1–9.

Kauvar, Elaine M. *Cynthia Ozick's Fiction* . . . , 179–184.
Strandberg, Victor. *Greek Mind* . . . , 139–151.

"Shots"
Kauvar, Elaine M. *Cynthia Ozick's Fiction* . . . , 119–122.
Strandberg, Victor. *Greek Mind* . . . , 98–100.

"The Suitcase"
Kauvar, Elaine M. *Cynthia Ozick's Fiction* . . . , 62–66.
Klingenstein, Susanne. "Visits to Germany in Recent Jewish-American Writing," *Contemporary Lit*, 34 (1993), 543–544.
Strandberg, Victor. *Greek Mind* . . . , 87–88.

"Usurpation (Other People's Stories)"
Cohen, Sarah B. *Cynthia Ozick's Comic Art* . . . , 72–81.
Kauvar, Elaine M. *Cynthia Ozick's Fiction* . . . , 99–110.
Strandberg, Victor. *Greek Mind* . . . , 90–92.

"Virility"
Cohen, Sarah B. *Cynthia Ozick's Comic Art* . . . , 83–85.
Kauvar, Elaine M. *Cynthia Ozick's Fiction* . . . , 70–73.
Strandberg, Victor. *Greek Mind* . . . , 85.

CRISTINA PACHECO

"La dicha conyugal"
Valdés, María Elena de. "La obra de Cristina Pacheco: Ficción testimonial de la mujer mexicana," *Escritura*, 16 (1991), 276.

"Esposa y mártir"
Valdés, María Elena de. "La obra . . . ," 275–276.

PAI HSIEN-YUNG

"Ashes"
Wong, Wai-leung. " 'Rediscovering the Use of Ancient Chinese Culture': A Look at Pai Hsien-yung's 'Ashes' through Liu Hsieh's 'Six Points' Theory," *Tamkang R*, 23, i (1992–1993), 759–777.

PABLO PALACIO

"Un hombre muerto a puntapiés"
Dahl, Mari. "Reacciones frente al espejo palaciano: La condena, la locura y la modernidad," *Dactylus*, 12 (1993), 73–77.

GRACE PALEY

"A Conservation with My Father"
Arcana, Judith. *Grace Paley's Life Stories* . . . , 89–91.
+Bohner, Charles H. *Instructor's Manual* . . . , 3rd ed., 113–114.
Charters, Ann. *Resources* . . . , 144–145.

"Dreamer in a Dead Language"
Arcana, Judith. *Grace Paley's Life Stories . . .*, 89, 111–112, 172, 207.

"Enormous Changes at the Last Minute"
Arcana, Judith. *Grace Paley's Life Stories . . .*, 104–105, 132–133.

"The Expensive Moment"
Arcana, Judith. *Grace Paley's Life Stories . . .*, 112–113.

"Faith in a Tree"
Arcana, Judith. *Grace Paley's Life Stories . . .*, 56, 58, 72, 109–110, 133, 207.
Meyer, Adam. "Faith and the 'Black Thing': Political Action and Self-Questioning in Grace Paley's Short Fiction," *Stud Short Fiction*, 31 (1994), 81–82.

"The Floating Truth"
Arcana, Judith. *Grace Paley's Life Stories . . .*, 131–132.

"Friends"
Arcana, Judith. *Grace Paley's Life Stories . . .*, 49, 64, 172–173, 188–189.

"Gloomy Tune"
Arcana, Judith. *Grace Paley's Life Stories . . .*, 73–74.

"Goodbye and Good Luck"
Arcana, Judith. *Grace Paley's Life Stories . . .*, 85.

"The Immigrant Story"
Arcana, Judith. *Grace Paley's Life Stories . . .*, 111, 132–133, 176–177.

"Lavinia: An Old Story"
Arcana, Judith. *Grace Paley's Life Stories . . .*, 39, 133–134, 172.

"Listening"
Arcana, Judith. *Grace Paley's Life Stories . . .*, 209–210.

"The Little Girl"
Arcana, Judith. *Grace Paley's Life Stories . . .*, 106–108.

"The Long Distance Runner"
Arcana, Judith. *Grace Paley's Life Stories . . .*, 109, 157–158, 161, 176–177, 193–194.
Baumgarten, Murray. "Urban Rites and Civic Premises in the Fiction of Saul Bellow, Grace Paley, and Sandra Schor," *Contemp Lit*, 34 (1993), 407–409.
Lidoff, Joan. "Fluid Boundaries: The Mother-Daughter Story, the Story-Reader Matrix," *Texas Stud Lit & Lang*, 35 (1993), 412–415.
Meyer, Adam. "Faith and the 'Black Thing' . . . ," 82–84.

"The Loudest Voice"
Charters, Ann. *Resources . . .*, 146.
Pinsker, Sanford. "Grace Paley's Book of the Ordinary," *Gettysburg R*, 7 (1994), 698–700.

"Love"
Arcana, Judith. *Grace Paley's Life Stories . . .*, 110–111.

"Mom"
Arcana, Judith. *Grace Paley's Life Stories* . . . , 172.

"Mother"
Arcana, Judith. *Grace Paley's Life Stories* . . . , 187.

"Northeast Playground"
Arcana, Judith. *Grace Paley's Life Stories* . . . , 161, 206.

"Politics"
Arcana, Judith. *Grace Paley's Life Stories* . . . , 94–95, 144.

"Ruthy and Edie"
Arcana, Judith. *Grace Paley's Life Stories* . . . , 162.

"The Sad Story About the Six Boys About to Be Drafted in Brooklyn"
Arcana, Judith. *Grace Paley's Life Stories* . . . , 144–145.

"Samuel"
Arcana, Judith. *Grace Paley's Life Stories* . . . , 72–73.

"Somewhere Else"
Arcana, Judith. *Grace Paley's Life Stories* . . . , 198–199.
Pinsker, Sanford. "Grace Paley's Book . . . ," 701.

"The Story Hearer"
Arcana, Judith. *Grace Paley's Life Stories* . . . , 108–109, 209.

"Wants"
Arcana, Judith. *Grace Paley's Life Stories* . . . , 157.

"A Woman, Young and Old"
Arcana, Judith. *Grace Paley's Life Stories* . . . , 47–48.

"Zagrowsky Tells"
Arcana, Judith. *Grace Paley's Life Stories* . . . , 162–163, 208, 211.
Meyer, Adam. "Faith and the 'Black Thing' . . . ," 85–88.

CLEMENTE PALMA

"Mors ex vita"
Burgos, Fernando. "Modos de lo fantástico en la cuentística de Clemente Palma y Julio Garmendia," in Tyler, Joseph, Ed. *Selected Essays* . . . , 128–131.

AVDOTYA PANAEVA

"The Talnikov Family"
Kelly, Catriona. *A History of Russian* . . . , 62–63, 195.

BREECE D'J PANCAKE

"Hollow"
Douglass, Thomas E. "Breece Pancake and the Problem with Place: A West Virginia State of Mind," *Appalachian J*, 22, i (1994), 65.

"The Salvation of Me"
Douglass, Thomas E. "Breece Pancake . . . ," 64–65, 71–72.

EMILIA PARDO BAZÁN

"La Mayorazga de Bouzas"
Pérez, Janet. "Winners, Losers and Casualities in Pardo Bazán's Battle of the Sexes," *Letras Peninsulares*, 5, iii (1992–1993), 350.

"Mi suicidio"
Tolliver, Joyce. "Discourse Analysis and the Interpretation of Literary Narrative," *Style*, 24 (1990), 273–278.
———. "Script Theory, Perspective, and Message in Narrative: The Case of 'Mi suicidio,' " in Bernstein, Cynthia G., Ed. *The Text Beyond* . . . , 97–119.

"La mirada"
Tolliver, Joyce. " 'La que entrega la mirada, lo entrega todo': The Sexual Economy of the Gaze in Pardo Bazán's 'La mirada,' " *Romance Lang Annual*, 4 (1992), 620–626.

"Sor Aparición"
Tolliver, Joyce. " 'Sor Aparición' and the Gaze: Pardo Bazán's Gendered Reply to the Romantic Don Juan," *Hispania*, 77 (1994), 394–405.

WALKER PERCY

"The Message in the Bottle"
Futrell, Ann M. *The Signs* . . . , 36–38.

IZHAK [ITZHAK] LEIB PERETZ

"Bontsha the Silent"
Zuckerman, Bruce. *Job the Silent* . . . , 34–46, 58–81.

BENITO PÉREZ GALDOS

"¿Dónde está mi cabeza?"
Willem, Linda M. "Anticipating Postmodernism in Two Galdosian Fantasies: 'Dónde está mi cabeza?' and the Final *Episodios Nacionales*," in Willem, Linda M., Ed. *A Sesquicentennial* . . . , 250–254.

CRISTINA PERI-ROSSI

"El ángel caído"
Olivera-Williams, María R. " 'El derrumbamiento' de Armonía

Somers y 'El ángel caído' de Cristina Peri-Rossi: Dos Manifestaciones de la narrative imaginaria," *Revista Chilena*, 42 (1993), 179–180.

LYUDMILA PETRUSHEVSKAYA

"Dark Fate"

Kustanovich, Konstantin. "Erotic Glasnost: Sexuality in Recent Russian Literature," *World Lit Today*, 67 (1993), 141.

"The Isolation Box"

Wool, Josephine. "The Minotaur in the Maze: Remarks on Lyudmila Petrushevskaya," *World Lit Today*, 67 (1993), 128–129.

"Night Time"

Wool, Josephine. "The Minotaur . . . ," 129.

"Our Crowd"

Kelly, Catriona. *A History of Russian . . .* , 364.
Porter, Robert. *Russia's Alternative Prose*, 55–58.
Wool, Josephine. "The Minotaur . . . ," 126–128, 129.

"That Kind of Girl"

Aiken, Susan H. "Telling the Other('s) Story, or, the Blues in Two Languages," in Aiken, Susan H., Adele M. Barker, Maya Koreneva, and Ekaterina Stetsenko, Eds. *Dialogues/Dialogi . . .* , 215–221.
Koreneva, Maya. "Children of the Sixties," in Aiken, Susan H., Adele M. Barker, Maya Koreneva, and Ekaterina Stetsenko, Eds. *Dialogues/Dialogi . . .* , 194–199.

"Two Sisters"

Porter, Robert. *Russia's Alternative Prose*, 62.

ANN PETRY

"Miss Muriel"

Holladay, Hilary. "Creative Prejudice in Ann Petry's 'Miss Muriel,' " *Stud Short Fiction*, 31 (1994), 667–674.

JAYNE ANN PHILLIPS

"Home"

Barker, Adele M. "The World of Our Mothers," in Aiken, Susan H., Adele M. Barker, Maya Koreneva, and Ekaterina Stetsenko, Eds. *Dialogues/Dialogi . . .* , 253–258.
Koreneva, Maya. "Hopes and Nightmares of the Young," in Aiken, Susan H., Adele M. Barker, Maya Koreneva, and Ekaterina Stetsenko, Eds. *Dialogues/Dialogi . . .* , 267–273.

LOUISE PICHLER

"Der Sohn der Wittwe"
Peterson, Brent O. "The 'Political' and the German-American Press," *Yearbook Germ-Am Stud*, 23 (1988), 45–47.

VIRGILIO PIÑERA

"El álbum"
Osuna de Esteguy, María L. "La intertextualidad en 'El álbum' de Virgilio Piñera," in Arancibia, Juana Alcira, Ed. *Literatura como . . .*, 457–465.

"Cómo viví y cómo morí"
Chichester, Ana G. "Metamorphosis in Two Short Stories of the Fantastic by Virgilio Piñera and Felisberto Hernández," *Stud Short Fiction*, 31 (1994), 388–390.

"El filántropo"
McQuade, Frank. "Making Sense Out of Non-Sense: Virgilio Piñera and the Short Story of the Absurd," in Macklin, John, Ed. *After Cervantes . . .*, 206–207.

"El infierno"
McQuade, Frank. "Making Sense Out . . . ," 215–216.

"El señor Ministro"
McQuade, Frank. "Making Sense Out . . . ," 209–210.

P'ING LU

"The Taiwan Miracle"
Wang, David Der-wei. "*Fin-de-siècle* Splendor: Contemporary Women Writers' Vision of Taiwan," *Mod Chinese Lit*, 6, i–ii (1992), 47–52.

NÉLIDA PIÑON

"I Love My Husband"
Schmidt, Rita T. "Un juego de máscaras: Nelida Piñon y Mary McCarthy," *Escritura*, 16 (1991), 263–266, 267–270.

LUIGI PIRANDELLO

"Acqua amara"
Caesar, Ann H. "Telling Tales: Pirandello and the Short Story," *Yearbook Soc Pirandello Stud*, 13 (1993), 6.

"L'altro figlio"
Caesar, Ann H. "Telling Tales . . . ," 5.

"La carriola"
Caesar, Ann H. "Telling Tales . . . ," 6–7.

"Certi obblighi"
Caesar, Ann H. "Telling Tales . . . ," 9.

"Felicità"
Grazia Di Paolo, Maria. "Women's Marginality and Self-Obliteration in Some of Pirandello's *Novelle*," *Forum Italicum*, 27, i–ii (1993), 210–211.

"Ho tante cose da dirvi"
Grazia Di Paolo, Maria. "Women's Marginality . . . ," 211–212.

"Lucilla"
Grazia Di Paolo, Maria. "Women's Marginality . . . ," 207–208.

"La maschera dimenticata"
Caesar, Ann H. "Telling Tales . . . ," 10–11.

"Il ventaglino"
Grazia Di Paolo, Maria. "Women's Marginality . . . ," 208–210.

"La verità"
Caesar, Ann H. "Telling Tales . . . ," 9–10.

"La veste lungo"
Grazia Di Paolo, Maria. "Women's Marginality . . . ," 204–205, 207.

"I viaggio"
Grazia Di Paolo, Maria. "Women's Marginality . . . ," 205–207.

"War"
+Bohner, Charles H. *Instructor's Manual* . . . , 3rd ed., 114–115.

EDGAR ALLAN POE

"The Balloon Hoax"
Alkon, Paul K. *Science Fiction* . . . , 102–103.

"Berenice"
Doyle, Jacqueline. "(Dis)Figuring Woman: Edgar Allan Poe's 'Berenice,' " *Poe Stud*, 26 (1993), 13–21.
Irwin, John T. *The Mystery to a Solution* . . . , 231–232, 234.
Voller, Jack G. *The Supernatural Sublime* . . . , 226–229.

"The Black Cat"
Benfey, Christopher. "Poe and the Unreadable: 'The Black Cat' and 'The Tell-Tale Heart,' " in Silverman, Kenneth, Ed. *New Essays* . . . , 29, 32, 35–43.
Madden, Fred. "Poe's 'The Black Cat' and Freud's 'The Uncanny,' " *Lit & Psych*, 39, i–ii (1993), 52–62.
Voller, Jack G. *The Supernatural Sublime* . . . , 234–235.

"The Cask of Amontillado"
+Bohner, Charles H. *Instructor's Manual* . . . , 3rd ed., 115–116.
Cervo, Nathan. "Poe's 'The Cask of Amontillado,' " *Explicator*, 51 (1993), 155–156.

Charters, Ann. *Resources . . .* , 148–149.
Pickering, James H., and Jeffrey D. Hoeper. *Instructor's Manual . . .* , 12–13.
Reynolds, David S. "Poe's Art of Transformation: 'The Cask of Amontillado' in Its Cultural Context," in Silverman, Kenneth, Ed. *New Essays . . .* , 93–112.
Voller, Jack G. *The Supernatural Sublime . . .* , 233–234.

"A Descent into the Maelström"
Person, Leland S. "Trusting the Tellers: Paradoxes of Narrative Authority in Poe's 'A Descent into the Maelström,' " *J Narrative Technique*, 23 (1993), 46–56.

"Eleonora"
Elbert, Monika. "Poe's Gothic Mother and the Incubation of Language," *Poe Stud*, 26 (1993), 29.
Irwin, John T. *The Mystery to a Solution . . .* , 231, 238–240.

"The Facts in the Case of M. Valdemar"
Ware, Tracy. "The 'Salutary Discomfort' in the Case of M. Valdemar," *Stud Short Fiction*, 31 (1994), 471–480.

"The Fall of the House of Usher"
+Bohner, Charles H. *Instructor's Manual . . .* , 3rd ed., 116–117.
Bradfield, Scott. *Dreaming . . .* , 86–92.
Coss, David L. "Art and Sentience in 'The Fall of the House of Usher,' " *Pleiades*, 14, i (1993), 93–106.
Elbert, Monika. "Poe's Gothic . . . ," 24–28.
Irwin, John T. *The Mystery to a Solution . . .* , 213–214, 231.
Kaplan, Louise J. "The Perverse Strategy in 'The Fall of the House of Usher,' " in Silverman, Kenneth, Ed. *New Essays . . .* , 45–64.
May, Leila S. " 'Sympathies of a Scarcely Intelligible Nature': The Brother-Sister Bond in Poe's 'The Fall of the House of Usher,' " *Stud Short Fiction*, 30 (1993), 387–396.
Pickering, James H., and Jeffrey D. Hoeper. *Instructor's Manual . . .* , 9–10.
Schneider, Kirk J. *Horror and the Holy . . .* , 50–54.
Tallack, Douglas. *The Nineteenth-Century American Short Story . . .* , 45–46, 48–60.

"The Gold Bug"
Tallack, Douglas. *The Nineteenth-Century American Short Story . . .* , 85–98.
Toner, Jennifer D. "The 'Remarkable Effect' of 'Silly Words': Dialect and Signature in 'The Gold Bug,' " *Arizona Q*, 49, i (1993), 1–20.
Whalen, Terence. "The Code for Gold: Edgar Allen Poe and Cryptography," *Representations*, 46 (Spring, 1994), 46–54.

"Hop-Frog"
Kowalewski, Michael. *Deadly Musings . . .* , 98–101.

"The Imp of the Perverse"
Brown, Arthur A. "Death and Telling in Poe's 'The Imp of the Perverse,' " *Stud Short Fiction*, 31 (1994), 197–205.

Kowalewski, Michael. *Deadly Musings* . . . , 86–87.
Loving, Jerome. *Lost in the Customhouse* . . . , 55–56.

"Ligeia"
Andriano, Joseph. *Our Ladies* . . . , 84–90.
Charters, Ann. *Resources* . . . , 149–150.
Del Principe, David. "Heresy and 'Hair-esy' in Ugo Tarchetti's *Fosca*," *Italica*, 71, i (1994), 48–49.
Elbert, Monika. "Poe's Gothic . . . ," 28.
Herndl, Diane P. *Invalid Women* . . . , 91–94.
Kennedy, J. Gerald. "Poe, 'Ligeia,' and the Problem of Dying Women," in Silverman, Kenneth, Ed. *New Essays* . . . , 119–127.

"The Man of the Crowd"
Minter, David. *A Cultural History* . . . , 35–36.

"MS. Found in a Bottle"
Friedl, Herwig. "Edgar Allan Poe: 'MS. Found in a Bottle,' " in Lubbers, Klaus, Ed. *Die Englische* . . . , 40–51.

"Masque of the Red Death"
Dudley, David R. "Dead or Alive: The Booby-Trapped Narrator of Poe's 'Masque of the Red Death,' " *Stud Short Fiction*, 30 (1993), 169–173.

"Mellonta Tauta"
Alkon, Paul K. *Science Fiction* . . . , 103–104.
Bradfield, Scott. *Dreaming* . . . , 96.

"Morella"
Elbert, Monika. "Poe's Gothic . . . ," 28–29.
Irwin, John T. *The Mystery to a Solution* . . . , 231, 373–374.

"The Murders in the Rue Morgue"
Bradfield, Scott. *Dreaming* . . . , 100–106.
Irwin, John T. *The Mystery to a Solution* . . . , 11–12, 27, 65–67, 133–134, 168, 178–180, 187–188, 195–200, 227–228, 229–231, 234–235, 236–237, 291–292, 318–319, 328–329, 354–356, 411, 414–415.
La Monthe, Jacques. "L'Etre en suspens," *Tangence*, 38 (1992), 65–73.
Leer, David V. "Detecting Truth: The World of the Dupin Tales," in Silverman, Kenneth, Ed. *New Essays* . . . , 65, 66, 68, 69–71, 73, 74–75, 78, 79.
Loving, Jerome. *Lost in the Customhouse* . . . , 67–69.

"The Mystery of Marie Rogêt"
Dayan, Joan. "Poe's Women: A Feminist Poe?" *Poe Stud*, 26 (1993), 11.
Irwin, John T. *The Mystery to a Solution* . . . , 237, 319, 321–329, 414–415, 420–421.
Leer, David V. "Detecting Truth . . . ," 65, 66, 67, 72, 79–88.

"The Narrative of Arthur Gordon Pym"
Loving, Jerome. *Lost in the Customhouse* . . . , 53–71.
Mainville, Stephen. "Language and the Void: Gothic Landscapes in

the Frontiers of Edgar Allan Poe,'' in Mogen, David, Scott P. Sanders, and Joanne B. Karpinski, Eds. *Frontier Gothic . . .*, 187–201.

Tallack, Douglas. *The Nineteenth-Century American Short Story . . .*, 27–41.

Whalen, Terence. ''Subtle Barbarians: Poe, Racism, and the Political Economy of Adventure,'' in Goldstein, Philip, Ed. *Styles of Cultural Activism . . .*, 169–172, 174–177, 180–182.

''The Oblong Box''

Dayan, Joan. ''Poe's Women . . .,'' 10.

''The Oval Portrait''

Herndl, Diane P. *Invalid Women. . .*, 87–90.

Rothberg, Michael. ''The Prostitution of Paris: Late Capital of the Twentieth Century,'' *Found Object*, 1 (Fall, 1992), 2–4, 7.

''The Premature Burial''

Loving, Jerome. *Lost in the Customhouse . . .*, 59–60.

Voller, Jack G. *The Supernatural Sublime . . .*, 236–237.

''The Purloined Letter''

Charters, Ann. *Resources . . .*, 151–152.

Irwin, John T. *The Mystery to a Solution . . .*, 2–12, 22–29, 82, 96–97, 115–117, 126–127, 177–178, 180–184, 191–192, 237–238, 319–321, 328–329, 331–332, 341–344, 359, 385–390, 391–397, 401–415.

Leer, David V. ''Detecting Truth . . .,'' 65, 66, 68, 72.

''Some Words with a Mummy''

Alkon, Paul K. *Science Fiction . . .*, 104–105.

Long, David A. ''Poe's Political Identity: A Mummy Unswathed,'' *Poe Stud*, 23, i (1990), 1–22.

''The Tell-Tale Heart''

Benfey, Christopher. ''Poe and the Unreadable . . .,'' 30–35, 37, 38, 39, 40–41.

''Thou Art the Man''

Irwin, John T. *The Mystery to a Solution . . .*, 202–206.

''William Wilson''

Bradfield, Scott. *Dreaming . . .*, 97–99.

Elmer, Jonathan. ''Poe, Plagiarism, and the Prescriptive Right of the Mob,'' in Lohmann, Christoph K., Ed. *Discovering Difference . . .*, 72–84.

Irwin, John T. *The Mystery to a Solution . . .*, 214–215, 296.

JOHN WILLIAM POLIDORI

''The Vampyre''

Gelder, Ken. *Reading the Vampire*, 31–34.

Macdonald, D. L., and Kathleen Scherf. ''Introduction,'' in Polidori, John William. *The Vampyre . . .*, 1–9.

MARY HELEN PONCE

"La Doctora Barr"
Wear, Delese, and Lois L. Nixon. *Literary Anatomies* . . . , 43–44.

ELENA PONIATOWSKA

"De Gaulle en minería"
Jörgensen, Beth E. *The Writings of* . . . , 126–127.

"De noche vienes"
Jörgensen, Beth E. *The Writings of* . . . , 104–105.

"El inventario"
Jörgensen, Beth E. *The Writings of* . . . , 130–131.

"El limbo"
Jörgensen, Beth E. *The Writings of* . . . , 116–117.

"The Night Visitor"
Moorhead, Florence. "Subversion with a Smile: Elena Poniatowska's 'The Night Visitor,' " *Letras Femeninas*, 20, i–ii (1994), 131–140.

VALERII POPOV

"Superfluous Virtuosity"
Brown, Deming. *The Last Years* . . . , 108.

YEVGENY POPOV

"Concentration"
Porter, Robert. *Russia's Alternative Prose*, 108.

"Denying the Waistcoat"
Porter, Robert. *Russia's Alternative Prose*, 102.

"Electronic Accordion"
Porter, Robert. *Russia's Alternative Prose*, 97–98, 100.

"Emanation"
Porter, Robert. *Russia's Alternative Prose*, 98–99, 100.

"Five Songs About Vodka"
Porter, Robert. *Russia's Alternative Prose*, 108–109.

"Grand Reception"
Porter, Robert. *Russia's Alternative Prose*, 106–108.

"I Await a Love That's True"
Porter, Robert. *Russia's Alternative Prose*, 90–92.

"Laughing—Smiling"
Porter, Robert. *Russia's Alternative Prose*, 99–100.

"The Plane for Cologne"
Kustanovich, Konstantin. "Erotic Glasnost: Sexuality in Recent Russian Literature," *World Lit Today*, 67 (1993), 141.

Vanchu, Anthony J. "Cross(-Dressing)ing One's Way to Crisis: Yevgeny Popov and Lyudmila Petrushevskaya and the Crisis of Category in Contemporary Russian Culture," *World Lit Today*, 67 (1993), 108–113.

"Pork Kebabs"
Brown, Deming. *The Last Years . . .*, 159.
Porter, Robert. *Russia's Alternative Prose*, 110.

"The Reservoir"
Brown, Deming. *The Last Years . . .*, 159–160.

"The Spiritual Effusions and Unexpected Death of Fetisov"
Porter, Robert. *Russia's Alternative Prose*, 104–106.

"The Statistician and We, Brother Slavs"
Porter, Robert. *Russia's Alternative Prose*, 101–102.

"Two Dried Fingers out of Five Former Ones"
Porter, Robert. *Russia's Alternative Prose*, 112–114.

HAL PORTER

"Gretel"
+Bohner, Charles H. *Instructor's Manual . . .*, 3rd ed., 117–118.

KATHERINE ANNE PORTER

"The Circus"
Brinkmeyer, Robert H. *Katherine Anne Porter's Artistic Development . . .*, 157–160.

"The Fig Tree"
Brinkmeyer, Robert H. *Katherine Anne Porter's Artistic Development . . .*, 162–165.

"Flowering Judas"
+Bohner, Charles H. *Instructor's Manual . . .*, 3rd ed., 119–120.
Brinkmeyer, Robert H. *Katherine Anne Porter's Artistic Development . . .*, 71–83.
———. "Mexico, Memory, and Betrayal: Katherine Anne Porter's 'Flowering Judas,' " in Carr, Virginia S., Ed. *Katherine Anne Porter . . .*, 200–209.
Carr, Virginia S. "Introduction," in Carr, Virginia S., Ed. *Katherine Anne Porter . . .*, 14–19.
Charters, Ann. *Resources . . .*, 153–155.
DeMouy, Jane K. . . . *Porter's Women . . .*, 79–92; rpt. " 'Flowering Judas': Psyche, Symbol, and Self-Betrayal," in Carr, Virginia S., Ed. *Katherine Anne Porter . . .*, 153–170.
+Gottfried, Leon. "Death's Other Kingdom: Dantesque and Theological Symbolism in 'Flowering Judas,' " in Carr, Virginia S., Ed. *Katherine Anne Porter . . .*, 99–120.
+Madden, David. "The Charged Image in Katherine Anne Porter's

'Flowering Judas,' " in Carr, Virginia S., Ed. *Katherine Anne Porter* . . . , 121–135.

Nilsen, Helge N. "Laura Against Sexism: A Feminist Reading of Katherine Anne Porter's 'Flowering Judas,' " in Kennedy, Andrew, and Orm Øverland, Eds. *Excursions in Fiction* . . . , 145–156.

Unrue, Darlene H. "Revolution and the Female Principle in 'Flowering Judas,' " in Carr, Virginia S., Ed. *Katherine Anne Porter* . . . , 137–152.

+West, Ray B. "Katherine Anne Porter: Symbol and Theme in 'Flowering Judas,' " in Carr, Virginia S., Ed. *Katherine Anne Porter* . . . , 89–97.

"The Grave"

+Bohner, Charles H. *Instructor's Manual* . . . , 3rd ed., 120–121.

Brinkmeyer, Robert H. *Katherine Anne Porter's Artistic Development* . . . , 179–181.

Pickering, James H., and Jeffrey D. Hoeper. *Instructor's Manual* . . . , 74–75.

"Hacienda"

Brinkmeyer, Robert H. *Katherine Anne Porter's Artistic Development* . . . , 62–69.

Stout, Janis P. " 'Something of a Reputation as a Radical': Katherine Anne Porter's Shifting Politics," *So Central R*, 10, i (1993), 55–57.

"He"

Brinkmeyer, Robert H. *Katherine Anne Porter's Artistic Development* . . . , 102–107.

"Holiday"

Brinkmeyer, Robert H. *Katherine Anne Porter's Artistic Development* . . . , 109–114.

"The Jilting of Granny Weatherall"

Brinkmeyer, Robert H. *Katherine Anne Porter's Artistic Development* . . . , 134–139.

"The Journey"

Brinkmeyer, Robert H. *Katherine Anne Porter's Artistic Development* . . . , 153–154.

"The Last Leaf"

Brinkmeyer, Robert H. *Katherine Anne Porter's Artistic Development* . . . , 161–162.

"The Leaning Tower"

Brinkmeyer, Robert H. *Katherine Anne Porter's Artistic Development* . . . , 211–214.

"The Man in the Tree"

Gretlund, Jan N. " 'The Man in the Tree': Katherine Anne Porter's Unfinished Lynching," *Southern Q*, 31, iii (1993), 7–16.

"María Concepción"

Brinkmeyer, Robert H. *Katherine Anne Porter's Artistic Development* . . . , 44–48.

Moddelmog, Debra. "Concepts of Justice in the Works of Katherine Anne Porter," *Mosaic*, 26, iv (1993), 44–45, 46.

"The Martyr"

Brinkmeyer, Robert H. *Katherine Anne Porter's Artistic Development* . . . , 52–54.

"Noon Wine"

Brinkmeyer, Robert H. *Katherine Anne Porter's Artistic Development* . . . , 140–145.

Charters, Ann. *Resources* . . . , 155–157.

Moddelmog, Debra. "Concepts of Justice . . . ," 45–46.

Page, Philip. "The Failure of Language and Vision in 'Noon Wine,' " *Short Story*, 1, ii, N.S. (1993), 57–63.

Sterne, Richard C. *Dark Mirror* . . . , 247–249.

"Old Mortality"

Brinkmeyer, Robert H. *Katherine Anne Porter's Artistic Development* . . . , 165–174.

Jones, Suzanne W. "Reading the Endings in Katherine Anne Porter's 'Old Mortality,' " in Booth, Alison, Ed. *Famous Last Words* . . . , 280–299. [See also *Southern Q*, 31, iii (1993), 29–44.]

Schulz, Joan. "Orphaning as Resistance," in Manning, Carol S., Ed. *The Female Tradition* . . . , 93–95.

Vande Kieft, Ruth H. "The Love Ethos of Porter, Welty, and McCullers," in Manning, Carol S., Ed. *The Female Tradition* . . . , 238–240.

"Pale Horse, Pale Rider"

Brinkmeyer, Robert H. *Katherine Anne Porter's Artistic Development* . . . , 174–179.

"That Tree"

Brinkmeyer, Robert H. *Katherine Anne Porter's Artistic Development* . . . , 69–73.

"Theft"

Brinkmeyer, Robert H. *Katherine Anne Porter's Artistic Development* . . . , 107–109.

Unrue, Darlene H. "Katherine Anne Porter, Politics, and Another Reading of 'Theft,' " *Stud Short Fiction*, 30 (1993), 119–126.

"Virgin Violeta"

Brinkmeyer, Robert H. *Katherine Anne Porter's Artistic Development* . . . , 48–52.

J. F. POWERS

"The Valiant Woman"

+Bohner, Charles H. *Instructor's Manual* . . . , 3rd ed., 121–122.

GERSON POYK

"Matias Akankari"

Hill, David T. "Writing on the Border: Irian, Indonesian Literature and Gerson Poyk's 'Matias Akankari,' " *SPAN*, 34–35 (1992–1993), 176–177.

V[ICTOR] S[AWDON] PRITCHETT

"The Diver"
+Bohner, Charles H. *Instructor's Manual* . . . , 3rd ed., 122–123.

MARÍA LUISA PUGA

"Inmóvil sol secreto"
Valdés, María Elena de. "Crítica feminista de la identidad en 'Inmóvil sol secreto,' " *J Hispanic Research*, 1 (1992–1993), 241–247.

ALEXANDER PUSHKIN

"The Captain's Daughter"
Reyfman, Irina. "Poetic Justice and Injustice: Autobiographical Echoes in Pushkin's 'The Captain's Daughter,' " *Slavic & East European J*, 38 (1994), 463–478.
Wachtel, Andrew B. *An Obsession* . . . , 71–78.

"The Queen of Spades"
Anikin, Andrei. "Money in Alexander Pushkin's 'The Queen of Spades,' " in DiGaetani, John L., Ed. *Money* . . . , 106–108.
Emerson, Caryl. " 'The Queen of Spades' and the Open End," in Bethea, David M., Ed. *Puškin Today*, 31–37.
Gregg, Richard. "Puškin, Victor Hugo, the Perilous Ordeal, and the True-Blue Hero," *Slavic & East European J*, 38 (1994), 438–439.
Leighton, Lauren G. *The Esoteric Tradition* . . . , 132–194.
Rosenshield, Gary. "Choosing the Right Card: Madness, Gambling, and the Imagination in Pushkin's 'The Queen of Spades,' " *PMLA*, 109 (1994), 995–1008.

THOMAS PYNCHON

"Entropy"
DeZwann, Victoria. "Pynchon's 'Entropy,' " *Explicator*, 51 (1993), 194–196.
Pérez-Llantada Auría, Carmen. "Beyond Linguistic Barriers: The Musical Fugue Structure of Thomas Pynchon's 'Entropy,' " *Cuadernos de Investigación*, 17 (1991), 127–140.

MUḤAMMAD 'ABD AL-QUDDŪS

"Inside the Belly of the Whale"
Hussein, Ayman. " 'Inside the Belly of the Whale': A Case Study," *Edebiyât*, 5, ii (1994), 309–313.

HORACIO QUIROGA

"El almohadón de pluma"
Holland, Norman S. " 'Doctoring' in Quiroga," *Confluencia*, 9, ii (1994), 64–66.

"Anaconda"
Boix, Christian. "Enonciation et représentation dans 'Anaconda,' de H. Quiroga et *El llano en llamas* de J. Rulfo," *Cahiers d'Etudes Romanes*, 12 (1987), 129–144.
Esquerro, Milagros. " 'Anaconda' c'est moi," *Cahiers d'Etudes Romanes*, 12 (1987), 100–113.

"The Dead Man"
Lindstrom, Naomi. *Twentieth-Century . . .* , 55–56.

"Una estación de amor"
Holland, Norman S. " 'Doctoring' . . . ," 67–69.

"La gallina degollada"
Holland, Norman S. " 'Doctoring' . . . ," 66–67.

"Gloria tropical"
Souměrou, Raúl V. "Intrusos en el trópico: A propósito de *Anaconda* de Horacio Quiroga," *Cahiers d'Etudes Romanes*, 12 (1987), 125.

"Miss Dorothy Phillips, mi esposa"
Soumerous, Raúl V. "Intrusos en el trópico . . . ," 125–126.

"Polea loca"
Soumerous, Raúl V. "Intrusos en el trópico . . . ," 123.

"El salvaje"
Llano, Dante. "Estilo y técnica en 'El salvaje' de Horacio Quiroga," *Quaderni Ibero-Americani*, 73 (1993), 37–48.

"El simún"
Soumerous, Raúl V. "Intrusos en el trópico . . . ," 123–124.

"El solitario"
Holland, Norman S. " 'Doctoring' . . . ," 70–71.

WILHELM RAABE

"Fabian und Sebastian"
Henkel, Gabriele. "Lautwelt als Element literarischer Wirklichkeit: Überlegungen zu Raabes 'Wer kann es wenden' und 'Fabian und Sebastian,' " *Jahrbuch der Raabe-Gesellschaft*, [n.v.] (1994), 26–40.

"Die Innerste"
Stern, Martin. "Raabe gegen ihn selbst in Schutz genommen: Gedanken zu seiner Erzählung 'Die Innerste,' " *Jahrbuch der Raabe-Gesellschaft*, [n.v.] (1994), 3–21.

"Wer kann es wenden?"
Henkel, Gabriele. "Lautwelt . . . ," 23–27.

"Zum wilden Mann"
Muschg, Adolf. "Der leere Blutstuhl: Einige Bemerkungen über Wilhelm Raabes Erzählung 'Zum wilden Mann,'" *Jahrbuch der Raabe-Gesellschaft*, [n.v.] (1994), 85–93.

MANUEL RAMOS OTERO

"El cuento de la Mujer del Mar"
Cruz-Malavé, Arnaldo. "Para virar al macho: La autobiografía como subversión en la cuentística de Manuel Ramos Otero," *Revista Iberoamericana*, 59 (1993), 260–262.

"Hollywood Memorabilia"
Cruz-Malavé, Arnaldo. "Para virar al macho . . . ," 259–260.

"Página en blanco y stacatto"
Cruz-Malavé, Arnaldo. "Para virar al macho . . . ," 262.

VALENTIN RASPUTIN

"The Fire"
Brown, Deming. *The Last Years* . . . , 85–86.
Diment, Galya. "Valentin Rasputin and Siberian Nationalism," *World Lit Today*, 67 (1993), 71–72.
Parthé, Kathleen. "The Righteous Brothers (and Sisters) of Contemporary Russian Literature," *World Lit Today*, 67 (1993), 91–92.
Walsh, Harry. "Shamanism and Animistic Personification in the Writings of Valentin Rasputin," *So Central R*, 10, i (1993), 80, 81–82, 88.

WALTER RATHENAU

"The Resurrection Co."
Kaplan, Louis. "Walter Rathenau's Media Technological Turn as Mediated through W. Hartenau's 'Die Resurrection Co.': An Essay at Resurrection," *New Germ Critique*, 62 (1994), 39–62.

MARJORIE KINNAN RAWLINGS

"Black Secret"
Parry, Sally E. " 'Make the Message Clear': The Failure of Language in Marjorie Kinnan Rawlings's *New Yorker* Stories," *Marjorie Kinnan Rawlings J*, 5 (1993), 40–42.

"Jassamine Springs"
Parry, Sally E. " 'Make the Message . . . ,'' 46–48.

"Miriam's Houses"
Parry, Sally E. " 'Make the Message . . . ,'' 42–43.

"The Pelican's Shadow"
Parry, Sally E. " 'Make the Message . . . ,'' 45–46.

"The Shell"
Parry, Sally E. " 'Make the Message . . . ,'' 43–45.

RUTH RENDELL

"The New Girlfriend"
Hendershot, Cyndy. "Gender and Subjectivity in Ruth Rendell's 'The New Girlfriend,' " *Clues*, 15, ii (1994), 75–83.

WILLIAM HENRY RHODES

"The Case of Summerfield"
Haynes, Roslynn D. *From Faust* . . . , 193.

JEAN RHYS [ELLA GWENDOLEN REES WILLIAMS]

"The Day They Burned the Books"
Lonsdale, Thorunn. "The Female Child in Jean Rhys," *Commonwealth Essays & Stud*, 15, i (1992), 66–67.
Raiskin, Judith. "7 Days/6 Nights at 'Plantation Estates': A Critique of Cultural Colonialism by Caribbean Writers," in Rudin, Ernest, and Gert Buelens, Eds. *Deferring a Dream* . . . , 87–89.

"Goodbye Marcus, Goodbye Rose"
Lonsdale, Thorunn. "The Female Child . . . ," 62–63.

"The Imperial Road"
O'Connor, Teresa F. "Jean Rhys, Paul Theroux, and the Imperial Road," *Twentieth Century Lit*, 38 (1992), 404–414.

"Let Them Call It Jazz"
Thomas, Sue. "Modernity, Voice, and Window-Breaking: Jean Rhys's 'Let Them Call It Jazz,' " in Tiffin, Chris, and Alan Lawson, Eds. *De-scribing* . . . , 186–191, 194–197.

JULIO RAMÓN RIBEYRO

"Al pie del acantilado"
Andreu, Alicia G. "Legitimidad literaria y legitimidad socio-económica en el relato de Julio Ramón Ribeyro," *Revista de Crítica*, 39 (1994), 169–176.

JULIO RICCI

"La baba"
Canfield, Martha L. "Lo específico esperpéntico en la obra de Julio Ricci," in Jordan, Isolde J., Ed. *El Inmovilismo* . . . , 98–99.

"La carta"
Angeles, José. "La narrativa desarraigada de Julio Ricci," in Jordan, Isolde J., Ed. *El Inmovilismo* . . . , 162–163.

"El concierto"
Walker, John. "From *maniáticos* to *mareados*: The Fictional World of Julio Ricci," *Revista Canadiense*, 18 (1993), 101.

"Cuchi"
Walker, John. "From *maniáticos* . . . ," 102–103.

"El cumpleaños de Lina"
Corredera, Ketty. "El 'Homo Uruguayensis' en la mirada de Julio Ricci," in Jordan, Isolde J., Ed. *El Inmovilismo* . . . , 30–31.
Walker, John. "From *maniáticos* . . . ," 100.

"El discurso"
Walker, John. "From *maniáticos* . . . ," 102.

"Historia de amor"
Canfield, Martha L. "Lo específico . . . ," 104–105, 111–112.

"La jeraquía"
Canfield, Martha L. "Lo específico . . . ," 99–100.

"El marcapaso"
Castelao, Estela. "La ironía como recurso en la narrative de Julio Ricci," in Jordan, Isolde J., Ed. *El Inmovilismo* . . . , 86–91.

"Las operaciones del amor"
Canfield, Martha L. "Lo específico . . . ," 101, 116–117, 118–119.

"La pieza"
Canfield, Martha L. "Lo específico . . . ," 109–110.
Walker, John. "From *maniáticos* . . . ," 101.

"El shoijet"
Zlotchew, Clark M. "Desde el infierno al paraiso: La búsqueda en Julio Ricci," in Jordan, Isolde J., Ed. *El Inmovilismo* . . . , 123, 129–136, 138.

"El viaje a Pocitas"
Canfield, Martha L. "Lo específico . . . ," 101–104.
Walker, John. "From *maniáticos* . . . ," 98–99.

"El viaje a Tumba"
Walker, John. "From *maniáticos* . . . ," 99–100.

"El viaje al suelo–I"
Walker, John. "From *maniáticos* . . . ," 99–100.

"El viaje de retorno"
Walker, John. "From *maniáticos* . . . ," 99.

HENRY HANDEL RICHARDSON [ETHEL FLORENCE LINDESAY RICHARDSON]

"The Bathe: A Grotesque"
Franklin, Carol. " 'A Depressed Amor': Richardson's 'The Bathe: A Grotesque,' " *Australian Lit Stud*, 15, iii (1992), 165–178.

"Two Hanged Women"
Franklin, Carol. "H. H. Richardson's 'Two Hanged Women': Our Own True Selves and Compulsory Heterosexuality," *Kunapipi*, 14, i (1992), 41–52.

CARME RIERA

"Te deix, amor, la mar com a penyora"
Nichols, Geraldine C. "Limits Unlimited: The Strategic Use of Fantasy in Contemporary Women's Fiction of Spain," in Vidal, Hernán, Ed. *Cultural and Historical* . . . 120–121.

PEDRO RIVERA

"La ventana"
Birmingham-Pokorny, Elba. "The Emergence of the New Afro-Hispanic Woman in Carlos Guillermo Wilson's *Cuentos del Negro Cubena* and *Chombo*," in Birmingham-Porkorny, Elba, Ed. *Denouncement* . . . , 112.

ALAIN ROBBE-GRILLET

"La Plage"
Milman, Yoseph. "Absurdist Estrangement and the Subversion of Narrativity in 'La Plage,' " *Mod Lang R*, 89, i (1994), 50–60.

"The Secret Room"
Caldwell, Roy C. "Ludic Narrative in 'La Chambre secrète,' " *French Forum*, 18 (1993), 59–75.

CHARLES G. D. ROBERTS

"Black Swamp"
Scholtmeijer, Marian. *Animal Victims* . . . , 116–117.

"Do Seek Their Meat from God"
Scholtmeijer, Marian. *Animal Victims* . . . , 113–114.

"The Homesickness of Kehonka"
Scholtmeijer, Marian. *Animal Victims* . . . , 117–118.

ELIZABETH ROBINS

"Aphrodite of the West"
Gates, Joanne E. *Elizabeth Robins* . . . , 114–116.

"The Coming Woman"
Gates, Joanne E. *Elizabeth Robins* . . . , 49–52.

"A Lucky Sixpence"
Gates, Joanne E. *Elizabeth Robins* . . . , 69–71.

"Miss de Maupassant"
Gates, Joanne E. *Elizabeth Robins* . . . , 86–87.

"Monica's Village"
Gates, Joanne E. *Elizabeth Robins* . . . , 135–136.

"Under His Roof"
Gates, Joanne E. *Elizabeth Robins* . . . , 200–201.

"White Violets"
Gates, Joanne E. *Elizabeth Robins* . . . , 178–179.

KIM STANLEY ROBINSON

"Exploring Fossil Canyon"
Franko, Carol. "Working the 'In-Between': Kim Stanley Robinson's Utopian Fiction," *Sci-Fiction Stud*, 21 (1994), 199–201.

"Green Mars"
Franko, Carol. "Working . . . ," 201–203.

ALEJANDRO R. ROCES

"Of Cocks and Choreographers"
Grow, L. M. "The Durian Humour of Alejandro R. Roces," *Philippine Q*, 20 (1992), 264–265.

"Of Cocks and Hens"
Grow, L. M. "The Durian . . . ," 266–267.

"We Filipinos Are Mild Drinkers"
Grow, L. M. "The Durian . . . ," 263–264.

MERCÈ RODOREDA

"La brusa vermella"
Sobrer, Josep M. "Gender and Personality in Rodoreda's Short Fiction," in McNerney, Kathleen, and Nancy Vosburg, Eds. *The Garden Across* . . . , 193–195.

"Camí de la guerra"
Bergmann, Emilie L. "Fragments of Letters: Mercè Rodoreda's Wartime Fiction," in McNerney, Kathleen, and Nancy Vosburg, Eds. *The Garden Across* . . . , 233–234.

"Els carrers blaus"
Bergmann, Emilie L. "Fragments . . . ," 229–233.

"Una carta"
Nichols, Geraldine C. "Limits Unlimited: The Strategic Use of Fantasy in Contemporary Women's Fiction of Spain," in Vidal, Hernán, Ed. Cultural and Historical . . . 118–119.

"En una nit obscura"
Sobrer, Josep M. "Gender and Personality . . . ," 196–198.

"Fil a l'agulla"
Claraśo, Mercè. "The Two Worlds of Mercè Rodoreda," in Davis, Catherine, Ed. *Women Writers* . . . , 44–45.

"La gallina"
Sobrer, Josep M. "Gender and Personality . . . ," 195–196.

"La meva Christina"
Rueda, Ana. "Mercè Rodoreda: From Traditional Tales to Modern Fantasy," in McNerney, Kathleen, and Nancy Vosburg, Eds. *The Garden Across* . . . , 203–210.

"La noieta bruna"
Bergmann, Emilie L. "Fragments . . . ," 228–229.

"Uns quants mots a una rosa"
Bergmann, Emilie L. "Fragments . . . ," 236–237.

"La salamandra"
Claraśo, Mercè. "The Two Worlds . . . ," 45–56.
Rhodes, Elizabeth. "The Salamander and the Butterfly," in McNerney, Kathleen, and Nancy Vosburg, Eds. *The Garden Across* . . . , 167–183.
Rueda, Ana. "Mercè Rodoreda . . . ," 210–219.

"Sònia"
Bergmann, Emilie L. "Fragments . . . ," 225–228.

"Tres cartes"
Bergmann, Emilie L. "Fragments . . . ," 235–236.

"Trossos de cartes"
Bergmann, Emilie L. "Fragments . . . ," 234–235.

REGINA RÖHNER

"Undine"
Hempen, Daniela. "Das Bild der Wasserfrau bei Meyerhof, Bachmann und Röhner," *Seminar*, 30 (1994), 388–391.

JOÃO GUIMARÃES ROSA

"My Uncle the True Jaguar"
Perrone, Charles A. "Guimarães Rosa through the Prism of Magic Realism," in Johnson, Randal, Ed. *Tropical Paths* . . . , 114–116.

"São Marcos"
Perrone, Charles A. "Guimarães Rosa . . . ," 109–110.

ANA ROSSETTI

"La cara oculta del amor"
Alborg, Concha. "Ana Rossetti y el relato erótico," *Hispanic J*, 15, ii (1994), 372–373.

"La castigadora"
Alborg, Concha. "Ana Rossetti . . . ," 375–376.

"Del diablo y sus hazañas"
Alborg, Concha. "Ana Rossetti . . . ," 371–372, 375.

"Et ne nos inducas"
Alborg, Concha. "Ana Rossetti . . . ," 374.

"La noche de aquel día"
Alborg, Concha. "Ana Rossetti . . . ," 373–374, 375.

"La sortija y el sortilegio"
Alborg, Concha. "Ana Rossetti . . . ," 370–371.

"La vengadora"
Alborg, Concha. "Ana Rossetti . . . ," 376–377.

ALEJANDRO ROSSI

"Un café con Gorrondona"
Ortega, Julio. "Alejandro Rossi: la fábula de las regiones," *Revista Iberoamericana*, 60 (1994), 528–529.

"El cielo de Sotero"
Ortega, Julio. "Alejandro Rossi . . . ," 529–531.

"En plena fuga"
Ortega, Julio. "Alejandro Rossi . . . ," 525–526.

"Sueños de Occam"
Ortega, Julio. "Alejandro Rossi . . . ," 526.

PHILIP ROTH

"The Conversion of the Jews"
+Bohner, Charles H. *Instructor's Manual* . . . , 3rd ed., 124.
Michel, Pierre. "Philip Roth: 'The Conversion of the Jews,' " in Lubbers, Klaus, Ed. *Die Englische* . . . , 427–435.

"On the Air"
Pughe, Thomas. *Comic Sense* . . . , 8–13.
———. "Why Is Everybody Laughing? Roth, Coover, and Meta-Comic Narrative," *Critique*, 35 (1994), 69–73.

SAMUEL ROVINSKI

"Change of Identity"
Rojas, Mario A. "Samuel Rovinski and the Dual Identity," in

JANE RULE

JUAN RULFO

JOANNA RUSS

"The Mystery of the Young Gentleman"
Griffin, Gabriele. *Heavenly Love? . . .*, 100–101.

"Souls"
Griffin, Gabriele. *Heavenly Love? . . .*, 99–100.

"What did you do during the revolution, Grandma?"
Griffin, Gabriele. *Heavenly Love? . . .*, 102–103.

NAWAL EL SAADAWI

"The Man with the Buttons"
Whelan, P. T. "Women's Domestic Quest: Minimal Journeys and Their Frames in the *Thousand and One Nights*, 'The Mark on the Wall' and 'The Man with the Buttons,' " *Comparatist*, 18 (1994), 156–160.

ERNESTO SÁBATO

"The Tunnel"
Busette, Cedric. *"La Familia . . .,"* 9–10, 13–25, 28–38, 43–45, 52–61, 63–65, 70–82, 84–87, 91–94, 102–118, 123–125, 127–143, 147–151.
Herpoel, Sonja. "El crimen de Juan Pablo Castel," *Romanische Forschungen*, 105, i–ii (1993), 127–132.
Lindstrom, Naomi. *Twentieth-Century . . .*, 107–108.
Wiman, Björn. "La mujer como objeto—una lectura actancial de Ernest Sábato," *Moderna Spraåk*, 88, ii (1994), 203–204, 207–210.

ASENSIO SÁEZ GARCÍA

"Bien estamos"
Dean-Thacker, Veronica, and Jack Girard. "Asensio Sáez, Symbiosis of Word and Image," *Letras Peninsulares*, 7, i (1994), 47–48.

"Bodegón con sandia"
Dean-Thacker, Veronica, and Jack Girard. "Asensio Sáez, Symbiosis . . .," 51–53.

"La sequía"
Dean-Thacker, Veronica, and Jack Girard. "Asensio Sáez, Symbiosis . . .," 47.

'ALI-AKBAR SA'IDI-SIRJANI

"Skaykh San'an"
Karimi-Hakkak, Ahmad. "A Storyteller and His Times: 'Ali-Akbar Sa'idi-Sirjani of Iran," *World Lit Today*, 68 (1994), 518–520.

SAKI [HECTOR HUGH MUNRO]

"Gabriel-Ernest"
Stern, Simon. "Saki's Attitude," *J Lesbian & Gay Stud*, 1, iii (1994), 284.

"The Music on the Hill"
Stern, Simon. "Saki's Attitude," 284–285.

AL-TAYYIB SÂLIH

"The Doum Tree of Wad Hâmid"
Elad, Ami. "Fiction and Reality in al-Tayyib Sâlih's 'Dawmat Wad Hâmid,' " in Elad, Ami, Ed. *Writer* . . . , 64–68, 69–73.

EDGARDO SANABRIA SANTALIZ

"Antes del último día"
Negrón-Muntaner, Frances. "Sanabria Santaliz, Edgardo (Puerto Rico, 1951)," in Foster, David W., Ed. *Latin American Writers* . . . , 397–399.

"La tercera noche"
Negrón-Muntaner, Frances. "Sanabria Santaliz . . . ," 399–400.

LUIS RAFAEL SÁNCHEZ

"Que sabe a paraíso"
Cachán, Manuel. "*En cuerpo de camisa* de Luis Rafael Sánchez: La antiliteratura alegórica del otro puertorriqueño," *Revista Iberoamericana*, 59 (1993), 182–184.

"La recién nacida sangre"
Vázquez Arce, Carmen. "Los desastres de la guerra: Sobre la articulación de la ironía en los cuentos 'La recién nacida sangre,' de Luis Rafael Sánchez y 'El momento divino de Caruso Llompart,' de Félix Córdova Iturregui," *Revista Iberoamericana*, 59 (1993), 193–195, 199–200.

GEORGE SAND [ARMANDINE AURORE LUCILE DUPIN]

"Carl"
Glasgow, Janis. "Sand's Imaginary Travels in 'Carl,' " in Alvarez-Detrell, Tamara, and Michael G. Paulson, Eds. *The Traveler* . . . , 97–106.

"Pierre Bonnin"
Sourian Eve. "Pierre Bonnin: Le Rêve du paysan français," in

Alvarez-Detrell, Tamara, and Michael G. Paulson, Eds. *The Traveler* . . . , 151–157.

"La Prima donna"

Powell, David A. "Nous et eux: Le Narrateur français dans un text italien: 'La Prima donna,' " in Gorilovics, Tivadar, and Anna Szabo, Eds. *Le Chantier* . . . , 285–293.

CORA SANDEL [SARA FABRICIUS]

"En gaåte"

Rees, Ellen. "The Riddle Solved: Cora Sandel's 'En gaåte,' " *Stud Short Fiction*, 31 (1994), 13–21.

WILLIAM SANSON

"Various Temptations"

+Bohner, Charles H. *Instructor's Manual* . . . , 3rd ed., 125.

"The Wall"

Bergonzi, Bernard. *Wartime* . . . , 43–44.

BIENVENIDO N. SANTOS

"Immigration Blues"

Wong, Sau-ling C. *Reading Asian American Literature* . . . , 51–53, 54–55.

FRANK SARGESON

"The Hole that Jack Dug"

Wevers, Lydia. "The Short New Zealand Story," *Southerly*, 53, iii (1993), 126–129.

"In the Midst of Life"

Wevers, Lydia. "The Short . . . ," 126.

"I've Lost My Pal"

Wevers, Lydia. "The Short . . . ," 132–133.

"A Man and His Wife"

Dass, Veena N. "Human Relationships in the Stories of Frank Sargeson," in Dhawan, R. K., and Walter Tonetto, Eds. *New Zealand Literature Today*, 57–59.

"That Summer"

Wevers, Lydia. "The Short . . . ," 131–132, 133–134.
Dass, Veena N. "Human Relationships . . . ," 56–57.

"White Man's Burden"

Wevers, Lydia. "The Short . . . ," 130–131.

WILLIAM SAROYAN

"Around the World with General Grant"
Foster, Edward H. *William Saroyan* . . . , 43.

"Aspirin Is a Member of the N.R.A."
Foster, Edward H. *William Saroyan* . . . , 9–10.

"The Assyrian"
Foster, Edward H. *William Saroyan* . . . , 66–67.

"The Black Tartars"
Foster, Edward H. *William Saroyan* . . . , 22–23.

"The Daring Young Man on the Flying Trapeze"
Foster, Edward H. *William Saroyan* . . . , 4–6.

"The Living and the Dead"
Foster, Edward H. *William Saroyan* . . . , 32–33.

"The Man with the Heart in the Highlands"
Foster, Edward H. *William Saroyan* . . . , 29–30.

"The Poet at Home"
Foster, Edward H. *William Saroyan* . . . , 67–68.

"Seventy Thousand Assyrians"
Foster, Edward H. *William Saroyan* . . . , 7–9.

"The Trains"
Foster, Edward H. *William Saroyan* . . . , 44.

JEAN-PAUL SARTRE

"Erostatus"
Gordon, Haim, and Rivca Gordon. "Living with the Horror of Evil: A Sartrean Perspective," *Dalhousie R*, 72 (1992), 305–306.

"Le Mur"
Shryock, Richard. *Tales of Storytelling* . . . , 131–132, 133.

DOROTHY L. SAYERS

"The Fascinating Problem of Uncle Meleager's Will"
Keating, H. R. F. "Dorothy L.'s Mickey Finn," in Dale, Alzina S., Ed. *Dorothy L. Sayers* . . . , 130–134.

JOHN SAYLES

"I-80 Nebraska, M. 490—M. 205"
+Bohner, Charles H. *Instructor's Manual* . . . , 3rd ed., 126.

PETER SCHNEIDER

"Der Mauerspringer"
Anderson, Susan C. "Walls and Other Obstacles: Peter Schneider's

Critique of Unity in 'Der Mauerspringer,' " *Germ Q*, 66 (1993), 362–371.

"Vati"

Morgan, Peter. "The Sins of the Fathers: A Reappraisal of the Controversy about Peter Schneider's 'Vati,' " *Germ Life & Letters*, 47 (1994), 104–133.

ARTHUR SCHNITZLER

"Fräulein Else"

Raymond, Cathy. "Masked in Music: Hidden Meaning in Schnitzler's 'Fräulein Else,' " *Monatshefte,* 85 (1993), 171–186.

Sandberg, Glenn. "Freudian Elements in Arthur Schnitzler's 'Fräulein Else,' " *West Virginia Univ Philol Papers*, 39 (1993), 116–120.

"Spiel im Morgengrauen"

Panagl, Oswald. "Das Leben ein Spiel—Das Spiel ein Leben Zu Arthur Schnitzlers Novelle 'Spiel im Morgengrauen,' " *Moderne Sprachen*, 38, iii–iv (1994), 183–189.

HELGA SCHUBERT

"Knots"

Lawson, Ursula D. " 'So, We Are Condemned.' Cancer in the GDR Short Story Written by Women," in Adamson, Ginette, and Eunice Myers, Eds. *Continental, Latin-American . . .* , 83–89.

BRUNO SCHULZ

"Age of Genius"

Shallcross, Bożena. "Pencil, Pen, and Ink: Bruno Schulz's Art of Interference," Pula, James S., and M. B. Biskupski, Eds. *Heart of the Nation . . .* , 58–59.

"The Night of the Great Season"

Goldfarb, David A. "A Living Schulz: 'Noc wielkiego sezonu' ('The Night of the Great Season')," *Prooftexts*, 14, i (1994), 32–47.

"Spring"

Meer, Jan IJ. van der. "On the Influence of Thomas Mann's *Joseph und seine Brüder* on Bruno Schulz's Story 'Spring,' " in Weststeijn, Willem G., Ed. *Dutch Contributions . . .* , 246–255.

CHRISTINE SCHUTT

"Sisters"

Cosslett, Tess. *Women Writing Childbirth . . .* , 81–83.

GEORGE S. SCHUYLER

"The Ethiopian Murder Mystery: A Story of Love and International Intrigue"
Hill, Robert A. "Introduction," *Ethiopian Stories* [by George S. Schuyler], 3–5, 15, 19–20, 25, 28–29.

"Revolt in Ethiopia: A Tale of Black Insurrection Against Italian Imperialism"
Hill, Robert A. "Introduction," 5–6, 15–16, 25–26, 27–28, 29–30, 31, 35.

LYNNE SHARON SCHWARTZ

"So You're Going to Have a New Baby!"
Wear, Delese, and Lois L. Nixon. *Literary Anatomies* . . . , 100–102.

MOACYR SCLIAR

"Inside My Dirty Head"
DiAntonio, Robert. "Resonances of the Yiddishkeit Tradition in the Contemporary Brazilian Narrative," in DiAntonio, Robert, and Nora Glickman, Eds. *Tradition and Innovation*. . . , 54–55.

VICKIE SEARS

"Grace"
Gould, Janice. "Disobedience (in Language) in Texts by Lesbian Native Americans," *Ariel*, 25, i (1994), 34–36.

ANNA SEGHERS

"Der Ausflug der toten Mädchen
Schlossbauer, Frank. "Schreiben als Erinnern, Sehen als Schau: Anna Seghers' 'Der Ausflug der toten Mädchen' zwischen Requiem und Utopie," *Zeitschrift für Deutsche Philologie*, 113, iv (1994), 578–597.

"Das Ende"
Rützou Petersen, Vibeke. "Zillich's End: The Formation of a Fascist Character in Anna Segher's 'Das Ende,' " *Seminar*, 29 (1993), 374–381.

GEORGII SEMYONOV

"The Smell of Burnt Powder"
Brown, Deming. *The Last Years* . . . , 42–43.

OLIVE SENIOR

"The Arrival of the Snake-Woman"
Gafoor, Ameena. "The Image of the Indo-Caribbean Woman in Olive Senior's 'The Arrival of the Snake Woman,' " *Callaloo*, 16 (1993), 34–43.
Patteson, Richard F. "The Fiction of Olive Senior: Traditional Society and the Wider World," *Ariel*, 24, i (1993), 17.

"Ascot"
Patteson, Richard F. "The Fiction of Olive Senior . . . ," 17.

"Ballad"
Patteson, Richard F. "The Fiction of Olive Senior . . . ," 21–23.

"Bright Thursday"
Patteson, Richard F. "The Fiction of Olive Senior . . . ," 20–21.

"Lily, Lily"
Patteson, Richard F. "The Fiction of Olive Senior . . . ," 26–27.

"Real Old Time T'ing"
Condé, Mary. "Jamaica in the Fiction of Olive Senior," *Swansea R*, [n.v.] (1994), 157.
Patteson, Richard F. "The Fiction of Olive Senior . . . ," 17–18.

"The Tenantry of Birds"
Patteson, Richard F. "The Fiction of Olive Senior . . . ," 24–26.

"The View from the Terrace"
Condé, Mary. "Jamaica . . . ," 158, 159.
Patteson, Richard F. "The Fiction of Olive Senior . . . ," 23–24.

OLGA SHAPIR

"Avdotya's Daughters"
Kelly, Catriona. *A History of Russian* . . . , 189, 190–193.

"Dunechka"
Kelly, Catriona. *A History of Russian* . . . , 189, 190.

"The Funeral"
Kelly, Catriona. *A History of Russian* . . . , 186, 187.

"Indian Summer"
Kelly, Catriona. *A History of Russian* . . . , 186.

"The Return"
Kelly, Catriona. *A History of Russian* . . . , 185.

"The Settlement"
Kelly, Catriona. *A History of Russian* . . . , 187–189.

"They Did Not Believe Her"
Kelly, Catriona. *A History of Russian* . . . , 185.

"Veterans and Raw Recruits"
Kelly, Catriona. *A History of Russian* . . . , 186–187.

IRWIN SHAW

"Act of Faith"
Giles, James R. *Irwin Shaw* . . . , 62–65.

"Borough of Cemeteries"
Giles, James R. *Irwin Shaw* . . . , 15–16.

"The Boss"
Giles, James R. *Irwin Shaw* . . . , 34–35.

"Circle of Light"
Giles, James R. *Irwin Shaw* . . . , 40–43.

"The City Was in Total Darkness"
Giles, James R. *Irwin Shaw* . . . , 54–57.

"The Climate of Insomnia"
Giles, James R. *Irwin Shaw* . . . , 110–114.

"The Deputy Sheriff"
Giles, James R. *Irwin Shaw* . . . , 119.

"Dinner in a Good Restaurant"
Giles, James R. *Irwin Shaw* . . . , 99–100.

"The Dry Rock"
Giles, James R. *Irwin Shaw* . . . , 117–118.

"The Eighty-Yard Run"
Giles, James R. *Irwin Shaw* . . . , 20–23.

"Free Conscience, Void of Offence"
Giles, James R. *Irwin Shaw* . . . , 52–54.

"The Girls in Their Summer Dresses"
Giles, James R. *Irwin Shaw* . . . , 91–96.

"God Was Here but He Left Early"
Giles, James R. *Irwin Shaw* . . . , 136–141.

"Goldilocks at Graveside"
Giles, James R. *Irwin Shaw* . . . , 82–86.

"The Green Nude"
Giles, James R. *Irwin Shaw* . . . , 86–90.

"Gunners' Passage"
Giles, James R. *Irwin Shaw* . . . , 72–75.

"The House of Pain"
Giles, James R. *Irwin Shaw* . . . , 30–31.

"The Indian in Depth of Night"
Giles, James R. *Irwin Shaw* . . . , 38–39.

"The Inhabitants of Venus"
Giles, James R. *Irwin Shaw* . . . , 65–68.

"The Lament of Madame Rechevsky"
Giles, James R. *Irwin Shaw* . . . , 33–34.

"Lemkau, Pogran and Blaufox"
Giles, James R. *Irwin Shaw* . . . , 27–29.

"Little Henry Irving"
Giles, James R. *Irwin Shaw* . . . , 103–104.

"Love on a Dark Street"
Giles, James R. *Irwin Shaw* . . . , 129–132.

"Main Currents of American Thought"
Giles, James R. *Irwin Shaw* . . . , 23–26.

"The Man Who Married a French Wife"
Giles, James R. *Irwin Shaw* . . . , 125–126.

"Material Witness"
Giles, James R. *Irwin Shaw* . . . , 35–36.

"Medal from Jerusalem"
Giles, James R. *Irwin Shaw* . . . , 78–80.

"Mixed Doubles"
Giles, James R. *Irwin Shaw* . . . , 96–97.

"The Monument"
Giles, James R. *Irwin Shaw* . . . , 114–115.

"Night, Birth and Opinion"
Giles, James R. *Irwin Shaw* . . . , 50–52.

"Noises in the City"
Giles, James R. *Irwin Shaw* . . . , 39–40.

"Part in a Play"
Giles, James R. *Irwin Shaw* . . . , 75–77.

"Pattern of Love"
Giles, James R. *Irwin Shaw* . . . , 100–101.

"Peter Two"
Giles, James R. *Irwin Shaw* . . . , 104–105.

"The Priest"
Giles, James R. *Irwin Shaw* . . . , 77.

"Prize for Promise"
Giles, James R. *Irwin Shaw* . . . , 29–30.

"Residents of Other Cities"
Giles, James R. *Irwin Shaw* . . . , 57–59.

"Retreat"
Giles, James R. *Irwin Shaw* . . . , 60–62.

"Sailor off the Bremen"
Giles, James R. *Irwin Shaw* . . . , 44–47.

"Santa Claus"
Giles, James R. *Irwin Shaw* . . . , 16–17.

"Second Mortgage"
Giles, James R. *Irwin Shaw* . . . , 14–15.

"Select Clientele"
Giles, James R. *Irwin Shaw* . . . , 59–60.

"Small Saturday"
Giles, James R. *Irwin Shaw* . . . , 36–38.

"Strawberry Ice Cream Soda"
Giles, James R. *Irwin Shaw* . . . , 101–103.

"Then We Were Three"
Giles, James R. *Irwin Shaw* . . . , 126–129.

"Tip on a Dead Jockey"
Giles, James R. *Irwin Shaw* . . . , 132–135.

"Triumph of Justice"
Giles, James R. *Irwin Shaw* . . . , 115–117.

"Voyage Out, Voyage Home"
Giles, James R. *Irwin Shaw* . . . , 123–125.

"Walking Wounded"
Giles, James R. *Irwin Shaw* . . . , 69–72.

"Weep in Years to Come"
Giles, James R. *Irwin Shaw* . . . , 48–50.

"Welcome to the City"
Giles, James R. *Irwin Shaw* . . . , 17–19.

"Where All Things Wise and Fair Descend"
Giles, James R. *Irwin Shaw* . . . , 105–110.

"A Wicked Story"
Giles, James R. *Irwin Shaw* . . . , 97–99.

"Widows' Meetings"
Giles, James R. *Irwin Shaw* . . . , 80–81.

"Wistful, Delicately Gay"
Giles, James R. *Irwin Shaw* . . . , 31–33.

"A Year to Learn the Language"
Giles, James R. *Irwin Shaw* . . . , 120–123.

SHEN CONGWEN [SAME AS SHEN TS'UNG-WEN]

"Twilight"
Wang, David D. W. "Lu Xun, Shen Congwen, and Decapitation," in Liu Kang and Xiaobing Tang, Eds. *Politics, Ideology* . . . , 181–184.

VASILIJ MAKAROVICH SHUKSHIN

"Stradaniia molodogo Vaganova"
Ketchian, Sonia. "A Response to Goethe: Vasilij Šukšin's 'Stradaniia molodogo Vaganova,' " in Gribble, Charles E., Ed. *Alexander Lipson* . . . , 90–101.

LESLIE MARMON SILKO

"Buffalo Story"
Browdy de Hernandez, Jennifer. "Laughing, Crying, Surviving: The

Pragmatic Politics of Leslie Marmon Silko's *Storyteller*,'' *Auto/Bio Stud*, 9, i (1994), 30–32.

''Cliff Dweller''

Danielson, Linda. ''The Storytellers in *Storyteller*,'' *Stud Am Indian Lit*, 1, ii (1989), 25–26.

''Coyote Holds a Full House in His Hand''

Browdy de Hernandez, Jennifer. ''Laughing . . . ,'' 37–39.

''The Laguna People''

Nelson, Robert M. ''He Said/She Said: Writing Oral Tradition in John Gunn's 'Ko-pot Ka-nat' and Leslie Silko's *Storyteller*,'' *Stud Am Indian Lit*, 5, i (1993), 40–42.

''Long Time Ago''

Danielson, Linda. ''The Storytellers . . . ,'' 27.

''Lullaby''

Danielson, Linda. ''The Storytellers . . . ,'' 24.

''The Man to Send Rainclouds''

Browdy de Hernandez, Jennifer. ''Laughing . . . ,'' 27–28.

''Storyteller''

Barker, Adele M. ''Crossings,'' in Aiken, Susan H., Adele M. Barker, Maya Koreneva, and Ekaterina Stetsenko, Eds. *Dialogues/Dialogi* . . . , 341–352.

Browdy de Hernandez, Jennifer. ''Laughing . . . ,'' 24–26.

Danielson, Linda. ''The Storytellers . . . ,'' 23–24.

Langen, Toby C. S. ''*Storyteller* as Hopi Basket,'' *Stud Am Indian Lit*, 5, i (1993), 18–19.

Stetsenko, Ekaterina. ''Retelling the Legends,'' in Aiken, Susan H., Adele M. Barker, Maya Koreneva, and Ekaterina Stetsenko, Eds. *Dialogues/Dialogi* . . . , 333–338.

''Tony's Story''

Browdy de Hernandez, Jennifer. ''Laughing . . . ,'' 32–34.

Danielson, Linda. ''The Storytellers . . . ,'' 23–24.

''Yellow Woman''

Danielson, Linda. ''The Storytellers . . . ,'' 24–25.

Pickering, James H., and Jeffrey D. Hoeper. *Instructor's Manual* . . . , 109–111.

ALAN SILLITOE

''Noah's Ark''

Isernhagen, Hartwig. ''Alan Sillitoe: 'Noah's Ark'—Social Existence and Individual Consciousness,'' in Lubbers, Klaus, Ed. *Die Englische* . . . , 390–398.

WILLIAM GILMORE SIMMS

''The Snake of the Cabin''

Martzinek, Ulrich. ''William Gilmore Simms: 'The Snake of the Cabin,' '' in Lubbers, Klaus, Ed. *Die Englische* . . . , 70–78.

ISAAC BASHEVIS SINGER

"Androygenus"

Sherman, Joseph. "What's Jews? Isaac Bashevis Singer's 'Androygenus,' " *Prooftexts*, 14, ii (1994), 167–188.

"Gimpel the Fool"

+Bohner, Charles H. *Instructor's Manual* . . . , 3rd ed., 127–128.

Hadda, Janet. "Gimpel the Full," *Prooftexts*, 10, ii (1990), 283–295.

"Menaseh's Dream"

Lenz, Millicent. "Archetypal Images of Otherworlds in Singer's 'Menaseh's Dream' and Tolkien's 'Leaf by Niggle,' " *Children's Lit Assn Q*, 19, 1 (1994), 4–6.

KHUSHWANT SINGH

"Karma"

Chandran, K. Narayana. "The Education of Sir Mohan Lal: On Khushwant Singh's 'Karma,' " *Stud Short Fiction*, 30 (1993), 399–401.

ANDREJ SINJAVSKIJ [ABRAM TERC]

"Pchenc"

Artz, Martine. "Interpretations of 'Pchenc,' One of the Fantastic Stories of Andrej Sinjavskij/Abram Terc," in Weststeijn, Willem G., Ed. *Dutch Contributions* . . . , 13–22.

JOSEF ŠKVORECKÝ

"Emöke"

Brink, André. "The Girl and the Legend: Josef Škvorecký's 'Emöke,' " *World Lit Today*, 54 (1980), 552–555; rpt. Solecki, Sam, Ed. *The Achievement* . . . , 104–111.

CLARK ASHTON SMITH

"Xeethra"

Clore, Dan. "Loss and Recuperation: A Model for Reading Clark Ashton Smith's 'Xeethra,' " *Stud Weird Fiction*, 13 (1993), 16–18.

IAIN CRICHTON SMITH

"The Black and the Red"

Gifford, Douglas. "Bleeding from All That's Best: The Fiction of Iain Crichton Smith," in Wallace, Gavin, and Randall Stevenson, Eds. *The Scottish Novel* . . . , 26–27.

"The Brothers"
Gifford, Douglas. "Bleeding from All That's Best . . . ," 31.

"Murdo"
Gifford, Douglas. "Bleeding from All That's Best . . . ," 34.

LEE SMITH

"Bob, a Dog"
Teem, William M. "Let Us Now Praise the Other: Women in Lee Smith's Short Fiction," *Stud Lit Imagination*, 27, ii (1994), 66–68.

"Gulfport"
Teem, William M. "Let Us Now Praise . . . ," 65–66.

"Heat Lighting"
Teem, William M. "Let Us Now Praise . . . ," 68–69.

"Tongues of Fire"
Teem, William M. "Let Us Now Praise . . . ," 69–72.

PAULINE SMITH

"The Pain"
Cosser, Michael. "Undercurrent Dialogue: Free Indirect Discourse in Pauline Smith's 'The Pain,' " *Engl Africa*, 19, ii (1992), 85–100.

SOFIA SOBOLEVA

"A Hopeless Situation"
Costlow, Jane. "Love, Work, and the Woman Question in Mid Nineteen-Century Women's Writing," in Clyman, Toby W., and Diana Greene, Eds. *Women Writers* . . . , 67.

NADEZHDA SOKHANSKAIA [KOKHANOVSKAIA]

"An After-Dinner Call"
Zirin, Mary F. "Women's Prose Fiction in the Age of Realism," in Clyman, Toby W., and Diana Greene, Eds. *Women Writers* . . . , 82–83.

ALEXANDER SOLZHENITSYN

"Matryona's House"
Parthé, Kathleen. "The Righteous Brothers (and Sisters) of Contemporary Russian Literature," *World Lit Today*, 67 (1993), 94, 95–96.

ARMONÍA SOMERS

"El derrumbamiento"
Olivera-Williams, María R. " 'El derrumbamiento' de Armonía Somers y 'El ángel caído' de Cristina Peri-Rossi: Dos Manifestaciones de la narrative imaginaria," *Revista Chilena*, 42 (1993), 176–179.

SUSAN SONTAG

"The Way We Live Now"
Jones, James W. "Refusing the Name: The Absence of AIDS in Recent American Gay Male Fiction," in Murphy, Timothy F., and Suzanne Poirier, Eds. *Writing AIDS* . . . , 228–229.

VLADIMIR SOROKIN

"Traffic Accident"
Porter, Robert. *Russia's Alternative Prose*, 40–41.

MURIEL SPARK

"The House of the Famous Poet"
Barreca, Regina. *Untamed and Unabashed* . . . , 169–170.

"Portobello Road"
Barreca, Regina. *Untamed and Unabashed* . . . , 165–166.

RENNIE SPARKS

"Shanks"
Wear, Delese, and Lois L. Nixon. *Literary Anatomies* . . . , 59–61.

ELIZABETH SPENCER

"The Business Venture"
Roberts, Terry. *Self and Community* . . . , 102–103.

"The Cousins"
Roberts, Terry. *Self and Community* . . . , 103–104.

"The Finder"
Roberts, Terry. *Self and Community* . . . , 95–96.

"First Dark"
Roberts, Terry. *Self and Community* . . . , 90–91.

"I, Maureen,"
Roberts, Terry. *Self and Community* . . . , 101–102.

"Indian Summer"
Roberts, Terry. *Self and Community* . . . , 99, 100.

"Jean-Pierre"
Roberts, Terry. *Self and Community* . . . , 100–101.

"The Pincian Gate"
Roberts, Terry. *Self and Community* . . . , 94.

"Sharon"
Roberts, Terry. *Self and Community* . . . , 96–97.

"Ship Island"
Roberts, Terry. *Self and Community* . . . , 93–94.

"A Southern Landscape"
Roberts, Terry. *Self and Community* . . . , 91–92, 99–100.

HARRIET PRESCOTT SPOFFORD

"Desert Sands"
Fast, Robin R. "Killing the Angel in Spofford's 'Desert Sands' and 'The South Breaker,' " *Legacy*, 11, ii (1994), 37–45.

"Her Story"
Gold, Eva, and Thomas H. Fick. "A 'masterpiece' of 'the educated eye': Convention, Gaze, and Gender in Spofford's 'Her Story,' " *Stud Short Fiction*, 30 (1993), 511–523.

"The South Breaker"
Fast, Robin R. "Killing the Angel . . . ," 45–52.

JEAN STAFFORD

"Caveat Emptor"
Rochette-Crawley, Susan. " 'Enjoying the Conceit of Suddenness': An Analysis of Brevity, Context, and Textual 'Identity' in Jean Stafford's 'Caveat Emptor,' " *Short Story*, 2, i, N.S. (1994), 73–77.

EMILIIAN STANEV

"Le Voleur de pêches"
Foulliaron, E. "Le Personnage de l'étranger dans le récit de E. Stanev 'Le Voleur de pêches,' " *Cahiers Balkaniques*, 9 (1989), 125–138.

CHRISTINA STEAD

"Accents"
Blake, Ann. "Christina Stead's English Short Stories," *Southerly*, 53, iv (1993), 150–151.

"Lost American"
Bennett, Bruce. "Place and Moral Commitment: Judith Wright and Christina Stead," in Thumboo, Edwin, Ed. *Perceiving* . . . , 18–19.

"The Puzzleheaded Girl"
Gardiner, Judith K. " 'Caught but not caught': Psychology and Politics in Christina Stead's 'The Puzzleheaded Girl,' " *World Lit Written Engl*, 32, i (1992), 26–41.

"A Routine"
Blake, Ann. "Christina Stead's . . . ," 153–155, 156–157.

"Street Idyll"
Blake, Ann. "Christina Stead's . . . ," 157–160.

"U.N.O. 1945"
Bennett, Bruce. "Place and Moral . . . ," 21–22.

WALLACE STEGNER

"The Traveler"
Flora, Joseph. "Stegner and Hemingway as Short Story Writers: Some Parallels and Contrasts in Two Masters," *So Dakota R*, 30, i (1992), 111–112.

GERTRUDE STEIN

"The Good Anna"
Simmons, Diane. "The Mother Mirror in Jamaica Kincaid's 'Annie John' and Gertrude Stein's 'The Good Anna,' " in Pearlman, Mickey, Ed. *The Anna Book* . . . , 99–101.

"Melanctha"
Blackmer, Corinne E. "African Masks and the Arts of Passing in Gertrude Stein's 'Melanctha' and Nella Larsen's *Passing*," *J History Sexuality*, 4 (1993), 240–251, 262–263.
Broeck, Sabine. "Gertrude Steins 'Melanctha' in den Diskursen zur 'Natur der Frau,' " *Amerikastudien*, 37, iii (1992), 505–516.
Niemeyer, Mark. "Hysteria and the Normal Unconscious: Dual Natures in Gertrude Stein's 'Melanctha,' " *J Am Stud*, 28, i (1994), 77–83.

JOHN STEINBECK

"The Chrysanthemums"
+Bohner, Charles H. *Instructor's Manual* . . . , 3rd ed., 128–129.

"The Murder"
Frank, Armin P. " 'Längsachsen': Ein in der Textlinguistik vernachlässigtes Problem der Literarischen Übersetzung," in Arntz, Reiner, Ed. *Textlinguistik* . . . , 487–490.

"The Snake"
Meyer, Michael J. "Fallen Adam: Another Look at Steinbeck's 'The Snake,' " in Noble, Donald R., Ed. *The Steinbeck Question . . .*, 99–107.

"The White Quail"
Lutwack, Leonard. *Birds in Literature*, 203–205.
Scholtmeijer, Marian. *Animal Victims . . .*, 212–215.

KARLHEINZ and ANGELA STEINMÜLLER

"Der schwarze Kasten"
Stapleton, Amy. *Utopias for a Dying World . . .*, 70–75.

STENDHAL [MARIE HENRI BEYLE]

"Les Ceni"
Lukacher, Maryline. *Maternal Fictions . . .*, 52–59.

ROBERT LOUIS STEVENSON

"A Lodging for the Night"
Menikoff, Barry. "Introduction," *Tales from the Prince . . .* [by Robert Louis Stevenson], 12, 15, 18–26, 27.

"Markheim"
Menikoff, Barry. "Introduction," 29–30, 31–35.

"The Merry Men"
Menikoff, Barry. "Introduction," 27–28, 36.

"The Pavilion on the Link"
Menikoff, Barry. "Introduction," 14–15, 28–29.

"The Strange Case of Dr. Jekyll and Mr. Hyde"
Hendershot, Cyndy. "Overdetermined Allegory in 'Jekyll and Hyde,' " *Victorian News*, 84 (Fall, 1993), 35–38.
Kramer, Jürgen. "Multiple Selves in Nineteenth Century British Fiction," in Seeber, Hans U., and Walter Göbel, Eds. *Anglistentag 1992 . . .*, 393–394, 395–396.
Shaw, Marion. " 'To tell the truth of sex': Confession and Abjection in Late Victorian Writing," in Shires, Linda M., Ed. *Rewriting the Victorians . . .*, 95–96.
Wright, Daniel L. " 'The Prisonhouse of My Disposition: A Study of the Psychology of Addiction in 'Dr. Jekyll and Mr. Hyde,' " *Stud Novel*, 26 (1994), 254–267.

"Thrawn Janet"
Menikoff, Barry. "Introduction," 30–31.

ADALBERT STIFTER

"The Inscribed Fir Tree"
Schiffermüller, Isolde. "Adalbert Stifters deskriptive Prosa: Eine Modellanalyse der Novelle 'Der beschreibene Tännling,' " *Deutsche Vierteljahrsschrift für Literaturwissenschaft und Geistesgeschichte*, 67 (1993), 267–301.

"Nachkommenschaften"
Plumpe, Gerhard. "An der Grenze des Realismus: Eine Anmerkung zu Adalbert Stifters 'Nachkommenschaften' und Wilhelm Baabes 'Der Dräumling,' " *Jahrbuch der Raabe-Gesellschaft*, [n.v.] (1994), 73–84.

ELIZABETH DREW BATSTOW STODDARD

"Lemorne Versus Huell"
Humma, John B. "Realism and Beyond: The Imagery of Sex and Sexual Oppression in Elizabeth Stoddard's 'Lemorne Versus Huell,' " *So Atlantic R*, 58, i (1993), 33–47.

THEODOR STORM

"Aquis Submersus"
Nuber, Achim. "Ein Bilderrätsel: Emblematische Struktur und Autoreferentialität in Theodor Storms Erzählung 'Aquis Submersus,' " *Colloquia Germanica*, 26, iii (1993), 227–243.

"Im Schloss"
Roebling, Von Irmgard. "Storm und die weibliche Stimme," *Studia Germanica Gandensia*, 42 (1993), 54–62.

"The Rider of the White Horse"
Stiffler, Muriel W. *The German Ghost Story . . .*, 67–87.

BOTHO STRAUß

"Marlenes Schwester"
Braunbeck, Helga G. " 'Fly, little sister, fly': Sister Relationship and Identity in Three Contemporary German Stories," in Mink, JoAnna S., and Janet D. Ward, Eds. *The Significance of Sibling . . .*, 161–163.

SU T'UNG

"The Diaspora in 1934"
Xiaobing Tang. "The Mirror of History and History as Spectacle: Reflections on Hsiao Yeh and Su T'ung," *Mod Chinese Lit*, 6, i–ii (1992), 210–218.

ONG CHOO SUAT

"Checkmate"
Jarrett, Mary. "Teachers and Servants: Colliding Worlds in Short Stories by Malaysia-Singapore Women Writers," in Thumboo, Edwin, Ed. *Perceiving* . . . , 68–69.

"The Crooked Shrine"
Jarrett, Mary. "Teachers . . . ," 69–70.

ITALO SVEVO [ETTORE SCHMITZ]

"Short Sentimental Journey"
Moloney, Brian. "Ulysses by Train: James Joyce and Italo Svevo's 'Corto viaggio sentimentale,' " in Hanne, Michael, Ed. *Literature and Travel*, 277–284.
Weiss, Beno. "Italo Svevo's Sentimental Journey," in Martín, Gregorio C., Ed. *Selected Proceedings* . . . , 380–384.

GRAHAM SWIFT

"Seraglio"
Broich, Ulrich. "Muted Postmodernism: The Contemporary British Short Story," *Zeitschrift für Anglistik und Amerikanistik*, 41 (1993), 37–38.

HARDEN TALIAFERRO

"Ham Rachel"
Watson, Ritchie D. *Yeoman Versus Cavalier* . . . , 61–63.

ELIZABETH TALLENT

"No One's a Mystery"
+Bohner, Charles H. *Instructor's Manual* . . . , 3rd ed., 129–130.

TAMURA TOSHIKO

"Glory"
Nagamatsu, Kyoko. "Tamura Toshiko (1884–1945)," in Mulhern, Chieko I., Ed. *Japanese* . . . , 396–397.

"A Woman Writer"
Nagamatsu, Kyoko. "Tamura Toshiko . . . ," 395.

AMY TAN

"A Pair of Tickets"
+Bohner, Charles H. *Instructor's Manual . . .*, 3rd ed., 130–131.

NALLA TAN

"Heat Wave"
Jarrett, Mary. "Teachers and Servants: Colliding Worlds in Short Stories by Malaysia-Singapore Women Writers," in Thumboo, Edwin, Ed. *Perceiving . . .*, 72–73.

TANABE SEIKO

"Sentimental Journey"
Yamamoto, Fumiko Y. "Tanabe Seiko (1928—)," in Mulhern, Chieko I., Ed. *Japanese . . .*, 398–399.

TANIZAKI JUN'ICHIRŌ

"The Secret"
Chambers, Anthony H. "Translator's Introduction," " 'The Secret' by Tanizaki Jun'ichirō" [by Anthony H. Chambers], in Gatten, Aileen, and Anthony H. Chambers, Eds. *New Leaves . . .*, 157–158.

UGO TARCHETTI

"Le leggende del castello nero"
Del Principe, David. "Heresy and 'Hair-esy' in Ugo Tarchetti's *Fosca*," *Italica*, 71, i (1994), 47–48.

PAT ELLIS TAYLOR

"A Call from Brotherland"
Ryan, Maureen. "The Other Side of Grief: American Women Writers and the Vietnam War," *Critique*, 36 (1994), 47–48, 54.

"Descent into Brotherland"
Ryan, Maureen. "The Other . . .," 47.

PETER TAYLOR

"At the Drugstore"
+Schuler, Barbara. "The House of Peter Taylor," in McAlexander, Hubert H., Ed. *Critical Essays . . .*, 92–94.

"Cousin Aubrey"
Shepherd, Allen. " 'The Green Fields of Tennessee,' " *Southern R*, (1994), 162–163.

"Dean of Men"
Lynn, David H. "Telling Irony: Peter Taylor's Later Stories," *Virginia Q R*, 67 (1991), 512–515; rpt. McAlexander, Hubert H., Ed. *Critical Essays* . . . , 195–196.

"The Decline and Fall of the Episcopal Church (in the Year of Our Lord 1952)"
Shepherd, Allen. " 'The Green Fields . . . ,'' 159–160.

"Demons"
Shepherd, Allen. " 'The Green Fields . . . ,'' 160–162.

"The Fancy Woman"
+Brown, Ashley. "The Early Fiction of Peter Taylor," in McAlexander, Hubert H., Ed. *Critical Essays* . . . , 81–82.

"Guests"
Shear, Walter. "Women and History in Peter Taylor's Short Stories," *Southern Q*, 33, i (1994), 43.

"Her Need"
Kuehl, Linda K. "Peter Taylor's Women: Old and New," *Southern Q*, 33, i (1994), 47–50.

"In the Miro District"
Balthazor, Ron. "Digression and Meaning: A Reading of 'In the Miro District,' " in McAlexander, Hubert H., Ed. *Critical Essays* . . . , 216–226.
Lynn, David H. "Telling Irony: Peter Taylor's Later Stories," *Virginia Q R*, 67 (1991), 515–520; rpt. McAlexander, Hubert H., Ed. *Critical Essays* . . . , 196–200.
Wyatt-Brown, Bertram. "Aging, Gender, and the Deterioration of Southern Family Values in the Stories of Peter Taylor," in Wyatt-Brown, Anne M., and Janice Rossen, Eds. *Aging and Gender* . . . , 302–312.

"A Long Fourth"
+Brown, Ashley. "The Early Fiction . . . ," 83–85.
+Schuler, Barbara. "The House of . . . ," 94–95.
Shear, Walter. "Women and History . . . ," 43–45.

"Miss Leonora When Last Seen"
+Pinkerton, Jan. "The Non-Regionalism of Peter Taylor," in McAlexander, Hubert H., Ed. *Critical Essays* . . . , 111–112.
Shear, Walter. "Women and History . . . ," 45–46.

"The Old Forest"
Robinson, David M. "Engaging the Past: Peter Taylor's 'The Old Forest,' " *Southern Lit J*, 23 (Spring, 1990), 63–77; rpt. McAlexander, Hubert H., Ed. *Critical Essays* . . . , 180–192.
Shear, Walter. "Women and History . . . ," 41–43.

"The Oracle at Stoneleigh Court"
Shepherd, Allen. "The Green Fields . . . ," 156–158.

"The Party"
Metress, Christopher. "The Expenses of Silence in *A Summons to Memphis*," in McAlexander, Hubert H., Ed. *Critical Essays . . .*, 201–202.

"Porte Cochère"
Vauthier, Simone. "Peter Taylor's 'Porte Cochère': The Geometry of Generation," in Humphries, Jefferson, Ed. *Southern Literature . . .*, 318–338; rpt. McAlexander, Hubert H., Ed. *Critical Essays . . .*, 162–179.

"Sky Line"
+Brown, Ashley. "The Early Fiction . . . ," 79–80.
+Schuler, Barbara. "The House of . . . ," 90–91.

"A Spinster's Tale"
+Andrews, Maureen. "A Psychoanalytic Appreciation of Peter Taylor's 'A Spinster's Tale,' " in McAlexander, Hubert H., Ed. *Critical Essays . . .*, 154–161.
+Brown, Ashley. "The Early Fiction . . . ," 80–81.
+Sodowsky, Roland and Gargi. "Determined Failure, Self-Styled Success: Two Views of Betsy in Peter Taylor's 'Spinster's Tale,' " in McAlexander, Hubert H., Ed. *Critical Essays . . .*, 148–153.

"Their Losses"
+Pinkerton, Jan. "The Non-Regionalism . . . ," 112–113.

"Three Heroines"
Kuehl, Linda K. "Peter Taylor's Women . . . ," 51–53.
Wyatt-Brown, Bertram. "Aging, Gender . . . ," 298–302.

"The Throughway"
+Schuler, Barbara. "The House of . . . ," 94.

"Two Pilgrims"
+Schuler, Barbara. "The House of . . . ," 91–92.

"Venus, Cupid, Folly and Time"
Vauthier, Simone. "Facing Outward, Yet Twirling Inward: Mannerist Devices in 'Venus, Cupid, Folly and Time,' " in McAlexander, Hubert H., Ed. *Critical Essays . . .*, 227–253.

"A Wife of Nashville"
Bell, Madison S. "The Mastery of Peter Taylor," in McAlexander, Hubert H., Ed. *Critical Essays . . .*, 256–258.

"The Witch of Owl Mountain Springs: An Account of Her Remarkable Powers"
Shepherd, Allen. " 'The Green Fields . . . ," 158–159.

"A Woman of Means"
+Brown, Ashley. "The Early Fiction . . . ," 85–86.

NADEZHDA TEFFI

"Huron"
Kelly, Catriona. *A History of Russian . . .*, 197.

"Walled Up"
Kelly, Catriona. *A History of Russian* . . . , 197.

"When the Crayfish Whistles"
Kelly, Catriona. *A History of Russian* . . . , 202.

LYGIA FAGUNDES TELLES

"Tigrela"
Bueno, Eva P. "Telles, Lygia Fagundes (Brazil; 1923)," in Foster, David W., Ed. *Latin American Writers* . . . , 424–426.

VLADIMIR TENDRYAKOV

"The Clear Waters of Kitezh"
Brown, Deming. *The Last Years* . . . , 34.

"Donna Anna"
Brown, Deming. *The Last Years* . . . , 34–35.

ALEKSANDR TEREKHOV

"Zyoma, An Ironic Diary"
Brown, Deming. *The Last Years* . . . , 174.

GEORGE THOMPSON

"The House Breaker; or The Mysteries of Crime"
Looby, Christopher. "George Thompson's 'Romance of the Real': Transgression and Taboo in American Sensation Fiction," *Am Lit*, 65 (1993), 651–672.

THOMAS BANGS THORPE

"The Big Bear of Arkansas"
Blair, Walter. *Essays* . . . , 22–23, 90–97.

JAMES THURBER

"The Catbird Seat"
+Bohner, Charles H. *Instructor's Manual* . . . , 3rd ed., 131.
Nicholson, Mervyn. "Peripety Cues in Short Fiction," *CEA Critic*, 56, ii (1994), 50–51.

"The Secret Life of Walter Mitty"
Kaufman, Anthony. " 'Things Close In': Dissolution and

Misanthropy in 'The Secret Life of Walter Mitty,' " *Stud Am Fiction*, 22 (1994), 93–104.

LUDWIG TIECK

"Der Runenberg"
Gille, Klaus F. "Der Berg und die Seele: Überlegungen zu Tiecks 'Runenberg,' " *Neophilologus*, 77 (1993), 612–623.

J[OHN] R[ONALD] TOLKIEN

"Leaf by Niggle"
Lenz, Millicent. "Archetypal Images of Otherworlds in Singer's 'Menaseh's Dream' and Tolkien's 'Leaf by Niggle,' " *Children's Lit Assn Q*, 19, 1 (1994), 4–6.

TATYANA TOLSTAYA

"A Clean Sheet"
Porter, Robert. *Russia's Alternative Prose*, 69–70.

"The Fakir"
Goscilo, Helena. "Perspective in Tatyana Tolstaya's Wonderland of Art," *World Lit Today*, 67 (1993), 80–86.
Porter, Robert. *Russia's Alternative Prose*, 66–67.

"Loves Me, Loves Me Not"
Porter, Robert. *Russia's Alternative Prose*, 67–68.

"Okkervil River"
Goscilo, Helena. "Perspective . . . ," 86–88.

LEO TOLSTOY

"A Confession"
Briggs, A. D. P. "Introduction," in Briggs, A. D. P., Ed. *Notes from Underground* . . . , xxi–xxvii.

"The Cossacks"
Orwin, Donna T. *Tolstoy's Art* . . . , 85–98.

"The Death of Ivan Ilych"
+Bohner, Charles H. *Instructor's Manual* . . . , 3rd ed., 131–132.
Costa, Richard H. *An Appointment with* . . . , 22, 24.
Jahn, Gary R. *"The Death of* . . . , 11–21, 31–102.
Nicholson, Mervyn. "Peripety Cues in Short Fiction," *CEA Critic*, 56, ii (1994), 45–46, 50.
Pickering, James H., and Jeffrey D. Hoeper. *Instructor's Manual* . . . , 26–27.

"God Sees the Truth but Waits"
Sterne, Richard C. *Dark Mirror* . . . , 68–71.

"The Kreutzer Sonata"
Howe, Irving. . . . *A Critic's Notebook*, 318–319.
Isenberg, Charles. *Telling Silence* . . . , 79–108.
Shirer, William L. *Love and Hatred* . . . , 129–133.

"Lucerne"
Orwin, Donna T. *Tolstoy's Art* . . . , 68–72, 77–79.

"Notes of a Madman"
Orwin, Donna T. *Tolstoy's Art* . . . , 154–155.

"Polikushka"
Orwin, Donna T. *Tolstoy's Art* . . . , 70–71.

"The Raid"
Orwin, Donna T. *Tolstoy's Art* . . . , 43, 52–53.

"Sebastopol in December"
Le Gouis, Catherine. "Narrative Techniques in Tolstoy's 'Sebastopol in December' and Butor's *La Modification*," *Comp Lit*, 45 (1993), 346–360.

"Sevastopol in May"
Orwin, Donna T. *Tolstoy's Art* . . . , 24–26, 53.

"Three Deaths"
Orwin, Donna T. *Tolstoy's Art* . . . , 70, 162.

JEAN TOOMER

"Avey"
Whyde, Janet M. "Mediating Forms: Narrating the Body in Jean Toomer's *Cane*," *Southern Lit J*, 26, i (1993), 47–48.

"Becky"
Whyde, Janet M. "Mediating Forms . . . ," 44–45.

"Carma"
Whyde, Janet M. "Mediating Forms . . . ," 45–46.

"Karintha"
Whyde, Janet M. "Mediating Forms . . . ," 44.

"Theater"
Whyde, Janet M. "Mediating Forms . . . ," 48–49.

FRIEDRICH TORBERG

"Mein ist die Rache"
Thunecke, Jörg. " 'Man *wird* nicht Jude, man *ist* es': Zur Funktion der jüdischen Moral in Friedrich Torbergs Novelle 'Mein ist die Rache,' (1943)" *Mod Austrian Lit*, 27, iii–iv (1994), 19–36.

OMAR TORRES

"Fallen Angels Sing"
Alvarez-Borland, Isabel. "Displacements and Autobiography in Cuban-American Fiction," *World Lit Today*, 68 (1993), 45–46.

MICHEL TOURNIER

"L'Aire du Muguet"
Edwards, Rachel. "Initiation and Menstruation: Michel Tournier's 'Amandine ou les deux jardins,' " *Essays French Lit*, 27 (November, 1990), 76–77.

"Amandine ou les deux jardins"
Edwards, Rachel. "Initiation . . . ," 77–87.

"La Jeune Fille et la mort"
Redfern, W. D. "Something about nothing: Michel Tournier's 'La Jeune Fille et la mort,' " *J European Stud*, 23 (1993), 299–313.

"Tristan Vox"
Redfern, Walter. "Radio Daze and Imperishable Myth: Tournier's 'Tristan Vox,' " *French Cultural Stud*, 4, ii (1993), 185–190.

BRUNO TRAVEN

"Accomplices"
Mezo, Richard E. *A Study of B. Traven's Fiction* . . . , 158–59.

"Assembly Line"
Mezo, Richard E. *A Study of B. Traven's Fiction* . . . , 164–165.

"Conversion of Some Indians"
Mezo, Richard E. *A Study of B. Traven's Fiction* . . . , 155–156.

"The Diplomat"
Mezo, Richard E. *A Study of B. Traven's Fiction* . . . , 159–160.

"Effective Medicine"
Mezo, Richard E. *A Study of B. Traven's Fiction* . . . , 151–152.

"The Friendship"
Mezo, Richard E. *A Study of B. Traven's Fiction* . . . , 163.

"Frustration"
Mezo, Richard E. *A Study of B. Traven's Fiction* . . . , 163–164.

"The Kidnapped Saint"
Mezo, Richard E. *A Study of B. Traven's Fiction* . . . , 157–158.

"Macario"
Mezo, Richard E. *A Study of B. Traven's Fiction* . . . , 143–150.

"Midnight Call"
Mezo, Richard E. *A Study of B. Traven's Fiction* . . . , 152–153.

"A New God Was Born"
Mezo, Richard E. *A Study of B. Traven's Fiction* . . . , 156–157.

"The Night Visitor"
Mezo, Richard E. *A Study of B. Traven's Fiction* . . . , 137, 138–143.

"The Story of a Bomb"
Mezo, Richard E. *A Study of B. Traven's Fiction* . . . , 161–162.

"Submission"
Mezo, Richard E. *A Study of B. Traven's Fiction* . . . , 160–161.

"When the Priest Is Not at Home"
Mezo, Richard E. *A Study of B. Traven's Fiction* . . . , 157.

DALTON TREVISAN

"A Pinta Preta da Paixão"
Ledford-Miller, Linda. "The Perverse Passions of Dalton Trevisan," in Bevan, David, Ed. *Literature* . . . , 64.

"A Velha Querida"
Ledford-Miller, Linda. "The Perverse . . . ," 66–69.

"Noite da Paixão"
Ledford-Miller, Linda. "The Perverse . . . ," 70–71.

"Paixão de Corneteiro"
Ledford-Miller, Linda. "The Perverse . . . ," 62.

"Paixão de Palhaço"
Ledford-Miller, Linda. "The Perverse . . . ," 63–64.

"Paixão e Agonia da Cigarra"
Ledford-Miller, Linda. "The Perverse . . . ," 64–66.

"Paixão Segundo João"
Ledford-Miller, Linda. "The Perverse . . . ," 62–63.

WILLIAM TREVOR

"Another Christmas"
Tillinghast, Richard. " 'They were as good as we were': The Stories of William Trevor," *New Criterion*, 11, vi (1993), 14–15.

"Attracta"
Paulson, Suzanne M. *William Trevor* . . . , 21–23.

"The Ballroom of Romance"
Paulson, Suzanne M. *William Trevor* . . . , 58–65.
Tillinghast, Richard. " 'They were . . . ," 11.

"Beyond the Pale"
Paulson, Suzanne M. *William Trevor* . . . , 3–4.

"The Blue Dress"
Paulson, Suzanne M. *William Trevor* . . . , 23–28.

"Broken Homes"
Paulson, Suzanne M. *William Trevor* . . . , 98–101.

"A Choice of Butchers"
Paulson, Suzanne M. *William Trevor* . . . , 37–43.

"The Day We Got Drunk on Cake"
Paulson, Suzanne M. *William Trevor* . . . , 17–21.

"The Distant Past"
Tillinghast, Richard. " 'They were . . . ," 13–14.

YURI TRIFONOV

"Vera and Zoika"
Gillespie, David. *Iurii Trifonov* . . . , 48–50.

LIONEL TRILLING

"Of This Time, of That Place"
Agnihotri, Pratima. "The Politics of Pedagogy," in Plakkoottam, J. L., and Prashant K. Sinha, Eds. *Literature and Politics* . . . , 17–21.

ANTHONY TROLLOPE

"The Journey to Panama"
Kohn, Denise. " 'The Journey to Panama': One of Trollope's Best 'Tarts'—or, Why You Should Read 'The Journey to Panama' to Develop Your Taste for Trollope," *Stud Short Fiction*, 30 (1993), 15–22.

TSUBOI SAKAE

"Radish Leaves"
McDonald, Keiko. "Tsuboi Sakae (1899–1967)," in Mulhern, Chieko I., Ed. *Japanese* . . . , 417–418.

"Umbrella on a Moonlit Night"
McDonald, Keiko. "Tsuboi Sakae . . . ," 422–423.

TSUMURA SETSUKO

"The Blue Surgical Knife"
Yoshida, Sanroka. "Tsumura, Setsuko (1928–)," in Mulhern, Chieko I., Ed. *Japanese* . . . , 427–428.

"Luminous Watch"
Yoshida, Sanroka. "Tsumura, Setsuko . . . ," 430.

"The Toy"
Yoshida, Sanroka. "Tsumura, Setsuko . . . ," 427.

"An Unfamiliar Town"
Yoshida, Sanroka. "Tsumura, Setsuko . . . ," 428–429.

TSUSHIMA YŪKO

"Fusehime"
Monnet, Livia. "The Politics of Miscegenation: The Discourse of Fantasy in 'Fusehime' by Tsushima Yūko," *Japan Forum*, 5, i (1993), 53–73.

IVAN TURGENEV

"Bezhin Meadow"
Durkin, Andrew R. "The Generic Context of Rural Prose: Turgenev and the Pastoral Tradition," in Maguire, Robert A., and Alan Timberlake, Eds. *American Contributions* . . . , 48–49.

"First Love"
Isenberg, Charles. *Telling Silence* . . . , 22–49.

"Forest and Steppe"
Durkin, Andrew R. "The Generic Context . . . ," 45–46.

"Iakov Pasynkov"
Eidelman, Dawn D. *George Sand* . . . , 42–48.

"Khor and Kalinitch"
Durkin, Andrew R. "The Generic Context . . . ," 44–45.

"The Singers"
Durkin, Andrew R. "The Generic Context . . . ," 46–47.

"The Tryst"
+Bohner, Charles H. *Instructor's Manual* . . . , 3rd ed., 133–134.

MARK TWAIN [SAMUEL L. CLEMENS]

"Baker's Blue-Jay Yarn"
Blair, Walter. *Essays* . . . , 165–166, 168–178.

"The Celebrated Jumping Frog of Calavaras County"
+Bohner, Charles H. *Instructor's Manual* . . . , 3rd ed., 32–33.
Pickering, James H., and Jeffrey D. Hoeper. *Instructor's Manual* . . . , 22–23.

"Journalism in Tennessee"
Frank, Armin P. " 'Längsachsen': Ein in der Textlinguistik vernachlässigtes Problem der literarischen Übersetzung," in Arntz, Reiner, Ed. *Textlinguistik* . . . , 490–493.
Wetzel-Sahm, Birgit. "Zwischen Verfremdung, Weiterschreibung und Einbürgerung: Amerikanischer *humor* am Beispiel von Mark Twains 'Journalism in Tennessee' in deutschen Übersetzungen," in Frank, Armin P., Ed. *Die Literarische* . . . , 152–171.

"The Mysterious Stranger"
Kiely, Robert. *Reverse Tradition* . . . , 104–122.

"The Notorious Jumping Frog of Calaveras County"
Gibian, Peter. "Levity and Gravity in Twain: The Bipolar Dynamics of the Early Tales," *Stud Am Humor*, 3, i (1994), 89–91.
Wonham, Henry B. *Mark Twain* . . . , 66–69.

"Over the Mountains"
Wonham, Henry B. *Mark Twain* . . . , 64–66.

"River Intelligence"
Wonham, Henry B. *Mark Twain* . . . , 56–60.

"The Story of the Good Little Boy"
Britton, Wesley. "Mark Twain, 'Cradle Skeptic': High Spirits, Ghosts, and the Holy Spirit," *So Dakota R*, 30, iv (1992), 95–96.

"The Story of the Old Ram"
Gibian, Peter. "Levity and Gravity . . . ," 91–94.

ANNE TYLER

"Laura"
Nesanovich, Stella. "The Early Novels: A Reconsideration," in Salwak, Dale, Ed. *Anne Tyler as Novelist*, 15–16.

"The Lights on the River"
Nesanovich, Stella. "The Early Novels . . . ," 16.

"Nobody Answers the Door"
Nesanovich, Stella. "The Early Novels . . . ," 16–17.

MIGUEL DE UNAMUNO

"Abel Sánchez"
Cuppett. Cathleen G. "La salvación en 'Abel Sánchez' a través del *Diario íntimo* de Miguel de Unamuno," *Romance Notes*, 34 (1993), 23–29.

"Saint Manuel the Good, Martyr"
Cabañas, Miguel A. "San Manuel Bueno, mártir, budista," *Torre de Papel*, 3 (1993), 34–49.
Christie, Ruth. "The Cross of Language in 'San Manuel Bueno, mártir,' " in Macklin, John, Ed. *After Cervantes . . .* , 195–202.

"La tía Tula"
Bretz, Mary L. "The Role of Negativity in Unamuno's 'La tía Tula,' " *Revista Canadiense*, 18 (1993), 17–30.

JOHN UPDIKE

"A & P"
+Bohner, Charles H. *Instructor's Manual* . . . , 3rd ed., 134–135.
Pickering, James H., and Jeffrey D. Hoeper. *Instructor's Manual* . . . , 96–97.
Wells, Walter. "John Updike's 'A & P': A Return to Araby," *Stud Short Fiction*, 30 (1993), 127–133.

"Ace in the Hole"
Ford, Thomas W. "Updike's 'Ace in the Hole,' " *Explicator*, 52 (1994), 122–125.

"The Music School"
Detweiler, Robert. "John Updike: 'The Music School'—A Quartet of Readings," in Lubbers, Klaus, Ed. *Die Englische* . . . , 409–420.

"Separating"
Charters, Ann. *Resources* . . . , 159–160.

"Wife-Wooing"
Charters, Ann. *Resources* . . . , 158–159.

LUISA VALENZUELA

"Cambio de armas"
Magnarelli, Sharon. "El significante deseo en *Cambio de armas* de Luisa Valenzuela," *Escritura*, 16 (1991), 168.
Rojas-Trempe, Lady. "Apuntes sobre *Cambio de armas* de Luisa Valenzuela," *Letras Femeninas*, 19, i–ii (1993), 81–82.

"Ceremonias de rechazo"
Magnarelli, Sharon. "El significante . . . ," 166.
Rojas-Trempe, Lady. "Apuntes sobre . . . ," 80–81.

"Cuarta versión"
Boling, Becky. " 'Cuarta versión': Implicit Subjects/Complicit Readings," *Hispanic J*, 14, ii (1993), 105–115.
Magnarelli, Sharon. "El significante . . . ," 164–165.
Rojas-Trempe, Lady. "Apuntes sobre . . . ," 74–79.

"De noche soy tu caballo"
Magnarelli, Sharon. "El significante . . . ," 166–167.

"La palabra asesino"
Bilbija, Ksenija. " 'La palabra asesino' de Luisa Valenzuela: La entrada en la lengua," *Confluencia*, 8, i (1992), 159–164.
+Bohner, Charles H. *Instructor's Manual* . . . , 3rd ed., 135–136.
Magnarelli, Sharon. "El significante . . . ," 165–166.
Rojas-Trempe, Lady. "Apuntes sobre . . . ," 79–80.

RIMA DE VALLBONA

"Balada de un sueño"
Gómez Parham, Mary. "Men in the Short Stories of Rima de Vallbona," *Confluencia*, 8, i (1992), 42–43.

"Infame retorno"
Gómez Parham, Mary. "Men . . . ," 41.

"Lo inconfesable"
Gómez Parham, Mary. "Men . . . ," 40–41.

"Más allá de la carne"
Gómez Parham, Mary. "Men . . . ," 41–42.

"Parábola del edén imposible"
Gómez Parham, Mary. "Men . . . ," 42.

"Penélope en sus bodas de plata"
Gómez Parham, Mary. "Men . . . ," 43–47.

"Tierra de secano"
Gómez Parham, Mary. "Men . . . ," 43.

RAMÓN MARÍA DEL VALLE-INCLÁN

"La adoración de los Reyes"
Pollack, Beth. "La dualidad oculto-cristiana en *Jardín umbrío*," in Gabriele, John P., Ed. *Suma* . . . , 527.

"Beatriz"
Pollack, Beth. "La dualidad . . . ," 527–528, 530–532.
Ramos, Rosa A. "Valle-Inclán's 'Beatriz': A Tale of the Symbolist Fantastic," *Discurso*, 9, ii (1992), 75–86.

"La Generala"
Nickel, Catherine. "Valle-Inclán's 'La General': Woman as Birdbrain," in Maier, Carol, and Roberta L. Salper, Eds. *Ramón María del Valle Inclán* . . . , 43–55.

"La Niña Chole"
Davies, Catherine. " 'Venus impera'? Women and Power in *Femeninas* and *Epitalamio*," in Maier, Carol, and Roberta L. Salper, Eds. *Ramón María del Valle Inclán* . . . , 140–142.

"Octavia Santino"
Addis, Mary K., and Roberta L. Salper. "Modernism and Margins: Valle-Inclán and the Politics of Gender, Nation, and Empire," in Maier, Carol, and Roberta L. Salper, Eds. *Ramón María del Valle Inclán* . . . , 108, 109–111.
Davies, Catherine. " 'Venus . . . ," 108, 109, 111, 136–137.

"El rey de la máscara"
Pollack, Beth. "La dualidad . . . ," 528–530.

"Rosarito"
Davies, Catherine. " 'Venus . . . ," 144–146.
Predmore, Michael P. "La literatura y la sociedad de Valle-Inclán: Concepciones liberal y popular del arte," in Gabriele, John P., Ed. *Suma* . . . , 106–109.

"Tula Varona"
Davies, Catherine. " 'Venus . . . ," 142–144.

WARREN VAN DINE

"The Poet"
Hallwas, John E. "Midwestern Writer: A Memoir," in Noe, Marcia, Ed. *Exploring the Midwestern* . . . , 120–121.

MARIO VARGAS LLOSA

"Día domingo"
Arrington, Melvin S. "El arquetipo de iniciación en 'Día domingo,' "

in Hernández de López, Ana María, Ed. *Mario Vargas Llosa . . .*, 333–340.

"In Praise of the Stepmother"
Booker, M. Keith. *Vargas Llosa Among the Postmodernists*, 162–182.

ANA VASQUEZ

"Las dudas de la mujer bígama"
Araujo, Helena. "Las huellas del 'propio camino' en los relatos de Ana Vasquez," *Escritura*, 16, (1991), 13.

"El hotel de la ballena verde"
Araujo, Helena. "Las huellas . . . ," 13–14.

"Pequeñas revoluciones sin importancia"
Araujo, Helena. "Las huellas . . . ," 12–13.

ANA LYDIA VEGA

"Ahí viene Mamá Yona"
González, Aníbal. "Ana Lydia Pluravega: unidad y multiplicidad caribeñas en la obra de Ana Lydia Vega," *Revista Iberoamericana*, 59 (1993), 296–299.

"El baúl de Miss Florence: fragmentos para un novelón romántico"
Olazagasti-Segovia, Elena. "Ana Lydia Vega y la re-escritura de la historia," *Letras Femeninas*, Número Extraordinario Conmemorativo: 1974–1994 (1994), 87–93.

"Despojo"
Daroqui, María S. "Palabra de mujer," *Escritura*, 16 (1991), 62.

"Dos"
Daroqui, María S. "Palabra . . . ," 61.

"Encancaranublado"
González, Aníbal. "Ana Lydia Pluravega . . . ," 293–294.
Vélez, Diana L. "We Are (Not) in This Together: The Caribbean Imaginary in 'Encancaranublado,' by Ana Lydia Vega," *Callaloo*, 17 (1994), 826–833.

"Letra para salsa y tres soneos por encargo"
Captain-Hidalgo, Yvonne. "El espíritu de la risa en el cuento de Ana Lydia Vega," *Revista Iberoamericana*, 59 (1993), 306–307.
Daroqui, María S. "Palabra . . . ," 59–60.
Den Tandt, Catherine. "Tracing Nation and Gender: Ana Lydia Vega," *Revista de Estudios Hispánicos*, 28 (1994), 13–21.

"Puerto Rican Syndrome"
Captain-Hidalgo, Yvonne. "El espíritu . . . ," 307.

"Sobre tumbas y héroes"
Acosta Cruz, María I. "Historia y escritura femenina en Olga Nolla,

Magali García Ramis, Rosario Ferré y Ana Lydia Vega," *Revista Iberoamericana*, 59 (1993), 273–276.

"Tres"
Daroqui, María S. "Palabra . . . ," 61.

"Una"
Daroqui, María S. "Palabra . . . ," 60–61.

ANASTASIYA VERBITSKAYA

"First Signs"
Rosenthal, Charlotte. "Achievement and Obscurity: Women's Prose in the Silver Age," in Clyman, Toby W., and Diana Greene, Eds. *Women Writers* . . . , 153–154.

"Sara Eizman"
Kelly, Catriona. *A History of Russian* . . . , 139–140.

JOSÉ GARCÍA VILLA

"Death Into Manhood"
Bresnahan, Roger J. "José García Villa and Sherwood Anderson: A Study in Influence," in Noe, Marcia, Ed. *Exploring the Midwestern* . . . , 65.

"The Fence"
Bresnahan, Roger J. "José García Villa . . . ," 62.

"Kamya"
Bresnahan, Roger J. "José García Villa . . . ," 61.

"Malakas"
Bresnahan, Roger J. "José García Villa . . . ," 60–61.

"Story for My Country"
Bresnahan, Roger J. "José García Villa . . . ," 64.

"Valse Triste"
Bresnahan, Roger J. "José García Villa . . . ," 61–62.

"The Woman Who Looked Like Christ"
Bresnahan, Roger J. "José García Villa . . . ," 63.

HELENA MARÍA VIRAMONTES

"The Cariboo Cafe"
Fernández, Roberta. " 'The Cariboo Cafe': Helena María Viramontes Discourses with her Social and Cultural Contexts," *Women's Stud*, 17, i–ii (1989), 72–85.

"Neighbors"
Pavletich, JoAnn, and Margot G. Backus. "With His Pistol in *Her* Hand: Rearticulating the Corrido Narrative in Helena María

Viramontes' 'Neighbors,' " *Cultural Critique*, 27 (Spring, 1994), 127–152.

GERALD VIZENOR

"Thomas White Hawk"
Stevenson, Winona. "Suppressive Narrator and Multiple Narratees in Gerald Vizenor's 'Thomas White Hawk,' " *Stud Am Indian Lit*, 5, iii (1993), 36–42.

ZINAIDA VOLKONSKAYA

"Laure"
Kelly, Catriona. *A History of Russian* . . . , 55–56.

ALICE WALKER

"The Abortion"
Wear, Delese, and Lois L. Nixon. *Literary Anatomies* . . . , 36–37.

"Everyday Use"
Charters, Ann. *Resources* . . . , 161–163.
Tuten, Nancy. "Alice Walker's 'Everyday Use,' " *Explicator*, 51 (1993), 125–128.

"Nineteen Fifty-Five"
Pickering, James H., and Jeffrey D. Hoeper. *Instructor's Manual* . . . , 105–106.

"Roselily"
+Bohner, Charles H. *Instructor's Manual* . . . , 3rd ed., 136–137.
Charters, Ann. *Resources* . . . , 163–164.

"To Hell With Dying"
+Bohner, Charles H. *Instructor's Manual* . . . , 3rd ed., 137.
Pickering, James H., and Jeffrey D. Hoeper. *Instructor's Manual* . . . , 103–104.

DAVID FOSTER WALLACE

"Little Expressionless Animals"
Rother, James. "Reading and Riding the Post-Scientific Wave: The Shorter Fiction of David Foster Wallace," *R Contemp Fiction*, 13, ii (1993), 230.

"Order and Flux in Northampton"
Rother, James. "Reading . . . ," 220–228.

MYRIAM WARNER-VIEYRA

"Sidonie"
Lionnet, Françoise. "Geographies of Pain: Captive Bodies and Violent Acts in the Fictions of Myriam Warner-Vieyra, Gayl Jones, and Bessie Head," *Callaloo*, 16 (1993), 141–143.

ROBERT PENN WARREN

"Blackberry Winter"
+Bohner, Charles H. *Instructor's Manual* . . . , 3rd ed., 138–139.

SHEILA WATSON

"Antigone"
Kuester, Martin. "(Post-) Modern Bricolage: Classical Mythology in Sheila Watson's Short Stories," *Zeitschrift für Anglistik und Amerikanistik*, 43 (1994), 230–231.

"The Black Farm"
Kuester, Martin. "(Post-) Modern Bricolage . . . ," 229–230.

"Brother Oedipus"
Kuester, Martin. "(Post-) Modern Bricolage . . . ," 227–229.

"The Rumble Seat"
Kuester, Martin. "(Post-) Modern Bricolage . . . ," 231–232.

FAY WELDON

"Un Crime Maternel"
Jacobus, Lee A. "The Monologic Narrator in Fay Weldon's Short Fiction," in Barreca, Regina, Ed. *Fay Weldon's* . . . , 169.

"A Gentle Tonic Effect"
Jacobus, Lee A. "The Monologic . . . ," 167–168.

"I do what I can and I am what I am"
Jacobus, Lee A. "The Monologic . . . ," 163–164.

"Ind Aff"
Jacobus, Lee A. "The Monologic . . . ," 165–166.

"A Libration of Blood"
Glavin, John. "Fay Weldon, Leader of the Frivolous Band," in Barreca, Regina, Ed. *Fay Weldon's* . . . , 139.

"Moon Over Minneapolis"
Jacobus, Lee A. "The Monologic . . . ," 168–169.

"A Pattern of Cats"
Jacobus, Lee A. "The Monologic . . . ," 169–171.

"Pumpkin Pie"
Jacobus, Lee A. "The Monologic . . . ," 166–167.

Walker, Nancy A. "Witch Weldon: Fay Weldon's Use of the Fairy Tale Tradition," in Barreca, Regina, Ed. *Fay Weldon's* . . . , 11–12.

"The Year of the Green Pudding"
Jacobus, Lee A. "The Monologic . . . ," 164–165.

"Watching Me, Watching You"
Broich, Ulrich. "Muted Postmodernism: The Contemporary British Short Story," *Zeitschrift für Anglistik und Amerikanistik*, 41 (1993), 34.

ARCHIE WELLER

"Going Home"
Little, Janine. " 'Deadly' Work: Reading the Short Fiction of Archie Weller," *Australian Lit Stud*, 16 (1993), 194, 195–196.

"Homelands"
Little, Janine. " 'Deadly' Work . . . ," 195.

"Johnny Blue"
Little, Janine. " 'Deadly' Work . . . ," 197, 198.

"Pension Day"
Little, Janine. " 'Deadly' Work . . . ," 193, 194–195.

H. G. WELLS

"The Country of the Blind"
Alkon, Paul K. *Science Fiction* . . . , 44–45.

"The Time Machine"
Haynes, Roslynn D. *From Faust* . . . , 150–153.

EUDORA WELTY

"Acrobats in a Park"
Gretlund, Jan N. *Eudora Welty's Aesthetics* . . . , 21–30, 33–36, 347.

"Asphodel"
Gretlund, Jan N. *Eudora Welty's Aesthetics* . . . , 125–128.
Mortimer, Gail L. *Daughter of the Swan* . . . , 114–116.

"At the Landing"
+Jones, William M. "Name and Symbol in the Prose of Eudora Welty," in Champion, Laurie, Ed. *The Critical Response* . . . , 177.
Pollack, Harriet. "On Welty's Use of Allusion: Expectations and Their Revision in 'The Wide Net,' *The Robber Bridegroom* and 'At the Landing,' " *Southern Q*, 29, i (1990), 22–29; rpt. Champion, Laurie, Ed. *The Critical Response* . . . , 327–332.
Weston, Ruth D. *Gothic Traditions* . . . , 40–42, 136–137, 179–181.

"The Bride of Innisfallen"
Gretlund, Jan N. *Eudora Welty's Aesthetics* . . . , 138–141, 339–340.

"The Burning"
Charters, Ann. *Resources* . . . , 166–167.
Weston, Ruth D. *Gothic Traditions* . . . , 76–78.

"Circe"
Mortimer, Gail L. *Daughter of the Swan* . . . , 88–91, 94, 119.
Trouard, Dawn. "Diverting Swine: The Magical Relevancies of Eudora Welty's Ruby Fisher and Circe," in Champion, Laurie, Ed. *The Critical Response* . . . , 344–352.

"Clytie"
+Jones, William M. "Name and Symbol . . . ," 175.
Weston, Ruth D. *Gothic Traditions* . . . , 31–32.

"A Curtain of Green"
Brown, Alan. "Welty's 'A Curtain of Green,' " *Explicator*, 51 (1993), 242–243.
Gretlund, Jan N. *Eudora Welty's Aesthetics* . . . , 335.
Mortimer, Gail L. *Daughter of the Swan* . . . , 55–58.

"Death of a Traveling Salesman"
Gretlund, Jan N. *Eudora Welty's Aesthetics* . . . , 49–60, 85, 341–342.
Mortimer, Gail L. *Daughter of the Swan* . . . , 77–78.
Weston, Ruth D. *Gothic Traditions* . . . , 28–29.

"First Love"
Mortimer, Gail L. *Daughter of the Swan* . . . , 85–88.
Weston, Ruth D. *Gothic Traditions* . . . , 34–37.

"Flowers for Marjorie"
Gretlund, Jan N. *Eudora Welty's Aesthetics* . . . , 99–104.
Weston, Ruth D. "Images of the Depression in the Fiction of Eudora Welty," *Southern Q*, 32, i (1993), 85.

"Going to Naples"
Weston, Ruth D. *Gothic Traditions* . . . , 79–88.

"The Hitchhikers"
Weston, Ruth D. "Images of the Depression . . . ," 84–85.

"June Recital"
Gretlund, Jan N. *Eudora Welty's Aesthetics* . . . , 191–193, 197, 211–212.
+Harris, Wendell V. "The Thematic Unity in Welty's *The Golden Apples*," in Champion, Laurie, Ed. *The Critical Response* . . . , 131–132.
+Jones, William M. "Name and Symbol . . . ," 181.
Mark, Rebecca. *The Dragon's Blood* . . . , 51–94.
Mortimer, Gail L. *Daughter of the Swan* . . . , 125–132.
Verley, Claudine. "Décentrement et excentrement: *The Golden Apples* de Eudora Welty," *Études Anglaises*, 47 (1994), 36–37, 38–39.
Weston, Ruth D. *Gothic Traditions* . . . , 114–118.

"Keela, the Outcast Indian Maiden"
Gretlund, Jan N. *Eudora Welty's Aesthetics* . . . , 321.
Mortimer, Gail L. *Daughter of the Swan* . . . , 64–65.

"The Key"
Mortimer, Gail L. *Daughter of the Swan* . . . , 39–42.

"Kin"
Mortimer, Gail L. *Daughter of the Swan* . . . , 78–83.
Prenshaw, Peggy W. "Southern Ladies and the Southern Literary Renaissance," in Manning, Carol S., Ed. *The Female Tradition* . . . , 84–86.

"Ladies in Spring"
Mortimer, Gail L. *Daughter of the Swan* . . . , 117–120.

"Lily Daw and the Three Ladies"
Weston, Ruth D. *Gothic Traditions* . . . , 68–76.

"Livvie"
+Prenshaw, Peggy W. "Persephone in Eudora Welty's 'Livvie,' " in Champion, Laurie, Ed. *The Critical Response* . . . , 91–97.

"A Memory"
Mortimer, Gail L. *Daughter of the Swan* . . . , 54–56.

"Moon Lake"
Arnold, Marilyn. "The Edge of Adolescence in Eudora Welty's 'Moon Lake,' " *Southern Q*, 32, i (1993), 49–61.
Gretlund, Jan N. *Eudora Welty's Aesthetics* . . . , 131–134, 212–213.
Mark, Rebecca. *The Dragon's Blood* . . . , 112–144.
Mortimer, Gail L. *Daughter of the Swan* . . . , 133–135.
Verley, Claudine. "Décentrement et excentrement . . . ," 33.

"Music from Spain"
Gretlund, Jan N. *Eudora Welty's Aesthetics* . . . , 89–97.
Mark, Rebecca. *The Dragon's Blood* . . . , 177–231.
Mortimer, Gail L. *Daughter of the Swan* . . . , 96–105.
Pingree, Allison. "The Circles of Ran and Eugene MacLain: Welty's Twin Plots in *The Golden Apples*," in Mink, JoAnna S., and Janet D. Ward, Eds. *The Significance of Sibling* . . . , 89–93.
Weston, Ruth D. *Gothic Traditions* . . . , 121–124.

"No Place for You, My Love"
Devlin, Albert J. " 'The Sharp Edge of Experiment': The Poetics of 'No Place for You, My Love,' " in Champion, Laurie, Ed. *The Critical Response* . . . , 165–169.
Gretlund, Jan N. *Eudora Welty's Aesthetics* . . . , 86–87.
Weston, Ruth D. *Gothic Traditions* . . . , 37–39.

"Old Mr. Marblehall"
Mortimer, Gail L. *Daughter of the Swan* . . . , 63–64.

"Petrified Man"
+Bohner, Charles H. *Instructor's Manual* . . . , 3rd ed., 139–140.

"A Piece of News"
Gretlund, Jan N. *Eudora Welty's Aesthetics* . . . , 338.
Mortimer, Gail L. *Daughter of the Swan* . . . , 65–66.
Trouard, Dawn. "Diverting Swine . . . ," 339–344.

"Powerhouse"
Gretlund, Jan N. *Eudora Welty's Aesthetics . . .*, 17–18, 326–327.

"The Purple Hat"
Weston, Ruth D. *Gothic Traditions . . .*, 33–34.

"Shower of Gold"
+Jones, William M. "Name and Symbol . . .," 180–181.
Mark, Rebecca. *The Dragon's Blood . . .*, 31–50.
Pingree, Allison. "The Circles . . .," 86–87.
Verley, Claudine. "Décentrement et excentrement . . .," 34.

"Sir Rabbit"
Gretlund, Jan N. *Eudora Welty's Aesthetics . . .*, 200–201.
Mark, Rebecca. *The Dragon's Blood . . .*, 101–109.
Mortimer, Gail L. *Daughter of the Swan . . .*, 132–133.
Pingree, Allison. "The Circles . . .," 87–88.

"A Still Moment"
Mortimer, Gail L. *Daughter of the Swan . . .*, 66–74.

"A Visit of Charity"
Weston, Ruth D. *Gothic Traditions . . .*, 32–33.

"The Wanderers"
Gretlund, Jan N. *Eudora Welty's Aesthetics . . .*, 194–197, 198–202, 208–210.
+Jones, William M. "Name and Symbol . . .," 183–184.
Mark, Rebecca. *The Dragon's Blood . . .*, 232–260.
Mortimer, Gail L. *Daughter of the Swan . . .*, 135–140.
Weston, Ruth D. *Gothic Traditions . . .*, 124–128.

"Where Is the Voice Coming from?"
Gretlund, Jan N. *Eudora Welty's Aesthetics . . .*, 9–10, 227–242, 328, 353–354.

"The Whistle"
Gretlund, Jan N. *Eudora Welty's Aesthetics . . .*, 62–66.
Weston, Ruth D. "Images of the Depression . . .," 84.

"The Whole World Knows"
Gretlund, Jan N. *Eudora Welty's Aesthetics . . .*, 202–208.
Mark, Rebecca. *The Dragon's Blood . . .*, 145–174.
Mortimer, Gail L. *Daughter of the Swan . . .*, 96–101.
Weston, Ruth D. *Gothic Traditions . . .*, 119–120.

"Why I Live at the P.O."
Charters, Ann. *Resources . . .*, 168.
Gretlund, Jan N. *Eudora Welty's Aesthetics . . .*, 118–121.
+Jones, William M. "Name and Symbol . . .," 178–179.
May, Charles E. "Why Sister Lives at the P.O.," *Southern Hum R*, 12 (1978), 243–249; rpt. Champion, Laurie, Ed. *The Critical Response . . .*, 43–49.
Nissen, Axel. "Occasional Travelers in China Grove: Welty's 'Why I Live at the P.O.' Reconsidered," *Southern Q*, 32, i (1993), 72–79.
Pickering, James H., and Jeffrey D. Hoeper. *Instructor's Manual . . .*, 72–73.

"The Wide Net"

Orr, Linda. "The Duplicity of the Southern Story: Reflections on Reynolds Price's *The Surface of Earth* and Eudora Welty's 'The Wide Net,' " in Torgovnick, Marianna, Ed. *Eloquent Obsessions* . . . , 60–67.

Pollack, Harriet. "On Welty's Use of Allusion . . . ," 314–318; rpt. Champion, Laurie, Ed. *The Critical Response* . . . , 327–332.

"The Winds"

Mortimer, Gail L. *Daughter of the Swan* . . . , 142–144.

"A Worn Path"

+Bohner, Charles H. *Instructor's Manual* . . . , 3rd ed., 140–141.

Charters, Ann. *Resources* . . . , 169.

+Isaacs, Neil D. "Life for Phoenix," in Champion, Laurie, Ed. *The Critical Response* . . . , 37–42.

+Jones, William M. "Name and Symbol . . . ," 174.

Weston, Ruth D. *Gothic Traditions* . . . , 29–30.

FRANZ WERFEL

"Cabrinowitsch"

Michaels, Jennifer E. *Franz Werfel* . . . , 66–67.

"Estrangement"

Wagener, Hans. *Understanding* . . . , 90–91.

"The House of Mourning"

Wagener, Hans. *Understanding* . . . , 94–95.

"The Man Who Conquered Death"

Wagener, Hans. *Understanding* . . . , 84–90.

"Nicht der Mörder, der Ermordete ist schuldig"

Michaels, Jennifer E. *Franz Werfel* . . . , 67–70.

Wagener, Hans. *Understanding* . . . , 73–77.

"Pogrom"

Wagener, Hans. *Understanding* . . . , 140.

"Poor People"

Wagener, Hans. *Understanding* . . . , 106–109.

"Saverio Secret"

Wagener, Hans. *Understanding* . . . , 91–92.

"Spielhof, eine Phantasie"

Wallas, Armin A. "Franz Werfel—Kulturkritik und Mythos 1918/19," *Jahrbuch des Wiener Goethe-Vereins*, 94 (1990), 75–137.

"The Staircase"

Wagener, Hans. *Understanding* . . . , 92–94.

"Der Tod des Kleinbürgers"

Ingalsbe, Lori A. "Pieces of Broken Dreams: Franz Werfel's 'Der Tod des Kleinbürgers' and the *Habsburger Mythos*," *New Germ R*, 8 (1992), 47–60.

Michaels, Jennifer E. *Franz Werfel* . . . , 74–76.

GLENWAY WESCOTT

"In a Thicket"

Baker, Jennifer J. " 'In a Thicket': Glenway Wescott's Pastoral Vision," *Stud Short Fiction*, 31 (1994), 187–195.

NATHANAEL WEST

"The Adventurer"

Barnard, Rita. " 'When You Wish Upon a Star': Fantasy, Experience, and Mass Culture in Nathanael West," *Am Lit*, 66 (1994), 330–331.

"Miss Lonelyhearts"

Barnett, Louise K. *Authority and Speech . . .* , 186–194.

Lynch, Richard P. "Saints and Lovers: 'Miss Lonelyhearts' in the Tradition," *Stud Short Fiction*, 31 (1994), 225–235.

"Mr. Potts of Pottstown"

Barnard, Rita. " 'When You Wish . . . ,' " 332–333.

REBECCA WEST

"Elegy"

Stetz, Margaret D. "Rebecca West's 'Elegy': Women's Laughter and Loss," *J Mod Lit*, 18 (1993), 369–380.

EDITH WHARTON

"Afterward"

Banta, Martha. "The Ghostly Gothic of Wharton's Everyday World," *Am Lit Realism*, 27, i (1994), 3–5.

Heller, Janet R. "Ghosts and Marital Estrangement: An Analysis of 'Afterward,' " *Edith Wharton R*, 10, i (1993), 18–19.

"Autres Temps . . ."

Charters, Ann. *Resources . . .* , 171–172.

Raub, Patricia. *Yesterday's Stories . . .* , 33–34.

"Bewitched"

Fedorko, Kathy A. " 'Forbidden Things': Gothic Confrontation with the Feminine in 'The Young Gentleman' and 'Bewitched,' " *Edith Wharton R*, 11, i (1994), 5–8.

"Duration"

Fracasso, Evelyn E. "Images of Imprisonment in Two Tales of Edith Wharton," *Coll Lang Assoc J*, 36 (1993), 323–326.

"Kerfol"

Killoran, Helen. "Pascal, Brontë, and 'Kerfol': The Horrors of a Foolish Quartet," *Edith Wharton R*, 10, i (1993), 12–17.

"The Looking Glass"

Inness, Sherrie A. "An Economy of Beauty: The Beauty System in Edith Wharton's 'The Looking Glass' and 'Permanent Wave,' " *Stud Short Fiction*, 30 (1993), 137–140. [see also *Edith Wharton R*, 10, i (1993), 8–9.]

"Mrs. Manstey's View"

Campbell, Donna M. "Edith Wharton and the 'Authoresses': The Critique of Local Color in Wharton's Early Fiction," *Stud Am Fiction*, 22 (1994), 171–173.

Fracasso, Evelyn E. "Images . . . ," 319–323.

"The Muse's Tragedy"

Levy, Andrew. *The Culture* . . . , 71–72.

Nettels, Elsa. "Texts Within Texts: The Power of Letters in Edith Wharton's Fiction," in Prier, Raymond A., Ed. *Countercurrents* . . . , 194–200.

"The Other Two"

+Bohner, Charles H. *Instructor's Manual* . . . , 3rd ed., 141–143.

Inverso, Mary B. "Performing Women: Semiotic Promiscuity in 'The Other Two,' " *Edith Wharton R*, 10, i (1993), 3–6.

Raub, Patricia. *Yesterday's Stories* . . . , 29.

"Permanent Wave"

Inness, Sherrie A. "An Economy of Beauty . . . ," 140–143. [See also *Edith Wharton R*, 10, i (1993), 9–11.]

"Pomegranate Seed"

Friedl, Bettina. "Edith Wharton: 'Pomegranate Seed'—The Verge of Being," in Lubbers, Klaus, Ed. *Die Englische* . . . , 120–133.

Singley, Carol J., and Susan E. Sweeney. "Forbidden Reading and Ghostly Writing in Edith Wharton's 'Pomegranate Seed,' " in Singley, Carol J., and Susan E. Sweeney, Eds. *Anxious Power* . . . , 197–217.

"Roman Fever"

Berkove, Lawrence I. " 'Roman Fever': A Mortal Malady," *CEA Critic*, 56, ii (1994), 56–60.

+Bohner, Charles H. *Instructor's Manual* . . . , 3rd ed., 143–144.

Charters, Ann. *Resources* . . . , 172–173.

Levy, Andrew. *The Culture* . . . , 72–74.

Wheeler, Kathleen. *'Modernist' Women* . . . , 82, 83, 88–98.

"The Young Gentleman"

Fedorko, Kathy A. " 'Forbidden Things' . . . ," 4–5.

EDMUND WHITE

"An Oracle"

Dellamora, Richard. "Apocalyptic Utterance in Edmund White's 'An Oracle,' " in Murphy, Timothy F., and Suzanne Poirier, Eds. *Writing AIDS* . . . , 98–116.

"Palace Days"
Clum, John M. " 'And Once I Had It All': AIDS Narratives and Memories of an American Dream," in Murphy, Timothy F., and Suzanne Poirier, Eds. *Writing AIDS* . . . , 213–214.

PATRICK WHITE

"The Cockatoos"
Gowda, H. H. Anniah. "R. K. Narayan and Patrick White as Short-Story Tellers," in McLeod, A. L., Ed. *R. K. Narayan* . . . , 57, 58.

"The Night of the Prowler"
Gowda, H. H. Anniah. "R. K. Narayan . . . ," 55–56.

"The Twitching Colonel"
Gowda, H. H. Anniah. "R. K. Narayan . . . ," 54.

ELIE WIESEL

"Une vieille connaissance"
Davis, Colin. *Elie Wiesel's Secretive Texts*, 7–12.

WILLIAM CARLOS WILLIAMS

"At the Front"
Witemeyer, Hugh. "William Carlos Williams' Introduction to His Short Stories: A History and Some Interpretive Uses," *J Mod Lit*, 18 (1993), 438–439.

"The Dawn of Another Day"
Witemeyer, Hugh. "William Carlos Williams' . . . ," 444–445.

"The Girl with a Pimply Face"
Witemeyer, Hugh. "William Carlos Williams' . . . ," 442.

"The Insane"
Bremen, Brian A. *William Carlos Williams* . . . , 102–103.

"Jean Beicke"
Bremen, Brian A. *William Carlos Williams* . . . , 105–106.

"The Knife of the Time"
Witemeyer, Hugh. "William Carlos Williams' . . . ," 440–441.

"In Northern Waters"
Witemeyer, Hugh. "William Carlos Williams' . . . ," 439–440.

"Pink and Blue"
Witemeyer, Hugh. "William Carlos Williams' . . . ," 442–444.

"The Use of Force"
+Bohner, Charles H. *Instructor's Manual* . . . , 3rd ed., 144–145.
Bremen, Brian A. *William Carlos Williams* . . . , 87, 98–102.
Witemeyer, Hugh. "William Carlos Williams' . . . ," 441–442.

ANGUS WILSON

"Realpolitik"
Bergonzi, Bernard. *Wartime* . . . , 95.

"A Story of Historical Interest"
Bergonzi, Bernard. *Wartime* . . . , 93–94.

"The Wrong Set"
Bergonzi, Bernard. *Wartime* . . . , 94.

CARLOS GUILLERMO WILSON

"Carbón y Leche"
Birmingham-Pokorny, Elba. "The Emergence of the New Afro-Hispanic Woman in Carlos Guillermo Wilson's *Cuentos del Negro Cubana* and *Chombo*," in Birmingham-Porkorny, Elba D., Ed. *Denouncement* . . . , 114, 115–116.

"La familia"
Birmingham-Pokorny, Elba. "The Emergence of the New . . . ," 113, 115–116.

HARRIET E. WILSON

"Our Nig"
Breau, Elizabeth. "Identifying Satire: *Our Nig*," *Callaloo*, 16 (1993), 455–465.
Davis, Cynthia J. "Speaking the Body's Pain: Harriet Wilson's 'Our Nig,' " *African Am R*, 27 (1993), 396–402.
Ernest, John. "Economies of Identity: Harriet E. Wilson's 'Our Nig,' " *PMLA*, 109 (1994), 424–438.
Mitchell, Angelyn. "Her Side of His Story: A Feminist Analysis of Two Nineteenth-Century Antebellum Novels—William Wells Brown's *Clotel* and Harriet E. Wilson's 'Our Nig,' " *Am Lit Realism*, 24, iii (1992), 12–19.

TIM WINTON

"Bay of Angels"
Bruce Bennett. "Nostalgia for Community: Tim Winton's Essay and Stories," in Haskell, Dennis, Ed. *Tilting at Matilda* . . . , 71–72.

"Gravity"
Bruce Bennett. "Nostalgia . . . ," 69.

"Lantern Stalk"
Bruce Bennett. "Nostalgia . . . ," 67–68.

"Laps"
Bruce Bennett. "Nostalgia . . . ," 70–71.

"My Father's Axe"
Bruce Bennett. "Nostalgia . . . ," 63–65.

"The Oppressed"
Bruce Bennett. "Nostalgia . . . ," 66–67.

"Scission"
Bruce Bennett. "Nostalgia . . . ," 65.

"Wake"
Bruce Bennett. "Nostalgia . . . ," 66.

GABRIELE WOHMANN

"Das enttäuschte Kind"
Geldrich-Leffman, Hanna. "Together Alone: Marriage in the Short Stories of Gabriele Wohmann," *Germ R*, 69 (1994), 137–138.

"Friendenstage"
Geldrich-Leffman, Hanna. "Together . . . ," 138.

"Guilty"
Geldrich-Leffman, Hanna. "Together . . . ," 137.

"Hamster, Hamster!"
Geldrich-Leffman, Hanna. "Together . . . ," 134–135.

"Das Oberhapt"
Geldrich-Leffman, Hanna. "Together . . . ," 137.

"Eine Okkasion"
Geldrich-Leffman, Hanna. "Together . . . ," 132–133.

"Paarlauf"
Geldrich-Leffman, Hanna. "Together . . . ," 136–137.

"Rudolph und Aline"
Geldrich-Leffman, Hanna. "Together . . . ," 136.

"Scherben"
Geldrich-Leffman, Hanna. "Together . . . ," 135–136.

"Spätherbst"
Geldrich-Leffman, Hanna. "Together . . . ," 137.

"Verjährt"
Geldrich-Leffman, Hanna. "Together . . . ," 134.

"Wer spricht denn da"
Geldrich-Leffman, Hanna. "Together . . . ," 133–134.

"Willkommen—herzlich willkommen"
Geldrich-Leffman, Hanna. "Together . . . ," 136.

CHRISTA WOLF

"Juninachmittag"
Rey, William H. "Christa Wolfs 'Juninachmittag': Vorspiel zu den letzten Erzählungen," *Weimarer Beiträge*, 38, i (1992), 85–103.

"Selbstversuch"
Haynes, Roslynn D. *From Faust* . . . , 232.
Henderson, Gary. "Christa Wolfs Erkenntnistheoretischer Übergang," *Seminar*, 30 (1994), 171–173.

"Stöfall"
Haynes, Roslynn D. *From Faust* . . . , 232–333, 264.

"Was bleibt"
Andress, Reinhard. " 'Lossprechungen sind nicht in Sicht'—Christa Wolf und 'Was bleibt,' " in Gerber, Margy, and Roger Wood, Eds. *The End of the GDR* . . . , 143–155.
Brockmann, Stephen. "Preservation and Change in Christa Wolf's 'Was bleibt,' " *Germ Q*, 67 (1994), 73–85.
Konzett, Matthias. "Christa Wolf's 'Was bleibt': The Literary Utopia and Its Remaining Significance," *Monatshefte*, 85 (1993), 438–452.
Lehnert, Herbert. "Spuren von Ingeborg Bachmann in Christa Wolfs 'Was bleibt,' " *Zeitschrift für Deutsche Philologie*, 112 (1994), 598–613.
Pakendorf, Gunther. " 'Was bliebt': DDR-Erfahrung als Geschichtserfahrung," *Acta Germanica*, 21 (1992), 247–260.
Romero, Christiane Z. "Sexual Politics and Christa Wolf's 'Was bleibt,' " in Gerber, Margy, and Roger Woods, Eds. *The End of the GDR* . . . , 169–177.

GENE WOLFE

"Seven American Nights"
Aichele, George. "Self-Referentiality in Gene Wolfe's 'Seven American Nights,' " *J Fantastic Arts*, 3, ii (1991), 37–47.

THOMAS KENNERLY WOLFE

"The Child by Tiger"
Gantt, Patricia. "Weaving Discourse in Thomas Wolfe's 'The Child by Tiger,' " *Southern Q*, 31, iii (1993), 45–57.

"I Have a Thing to Tell You"
Idol, John L. "The Narrative Discourse of Thomas Wolfe's 'I Have a Thing to Tell You,' " *Stud Short Fiction*, 30 (1993), 43–52.

"The Lost Boy"
Bentz, Joseph. "The Influence of Modernist Structure in the Short Fiction of Thomas Wolfe," *Stud Short Fiction*, 31 (1994), 155–160.

"No Cure for It"
Bentz, Joseph. "The Influence . . . ," 154–155.

TOBIAS WOLFF

"Smokers"
+Bohner, Charles H. *Instructor's Manual* . . . , 3rd ed., 145–146.

CONSTANCE FENIMORE WOLLSON

"Miss Grief"

Grasso, Linda. " 'Thwarted Life, Mighty Hunger, Unfinished Work': The Legacy of Nineteenth-Century Women Writing in America," *ATQ*, 8, N.S. (1994), 106–107.

VIRGINIA WOOLF

"The Evening Party"

Broughton, Panthea R. "The Blasphemy of Art: Fry's Aesthetics and Woolf's Non-'Literary' Stories," in Gillespie, Diane F., Ed. *The Multiple Muses* . . . , 52.

Levy, Heather. "Gender Crossings: The Short Fiction," in Hussey, Mark, and Vara Neverow, Eds. *Virginia Woolf: Emerging* . . . , 84–85, 86.

"The Journal of Mistress Joan Martyn"

Levy, Heather. "Gender Crossings . . . ," 87.

VanStavern, Jan. "Back Talk: Writing Empires in Woolf's Fiction," in Hussey, Mark, and Vara Neverow, Eds. *Virginia Woolf: Emerging* . . . , 254–258.

"Kew Gardens"

+Bohner, Charles H. *Instructor's Manual* . . . , 3rd ed., 146–147.

Broughton, Panthea R. "The Blasphemy . . . ," 50–52.

"The Lady in the Looking Glass"

Kemp, Sandra. "Selected Short Stories," in Briggs, Julia, Ed. *Virginia Woolf* . . . , 67–68.

Reynier–Girardin, Christine. " 'The Lady in the Looking Glass' de Virginia Woolf: Reflexions sur un miroir," *Cahiers Victoriens et Edouardiens*, 37 (1993), 121–128.

"Lappin and Lapinova"

Campbell, Ann G. "Virginia Woolf and Hélène Cixous: Female Fantasy in Two of Woolf's Short Stories," in Hussey, Mark, and Vara Neverow, Eds. *Virginia Woolf: Emerging* . . . , 72–74.

"The Mark on the Wall"

Broughton, Panthea R. "The Blasphemy . . . ," 44–45.

Kemp, Sandra. "Selected . . . ," 71–73, 74–75, 76.

Whelan, P. T. "Women's Domestic Quest: Minimal Journeys and Their Frames in the *Thousand and One Nights*, 'The Mark on the Wall' and 'The Man with the Buttons,' " *Comparatist*, 18 (1994), 153–156.

"Moments of Being: 'Slater's Pins Have No Points' "

Levy, Heather. "Gender Crossings . . . ," 89.

"Mrs. Dalloway in Bond Street"

Levy, Heather. "Gender Crossings . . . ," 87–88.

"Phyllis and Rosamond"

VanStavern, Jan. "Back Talk . . . ," 253–254.

"Portrait 3"
Levy, Heather. "Gender Crossings . . . ," 89–90.

"The Searchlight"
Campbell, Ann G. "Virginia Woolf . . . ," 74–76.

"The Shooting Party"
Levy, Heather. "Gender Crossings . . . ," 85.

"Solid Objects"
Broughton, Panthea R. "The Blasphemy . . . ," 54–56.

"The String Quartet"
Jacobs, Peter. " 'The Second Violin Tuning in the Ante-room': Virginia Woolf and Music," in Gillespie, Diane F., Ed. *The Multiple Muses* . . . , 242–244.

"Time Passes"
Hankins, Leslie K. "A Splice of Reel Life in Virginia Woolf's 'Time Passes': Censorship, Cinema and 'the usual battlefield of emotions,' " *Criticism*, 35 (1993), 106–111.

"An Unwritten Novel"
Reed, Christopher. "Through Formalism: Feminism and Virginia Woolf's Relation to Bloomsbury Aesthetics," in Gillespie, Diane F., Ed. *The Multiple Muses* . . . , 26–27.

"A View of a Woman's College from the Outside"
Levy, Heather. "Gender Crossings . . . ," 88–89.

JUDITH WRIGHT

"Eighty Acres"
Bennett, Bruce. "Place and Moral Commitment: Judith Wright and Christina Stead," in Thumboo, Edwin, Ed. *Perceiving* . . . , 14–16.

RICHARD WRIGHT

"Big Black Good Man"
Charters, Ann. *Resources* . . . , 175.

"Down by the Riverside"
Hakutani, Yoshinobu. "Racial Oppression and Alienation in Richard Wright's 'Down by the Riverside' and 'Long Black Song,' " *Mississippi Q*, 46 (1993), 232–235.

"Fire and Cloud"
Shulman, Robert. "Subverting and Reconstructing the Dream: The Radical Voices of Le Sueur, Herbst, and Wright," in Rudin, Ernest, and Gert Buelens, Eds. *Deferring a Dream* . . . , 29–35.

"Long Black Song"
Clinton, Catherine. " 'With a Whip in His Hand': Rape, Memory, and African-American Women," in Fabre, Geneviève, and Robert O'Meally, Eds. *History* . . . , 213–214.

Hakutani, Yoshinobu. "Racial Oppression and Alienation . . . ," 235–238.

"The Man Who Lived Underground"

Hakutani, Yoshinobu. "Richard Wright's 'The Man Who Lived Underground,' Nihilism, and Zen," *Mississippi Q*, 47 (1994), 201–213.

Peterson, Dale E. "Richard Wright's Long Journey from Gorky to Dostoevsky," *African Am R*, 28 (1994), 383–384.

"The Man Who Was Almost a Man"

+Bohner, Charles H. *Instructor's Manual* . . . , 3rd ed., 147–148.

Charters, Ann. *Resources* . . . , 176.

Pickering, James H., and Jeffrey D. Hoeper. *Instructor's Manual* . . . , 71–72.

WILLIAM WRIGHT [DAN DE QUILLE]

"The Sorceress of Attu"

Berkove, Lawrence I. "Introduction," in Berkove, Lawrence, Ed. *The Sorceress of Attu* [by Dan De Quille], 12–15.

LILLIE BUFFUM CHACE WYMAN

"The Child of the State"

Rose, Jane A. "Recovering Lillie Buffum Chace Wyman and 'The Child of the State,' " *Legacy*, 7 (1990), 39–43.

YAMADA EIMI

"Jessie's Spine"

Samuel, Yoshiko Y. "Yamada Eimi (1959–)," in Mulhern, Chieko I., Ed. *Japanese* . . . , 460–461.

HISAYE YAMAMOTO

"The Brown House"

Crow, Charles L. "The *Issei* Father in the Fiction of Hisaye Yamamoto," in Truchlar, Leo, Ed. *Für eine offene Literaturwissenschaft* . . . , 38; rpt. Cheung, King-Kok, Ed. *Hisaye Yamamoto* . . . , 125.

Kim, Elaine H. *Asian American Literature* . . . , 158–159; rpt. in his "Hisaye Yamamoto: A Woman's View," in Cheung, King-Kok, Ed. *Hisaye Yamamoto* . . . , 110–111.

McDonald, Dorothy R., and Katharine Newman. "Relocation and Dislocation: The Writings of Hisaye Yamamoto and Wakako Yamauchi," *MELUS*, 7, iii (1980), 26; rpt. Cheung, King-Kok, Ed. *Hisaye Yamamoto* . . . , 134–135.

"Epithalamium"
McDonald, Dorothy R., and Katharine Newman. "Relocation . . . ," 29; rpt. Cheung, King-Kok, Ed. *Hisaye Yamamoto* . . . , 138–139.

"The High-Heeled Shoes"
McDonald, Dorothy R., and Katharine Newman. "Relocation . . . ," 24–25; rpt. Cheung, King-Kok, Ed. *Hisaye Yamamoto* . . . , 133–134.

"Las Vegas Charley"
Crow, Charles L. "The *Issei* Father . . . ," 38–40; rpt. Cheung, King-Kok, Ed. *Hisaye Yamamoto* . . . , 125–127.
McDonald, Dorothy R., and Katharine Newman. "Relocation . . . ," 26–27; rpt. Cheung, King-Kok, Ed. *Hisaye Yamamoto* . . . , 135–136.

"The Legend of Miss Sasagawara"
Cheung, King-kok. "Thrice Muted Tale: Interplay of Art and Politics in Hisaye Yamamoto's 'The Legend of Miss Sasagawara,' " *MELUS*, 17, iii (1991), 109–125.
Crow, Charles L. "The *Issei* Father . . . ," 36–38; rpt. Cheung, King-Kok, Ed. *Hisaye Yamamoto* . . . , 123–124.
McDonald, Dorothy R., and Katharine Newman. "Relocation . . . ," 27–28; rpt. Cheung, King-Kok, Ed. *Hisaye Yamamoto* . . . , 136–137.

"Seventeen Syllables"
Crow, Charles L. "The *Issei* Father . . . ," 34–35; rpt. Cheung, King-Kok, Ed. *Hisaye Yamamoto* . . . , 120–121.
Goellnicht, Donald C. "Transplanted Discourse in Yamamoto's 'Seventeen Syllables,' " in Cheung, King-Kok, Ed. *Hisaye Yamamoto* . . . , 181–193.
Kim, Elaine H. *Asian American Literature* . . . , 159–160, 161–163; rpt. in his "Hisaye Yamamoto . . . ," 111–112, 113–114, 116.
Wong, Sau-ling C. *Reading Asian American Literature* . . . , 167–169.

"Yoneko's Earthquake"
Crow, Charles L. "The *Issei* Father . . . ," 35–36; rpt. Cheung, King-Kok, Ed. *Hisaye Yamamoto* . . . , 121–123.
Kim, Elaine H. *Asian American Literature* . . . , 160–161; rpt. in his "Hisaye Yamamoto . . . ," 113.
Payne, Robert M. "Adapting (to) the Margins: *Hot Summer Winds* and the Stories of Hisaye Yamamoto," *East-West Film J*, 7, ii (1993), 40–42.
Wong, Sau-ling C. *Reading Asian American Literature* . . . , 169–170, 172–173.

YAMAMOTO MICHIKO

"Chair in the Rain"
Wilson, Michiko N. "Yamamoto Michiko (1936–)," in Mulhern, Chieko I., Ed. *Japanese* . . . , 470–471.

"Father Goose"
Wilson, Michiko N. "Yamamoto Michiko . . . ," 470.

"The Man Who Cut the Grass"
Wilson, Michiko N. "Yamamoto Michiko . . . ," 469–470.

YAMAUCHI WAKAKO

"And the Soul Shall Dance"
Hongo, Garrett. "Introduction," *Songs My Mother* . . . [by Yamauchi Wakako], 8–9.

"Charted Lives"
Hongo, Garrett. "Introduction," 13–14.

"The Coward"
Hongo, Garrett. "Introduction," 14–15.

"Ōtōkō"
Hongo, Garrett. "Introduction," 9–10.

"The Sensei"
Hongo, Garrett. "Introduction," 12–13.

"Songs My Mother Taught Me"
Wong, Sau-ling C. *Reading Asian American Literature* . . . , 169, 172.

"That Was All"
Hongo, Garrett. "Introduction," 11.

ABRAHAM B. YEHOSHUA

"Facing the Forests"
Frieden, Ken. "A. B. Yehoshua: Arab Dissent in His Early Fiction," in Yudkin, Leon I., Ed. *Israeli Writers* . . . , 113–118.

"Three Days and a Child"
Frieden, Ken. "A. B. Yehosua: Arab . . . ," 118–123.

YÜ TA-FU

"Sinking"
Gu Ming Dong. "A Chinese Oedipus in Exile," *Lit & Psych*, 39, i–ii (1993), 1–19.

CARLOS EDUARDO ZAVALETA

"El cuervo blanco"
González Montes, Antonio. "Notas sobre *Vestido de luto* de C. E. Zavaleta," *Lexis*, 16, ii (1992), 257, 258.

"Los dos cocineritas del rey"
González Montes, Antonio. "Notas sobre . . . ," 257.

"Vestido de luto"
González Montes, Antonio. "Notas sobre . . . ," 257–258.

ROGER ZELAZNY

"He Who Shapes"
Goodrich, Peter H. "The Lineage of Mad Scientists: Anti-types of Merlin," in Rieger, Branimir M., Ed. *Dionysus in Literature* . . . , 81.

"The Last Defender of Camelot"
Goodrich, Peter H. "The Lineage . . . ," 81.

CYNTHIA M. ZELMAN

"Our Menstruation"
Wear, Delese, and Lois L. Nixon. *Literary Anatomies* . . . , 56–59.

PATRICIA ZELVER

"Love Letters"
Pickering, James H., and Jeffrey D. Hoeper. *Instructor's Manual* . . . , 111–112.

MARIYA ZHUKOVA

"Baron Reichman"
Kelly, Catriona. *A History of Russian* . . . , 84–87, 88.

"Self-Sacrifice"
Kelly, Catriona. *A History of Russian* . . . , 83.

WILHELM ZIETHE

"The Locksmith from Philadelphia"
Peterson, Brent O. "The 'Political' and the German-American Press," *Yearbook Germ-Am Stud*, 23 (1988), 43–44, 46–47.

LIDIYA ZINOVEVA-ANNIBAL

"The Red Spider"
Kelly, Catriona. *A History of Russian* . . . , 159–160.

ZITKALA-ŠA

"The Soft-Hearted Sioux"
Okker, Patricia "Native American Literatures and the Canon: The

Case of Zitkala-Ša,'' in Quirk, Tom, and Gary Scharnhorst, Eds. *American Realism* . . . , 91–94.

ÉMILE ÉDOUARD CHARLES ANTOINE ZOLA

''L'Attaque du moulin''
Viti, Robert M. ''Myth, Time and History in Zola's 'L'Attaque du moulin,' '' *Romance Notes*, 34 (1993), 177–183.

MIKHAIL ZOSHCHENKO

''The Adventures of a Monkey''
Scatton, Linda H. *Mikhail Zoshchenko* . . . , 157–159.

''The Black Prince''
Scatton, Linda H. *Mikhail Zoshchenko* . . . , 113–118.

''The Christmas Tree''
Scatton, Linda H. *Mikhail Zoshchenko* . . . , 149–152.

''A Find''
Scatton, Linda H. *Mikhail Zoshchenko* . . . , 148–149.

''Galoshes and Ice-Cream''
Scatton, Linda H. *Mikhail Zoshchenko* . . . , 143–144.

''The Goat''
Scatton, Linda H. *Mikhail Zoshchenko* . . . , 86–88.

''Golden Words''
Scatton, Linda H. *Mikhail Zoshchenko* . . . , 152–155.

''Grandmother's Gift''
Scatton, Linda H. *Mikhail Zoshchenko* . . . , 144–145.

''Lenin and the Sentry''
Scatton, Linda H. *Mikhail Zoshchenko* . . . , 137–138.

''Mishel Sinyagin''
Scatton, Linda H. *Mikhail Zoshchenko* . . . , 99–101.

''No Need to Lie''
Scatton, Linda H. *Mikhail Zoshchenko* . . . , 142–143.

''A Relatively Clever Kitty''
Scatton, Linda H. *Mikhail Zoshchenko* . . . , 138–140.

''Thirty Years Later''
Scatton, Linda H. *Mikhail Zoshchenko* . . . , 145–148.

A Checklist of Books Used

Achberger, Karen R. *Understanding Ingeborg Bachmann*. Columbia: Univ. of South Carolina Press, 1995.

Actas del IV simposio internacional de la Asociación Española de Semiótica: Describir, inventar, transcribir el mundo, I & II. Madrid: Visor, 1992.

Adamson, Ginette, and Eunice Myers, Eds. *Continental, Latin-American, and Francophone Women Writers: Selected Papers from the Wichita State University Conference on Foreign Literature, 1986–1987*, II. Lanham, Md.: Univ. Press of America, 1990.

Aiken, Susan H., Adele M. Barker, Maya Koreneva, and Ekaterina Stetsenko, Eds. *Dialogues/Dialogi: Literary and Cultural Exchanges Between (ex)Soviet and American Women*. Durham: Duke Univ. Press, 1994.

Alkon, Paul K. *Science Fiction Before 1900: Imagination Discovers Technology*. New York: Twayne, 1994.

Allen, Roger, Ed. *Critical Perspectives on Yusuf Idris*. Colorado Springs: Three Continents Press, 1994.

Alvarez-Detrell, Tamara, and Michael G. Paulson, Eds. *The Traveler in the Life and Works of George Sand*. Troy, N.Y.: Whitson, 1994.

Amoia, Alba. *Feodor Dostoevsky*. New York: Continuum, 1993.

Anderson, Roger, and Paul Debreczeny, Eds. *Russian Narrative and Visual Art: Varieties of Seeing*. Gainesville: Univ. Press of Florida, 1994.

Andrews, William L., Ed. *Classic Fiction of the Harlem Renaissance*. Oxford: Oxford Univ. Press, 1994.

Andriano, Joseph. *Our Ladies of Darkness: Feminine Daemonology in Male Gothic Fiction*. University Park: Pennsylvania State Univ. Press, 1993.

Anisfield, Nancy, Ed. *The Nightmare Considered: Critical Essays on Nuclear War Literature*. Bowling Green, Ohio: Popular, 1991.

Arancibia, Juana Alcira, Ed. *Literatura como intertextualidad: IX Simposio Internacional de Literatura*. Buenos Aires: Instituto Literario y Cultural Hispánico, 1993.

———. *Literatura del Mundo Hispánico: VIII Simposio International de Literatura*. Quito: Instituto Literario y Cultural Hispánico, 1992.

Arcana, Judith. *Grace Paley's Life Stories: A Literary Biography*. Urbana: Univ. of Illinois Press, 1993.

Arntz, Reiner, Ed. *Textlinguistik und Fachsprache*. Hildesheim: Olms, 1988.

Asals, Frederick, Ed. *Flannery O'Connor, "A Good Man Is Hard to Find."* New Brunswick, N. J.: Rutgers Univ. Press, 1993.

Badawi, M. M. *A Short History of Modern Arabic Literature*. Oxford: Clarendon Press, 1993.

Bailin, Miriam. *The Sickroom in Victorian Fiction*. Cambridge: Cambridge Univ. Press, 1994.

Balat, Michel, and Janice Deledalle-Rhodes, Eds. *Signs of Humanity/ L'homme et ses signes*, II. Berlin: Mouton de Gruyter, 1992.

Balderston, Daniel. *Out of Context: Historical Reference and the Representation of Reality in Borges*. Durham: Duke Univ. Press, 1993.

Barnett, Louise K. *Authority and Speech: Language, Society, and Self in the American Novel*. Athens: Univ. of Georgia Press, 1993.

Barreca, Regina. *Untamed and Unabashed: Essays on Women and Humor in British Literature*. Detroit: Wayne State Univ. Press, 1994.
———, Ed. *Fay Weldon's Wicked Fictions*. Hanover, N.H. : Univ. Press of New England, 1994.
Baskin, Judith R., Ed. *Women of the Word: Jewish Women and Jewish Writing*. Detroit: Wayne State Univ. Press, 1994.
Bauer, Helen P. *Rudyard Kipling: A Study of the Short Fiction*. New York: Twayne, 1994.
Bell, David F. *Circumstances: Chance in the Literary Text*. Lincoln: Univ. of Nebraska Press, 1993.
Bell, Michael. *Gabriel García Márquez: Solitude and Solidarity*. New York: St. Martin's Press, 1993.
Bell, Michael D. *The Problem of American Realism: Studies in the Cultural History of a Literary Idea*. Chicago: Univ. of Chicago Press, 1993.
Bergonzi, Bernard. *Wartime and Aftermath: English Literature and its Background, 1939–60*. Oxford: Oxford Univ. Press, 1993.
Berkove, Lawrence I., Ed. *The Sorceress of Attu* [by Dan De Quille]. Dearborn, Mich.: Madrigan Library, 1994.
Bernstein, Cynthia G. *The Text & Beyond: Essays in Literary Linguistics*. Tuscaloosa: Univ. of Alabama Press, 1994.
Bestard Vázquez, Joaquín. *Cuentos de Beyhualé: Doce cuentos de Joaquín Bestard Vázquez*, ed. Lee A. Daniel. Fredericton, Canada: York Press, 1994.
Bethea, David M., Ed. *Pukin Today*. Bloomington: Indiana Univ. Press, 1993.
Bevan, David, Ed. *Literature and the Bible*. Amsterdam: Rodopi, 1993.
Birmingham-Pokorny, Elba D., Ed. *Denouncement and Reaffirmation of the Afro-Hispanic Identity in Carlos Guillermo Wilson's Works*. Miami: Ediciones Universal, 1993.
Björklund, Martina. *Narrative Strategies in Čechov's 'The Steppe': Cohesion, Grounding and Point of View*. Aåbo: Aåbo Univ. Press, 1993.
Blair, Walter. *Essays on American Humor: Blair Through the Ages*. Madison: Univ. of Wisconsin Press, 1993.
Bloom, Clive, Ed. *Creepers: British Horror and Fantasy in the Twentieth Century*. London: Pluto Press, 1993.
———. *Twentieth-Century Suspense: The Thriller Comes of Age*. New York: St. Martin's Press, 1990.
Bloom, Harold. *The Western Canon: The Books and School of the Ages*. New York: Harcourt Brace & Co., 1994.
Blüher, Karl A., and Alfonso de Toro, Eds. *Jorge Luis Borges: Variaciones interpretativas sobre sus procedimientos literarios y bases epistemológicas*. Frankfurt am Main: Vervuert, 1992.
Booker, M. Keith. *Vargas Llosa Among the Postmodernists*. Gainesville: Univ. Press of Florida, 1994.
Booth, Alison, Ed. *Famous Last Words: Changes in Gender and Narrative Closure*. Charlottesville: Univ. Press of Virginia, 1993.
Boschetto-Sandoval, Sandra M., and Marcia P. McGowan, Eds. *Claribel Alegría and Central American Literature: Critical Essays*. Athens: Ohio Univ. Center for International Studies, 1994.
Bourquin, Jacques, and Daniel Jacobi, Eds. *Mélanges offerts à Jean Peytard, I & II*. Paris: Belles Lettres, 1993.
Bowen, Zack. *A Reader's Guide to John Barth*. Westport: Greenwood Press, 1994.
Bradfield, Scott. *Dreaming Revolution: Transgression in the Development of American Romance*. Iowa City: Univ. of Iowa Press, 1993.
Brand, Max [Frederick Schiller Faust]. *The Collected Stories of Max Brand*, ed. Robert and Jane Easton. Lincoln: Univ. of Nebraska Press, 1994.
Bremen, Brian A. *William Carlos Williams and the Diagnostics of Culture*. New York: Oxford Univ. Press, 1993.

Briggs, A. D. P., Ed. *Notes from Underground* [Dostoevsky] [and] *A Confession* [Tolstoy]. London: Dent, 1994; Am. ed. Rutland, Vt.: Charles E. Tuttle, 1994.
Briggs, Julia, Ed. *Virginia Woolf: Introduction to the Major Works*. London: Virago Press, 1994.
Brinkmeyer, Robert H. *Katherine Anne Porter's Artistic Development: Primitivism, Traditionalism, and Totalitarianism*. Baton Rouge: Louisiana State Univ. Press, 1993.
Bromell, Nicholas K. *By the Sweat of the Brow: Literature and Labor in Antebellum America*. Chicago: Univ. of Chicago Press, 1993.
Brooks, Peter. *Body Work: Objects of Desire in Modern Narrative*. Cambridge: Harvard Univ. Press, 1993.
Brown, Deming. *The Last Years of Soviet Russian Literature*. Cambridge: Cambridge Univ. Press, 1993.
Brunsdale, Mitzi M. *James Joyce: A Study of the Short Fiction*. New York: Twayne, 1993.
Bryan, Violet H. *The Myth of New Orleans in Literature: Dialogues of Race and Gender*. Knoxville: Univ. of Tennessee Press, 1993.
Bunge, Nancy. *Nathaniel Hawthorne: A Study of the Short Fiction*. New York: Twayne, 1993.
Busette, Cedric. *"La familia de Pascual Duarte" and "El túnel": Correspondences and Divergencies in the Exercise of Craft*. Lanham, Md.: Univ. Press of America, 1994.
Butler, Pierce. *Sean O'Faolain: A Study of the Short Fiction*. New York: Twayne, 1993.
Buzard, James. *The Beaten Track: European Tourism, Literature, and the Ways to Culture, 1800–1918*. Oxford: Oxford Univ. Press, 1993.
Cahalan, James M. *Liam O'Flaherty: A Study of the Short Fiction*. Boston: Twayne, 1991.
Calinescu, Matei. *Rereading*. New Haven: Yale Univ. Press, 1993.
Capozzi, Rocco, and Mario B. Mignone, Eds. *Homage to Moravia*. Stony Brook: Forum Italicum, 1993.
Captain-Hidalgo, Yvonne. *The Culture of Fiction in the Works of Manuel Zapata Olivella*. Columbia: Univ. of Missouri Press, 1993.
Carabine, Keith, Owen Knowles, and Wiesław Krajka, Eds. *Conrad's Literary Career*. Lubin: Maria Curie-Skłodowska Univ. Press, 1992.
———. *Contexts for Conrad*. New York: Columbia Univ. Press, 1993.
Carmean, Karen. *Toni Morrison's World of Fiction*. Troy, N.Y.: Whitson, 1993.
Carr, Virginia S, Ed. *Katherine Anne Porter, "Flowering Judas."* New Brunswick, N.J.: Rutgers Univ. Press, 1993.
Carscallen, James. *The Other Country: Patterns in the Writing of Alice Munro*. Toronto: ECW Press, 1993.
Champion, Laurie, Ed. *The Critical Response to Eudora Welty's Fiction*. Westport: Greenwood Press, 1994.
Charters, Ann. *Resources for Teaching: "Major Writers of Short Fiction."* Boston: St Martin's Press, 1993.
Cheng, Vincent J., and Timothy Martin, Eds. *Joyce in Context*. Cambridge: Cambridge Univ. Press, 1992.
Cheung, King-Kok, Ed. *Hisaye Yamamoto "Seventeen Syllables."* New Brunswick, N.J.: Rutgers Univ. Press, 1994.
Clark, Robert, and Piero Boitani, Eds. *English Studies in Transition: Papers from the ESSE Inaugural Conference*. London: Routledge, 1993.
Clayton, Douglas. *Floyd Dell: The Life and Times of an American Rebel*. Chicago: Ivan R. Dee, 1994.
Clyman, Toby W., and Diana Greene, Eds. *Women Writers in Russian Literature*. Westport: Greenwood Press, 1994.

Cohen, Sarah B. *Cynthia Ozick's Comic Art: From Levity to Liturgy*. Bloomington: Indiana Univ. Press, 1994.
Coloquio internacional: El texto latinamericano, I. Madrid: Espiral, 1994.
Cortázar, Julio. *Siete cuentos*, ed. Peter Beardsell. Manchester: Manchester Univ. Press, 1994.
Cosslett, Tess. *Women Writing Childbirth: Modern Discourses of Motherhood*. Manchester: Manchester Univ. Press, 1994; Am. ed. New York: St. Martin's Press, 1994.
Costa, Richard H. *An Appointment with Somerset Maugham and Other Literary Encounters*. College Station: Texas A&M Univ. Press, 1994.
Current-Garcia, Eugene. *O. Henry: A Study of the Short Fiction*. New York: Twayne, 1993.
Dale, Alzina S., Ed. *Dorothy L. Sayers: The Centenary Celebration*. New York: Walker, 1993.
Davies, Carole B. *Black Women, Writing and Identity: Migrations of the Subject*. New York: Routledge, 1994.
Davis, Catherine, Ed. *Women Writers in Twentieth-Century Spain and Spanish America*. Lewiston, N.Y.: Edwin Mellen, 1993.
Davis, Colin. *Elie Wiesel's Secretive Texts*. Gainesville: Univ. Press of Florida, 1994.
Davis, Lloyd, Ed. *Virginal Sexuality and Textuality in Victorian Literature*. Albany: State Univ. of New York Press, 1993.
Davis, Thadious. *Nella Larsen, Novelist of the Harlem Renaissance: A Woman's Life Unveiled*. Baton Rouge: Louisiana State Univ. Press, 1994.
Death, Sarah, and Helena Forsaås-Scott, Eds. *A Century of Swedish Narrative: Essays in Honour of Karin Petherick*. Norwich, England: Norvik Press, 1994.
D'haen, Theo, and Hans Bertens, Eds. *Postmodern Fiction in Canada*. Amsterdam: Rodopi, 1992.
Deiritz, Karl, and Hannes Krauss, Eds. *Verrat an der Kunst? Rückblicke auf die DDR-Literatur*. Berlin: Aufbau, 1993.
Delany, Paul, Ed. *Vancouver: Representing the Postmodern City*. Vancouver: Arsenal Pulp Press, 1994.
Delbaere, Jeanne, Ed. *William Golding: The Sound of Silence*. Liège: L^3-Liège Lang. and Lit., 1991.
DeMouy, Jane K. *Katherine Anne Porter's Women: The Eye of Her Fiction*. Austin: Univ. of Texas Press, 1983.
Dendle, Brian J., and José Belmonte Serrano, Eds. *Literatura de Levante*. Alicante: Fundación Cultural CAM, 1993.
Dhawan, R. K., and William Tonetto, Eds. *New Zealand Literature Today*. New Delhi: Indian Society for Commonwealth Studies, 1993.
DiAntonio, Robert, and Nora Glickman, Eds. *Tradition and Innovation: Reflections on Latin American Jewish Writing*. Albany: State Univ of New York Press, 1993.
DiGaetani, John L., Ed. *Money: Lure, Lore, and Literature*. Westport: Greenwood Press, 1994.
Dine, Philip. *Images of the Algerian War: French Fiction and Film, 1954–1992*. Oxford: Oxford Univ. Press, 1994.
Djebar, Assia. *Women of Algiers in Their Apartment*. Trans. Marjolija Jager. Charlottesville: Univ. of Virginia Press, 1992.
Dooley, Patrick. K. *The Pluralistic Philosophy of Stephen Crane*. Urbana: Univ. of Illinois Press, 1993.
Dubey, Madhu. *Black Women Novelists and the Nationalist Aesthetic*. Bloomington: Indiana Univ. Press, 1994.
Eidelman, Dawn D. *George Sand and the Nineteenth-Century Russian Love-Triangle Novels*. Cranbury, N.J.: Assoc. Univ. Presses [for Bucknell Univ. Press], 1994.
Elad, Ami, Ed. *Writer, Culture, Text: Studies in Modern Arabic Literature*. Fredericton, Canada: York, 1993.

England, Eugene, and Peter Makuck, Eds. *An Open World: Essays on Leslie Norris*. Columbia, S.C.: Camden House, 1994.

Erskine, Thomas L., and Connie L. Richards, Eds. *Charlotte Perkins Gilman, "The Yellow Wallpaper."* New Brunswick, N.J.: Rutgers Univ. Press, 1993.

Estes, David C., Ed. *Critical Reflections on the Fiction of Ernest J. Gaines*. Athens: Univ. of Georgia Press, 1994.

Ettin, Andrew V. *Betrayals of the Body Politic: The Literary Commitments of Nadine Gordimer*. Charlottesville: Univ. Press of Virginia, 1993.

Fabre, Geneviève, and Robert O'Meally, Eds. *History and Memory in African-American Culture*. Oxford: Oxford Univ. Press, 1994.

Faulkner, Mara. *Protest and Possibility in the Writing of Tillie Olsen*. Charlottesville: Univ. Press of Virginia, 1993.

Feldman, Jessica R. *Gender on the Divide: The Dandy in Modernist Literature*. Ithaca: Cornell Univ. Press, 1993.

Ferguson, Moira. *Jamaica Kincaid: Where the Land Meets the Body*. Charlottesville: Univ. Press of Virginia, 1994.

Fickert, Kurt. *End of a Mission: Kafka's Search for Truth in His Last Stories*. Columbia, S.C.: Camden House, 1993.

Finkelstein, Norman. *The Ritual of New Creation: Jewish Tradition and Contemporary Literature*. Albany: State Univ. of New York, 1992.

Firda, Richard A. *Peter Handke*. New York: Twayne, 1993.

Fischlin, Daniel, Ed. *Negation, Critical Theory, and Postmodern Textuality*. Dordrecht, The Netherlands: Kluwer, 1994.

Fleming, Robert E. *The Face in the Mirror: Hemingway's Writers*. Tuscaloosa: Univ. of Alabama Press, 1994.

Flynn, Elizabeth A., and Patrocinio P. Schweickart, Eds. *Gender and Reading: Essays on Readers, Texts, and Contexts*. Baltimore: Johns Hopkins Univ. Press, 1986.

Fogel, Daniel M., Ed. *A Companion to Henry James Studies*. Westport: Greenwood Press, 1993.

Foster, David W., Ed. *Latin American Writers on Gay and Lesbian Themes: A Bio-Critical Sourcebook*. Westport: Greenwood Press, 1994.

———, Ed. *Mexican Literature: A History*. Austin: Univ. of Texas Press, 1994.

Foster, Edward H. *William Saroyan: A Study of the Short Fiction*. New York: Twayne, 1991.

Foster, John B. *Nabokov's Art of Memory and European Modernism*. Princeton: Princeton Univ. Press, 1993.

Foster, Thomas C. *Understanding John Fowles*. Columbia: Univ. of South Carolina Press, 1994.

Frank, Armin P., Ed. *Die literarische Übersetzung—der lange Schatten kurzer Geschichten: Amerikanische Kurzprosa in deutschen Übersetzungen*. Berlin: Schmidt, 1989.

Freadman, Richard, and Lloyd Reinhardt, Eds. *On Literary Theory and Philosophy*. New York: St. Martin's Press, 1991.

Friedman, Lawrence S. *William Golding*. New York: Continuum, 1993.

Friedman, Susan S., Ed. *Joyce: The Return of the Repressed*. Ithaca: Cornell Univ. Press, 1993.

Frus, Phyllis. *The Politics and Poetics of Journalistic Narrative: The Timely and the Timeless*. Cambridge: Cambridge Univ. Press, 1994.

Frye, Northrop. *The Eternal Act of Creation: Essays, 1979–1990*, ed. Robert D. Denham. Bloomington: Indiana Univ. Press, 1993.

Fuchs, Gerhard, and Gerhard Melzer, Eds. *Peter Handke: Die Langsamkeit der Welt*. Graz: Droschl, 1993.

Furman, Necah S. *Caroline Lockhart: Her Life and Legacy*. Cody, Wyo.: Buffalo Bill Historical Center, 1994.

Fusco, Richard. *Maupassant and the American Short Story: The Influence of Form at the Turn of the Century*. University Park: Pennsylvania State Univ. Press, 1994.
Fussell, Edwin S. *The Catholic Side of Henry James*. Cambridge: Cambridge Univ. Press, 1993.
Fussell, Paul. *The Anti-Egotist: Kingsley Amis, Man of Letters*. London: Oxford Univ. Press, 1994.
Fusso, Susanne. *Designing Dead Souls: An Anatomy of Disorder in Gogol*. Stanford: Stanford Univ. Press, 1993.
Futrell, Ann M. *The Signs of Christianity in the Work of Walker Percy*. San Francisco: Catholic Scholars Press, 1994.
Gabriele, John P., Ed. *Suma valleinclaniana*. Barcelona: Anthropos, 1992.
Gabriele, Tommasina. *Italo Calvino: Eros and Language*. Cranbury, N.J.: Assoc. Univ. Presses [for Fairleigh Dickinson Univ. Press], 1994.
Galef, David. *The Supporting Cast: A Study of Flat and Minor Characters*. University Park: Pennsylvania State Univ. Press, 1993.
Gallagher, Susan V., Ed. *Postcolonial Literature and the Biblical Call for Justice*. Jackson: Univ. Press of Mississippi, 1994.
Gates, Henry L., and K. A. Appiah, Eds. *Langston Hughes: Critical Perspectives Past and Present*. New York: Amistad, 1993.
Gates, Joanne E. *Elizabeth Robins, 1862–1952: Actress, Novelist, Feminist*. Tuscaloosa: Univ. of Alabama Press, 1994.
Gatten, Aileen, and Anthony H. Chambers, Eds. *New Leaves: Studies and Translations of Japanese Literature in Honor of Edward Seidensticker*. Ann Arbor: Center for Japanese Studies, The Univ. of Michigan, 1993.
Gatrell, Simon, Ed. *The Ends of the Earth: 1876–1918*. London: Ashfield, 1992.
Gelder, Ken. *Reading the Vampire*. New York: Routledge, 1994.
Gerber, Margy, and Roger Woods, Eds. *The End of the GDR and the Problems of Integration*. Lanham, Md.: Univ. Press of America, 1993.
Giles, James R. *Irwin Shaw: A Study of the Short Fiction*. Boston: Twayne, 1991.
Gillespie, David. *Iurii Trifonov: Unity Through Time*. Cambridge: Cambridge Univ. Press, 1992.
Gillespie, Diane F. *The Multiple Muses of Virginia Woolf*. Columbia: Univ. of Missouri Press, 1993.
Gimbernat González, Ester, and Cynthia Tompkins, Eds. *Utopías, ojos azules, bacas suicidas: La narrativa de Alina Diaconú*. Buenos Aires: Editorial Fraterna, 1993.
Glantz, Margo. *Esguince de cintura: ensayos sobre narrativa Mexicana del siglo xx*. Coyoacán, Mexico: Consejo Nacional para la Cultura y las Artes, 1994.
Glasser, William A. *Reclaiming Literature: A Teacher's Dilemma*. Westport: Praeger, 1994.
Golden Catherine, Ed. *The Captive Imagination: A Casebook on "The Yellow Wallpaper."* New York: Feminist Press, 1992.
Goldstein, Philip, Ed. *Styles of Cultural Activism: From Theory and Pedagogy to Women, Indians, and Communism*. Cranbury, N.J.: Assoc. Univ Presses [for Univ. of Delaware Press], 1994.
Goodenough, Elizabeth, Mark A. Heberle, and Naomi Sokoloff, Eds. *Infant Tongues: The Voice of the Child in Literature*. Detroit: Wayne State Univ. Press, 1994.
Gorilovics, Tivadar, and Anna Szabo, Eds. *Le Chantier de George Sand: George Sand et l'étranger*. Debrecen: Kossuth Lajos Tudományegyetem, 1993.
Göttsche, Dirk, and Hubert Ohl, Eds. *Ingeborg Bachmann—Neue Beiträge zu ihrem Werk: Internationales Symposion Münster, 1991*. Würzburg: Königshausen & Neumann, 1993.
Gretlund, Jan N. *Eudora Welty's Aesthetics of Place*. Cranbury, N.J.: Assoc. Univ. Press [for Univ. of Delaware Press], 1994.
Gribble, Charles E., Ed. *Alexander Lipson: In Memoriam*. Columbus: Slavica Publishers, 1994.

Griffin, Gabriele. *Heavenly Love? Lesbian Images in Twentieth-Century Women's Writing*. Manchester: Manchester Univ. Press, 1993.
Groß, Konrad, Kurt Müller, and Meinhard Winkgens, Eds. *Das Natur/Kultur-Paradigma in der englischsprachigen Erzählliteratur des 19. und 10. Jahrhunderts: Festschrift zum 60. Geburtstag von Paul Goetsch*. Tübingen: Gunter Narr, 1994.
Gurewitch, Morton. *The Ironic Temper and the Comic Imagination*. Detroit: Wayne State Univ. Press, 1994.
Gurnah, Abdulrazak, Ed. *Essays on African Writing: A Re-evaluation*. Oxford: Heinemann, 1993.
Hahn, Gerhard, and Ernst Weber, Eds. *Zwischen den Wissenschaften: Beiträge zur deutschen Literaturgeschichte*. Regensburg: Pustet, 1994.
Hall, Joan W. *Shirley Jackson: A Study of the Short Fiction*. New York: Twayne, 1993.
Hanne, Michael, Ed. *Literature and Travel*. Amsterdam: Rodopi, 1994.
Harmon, Maurice. *Sean O'Faolain: A Critical Introduction*. Dublin: Wolfhound Press, 1984; Am. ed. Notre Dame: Univ. of Notre Dame Press, 1966.
Harper, Phillip B. *Framing the Margins: The Social Logic of Postmodern Culture*. Oxford: Oxford Univ. Press, 1994.
Harrison, Russell. *Against the American Dream: Essays on Charles Bukovski*. Santa Rosa, Calif.: Black Sparrow Press, 1994.
Harrow, Kenneth, Jonathan Ngaté, and Clarisse Zimra, Eds. *Crisscrossing Boundaries in African Literatures, 1986*. Washington: Three Continents Press, 1991.
———. *Thresholds of Change in African Literature: The Emergence of a Tradition*. London: James Currey Ltd., 1994; Am. ed. Portsmouth, N. H.: Heinemann, 1994.
Hart, Stephen M. *Gabriel García Márquez: "Crónica de una muerte anunciada."* London: Grant & Cutler, 1994.
———. *White Ink: Essays on Twentieth-Century Feminine Fiction in Spain and Latin America*. London: Tamesis Books Limited, 1994; Span. ed. Madrid: Editorial Támesis, 1994.
Haskell, Dennis, Ed. *Tilting at Matilda: Literature, Aborigines, Women and the Church in Contemporary Australia*. South Fremantle, Australia: Fremantle Arts Centre, 1994.
Hayashi, Tetsumaro, Ed. *A New Study Guide to Steinbeck's Major Works*. Metuchen, N.J.: Scarecrow Press, 1993.
Hayes, Elizabeth, Ed. *Images of Persephone: Feminist Readings in Western Literature*. Gainesville: Univ. Press of Florida, 1994.
Haynes, Roslynn D. *From Faust to Strangelove: Representations of the Scientist in Western Literature*. Baltimore: Johns Hopkins Univ. Press, 1994.
Head, Bessie. *The Cardinals: With Meditations and Short Stories*. Portsmouth, N.H.: Heinemann, 1993.
Heble, Ajay. *The Tumble of Reason: Alice Munro's Discourse of Absence*. Toronto: Univ. of Toronto Press, 1994.
Hedges, Elaine, and Shelley F. Fishkin, Eds. *Listening to Silences: New Essays in Feminist Criticism*. New York: Oxford Univ. Press, 1994.
Heidsieck, Arnold. *The Intellectual Contexts of Kafka's Fiction: Philosophy, Law, Religion*. Columbia, S.C.: Camden House, 1994.
Heinze, Denise. *The Dilemma of "Double-Consciousness": Toni Morrison's Novels*. Athens: Univ. of Georgia Press, 1993.
Hengen, Shannon. *Margaret Atwood's Power: Mirrors, Reflections and Images in Select Fiction and Poetry*. Toronto: Second Story Press, 1993.
Henriksen, Aage. *Isak Dinesen/Karen Blixen: The Work and the Life*, trans. William Mishler. New York: St. Martin's Press, 1988.
Hernández de López, Ana María, Ed. *Mario Vargas Llosa: Opera Omnia*. Madrid: Editorial Pliegos, 1994.
Herndl, Diane P. *Invalid Women: Figuring Feminine Illness in American Fiction and Culture, 1840–1940*. Chapel Hill: Univ. of North Carolina Press, 1993.

Heyns, Michiel. *Expulsion and the Nineteenth-Century Novel: The Scapegoat in English Realist Fiction*. Oxford: Clarendon Press, 1994.

Hibbard, Allen. *Paul Bowles: A Study of the Short Fiction*. New York: Twayne, 1994.

Hill, Leslie. *Marguerite Duras: Apocalyptic Desires*. London: Routledge, 1993.

Hillenaar, Henk, and Jan Versteeg, Eds. *George Bataille et la fiction*. Amsterdam: Rolopi, 1992.

Hillenaar, Henk, and Walter Schönau, Eds. *Fathers and Mothers in Literature*. Amsterdam: Rodopi, 1994.

Hönnighausen, Lothar, and Valeria G. Lerda, Eds. *Rewriting the South: History and Fiction*. Tübingen: Francke, 1993.

Hoppenstand, Gary. *Clive Barker's Short Stories: Imagination as Metaphor in the "Books of Blood" and Other Works*. Jefferson, N.C.: McFarland & Co., 1994.

Hosmer, Robert E., Ed. *Contemporary British Women Writers: Narrative Strategies*. New York: St. Martin's Press, 1993.

Howe, Irving. *Irving Howe: A Critic's Notebook*, ed. Nicholas Howe. New York: Harcourt Brace & Company, 1994.

Howell, John M. *Understanding John Gardner*. Columbia: Univ. of South Carolina Press, 1993.

Huet, Marie-Hélène. *Monstrous Imagination*. Cambridge: Harvard Univ. Press, 1993.

Humphries, Jefferson, Ed. *Southern Literature and Literary Theory*. Athens: Univ. of Georgia Press, 1980.

Hussey, Mark, and Vara Neverow, Eds. *Virginia Woolf: Emerging Perspectives, Selected Papers from the Third Annual Conference on Virginia Woolf*. New York: Pace Univ. Press, 1994.

Irwin, John T. *The Mystery to a Solution: Poe, Borges, and the Analytic Detective Story*. Baltimore: Johns Hopkins Univ. Press, 1994.

Isenberg, Charles. *Telling Silence: Russian Frame Narratives of Renunciation*. Evanston, Ill.: Northwestern Univ. Press, 1993.

Jackson, Robert L. *Dialogues with Dostoevsky: The Overwhelming Questions*. Stanford: Stanford Univ. Press, 1993.

———, Ed. *Reading Chekhov's Text*. Evanston, Ill.: Northwestern Univ. Press, 1993.

Jackson, Tony E. *The Subject of Modernism: Narrative Alterations in the Fiction of Eliot, Conrad, Woolf, and Joyce*. Ann Arbor: Univ. of Michigan Press, 1994.

Jacobson, Marcia. *Being a Boy Again: Autobiography and the American Boy Book*. Tuscaloosa: Univ. of Alabama Press, 1994.

Jahn, Gary R. *"The Death of Ivan Ilich": An Interpretation*. New York: Twayne, 1993.

Johnson, Greg. *Joyce Carol Oates: A Study of the Short Fiction*. New York: Twayne, 1994.

Johnson, Randal, Ed. *Tropical Paths: Essays on Modern Brazilian Literature*. New York: Garland, 1993.

Johnson, Ronald L. *Anton Chekhov: A Study of the Short Fiction*. New York: Twayne, 1993.

Jordan, Isolde J., Ed. *El inmovilismo existencial en la narrativa de Julio Ricci*. Montevideo: Editorial Graffiti, 1993.

Jörgensen, Beth E. *The Writings of Elena Poniatowska*. Austin: Univ. of Texas Press, 1994.

Joyce, James. *Dubliners*, eds. Hans W. Gabler and Walter Hettche. New York: Vintage, 1993.

Joyce, Joyce A. *Warriors, Conjurers, and Priests: Defining African-centered Literary Criticism*. Chicago: Third World Press, 1994.

Jurak, Mirko, Ed. *Literature, Culture, and Ethnicity: Studies on Medieval, Renaissance, and Modern Literatures*. Ljubljana: Author, 1992.

Kaiser, Herbert, and Gerhard Köpf, Eds. *Erzählen, Erinnern: Deutsche Prosa der Gegenwart: Interpretationen*. Frankfort: Diesterweg, 1992.

Karolides, Nicholas J., Lee Burress, and John M. Kean, Eds. *Censored Books: Critical Viewpoints*. Metuchen, N.J.: Scarecrow Press, 1993.

Karpinski, Joanne B., Ed. *Critical Essays on Charlotte Perkins Gilman*. New York: G. K. Hall, 1992.

Kauvar, Elaine M. *Cynthia Ozick's Fiction: Tradition and Invention*. Bloomington: Indiana Univ. Press, 1993.

Kaye, Frances W. *Isolation and Masquerade: Willa Cather's Women*. New York: Peter Lang, 1993.

Kelly, Catriona. *A History of Russian Women's Writing, 1820–1992*. Oxford: Clarendon Univ. Press, 1994.

Kennedy, Andrew, and Orm Øverland, Eds. *Excursions in Fiction: Essays in Honour of Professor Lars Hartveit on His 70th Birthday*. Oslo: Novus Press, 1994.

Kenwood, Alun, Ed. *Travellers' Tales, Real and Imaginary, in the Hispanic World and Its Literature*. Melbourne: Voz Hispánica, 1992.

Kiely, Robert. *Reverse Tradition: Postmodern Fictions and the Nineteenth-Century Novel*. Cambridge: Harvard Univ. Press, 1993.

Kim, Elaine H. *Asian American Literature: An Introduction to the Writings and Their Social Context*. Philadelphia: Temple Univ. Press, 1982.

King, Bruce, Ed. *The Later Short Fiction of Nadine Gordimer*. New York: St. Martin's Press, 1993.

———. *V. S. Naipaul*. New York: St. Martin's Press, 1993.

Klevar, Harvey L. *Erskine Caldwell: A Biography*. Knoxville: Univ. of Tennessee Press, 1993.

Kluback, William. *Franz Kafka: Challenges and Confrontations*. New York: Peter Lang, 1993.

Kowalewski, Michael. *Deadly Musing: Violence and Verbal Form in American Fiction*. Princeton: Princeton Univ. Press, 1993.

Krase, Jerome, and Judith N. DeSena, Eds. *Italian Americans in a Multicultural Society*. Stony Brook, N.Y.: *Forum Italicum*, 1994.

Kristeva, Julia. *Strangers to Ourselves*, trans. Leon S. Roudiez. New York: Columbia Univ. Press, 1991.

Kronegger, Marlies, and Anna-Teresa Tymieniecka, Eds. *Allegory Old and New in Literature, the Fine Arts, Music and Theatre, and Its Continuity in Culture*. Dordrecht: Kluwer Acad. Publishers, 1994.

Langford, Michele K., Ed. *Contours of the Fantastic: Selected Essays from the Eighth International Conference on the Fantastic in the Arts*. Westport: Greenwood Press, 1990.

Lassner, Phyllis. *Elizabeth Bowen: A Study of the Short Fiction*. New York: Twayne, 1991.

Leeming, David. *James Baldwin: A Biography*. New York: Alfred A. Knopf, 1994.

Le Fanu, Sheridan. *In a Glass Darkly*. ed. Robert Tracy. Oxford: Oxford Univ. Press, 1993.

Le Gassick, Trevor, Ed. *Critical Perspectives on Naguib Mahfouz*. Washington: Three Continents Press, 1991.

Leighton, Lauren G. *The Esoteric Tradition in Russian Romantic Literature: Decembrism and Freemasonry*. University Park: Pennsylvania State Univ. Press, 1994.

Leonard, Garry M. *Reading "Dubliners" Again: A Lacanian Perspective*. Syracuse: Syracuse Univ. Press, 1993.

Levine, Michael G. *Writing Through Repression: Literature, Censorship, Psychoanalysis*. Baltimore: Johns Hopkins Univ. Press, 1994.

Levy, Andrew. *The Culture and Commerce of the American Short Story*. Cambridge: Cambridge Univ. Press, 1993.

Lindstrom, Naomi. *Jorge Luis Borges: A Study of the Short Fiction*. Boston: Twayne, 1990.

———. *Twentieth-Century Spanish American Fiction*. Austin: Univ. of Texas Press, 1994.

Liu Kang and Xiaobing Tang, Eds. *Politics, Ideology, and Literary Discourse in Modern China: Theoretical Interventions and Cultural Critique*. Durham: Duke Univ. Press, 1993.

Logsdon, Loren, and Charles W. Mayer, Eds. *Since Flannery O'Connor: Essays on the Contemporary American Short Story*. Malcomb: Western Illinois Univ., 1987.

Lohmann, Christoph K., Ed. *Discovering Difference: Contemporary Essays in American Culture*. Bloomington: Indiana Univ. Press, 1993.

Loving, Jerome. *Lost in the Customhouse: Authorship in the American Renaissance*. Iowa City: Univ. of Iowa Press, 1993.

Lowe, James. *The Creative Process of James Agee*. Baton Rouge: Louisiana State Univ. Press, 1994.

Lu, Tonglin, Ed. *Gender and Sexuality in Twentieth-Century Chinese Literature and Society*. Albany: State Univ. of New York Press, 1993.

Lubbers, Klaus, Ed. *Die Englische und Amerikanische Kurzgeschichte*. Darmstadt: Wiss Buchgesellschaft, 1990.

Lucente, Carla E., Ed. *The Western Pennsylvania Symposium on World Literatures, Selected Proceedings: 1974–1991, a Retrospective*. Greensburg, Pa.: Eadmer Press, 1992.

Lugones, Leopoldo. *Las fuerzas extrañas: Cuentos fatales*, pref. Noé Jitrik. Mexico: Editorial Trillas, 1992.

Lukacher, Maryline. *Maternal Fictions: Stendhal, Sand, Rachilde, and Bataille*. Durham: Duke Univ. Press, 1994.

Lustig, T. J. *Henry James and the Ghostly*. Cambridge: Cambridge Univ. Press, 1994.

Lutwack, Leonard. *Birds in Literature*. Gainesville: Univ. Press of Florida, 1994.

McAlexander, Hubert H., Ed. *Critical Essays on Peter Taylor*. New York: G. K. Hall, 1993.

McCormack, W. J. *Dissolute Characters: Irish Literary History Through Balzac, Sheridan Le Fanu, Yeats and Bowen*. Manchester: Manchester Univ. Press, 1993.

Macklin, John, Ed. *After Cervantes: A Celebration of 75 Years of Iberian Studies at Leeds*. Leeds: Trinity and All Saints College, 1993.

McKnight, Phillip. *Understanding Christoph Hein*. Columbia: Univ. of South Carolina Press, 1995.

McLeod, A. L., Ed. *R. K. Narayan: Critical Perspectives*. New Delhi: Sterling Publishers, 1994.

McNerney, Kathleen, and Nancy Vosburg, Eds. *The Garden Across the Border: Mercè Rodoreda's Fiction*. Selinsgrove, Pa.: Susquehanna Univ. Press, 1994.

Magistrale, Tony, Ed. *The Dark Descent: Essays Defining Stephen King's Horrorscape*. New York: Greenwood, 1992.

Magliocchetti, Bruno, and Anthony Verna, Ed. *The Motif of the Journey in Nineteenth-Century Italian Literature*. Gainesville: Univ. Press of Florida, 1994.

Magnarelli, Sharon. *Understanding José Donoso*. Columbia: Univ of South Carolina Press, 1993.

Maguire, Robert A. *Exploring Gogol*. Stanford: Stanford Univ. Press, 1994.

Maguire, Robert A., and Alan Timberlake, Eds. *American Contributions to the Eleventh International Congress of Slavists*. Columbus, Ohio: Slavica, 1993.

Maier, Carol, and Roberta L. Salper, Eds. *Ramón María del Valle-Inclán: Questions of Gender*. Cranbury, N.J.: Assoc. Univ. Presses [for Bucknell Univ. Press], 1994.

Makowsky, Veronica. *Susan Glaspell's Century of American Woman*. New York: Oxford Univ. Press, 1993.

Manning, Carol S., Ed. *The Female Tradition in Southern Literature*. Urbana: Univ. of Illinois Press, 1993.

Marchalonis, Shirley, Ed. *Critical Essays on Mary Wilkins Freeman*. Boston: G. K. Hall, 1991.

Mark, Rebecca. *The Dragon's Blood: Feminist Intertextuality in Eudora Welty's "The Golden Apples."* Jackson: Univ. Press of Mississippi, 1994.

Marotin, François, and Jacques-Philippe Saint-Gérand, Eds. *Poétique et narration: Mélanges offerts à Guy Demerson.* Paris: Champion, 1993.

Martin, Carol A. *George Eliot's Serial Fiction.* Columbus: Ohio State Univ. Press, 1994.

Martín, Gregorio C., Ed. *Selected Proceedings of the Pennsylvania Foreign Language Conference.* Pittsburgh: Dept. of Mod. Langs., Duquesne Univ., 1988–1989.

Martínez Cuitiño, Luis, and Élida Lois, Eds. *Actas del III Congreso Argentino de Hispanistas "España en América y América en España."* Buenos Aires: Univ. de Buenos Aires, Instituto de Filología y Literaturas Hispánicas, 1992.

Massa, Ann, and Alistair Stead, Eds. *Forked Tongues? Comparing Twentieth-Century British and American Literature.* London: Longman, 1994.

Mata, Oscar, Ed.. *En torno a la literatura mexicana.* Mexico: Universidad Autónoma Metropolitana, 1989.

Matthews, Pamela R. *Ellen Glasgow and a Woman's Traditions.* Charlottesville: Univ. Press of Virginia, 1994.

May, Charles E., Ed. *The New Short Story Theories.* Athens: Ohio Univ. Press, 1994.

Meese, Elizabeth. *Crossing the Double-cross: The Practice of Feminist Criticism.* Chapel Hill: Univ. of North Carolina Press, 1986.

Meldrum, Barbara H., Ed. *Old West–New West: Centennial Essays.* Moscow: Univ. of Idaho Press, 1993.

Méndez-Clark, Ronald S. *Onetti y la (in)fidelidad a las reglas del juego.* Lanham, Md.: University Press of America, 1993.

Menton, Seymour. *Latin America's New Historical Novel.* Austin: Univ. of Texas Press, 1993.

Meslin, Michel, Ed. *Regards européenssur le monde anglo-américain.* Paris: Univ. Press of Paris, Sorbonne, 1992.

Mezo, Richard E. *A Study of B. Traven's Fiction: The Journey to Solipaz.* San Francisco: Edwin Mellen, 1993.

Michaels, Jennifer E. *Franz Werfel and the Critics.* Columbia, S.C.: Camden House, 1994.

Mickel, Emanuel J., Ed. *The Shaping of Text: Style, Imagery, and Structure in French Literature.* Cranbury, N.J.: Assoc. Univ. Presses [for Bucknell Univ. Press], 1993.

Mills, Bruce. *Cultural Reformations: Lydia Maria Child and the Literature of Reform.* Athens: Univ. of Georgia Press, 1994.

Mills, William, Ed. *John William Corrington: Southern Man of Letters.* Conway, Ark.: UCA Press, 1994.

Mink, JoAnna S., and Janet D. Ward, Eds. *The Significance of Sibling Relationships in Literature.* Bowling Green: Bowling Green State Univ. Press, 1993.

Minter, David. *A Cultural History of the American Novel: Henry James to William Faulkner.* Cambridge: Cambridge Univ. Press, 1994.

Misurella, Fred. *Understanding Milan Kundera: Public Events, Private Affairs.* Columbia: Univ. of South Carolina Press, 1993.

Mogen, David, Scott P. Sanders, and Joanne B. Karpinski, Eds. *Frontier Gothic: Terror and Wonder at the Frontier in American Literature.* Cranbury, N.J.: Assoc. Univ. Presses [for Fairleigh Dickinson Univ. Press], 1993.

Molloy, Sylvia. *Signs of Borges.* Trans. Oscar Montero. Durham: Duke Univ. Press, 1994.

Montresor, Jaye B., Ed. *The Critical Response to Ann Beattie.* Westport: Greenwood Press, 1993.

Morgan, Thaïs E., Ed. *Men Writing the Feminine: Literature, Theory, and the Question of Genders.* Albany: State Univ. of New York Press, 1994.

Morris, John. Ed. *Exploring Stereotyped Images in Victorian and Twentieth-Century Literature and Society.* Lewiston, N.Y.: Edwin Mellen, 1993.

Mortimer, Gail L. *Daughter of the Swan: Love and Knowledge in Eudora Welty's Fiction*. Athens: Univ. of Georgia Press, 1994.

Mosele, Elio, Ed. *George Sand et son temps*, I. Geneva: Slatkine, 1993.

Motte, Warren, and Gerald Prince, Eds. *Alteratives*. Lexington, Ky.: French Forum, 1993.

Mulhern, Chieko I., Ed. *Japanese Women Writers: A Bio-Critical Sourcebook*. Westport: Greenwood Press, 1994.

Murphy, Timothy F., and Suzanne Poirier, Eds. *Writing AIDS:Gay Literature, Language, and Analysis*. New York: Columbia Univ. Press, 1993.

Myers, Eunice, and Ginette Adamson, Eds. *Continental, Latin-American and Francophone Women Writers: Selected Papers from the Wichita State University Conference on Foreign Literature, 1984–1985*. Lanham, Md.: Univ. Press of America, 1987.

Nathan, Rhoda B., Ed. *Critical Essays on Katherine Mansfield*. New York: G. K. Hall, 1993.

Nelson, Kay H., and Nancy Huse, Eds. *The Critical Responses to Tillie Olsen*. Westport: Greenwood Press, 1994.

Nicholson, Colin, Ed. *Margaret Atwood: Writing and Subjectivity: New Critical Essays*. New York: St. Martin's Press, 1994.

Nicol, Charles, and Gennady Barabtarlo, Eds. *A Small Alpine Form: Studies in Nabokov's Short Fiction*. New York: Garland, 1993.

Noble, Donald R., Ed. *The Steinbeck Question: New Essays in Criticism*. Troy, N.Y.: Whitson, 1993.

Noe, Marcia, Ed., *Exploring the Midwestern Literary Imagination: Essays in Honor of David D. Anderson*. Troy, N.Y.: Whitston, 1993.

Oberhelman, Harley D. *The Presence of Hemingway in the Short Fiction of Gabriel García Márquez*. Fredericton, Canada: York Press, 1994.

Onetti, Juan Carlos. *'Esbjerg, en la costa' y otros cuentos*, ed. Peter Turton. Manchester: Manchester Univ. Press, 1994; Am. ed. New York: St. Martin's Press, 1994.

Orwin, Donna T. *Tolstoy's Art and Thought, 1847–1880*. Princeton: Princeton Univ. Press, 1993.

Owomoyela, Oyekan, Ed. *A History of Twentieth-Century African Literatures*. Lincoln: Univ. of Nebraska Press, 1993.

Paolini, Gilbert, Ed. *La Chispa '93: Selected Proceedings*. New Orleans: Tulane Univ., 1993.

Patterson, David, and Glenda Abramson, Eds. *Tradition and Trauma: Studies in the Fiction of S. J Agnon*. Boulder: Westview Press, 1994.

Patterson, Richard F., Ed. *Critical Essays on Donald Barthelme*. New York: G. K. Hall, 1992.

Paulson, Suzanne M. *William Trevor: A Study of the Short Fiction*. New York: Twayne, 1993.

Pavón, Alfredo, Ed. *Cuento contigo: La ficción en México*. Tlaxcala: Univ. Autónoma de Tlaxcala, 1993.

Peacock, Alan J., Ed. *The Achievement of Brian Friel*. Gerrards Cross, England: Colin Smythe, 1993.

Pearlman, Mickey, Ed. *The Anna Book: Searching for Anna in Literary History*. Westport: Greenwood Press, 1992.

Peixoto, Marta. *Passionate Fictions: Gender, Narrative, and Violence in Clarice Lispector*. Minneapolis: Univ. of Minnesota Press, 1994.

Pelensky, Olga A., Ed. *Isak Dinesen: Critical Views*. Athens: Ohio Univ. Press, 1993.

Penuel, Arnold M. *Intertextuality in García Márquez*. York, S.C.: Spanish Literature Publications, 1994.

Phelan, James, and Peter J. Rabinowitz, Eds. *Understanding Narrative*. Columbus: Ohio State Univ. Press, 1994.

Pickering, James H., and Jeffrey D. Hoeper. *Instructor's Manual to Accompany "Literature," Fourth Edition*. New York: Macmillan, 1994.

Pilling, John, Ed. *The Cambridge Companion to Beckett*. Cambridge: Cambridge Univ. Press, 1994.
Pizer, Donald. *The Theory and Practice of American Literary Naturalism: Selected Essays and Reviews*. Carbondale: Southern Illinois Univ. Press, 1993.
Plakkoottam, J. L., and Prashant K. Sinha, Eds. *Literature and Politics in Twentieth Century America*. Hyderabad, India: Amer. Studies Research Centre, 1993.
Polidori, John William. *"The Vampyre" and Ernestus Berchtold; or, The Modern Oedipus: Collected Fiction of John William Polidori*, eds. D. L. MacDonald and Kathleen Scherf. Toronto: Univ. of Toronto Press, 1994.
Pollak, Vivian R., Ed. *New Essays on "Daisy Miller" and "The Turn of the Screw."* Cambridge: Cambridge Univ. Press, 1993.
Porter, Robert. *Russia's Alternative Prose*. Oxford: Berg, 1994.
Prier, Raymond A., Ed. *Countercurrents: On the Primacy of Texts in Literary Criticism*. Albany: State Univ. of New York Press, 1992.
Pughe, Thomas. *Comic Sense: Reading Robert Coover, Stanley Elkin, Philip Roth*. Basel: Birkhäuser, 1994.
Pula, James S., and M. B. Biskupski, Eds. *Heart of the Nation: Polish Literature and Culture*, III. N.p.: East European Monographs, 1993.
Quirk, Tom, and Gary Scharnhorst, Eds. *American Realism and the Canon*. Cranbury, N.J.: Assoc. Univ. Presses [for Univ. of Delaware Press], 1994.
Rampton, David. *Vladimir Nabokov*. New York: St. Martin's Press, 1993.
Rao, E. Nageswara, Ed. *Mark Twain and Nineteenth Century American Literature*. Hyderabad: American Studies Research Centre, 1993.
Raub, Patricia. *Yesterday's Stories: Popular Women's Novels of the Twenties and Thirties*. Westport: Greenwood Press, 1994.
Reilly, Jim. *Shadowtime: History and Representation in Hardy, Conrad and George Eliot*. London: Routledge, 1993.
Renaux, Sigrid. *The Turn of the Screw: A Semiotic Reading*. New York: Peter Lang, 1993.
Ricks, Christopher. *Beckett's Dying Words: The Clarendon Lectures, 1990*. Oxford: Oxford Univ. Press, 1993.
Rieger, Branimir M. *Dionysus in Literature: Essays on Literary Madness*. Bowling Green: Bowling Green Univ. Popular Press, 1994.
Roberts, Diane. *The Myth of Aunt Jemima: Representations of Race and Region*. New York: Routledge, 1994.
Roberts, Terry. *Self and Community in the Fiction of Elizabeth Spencer*. Baton Rouge: Louisiana State Univ. Press, 1994.
Robinson, Roger, Ed. *Katherine Mansfield—In from the Margin*. Baton Rouge: Louisiana State Univ. Press, 1994.
Rogowski, Christian. *Distinguished Outsider: Robert Musil and His Critics*. Columbia, S.C.: Camden House, 1994.
Roloff, Volker, and Harald Wentzlaff-Eggebert, Eds. *Der Hispanoamerikanische Roman*, I. Darmstadt: Wissenschaftliche Buchgesellschaft, 1992.
Román-Lagunas, Jorge, Ed. *La literatura centroamericana: Visiones y revisiones*. Lewiston, N.Y.: Edwin Mellen, 1994.
Romera Castillo, José, Ed. *Actas del IV simposio internacional de la Asociación Española de Semiótica: Describir, inventar, transcribir el mundo*, II. Madrid: Visor, 1992.
Ross, Lena B., Ed. *To Speak or be Silent: The Paradox of Disobedience in the Lives of Women*. Wilmette, Ill.: Chiron Publications, 1993.
Rudin, Ernst, and Gert Buelens, Eds. *Deferring a Dream: Literary Sub-Versions of the American Columbiad*. Basel: Birkhäuser, 1994.
Russo, Mary. *The Female Grotesque: Risk, Excess and Modernity*. New York: Routledge, 1994.
Salwak, Dale, Ed. *Anne Tyler as Novelist*. Iowa City: Univ. of Iowa Press, 1994.

Sampson, Denis. *Outstaring Nature's Eye: The Fiction of John McGahern*. Washington: Catholic Univ. of America Press, 1993.

Sánchez, Reinaldo, Ed. *Reinaldo Arenas: Recuerdo y Presencia*. Miami: Ediciones Universal, 1994.

Sánchez Trigueros, Antonio, and Antonio Chicharro Chamorro, Eds. *Francisco Ayala, teórico y crítico literario*. Granada: Diputación Provincial de Granada, Biblioteca de Ensayo, 1992.

Sarlo, Beatriz. *Jorge Luis Borges: A Writer on the Edge*. London: Verso, 1993.

Scatton, Linda H. *Mikhail Zoshchenko: Evolution of a Writer*. Cambridge: Cambridge Univ. Press, 1993.

Schneider, Kirk J. *Horror and the Holy: Wisdom-Teachings and the Monster Tale*. Chicago: Open Court, 1993.

Scholtmeijer, Marian. *Animal Victims in Modern Fiction: From Sanctity to Sacrifice*. Toronto: Univ. of Toronto Press, 1993.

Schuster, Marilyn. *Marguerite Duras Revisited*. New York: Twayne, 1993.

Schuyler, George S. *Ethiopian Stories*, ed. Robert A. Hill. Boston: Northeastern Univ. Press, 1994.

Schwarz, Daniel R., Ed. *James Joyce: The Dead*. New York: St. Martin's Press, 1994.

Scruggs, Charles. *Sweet Home: Invisible Cities in the Afro-American Novel*. Baltimore: Johns Hopkins Univ. Press, 1993.

Seabrook, Jack. *Martians and Misplaced Clues: The Life and Work of Fredric Brown*. Bowling Green: Bowling Green State Univ. Popular Press, 1993.

Seeber, Hans U., and Walter Göbel, Eds. *Anglistentag 1992 Stuttgart: Proceedings*. Tübinger: Niemeyer, 1993.

Shaffer, Brian W. *The Blinding Torch: Modern British Fiction and the Discourse of Civilization*. Amherst: Univ. of Massachusetts Press, 1993.

Shaw, Peter. *Recovering American Literature*. Chicago: Ivan R. Dee, 1994.

Shelden, Michael. *Graham Greene: The Enemy Within*. New York: Random House, 1994.

Shirer, William L. *Love and Hatred: The Troubled Marriage of Leo and Sonya Tolstoy*. New York: Simon & Schuster, 1994.

Shires, Linda M., Ed. *Rewriting the Victorians: Theory, History, and the Politics of Gender*. New York: Routledge, 1992.

Showalter, Elaine, Ed. *Daughters of Decadence: Women Writers of the Fin-de-Siècle*. New Brunswick, N.J.: Rutgers Univ. Press, 1993.

———, Ed. *Joyce Carol Oates, "Where Are You Going, Where Have You Been?"* New Brunswick, N.J.: Rutgers Univ. Press, 1994.

Shryock, Richard. *Tales of Storytelling: Embedded Narrative in Modern French Fiction*. New York: Peter Lang, 1993.

Siegel, Carol. *Male Masochism: Modern Revisions of the Story of Love*. Bloomington: Indiana Univ. Press, 1995.

Silverman, Kenneth, Ed. *New Essays on Poe's Major Tales*. Cambridge: Cambridge Univ. Press, 1993.

Silverthorne, Elizabeth. *Sarah Orne Jewett: A Writer's Life*. Woodstock, N.Y.: Overlook Press, 1993.

Simpson, Lewis P. *The Fable of the Southern Writer*. Baton Rouge: Louisiana State Univ. Press, 1994.

Sinclair, John M., Michael Hoey, and Gwyneth Fox, Eds. *Techniques of Description: Spoken and Written Discourse*. London: Routledge, 1993.

Singh, Amritjit, Joseph T. Skerrett, and Robert E. Hogan, Eds. *Memory, Narrative, and Identity: New Essays in Ethnic American Literatures*. Boston: Northeastern Univ. Press, 1994.

Singley, Carol J., and Susan E. Sweeney, Eds. *Anxious Power: Reading, Writing, and Ambivalence in Narrative by Women*. Albany: State Univ. of New York Press, 1993.

Slethaug, Gordon E. *The Play of the Double in Postmodern American Fiction.* Carbondale: Southern Illinois Univ. Press, 1993.
Smith, Stephanie A. *Conceived by Liberty: Maternal Figures and Nineteenth-Century American Literature.* Ithaca: Cornell Univ. Press, 1994.
Smith, Virginia L. *Henry James and the Real Thing: A Modern Reader's Guide.* London: MacMillan Press, 1994.
Snodgrass, Kathleen. *The Fiction of Hortense Calisher.* Cranbury, N.J.: Associated Univ Presses [for Univ. of Delaware Press], 1993.
Solecki, Sam, Ed. *The Achievement of Josef kvorecký.* Toronto: Univ. of Toronto Press, 1994.
Spolsky, Ellen, Ed. *Summoning: Ideas of the Covenant and Interpretive Theory.* Albany: State Univ. of New York Press, 1993.
Stapleton, Amy. *Utopias for a Dying World: Contemporary German Science Fiction's Plea for a New Ecological Awareness.* New York: Peter Lang, 1993.
Steiner, Carl. *Of Reason and Love: The Life and Works of Marie von Ebner-Eschenbach (1830–1916).* Riverside, Calif.: Ariadne Press, 1994.
Stephens, Anthony. *Heinrich von Kleist: The Dramas and Stories.* Oxford: Berg, 1994.
Sterne, Richard C. *Dark Mirror: The Sense of Injustice in Modern European and American Literature.* New York: Fordham Univ. Press, 1994.
Stevenson, Robert Louis. *Tales From the Prince of Storytellers,* ed. Barry Menikoff. Evanston, Ill.: Northwestern Univ. Press, 1993.
Stiffler, Muriel W. *The German Ghost Story as Genre.* New York: Peter Lang, 1993.
Stivale, Charles. *The Art of Rupture: Narrative Desire and Duplicity in the Tales of Guy De Maupassant.* Ann Arbor: Univ. of Michigan Press, 1994.
Strandberg, Victor. *Greek Mind/Jewish Soul: The Conflicted Art of Cynthia Ozick.* Madison: Univ. of Wisconsin Press, 1994.
Sundquist, Eric J. *To Wake the Nations: Race in the Making of American Literature.* Cambridge: Harvard Univ. Press, 1993.
Takahashi, Teruaki, Ed. *Literarische Problematisierung der Moderne: Deutsche Aufklärung und Romantik in der japanischen Germanistik.* Munich: Iudicium, 1992.
Tallack, Douglas. *The Nineteenth-Century American Short Story: Language, Form and Ideology.* London: Routledge, 1993.
Tavernier-Courbin, Jacqueline. *The Call of the Wild: A Naturalistic Romance.* New York: Twayne, 1994.
Thompson, G. R. *The Art of Authorial Presence: Hawthorne's Provincial Tales.* Durham: Duke Univ. Press, 1993.
Thornton, Weldon. *D. H. Lawrence: A Study of the Short Fiction.* New York: Twayne, 1993.
Thumboo, Edwin, Ed. *Perceiving Other Worlds.* Singapore: Times Academic Press, 1991.
Tiffin, Chris, and Alan Lawson, Eds. *De-scribing Empire: Post-Colonialism and Textuality.* London: Routledge, 1994.
Timm, Eitel, and Kenneth Mendoza, Eds. *The Poetics of Reading.* Columbia, S.C.: Camden House, 1993.
Tintner, Adeline R. *Henry James and the Lust of the Eyes: Thirteen Artists in His Work.* Baton Rouge: Louisiana State Univ. Press, 1993.
Torgovnick, Marianna, Ed. *Eloquent Obsessions: Writing Cultural Criticism.* Durham: Duke Univ. Press, 1994.
Treglown, Jeremy. *Roald Dahl: A Biography.* New York: Farrar, Straus, Giroux, 1994.
Trotter, David. *The English Novel in History, 1895–1920.* London: Routledge, 1993.
Truchlar, Leo, Ed. *Für eine offene Literaturwissenschaft: Erkundungen und Erprobungen am Beispiel US-amerikanischer Texte/ Opening Up Literary Criticism: Essays on American Prose and Poetry.* Salzburg: Neugebauer, 1986.

TuSmith, Bonnie. *All My Relatives: Community in Contemporary Ethnic American Literatures*. Ann Arbor: Univ. of Michigan Press, 1993.
Tyler, Joseph, Ed. *Selected Essays from the International Conference on Myth and Fantasy, 1991*. Carrollton: West Georgia International Conference, 1994.
Tymieniecka, Anna-Teresa, Ed. *Allegory Revisted: Ideals of Mankind*. Dordrecht: Kluwer Acad. Publishers, 1994.
Vidal, Hernán, Ed. *Cultural and Historical Grounding for Hispanic and Luso-Brazilian Feminist Literary Criticism*. Minneapolis: Institute for the Study of Ideologies & Literature, 1989.
Vinken, Barbara, Ed. *Dekonstruktiver Feminismus: Literaturwissenschaft in Amerika*. Frankfurt: Suhrkamp, 1992.
Voller, Jack G. *The Supernatural Sublime: The Metaphysics of Terror in Anglo-American Romanticism*. DeKalb: Northern Illinois Univ. Press, 1994.
Wachtel, Andrew B. *An Obsession with History: Russian Writers Confront the Past*. Stanford: Stanford Univ. Press, 1994.
Wagener, Hans. *Understanding Franz Werfel*. Columbia: Univ. of South Carolina Press, 1993.
Wallace, Gavin, and Randall Stevenson, Eds. *The Scottish Novel since the Seventies: New Visions, Old Dreams*. Edinburgh: Edinburgh Univ. Press, 1993.
Waller, Margaret. *The Male Malady: Fictions of Impotence in the French Romantic Novel*. New Brunswick, N.J.: Rutgers Univ. Press, 1993.
Warren, Kenneth W. *Black and White Strangers: Race and American Literary Realism*. Chicago: Univ. of Chicago Press, 1993.
Wasserman, Renata R. M. *Exotic Nations: Literature and Cultural Identity in the United States and Brazil, 1830–1930*. Ithaca: Cornell Univ. Press, 1994.
Watson, Ritchie D. *Yeoman Versus Cavalier: The Old Southwest's Fictional Road to Rebellion*. Baton Rouge: Louisiana State Univ. Press, 1993.
Waxman, Barbara F., Ed. *Multicultural Literatures Through Feminist/Poststructuralist Lenses*. Knoxville: Univ. of Tennessee Press, 1993.
Wear, Delese, and Lois L. Nixon. *Literary Anatomies: Women's Bodies and Health in Literature*. Albany: State Univ. Press of New York, 1994.
Weinstein, Arnold. *Nobody's Home: Speech, Self, and Place in American Fiction from Hawthorne to DeLillo*. Oxford: Oxford Univ. Press, 1993.
Weiss, Beno. *Understanding Italo Calvino*. Columbia: Univ. of South Carolina Press, 1993.
Welch, Robert. *Changing States: Transformations in Modern Irish Writing*. London: Routledge, 1993.
Werner, Craig H. *Playing the Changes: From Afro-Modernism to the Jazz Impluse*. Urbana: Univ. of Illinois Press, 1994.
Wesley, Marilyn C. *Refusal and Transgression in Joyce Carol Oates' Fiction*. Westport: Greenwood Press, 1993.
Westarp, Karl-Heinz, and Jan N. Gretlund, Eds. *Realist of Distances: Flannery O'Connor Revisited*. Aarhus, Denmark: Aarhus Univ. Press, 1987.
Weston, Ruth D. *Gothic Traditions and Narrative Techniques in the Fiction of Eudora Welty*. Baton Rouge: Louisiana State Univ. Press, 1994.
Weststeijn, Willem G., Ed. *Dutch Contributions to the Eleventh International Congress of Slavists, Bratislava, August 30-September 9, 1993: Literature*. Amsterdam: Rodopi, 1994.
Wheeler, Kathleen. *'Modernist' Women Writers and Narrative Art*. New York: New York Univ. Press, 1994.
White, Andrea. *Joseph Conrad and the Adventure Tradition: Constructing and Deconstructing the Imperial Subject*. Cambridge: Cambridge Univ. Press, 1993.
White, Jonathan, Ed. *Recasting the World: Writing After Colonialism*. Baltimore: Johns Hopkins Univ. Press, 1993.
Whitt, Jan. *Allegory and the Modern Southern Novel*. Macon, Ga.: Mercer Univ. Press, 1994.

Willem, Linda M, Ed. *A Sesquicentennial Tribute to Galdós 1843–1993*. Newark, Del.: Juan de la Cuesta, 1993.
Wilson, Sharon R. *Margaret Atwood's Fairy-Tale Sexual Politics*. Jackson: Univ. Press of Mississippi, 1993.
Wisker, Gina, Ed. *Black Women's Writing*. New York: St. Martin's Press, 1993.
Wong, Sau-ling C. *Reading Asian American Literature: From Necessity to Extravagance*. Princeton: Princeton Univ. Press, 1993.
Wonham, Henry B. *Mark Twain and the Art of the Tall Tale*. Oxford: Oxford Univ. Press, 1993.
Wyatt-Brown, Anne M., and Janice Rossen, Eds. *Aging and Gender in Literature: Studies in Creativity*. Charlottesville: Univ. of Virginia Press, 1993.
Yamauchi, Wakako. *Songs My Mother Taught Me: Stories, Plays, and Memoir*, ed. Garrett Hongo. New York: Feminist Press at The City Univ. of New York, 1994.
Young, Philip. *The Private Melville*. University Park: Pennsylvania State Univ. Press, 1993.
Yudkin, Leon I., Ed. *Hebrew Literature in the Wake of the Holocaust*. Cranbury, N.J.: Assoc. Univ. Presses [for Fairleigh Dickinson Univ. Press], 1993.
———, Ed. *Israeli Writers Consider the "Outsider."* Rutherford, N.J.: Fairleigh Dickenson Univ. Press, 1993.
Zuckerman, Bruce. *Job the Silent: A Study in Historical Counterpoint*. New York: Oxford Univ. Press, 1991.

A Checklist of Journals Used

Acta Germanica	*Acta Germanica: Jahrbuch des Germanistenverbandes im Südlichen Afrika* [formerly *Acta Germanica: Jahrbuch des Südafrikanischen Germanistenverbandes*]
Acta Litteraria	*Acta Litteraria Academiae Scientiarum Hungaricae*
Aethlon	*Aethlon: The Journal of Sport Literature*
African Am R	*African American Review*
	Alba de América
Aligarh J Engl Stud	*The Aligarh Journal of English Studies*
Am Lit	*American Literature: A Journal of Literary History, Criticism, and Bibliography*
Am Lit Hist	*American Literary History*
Am Lit Realism	*American Literary Realism, 1870–1910*
Am Q	*American Quarterly*
Am Scholar	*The American Scholar*
Amerikastudien	*Amerikastudien/American Studies*
Anglia	*Anglia: Zeitschrift für Englische Philologie*
	L'Année Balzacienne
ANQ	*ANQ: A Quarterly Journal of Short Articles, Notes, and Reviews*
Anthropos	*Anthropos: Revista de Documentación Científica de la Cultura (Sant Cugat del Vallés, Spain)*
Antipodes	*Antipodes: A North American Journal of Australian Literature*
Appalachian J	*Appalachian Journal*
	Arbeiten aus Anglistik und Amerikanistik

Arcadia	*Arcadia: Zeitschrift für Vergleichende Literaturwissenschaft*
Arete	*Arete: The Journal of Sport Literature*
Ariel	*Ariel: A Review of International English Literature*
Arizona Q	*Arizona Quarterly*
Arkansas Q	*The Arkansas Quarterly: A Journal of Criticism*
Atlantis	*Atlantis: Revista de la Asociación Española de Estudios Anglo-Norteamericanos*
ATQ	*American Transcendental Quarterly*
Aurora	*Aurora: Jahrbuch der Eichendorff Gesellschaft*
Australian-Canadian Stud	*Australian-Canadian Studies: A Journal for the Humanities & Social Sciences*
Australian J of French Stud	*Australian Journal of French Studies*
Australian Lit Stud	*Australian Literary Studies*
Australian & New Zealand Stud	*Australian and New Zealand Studies in Canada*
Auto/Bio Stud	*Auto/Biography Studies*
Baker Street J	*The Baker Street Journal: An Irregular Quarterly of Sherlockiana*
Bestia	*Bestia: Yearbook of the Beast Fable Society*
Boundary 2	*Boundary 2: An International Journal of Literature and Culture*
British J Aesthetics	*British Journal of Aesthetics*
Bull des Amis d'André Gide	*Bulletin des Amis d'André Gide*
Bull des Etudes Valéryennes	*Bulletin des Etudes Valéryennes*
Bull Hispanique	*Bulletin Hispanique*
	Cahiers Balkaniques
Cahiers d'Etudes Germ	*Cahiers d'Etudes Germaniques*
Cahiers de la Nouvelle	*Les Cahiers de la Nouvelle: Journal of the Short Story in English*
	Cahiers d'Etudes Romanes

Cahiers Victoriens et Edouardiens	*Cahiers Victoriens et Edouardiens: Revue du Centre d'Études et de Recherches Victoriennes et Edouardiennes de l'Université Paul Valéry, Montpellier*
Callaloo	*Callaloo: An Afro-American and African Journal of Arts and Letters*
Cambridge Q	*The Cambridge Quarterly*
Canadian Lit	*Canadian Literature*
Canadian R Comp Lit	*Canadian Review of Comparative Literature*
	Canadian Slavonic Papers
Carleton Germ Papers	*Carleton Germanic Papers*
CEA Critic	*College English Association Critic*
Chasqui	*Chasqui: Revista de Literatura Latinoamericana*
Chesterton R	*Chesterton Review: The Journal of the Chesterton Society*
Children's Lit	*Children's Literature*
Children's Lit Assn Q	*Children's Literature Association Quarterly*
Círculo	*Círculo: Revista de Cultura*
Cithara	*Cithara: Essays in the Judaeo-Christian Tradition*
Classical & Mod Lit	*Classical and Modern Literature: A Quarterly*
Clio	*Clio: A Journal of Literature, History and the Philosophy of History*
Clues	*Clues: A Journal of Detection*
Colby Q	*Colby Quarterly [*formerly *Colby Library Quarterly]*
Coll Engl	*College English*
Coll Lang Assoc J	*College Language Association Journal*
Coll Lit	*College Literature*
Colloquia Germanica	*Colloquia Germanica: Internationale Zeitschrift für Germanische Sprach- und Literaturwissenschaft*
Commonwealth Essays & Studs	*Commonwealth Essays and Studies*

Comparatist	*The Comparatist: Journal of the Southern Comparative Literature Association*
Comp Lit	*Comparative Literature*
Comp Lit Stud	*Comparataive Literature Studies*
Conference Coll Teachers Engl Stud	*Conference of College Teachers of English Studies*
Confluencia	*Confluencia: Revista Hispánica de Cultura y Literatura*
Conradian	*The Conradian: Journal of the Joseph Conrad Society (*U. K.)
Conradiana	*Conradiana: A Journal of Joseph Conrad Studies*
Contemp Lit	*Contemporary Literature*
	Crítica Hispánica
	Critical Inquiry
Critical S	*Critical Survey*
Criticism	*Criticism: A Quarterly for Literature and the Arts* (Detroit, Mich)
Critique	*Critique: Studies in Contemporary Fiction*
	Cuadernos Americanos
Cuadernos Hispanoamericanos	*Cuadernos Hispanoamericanos: Revista Mensual de Cultura Hispanica*
Cuadernos de Investigación	*Cuadernos de Investigación Filológica*
	Cultural Critique
	Dactylus
D. H. Lawrence R	*The D. H. Lawrence Review*
Dalhousie R	*Dalhousie Review*
Dickensian	*The Dickensian*
Dionysos	*Dionysos: The Literature and Addiction TriQuarterly*
Discourse	*Discourse: Journal for Theoretical Studies in Media and Culture*
Discurso	*Discurso Literario: Revista de Estudios Iberoamericanos*

Durham Univ J	*Durham University Journal*
East-West Film J	*East-West Film Journal*
Edebiyât	*Edebiyât: The Journal of Middle Eastern Literatures*
Edith Wharton R	*Edith Wharton Review* [formerly *Edith Wharton Newsletter*]
Éire	*Éire-Ireland: A Journal of Irish Studies*
Engl Africa	*English in Africa*
Engl Lang Notes	*English Language Notes*
	ELH
Engl Lit Transition	*English Literature in Transition*
Engl Stud Canada	*English Studies in Canada*
Escritura	*Escritura: Revista de Teoría y Crítica Literaria*
ESQ: J Am Renaissance	*Emerson Society Quarterly: Journal of the American Renaissance*
	L'Epoque Conradienne
Essays French Lit	*Essays French Literature* (Nedlands, Western Australia)
Essays Lit	*Essays in Literature* (Western Illinois)
	Estudios Filológicos
Études Anglaises	*Études Anglaises: Grande-Bretagne, États-Unis*
	Études Française
Excavatio	*Excavatio: International Review for Multidisciplinary Approaches and Comparative Studies Related to Emile Zola and His Time, Naturalism, Naturalist Writers and Artists Around the World*
	Explicator
	Extrapolation
Faulkner J	*The Faulkner Journal*
Feminist Stud	*Feminist Studies*
Flannery O'Connor Bull	*Flannery O'Connor Bulletin*

Foro Lit	*Foro Literario: Revista de Literatura y Lenguaje*
Forum Mod Lang Stud	*Forum for Modern Language Studies*
	Forum Italicum
	Found Object
Foundation	*Foundation: Review of Science Fiction*
Frank Norris Stud	*Frank Norris Studies*
French Cultural Stud	*French Cultural Studies*
	French Forum
French R	*French Review: Journal of the American Association of Teachers of French*
Frontenac R	*Revue Frontenac*
Gaskell Soc J	*The Gaskell Society Journal*
George Eliot-George Henry Lewes Stud	*George Eliot-George Henry Lewes Studies* [formerly *The George Eliot-George Henry Lewes Newsletter*]
Georgetown Univ. Round Table	*Georgetown University Round Table on Language and Linguistics*
Germ Life & Letters	*German Life and Letters*
Germ Notes & R	*Germanic Notes and Reviews* [formerly *Germanic Notes*]
Germ Q	*German Quarterly*
Germ R	*The Germanic Review*
Germ Stud R	*German Studies Review*
	Germanisch-Romanische Monatsschrift
Gettysburg R	*The Gettysburg Review*
Hebrew Stud	*Hebrew Studies: A Journal Devoted to Hebrew Language and Literature*
Hemingway R	*Hemingway Review*
Henry James R	*Henry James Review*
Hispamérica	*Hispamérica: Revista de Literatura*
Hispania	*Hispania: A Journal Devoted to the Interests of the Teaching of Spanish and Portuguese*

Hispanic J	*Hispanic Journal*
Hispanic R	*Hispanic Review*
Hispano	*Hispanófila*
Hist European Ideas	*History of European Ideas*
Hudson R	*Hudson Review*
Iberoromania	*Iberoromania: Revista Dedicada a las Lenguas y Literaturas Iberorrománicas de Europa y America*
	Indian Scholar
Insula	*Insula: Revista de Letras y Ciencias Humanas*
Italianist	*The Italianist: Journal of the Department of Italian, University of Reading*
	Italica
Interpretation	*Interpretation: A Journal of Political Philosophy*
Inti	*Inti: Revista de Literatura Hispánica*
Int'l Fiction R	*International Fiction Review*
	Jahrbuch der Jean-Paul-Gesellschaft
	Jahrbuch der Raabe-Gesellschaft
	Jahrbuch des Wiener Goethe-Vereins
James Joyce Q	*James Joyce Quarterly*
	Japan Forum
J Am Culture	*Journal of American Culture*
J Am Stud	*Journal of American Studies*
J Commonwealth Lit	*The Journal of Commonwealth Literature*
J European Stud	*Journal of European Studies*
J Evolutionary Psych	*The Journal of Evolutionary Psychology*
J Fantastic Arts	*Journal of the Fantastic in the Arts*
J Hispanic Philol	*Journal of Hispanic Philology*
J Hispanic R	*Journal of Hispanic Research*
J History Sexuality	*Journal of the History of Sexuality*

J Interdisciplinary Lit Stud	*Journal of Interdisciplinary Literary Studies*
J Kafka Soc Am	*Journal of the Kafka Society of America*
J Lesbian & Gay Stud	*Journal of Lesbian and Gay Studies*
J Men's Stud	*Journal of Men's Studies: A Scholarly Journal about Men and Masculinities*
J Mod Lit	*Journal of Modern Literature*
J Narrative Technique	*Journal of Narrative Technique*
J Pop Culture	*Journal of Popular Culture*
Joyce Stud Annual	*Joyce Studies Annual*
Kentucky Philol R	*Kentucky Philological Review*
Kenyon R	*Kenyon Review*
Kipling J	*The Kipling Journal*
	Kunapipi
Landfall	*Landfall: A New Zealand Quarterly*
Lang Forum	*Language Forum: A Half-Yearly Journal of Language and Literature*
Lang & Lit	*Language and Literature: Journal of the Poetics and Linguistics Association*
Langston Hughes R	*The Langston Hughes Review*
Language and Lit	*Language and Literature (*San Antonio, Texas*)*
Latin Am Lit R	*Latin American Literary Review*
Legacy	*Legacy: A Journal of Nineteenth-Century American Women Writers*
Letras	*Letras (Univ. Católica Argentina)*
	Letras Femeninas
	Letras Peninsulares
Lexis	*Lexis: Revista de Lingüística y Literatura*
Lingüística y Lit	*Lingüística y Literatura* (Medellín, Colombia)
Lion & Unicorn	*The Lion and the Unicorn: A Critical Journal of Children's Literature*

Lit Int Theory	*LIT: Literature Interpretation Theory*
Lit Mexicana	*Literatura Mexicana*
Lit & Psych	*Literature and Psychology*
	Literatur in Wissenschaft und Unterricht
Louisiana Engl J	*Louisiana English Journal*
Louisiana Lit	*Louisiana Literature: A Review of Literature and Humanities*
Lovecraft Stud	*Lovecraft Studies*
Lucero	*Lucero: A Journal of Iberian and Latin American Studies*
Marjorie Kinnan Rawlings J	*Marjorie Kinnan Rawlings Journal of Florida Literature*
Malcolm Lowry R	*Malcolm Lowry Review*
Massachusetts R	*Massachusetts Review: A Quarterly of Literature, the Arts and Public Affairs*
MELUS	*MELUS: The Journal of the Society for the Study of the Multi-Ethnic Literature of the United States*
Melville Soc Extracts	*Melville Society Extracts* [supersedes *Extracts: An Occasional Newsletter*]
Merkur	*Merkur: Deutsche Zeitschrift für Europäisches Denken*
Midamerica	*Midamerica: The Yearbook of the Society for the Study of Midwestern Literature*
Midwest Q	*Midwest Quarterly: A Journal of Contemporary Thought*
Mississippi Q	*Mississippi Quarterly: A Journal of Contemporary Thought*
Mod Austrian Lit	*Modern Austrian Literature: Journal of the International Arthur Schnitzler Research Association*
Mod Chinese Lit	*Modern Chinese Literature*
Mod Lang Notes	*MLN: Modern Language Notes*
Mod Lang R	*Modern Language Review*
Mod Lang Stud	*Modern Language Studies*

Moderne Sprachen	*Moderne Sprachen: Zeitschrift des Verbandes der Österreichischen Neuphilologen*
	Moderna Spraåk
Monatshefte	*Monatshefte: Für Deutschen Unterricht, Deutsche Sprache und Literatur*
Mosaic	*Mosaic: A Journal for the Comparative Study of Literature and Ideas for the Interdisciplinary Study of Literature*
Mount Olive R	*Mount Olive Review*
Mythes	*Mythes, Croyances et Religions dans le Monde Anglo-Saxon*
Nanzan R Am Stud	*Nanzan Review of American Studies*
Narrative	*Narrative* (Columbus, Ohio)
Nathaniel Hawthorne R	*The Nathaniel Hawthorne Review*
	New Contrast
	Neophilologus
New Criterion	*The New Criterion*
New England R	*New England Review*
New Germ Critique	*New German Critique: An Interdisciplinary Journal of German Studies*
New Germ R	*New German Review: A Journal of Germanic Studies*
New Germ Stud	*New German Studies*
New Lit Hist	*New Literary History*
New Orleans R	*New Orleans Review*
New York R Sci Fiction	*The New York Review of Science Fiction*
New Zealand J French Stud	*New Zealand Journal of French Studies*
	New Zealand Literature Today
New Zealand Slavonic J	*New Zealand Slavonic Journal*
Nineteenth-Century French Stud	*Nineteenth-Century French Studies*
Nineteenth-Century Lit	*Nineteenth-Century Literature* [formerly *Nineteenth-Century Fiction*]

Notes Contemp Lit	*Notes on Contemporary Literature*
Notes Mod Irish Lit	*Notes on Modern Irish Literature*
Paidika	*Paidika: The Journal of Paedophilia*
La Palabra y el Hombre	*La Palabra y el Hombre: Revista de la Universidad Veracruzana*
Papers Lang & Lit	*Papers on Language and Literature: A Journal for Scholars and Critics of Language and Literature*
Philippine Q	*Philippine Quarterly of Culture and Society*
Philosophy & Lit	*Philosophy and Literature*
	Pleiades
PMLA	*PMLA: Publications of the Modern Language Association of America*
Poe Stud	*Poe Studies: Dark Romanticism: History, Theory, Interpretation*
Poetica	*Poetica: Zeitschrift für Sprach- und Literaturwissenschaft* (Munich, Germany)
Poétique	*Poétique: Revue de Théorie et d'Analyse Littéraires*
Poetics Today	*Poetics Today: Theory and Analysis of Literature and Communications* (Tel Aviv, Israel)
Prooftexts	*Prooftexts: A Journal of Jewish Literary History*
Psycho & Contemp Thought	*Psychoanalysis and Contemporary Thought*
Quaderni Ibero-Americani	*Quaderni Ibero-Americani: Attualità Culturale della Penisola Iberica e America Latina*
Raritan	*Raritan: A Quarterly Review*
Reader	*Reader: Essays in Reader-Oriented Theory, Criticism, and Pedagogy*
Religion & Lit	*Religion and Literature*
Renascence	*Renascence: Essays on Value in Literature*
	Representations
Research African Lit	*Research in African Literature*
R Contemp Fiction	*Review of Contemporary Fiction*

Revista Canadiense	*Revista Canadiense de Estudios Hispánicos*
Revista Chilena	*Revista Chilena de Literatura*
Revista de Crítica	*Revista de Crítica Literaria Latinoamericana*
	Revista de Estudios Colombianos
	Revista de Estudios Hispánicos
	Revista Iberoamericana
Revista Interamericana	*Revista Interamericana de Bibliografía/Inter-American Review of Bibliography*
Revista Lit Modernas	*Revista de Literaturas Modernas*
Revue d'Histoire Littéraire	*Revue d'Histoire Littéraire de la France*
R Lettres Modernes	*La Revue des Lettres Modernes: Histoire des Idées des Littératures*
Rocznik Orientalistyczny	*Rocznik Orientalistyczny* (Warsaw, Poland)
Roman 20–50	*Roman 20–50: Revue d'Etude du Roman du XX*[e] *Siècle*
Romance Lang Annual	*RLA: Romance Language Annual*
	Romance Notes
Romance Q	*Romance Quarterly*
Romanic R	*Romanic Review*
	Romanische Forschungen
Russian, Croatian	*Russian, Croatian and Serbian, Czech and Slovak, Polish Literature*
Russian R	*Russian Review: An American Quarterly Devoted to Russia Past and Present*
Saul Bellow J	*Saul Bellow Journal* [formerly *Saul Bellow Newsletter*]
San Jose Stud	*San Jose Studies*
Scandinavian Stud	*Scandinavian Studies*
Sci-Fiction Stud	*Science-Fiction Studies*
SECOLAS Annals	*SECOLAS Annals: Journal of the Southeastern Conference on Latin American Studies*

Seminar	*Seminar: A Journal of Germanic Studies*
	Sémiotiques
Sewanne R	*Sewanne Review*
	Short Story
Siglo	*Siglo XX/20th Century*
Simone de Beauvoir Stud	*Simone de Beauvoir Studies*
Slavic R	*Slavic Review: American Quarterly of Soviet and East European Studies*
Slavic & East European J	*Slavic and East European Journal*
So Central R	*South Central Review*
So Dakota R	*South Dakota Review*
So Eastern Latin Amer	*South Eastern Latin Americanist: Quarterly Review of the Southern Council of Latin American Studies*
Southerly	*Southerly: A Review of Australian Literature*
Southern Hum R	*Southern Humanities Review*
Southern Lit J	*Southern Literary Journal*
Southern Q	*The Southern Quarterly: A Journal of Arts in the South*
Southern R	*Southern Review*
SPAN	*SPAN: Journal of the South Pacific Association for Commonwealth Literature and Language Studies*
	Studia Slavica
Stud Am Fiction	*Studies in American Fiction*
Stud Am Humor	*Studies in American Humor*
Stud Am Indian Lit	*Studies in American Indian Literatures: The Journal of the Association for the Study of American Indian Literatures*
Stud Engl Lit	*Studies in English Literature* (Tokyo, Japan)
Stud Hum	*Studies in the Humanities*
Stud Lit Imagination	*Studies in the Literary Imagination*

Stud Novel	*Studies in the Novel*
Stud Short Fiction	*Studies in Short Fiction*
Stud Twentieth-Century Lit	*Studies in Twentieth-Century Literature*
Stud Weird Fiction	*Studies in Weird Fiction*
	Studia Germanica Gandensias
Studia Neophilologica	*Studia Neophilologica: A Journal of Germanic and Romance Languages and Literature*
	Style
Swansea R	*The Swansea Review: A Journal of Criticism*
Symposium	*Symposium: A Quarterly Journal of Modern Literatures*
	Taller de Letras
Tamkang R	*Tamkang Review*
	Tangence
	Tenggara
Texas Stud Lit & Lang	*Texas Studies in Literature and Languages: A Journal of the Humanities*
	Texto Crítico
	Textual Practice
Thomas Hardy J	*The Thomas Hardy Journal*
	Thomas Mann Jahrbuch
	Torre de Papel
La torre	*La torre: revista general de la Universidad de Puerto Rico*
Tulsa Stud Women's Lit	*Tulsa Studies in Women's Literature*
Twentieth Century Lit	*Twentieth Century Literature: A Scholarly and Critical Journal*
Universidad	*Universidad de La Habana*
Univ Dayton R	*University of Dayton Review*
Univ. Toronto Q	*University of Toronto Quarterly: A Canadian Journal of the Humanities*

Utah Foreign Lang R	*Utah Foreign Language Review*
Victorian News	*The Victorian Newsletter*
Victorian R	*Victorian Review: The Journal of the Victorian Studies Association of Western Canada*
Victorian Stud	*Victorian Studies: A Journal of the Humanities, Arts and Sciences*
Victorians Institute J	*Victorians Institute Journal*
Virginia Q R	*Virginia Quarterly Review: A National Journal of Literature and Discussion*
Voix et Images	*Voix et Images: Littérature Québécoise*
Wascana R	*Wascana Review of Contemporary Poetry and Short Fiction*
Weber Stud	*Weber Studies: An Interdisciplinary Humanities Journal*
Weimarer Beiträge	*Weimarer Beiträge: Zeitschrift für Literaturwissenschaft, Ästhetik und Kulturwissenschaften* [formerly *Weimarer Beiträge: Zeitschrift für Literaturwissenschaft, Ästhetik und Kulturtheorie*]
West Virginia Univ Philol Papers	*West Virginia University Philological Papers*
Western Am Lit	*Western American Literature*
Women Germ Yearbook	*Women in German Yearbook: Feminist Studies in German Literature and Culture*
Women's Stud	*Women's Studies: An Interdisciplinary Journal*
World Lit Today	*World Literature Today: A Literary Quarterly of the University of Oklahoma*
World Lit Written Engl	*World Literature Written in English*
Wirkendes Wort	*Wirkendes Wort: Deutsche Sprache in Forschung und Lehre*
Xavier R	*Xavier Review*
Yearbook Comp Gen Lit	*Yearbook of Comparative and General Literature*
Yearbook Engl Stud	*Yearbook of English Studies*
Yearbook Germ-Am Stud	*Yearbook of German-American Studies*

Yearbook Soc Pirandello Stud	*The Yearbook for the Society for Pirandello Studies*
	Zeitschrift für Anglistik und Amerikanistik
	Zeitschrift für Deutsche Philologie

Index of Short Story Writers